THE
MAYFLOWER
IN BRITAIN

THE
MAYFLOWER
IN BRITAIN

How an Icon was Made in London

GRAHAM TAYLOR

AMBERLEY

Back flap of jacket: The Statue to Captain John Smith (whose life was saved by Pocahontas, according to Smith's own account) next to Mary le Bow Church, Cheapside, London. Smith heavily criticised, but later praised, the Pilgrims.

First published 2020

Amberley Publishing
The Hill, Stroud
Gloucestershire, GL5 4EP

www.amberley-books.com

British Library Cataloguing in Publication Data.
A catalogue record for this book is available from the British Library.

ISBN 978 1 4456 9229 6 (hardback)
ISBN 978 1 4456 9230 2 (ebook)

Typesetting by Aura Technology and Software Services, India.
Printed in the UK.

Contents

Preface

The story of the *Mayflower* has been recounted from an American and a New England point of view, and from a Dutch and a Leiden point of view, but never from a British and a London point of view.

Given the origins, the circumstances and the significance of the expedition, this omission is surprising. The *Mayflower* was a London ship with a London crew, which in the summer of 1620 sailed from London to America with over 60 passengers recruited by London merchants. City of London investors had financed and organised the expedition; and even in America the colony was still dependent for a long time upon finance and supplies sent by London. The *Mayflower* expedition was a product of the City of London and, despite all its other achievements, the *Mayflower* voyage remains among the City's most celebrated contributions to history.

Since 1620 the shape, size and look of London have altered almost beyond recognition but the central core of Britain's capital, known as 'the City', still retains recognisable features. Inside the City's ancient walls (now more or less disappeared) there still lies the ward of Aldgate, where Pilgrim leaders in 1620 negotiated with the City merchants. On the western edge of the City is still the parish of St Bride where Pilgrim leader, Edward Winslow, served an apprenticeship and where his parents were married. Just outside the City in 1620, but inside the London of today, is Whitechapel, where Stephen Hopkins lived, and along the north bank of the Thames, in what is now the borough of Tower Hamlets, still stand Wapping and Blackwall where, in the estimation of the American historian, Charles Banks, the *Mayflower* must have embarked its passengers. On the south bank, within the modern Borough of Southwark, are the remains of ancient Southwark, which in 1620 was the 26th ward of the City of London and the home of Timothy Hatherley and John Harvard. To the east stands the district of Rotherhithe, which, although not part of London in 1620, was home to the *Mayflower* ship and probably to much of her crew, including the Master, Christopher Jones.

These circumstances alone would justify examining the *Mayflower* from a London, and British, perspective but the centrality of London to the *Mayflower* story is not just geographical. London holds all the *Mayflower* story together. After leaving London the ship called in at Southampton to take on supplies, but those supplies had already been organised from London. While docked in Southampton it rendezvoused with the *Speedwell*, carrying passengers from the Brownist church in Holland, but the rendezvous had been arranged in London. The Brownist church in Amsterdam and Leiden was itself descended from the Brownist church of 1592 in London. William Bradford and Pastor John Robinson traced back the ancestry of their church even beyond the London of 1592 to the London church of 1567. The political arrangements were also made in London. It was at the royal court in Whitehall, now part of London, that crucial decisions were taken about the *Mayflower* expedition, without which the voyage could not have taken place.

There is also a broader sense in which London holds together the *Mayflower* story and endows it with true significance. During the second half of the 16th century England in general, and London in particular, enjoyed a spectacular economic boom that by the end of the 17th century was to make London one of the greatest cities in the world and Britain one of the greatest countries. Contemporary with the Mayflower Pilgrims were the plays of Shakespeare, the poetry of Milton, the philosophy of Bacon, the science of Gilbert, and the architecture of Inigo Jones. This economic and cultural explosion put all the existing institutions under severe strain. The aristocracy, the monarchy and the church were barely able to cope with the demands by rich merchants and traders for freedom of trade, freedom of movement and freedom of opinion. In the 1640s the system of government finally imploded into revolution and civil war. The Archbishop of Canterbury and the king were both executed. At the centre of this uprising was London and its City merchants. During the Civil War the Pilgrims from the *Mayflower* and the subsequent ships, or their families, streamed back from New England to fight against the king and the Church on behalf of Parliament and the City of London. The narrative of the *Mayflower* came to represent liberty on both sides of the Atlantic.

Understanding the role of London and Britain in the *Mayflower* story is one thing but researching and presenting the material is quite another. I hope this book contains no inaccuracies but inevitably, I fear, it will. For these I apologise in advance. In the case of the *Mayflower* expedition such an apology is not just a formality. Few historical topics are so crisscrossed with vested interests, local loyalties, family loyalties (in respect of the millions of descendants) and political passions. The smallest details are supervised by eagle-eyed partisans. Lecturing or writing on the *Mayflower* is like walking through a minefield. All I can say is that I have done my best, everything is double-checked, and I have as far as possible used primary sources.

Vested interest and endemic partisanship are not the only problems. The literature of the *Mayflower* is too vast to read, let alone digest, except by the few outstanding scholars like Jeremy Bangs who have devoted their working lives to the topic. In addition, the glitter of the *Mayflower* has attracted large numbers of authors who are not historians. As Bangs says: 'The literature about the Pilgrims for the most part lacks academic focus; typically it is not written by trained historians or for an audience of historians.'[1] There is often no deference to primary sources and little understanding of the period, or of the underlying causes of events. Often this plethora of secondary literature creates more confusion than it dispels.

In the case of this particular work there is a final problem. There is a built-in bias against London in the literature and a consequent bias against Britain. The *Mayflower* is viewed, on both sides of the Atlantic, as part of American history. The less spectacular London passengers and the financiers behind them have not attracted such attention as the gripping tales of the Pilgrims. Similarly, the extraordinary genealogical interest in the *Mayflower* works to the detriment of London since it focuses on where people were born and not where they lived and worked. Even where London has been noticed, it has not usually been thoroughly researched, especially in the cases of East and South London. For example, Tai Liu in *Puritan London* (1986) says that the parishes of Southwark, Bermondsey and Rotherhithe lie 'outside the scope of this study', and even Charles Banks confesses to not having fully researched the parish registers of Bermondsey, St George, or St Saviour. There seems also to be insufficient research on Stepney, Ratcliff and the Isle of Dogs.

There are times when the aggregate weight of such formidable obstacles has proved challenging. On the other hand, there is a satisfaction in breaking new ground and portraying the *Mayflower* story in a brand new light. My thanks for help with the research go to staff at the British Library, the Guildhall Library, the Kent History and Library Centre, Lambeth Palace Library, London Metropolitan Archive, the National Archives, Southwark Local Studies Library and Tower Hamlets Local History Library. Above all, my thanks for help and inspiration must go to Sheila my wife, Jo my daughter and Mike my son, all of whom were pioneers and pilgrims in their own ways.

Notes on Calendars, Places and Terminology

The calendar used in this book is the modern, New Style Gregorian Calendar, which in September 1752 replaced the Old Style Julian Calendar used by the *Mayflower* passengers. Over many centuries the not very accurate Julian Calendar (introduced by Julius Caesar) had drifted away from astronomical reality. By 1752 the more accurate Gregorian Calendar (introduced by Pope Gregory) was 11 days ahead of the Julian and the government decided to switch to the Gregorian. The citizens of London, some with delivery dates to meet, went to bed on 2 September and woke up the next morning to find it was not 3 September but 14 September. In some places riots broke out. Transition to a modern calendar was also awkward in respect of years. The present British calendar begins its year on 1 January but the Old Style calendar began the year on 25 March.

At the time of the *Mayflower* the Old Style Julian calendar lagged 10 days behind the modern calendar, and the year still ended on 24 March. In the following examples the Old Style dates used in Britain in 1620 are on the left and the modern dates, used in this book, are on the right.

1620 August 05	1620 August 15
1620 November 11	1620 November 21
1620 January 09	1621 January 19
1620 March 22	1621 April 01

On places the preference in this book is, as with the calendar, for the modern version over the old. Thus 'London' means the city as it is today and not the 'City of London' as it was then. Similarly, 'New England' is in accordance with modern boundaries and so is the 'Netherlands'. Sometimes the reader may be reminded of the differences.

On terminology more precise definitions are preferred to the more general. Thus 'puritans' refers to those inside the Anglican Church who wished to stay inside and 'purify' it; 'separatists' refers to those – whether Anabaptists, Antinomians, Arians or Brownists – who rejected the idea of one state church and believed that separation was the only answer; 'Pilgrim' means those who felt their religious convictions obliged them to emigrate; while 'settler' refers to all emigrating, whether for religious motives or not.

1

The Origins of the *Mayflower*

England, and London, became involved in the exploration of North America immediately after Columbus had first landed in America. In 1497 John Cabot (Giovanni Caboto), an Italian partly funded by London merchants, sailed from Bristol with five ships, and reached Nova Scotia and Newfoundland in what is now Canada. The aim of Cabot and the Bristol mariners was trade but there was already an idea that in America might be found a 'North-West Passage' through to China and to the rich spice trade of what is now Indonesia. Spices were prized not just for flavouring food but as preservatives, and for making medicines and perfume. This dream of a passage to China was still a motive for the *Mayflower* in 1620, but Cabot found in the waters off Newfoundland another attraction – vast supplies of fish. The fish also became a factor in the *Mayflower* expedition, since investors believed such a rich food supply would guarantee that no colony on that coast could ever starve. In Cabot's time it did not attract much interest. It was not until 1527 that some English ships did fish off Newfoundland and the French were more active than the English in exploiting the discoveries of the Bristol sailors.

One problem was that England was not a major power and could not hope to compete with the Spanish and Portuguese Empires, or even with the French. Alford wrote: 'In European terms England in 1500 was a marginal backwater, London a solid enough but broadly unspectacular city, English was a minor language.'[1] England was still a developing country.

By the middle of the century this had begun to change. Previously England's economy had relied overwhelmingly on cloth production but now it started to turn to manufacture, and industry. From 1540 to 1640 coal production increased from 200,000 tons to 1.5

million. By 1640 England produced three times as much coal as the rest of Europe put together. Iron production increased fivefold. As an island crisscrossed with rivers, Britain had excellent water communications. Water provided the ideal means of transport for such heavy goods as coal and iron, though cloth still remained its main export.

The chief factor in England's upsurge was London. In 1500-1750 London's population soared from 50,000 to 500,000. It overtook Paris to become the largest city in Europe. By the time of the *Mayflower* the Thames in London was packed with ships bringing in coal from Newcastle. This coal was a prerequisite for all key industrial processes involving heat: soap-boiling, glass-blowing, dye-making, and salt-refining.

The standard of living soared. By the time of the *Mayflower* the private homes of London's upper middle class were visibly transformed: 'From their wills we can see a separate kitchen appear; ground-floor rooms are boarded over to create [upstairs] bedrooms; permanent stairs replace ladders; glass appears in windows ... chairs replace benches, knives and forks become necessities rather than luxuries.' London benefited most from the new technologies since 'London furnished most of the capital for industrial developments.' By 1640 most of the richest men of the land were in the City and 'London's economic dominance of the country was unique in Europe.'² It was this accumulation of capital in the hands of the London merchants that was to fund the ships of exploration and emigration, of which the *Mayflower* is the most famous.

Some of the institutions that underpinned the *Mayflower* voyage also took shape in the middle of the 16th century. One was the chartered monopoly. English trade expansion westwards towards America was blocked as a rule by the Portuguese and the Spanish Empires that dominated South and Central America, but the English did have one advantage. English traders, although they lacked freedom in absolute terms, possessed more freedom than most. In Portugal and Spain expansion of trade was dominated by the state while in England, France and the Netherlands there was state control but much more emphasis on private initiative. In England the Crown granted companies a charter, or patent, for certain trading activities. This charter dictated where a company could trade and how it was organised but on the other hand the company received monopoly rights for their specified area of activity and were allowed a large degree of autonomy in the conduct of their affairs. These monopolies were controversial later, but in the 16th century, when the English economy was weak, they were more help than hindrance.

The most powerful of the trading monopolies was the Company of Merchant Adventurers in London. The Merchant Adventurers were cloth exporters, and as cloth merchants ('mercers') they met in London at the Mercers' Hall. The name of 'adventurers' did not mean they were explorers, as might be thought, nor pirates like the privateers of Elizabeth's reign. They were financial risk-takers, as in the modern term, 'venture capital'. They 'adventured' their own capital in high-risk foreign trade. They were very important because woollen cloth was England's chief export by far. There were merchant adventurers in other major towns (notably, Bristol and York) but the overwhelming majority were in London. In 1620, when the *Mayflower* sailed out of London, three-quarters of London's total exports were cloth. The Merchant Adventurers, based partly in the City of London and partly abroad in Antwerp or Hamburg, were such a major part of the economy that the financial genius, Thomas Gresham, was able in a crisis to restore the financial credit of the country simply by working with them.

The geographical area assigned to the Merchant Adventurers by the Crown was a monopoly on trade between the River Somme in France and the Baltic (the 'Germane Sea'). No English company could sell or buy cloth in this zone except through them. From their continental headquarters – whether Antwerp, Emden, Hamburg or Middelburg – the company policed entry into the cloth exporting trade. It kept out interlopers; it chartered ships; it determined where and when ships sailed; it arranged for them to sail in convoy when necessary for self-protection; and it levied a charge on shipments ('conduit money') to finance such supervision.

Although the state laid down the constitution of the Merchant Adventurers, the merchants enjoyed a great deal of flexibility. As individuals they could be in 'livery companies' in the City or hold shares in 'joint-stock companies', as well as being Merchant Adventurers. Livery companies were the great chartered companies of the City which had evolved out of the mediaeval craft trades, such as Mercers (for cloth), Skinners (for animal furs), Grocers, Drapers, Fishmongers, Goldsmiths, Merchant Taylors and Haberdashers. They were entitled to parade in their own uniforms (or 'livery'). Many of the investors in the *Mayflower* expedition were members of the Skinners, Fishmongers, Haberdashers or Merchant Taylors companies.

Joint-stock companies allowed merchants to buy shares in a project and draw dividends from the company's profits without being liable individually for the whole of the company's debts. The company that financed the *Mayflower* was a joint-stock company. In the 16th century the joint-stock companies were the rising stars of the economy.

It was Sebastian Cabot, the son of Giovanni, who formed the first joint-stock company in England. Cabot's Muscovy Company was set up to establish trade with what is now Russia. Some 240 adventurers 'ventured' their capital (£6,000, a large sum) by buying shares in the Muscovy Company at £25 per share. A royal charter, prepared under King Edward VI in 1552 but later confirmed by Mary I, made Cabot the company's Governor. He aimed to find a 'North-East Passage', via the Baltic, to China and India and his first expedition departed from Deptford, now part of South-East London, in 1553. This was not to do with spices but with high quality luxury goods such as textiles. China and India were the great civilisations of the day and trade with them promised rich rewards.

Such were the economic institutions developed in the 16th century that constituted, as it were, the infrastructure of the *Mayflower* expedition. It may be asked, however, where the famous *Mayflower* Pilgrims fitted into this; how did a group of religious zealots insinuate themselves into this impressive array of economic institutions? In fact, religious dissent arose naturally out of the expansion of trade. It was in the great trading cities such as Amsterdam, Antwerp and London that dissent flourished. Trade had a social and cultural impact, firstly in prioritising literacy and secondly in bringing together by commerce all the religions of Europe.

Trade nationally could not be conducted without a certain level of literacy and education, and for international trade that was even more the case. Literacy caused more and more merchants and traders to read the Bible, now being printed in the English language for the first time. The merchants discovered that the Bible contained explosive material not previously suspected. Inside the Bible merchants found critiques of aristocracy, monarchy and even the church. In the Old Testament they found governments without kings, or with elected kings; there was an impressive parliament, the Sanhedrin; and there were denunciations by the Prophets of kings, queens and the super-rich. In the New Testament they found the ethical injunctions of the Sermon on the Mount and, although Jesus did not denounce any Roman emperors, they found denunciations on ethical grounds of the priests, lawyers and wealthy landowners who were still causing them so many problems in the 16th and 17th centuries. The Bible was topical.

This use of biblical ammunition to criticise the established church was first promoted in London by the 'Lollards' (a term said to be derived from a Dutch word for a subversive 'mutterer'). They were the followers of John Wyclif, the reformer who first translated parts of the Bible into English. The Lollards in London were heavily represented in the newly literate class, whether local traders or international merchants. As Peter Marshall wrote: 'Most London Lollards were artisans, but some were members of the prestigious livery companies who ran the city's economy.'[3] In the middle of the 16th century, for example, Lady Jane Younge, the widow of John Younge, former Mayor of the City of London, was also the daughter of Jone Boughton. Poor Jone had been arrested, taken to court, convicted of holding 'eight of Wickliffe's opinions' and, although an old woman in her 80s, she was burnt to death at the stake in Smithfield, London, in 1494.

As well as fostering literacy in London, trade also forced City merchants into contact with all sorts of religious tendencies in the cities of Europe. To trade abroad, merchants needed to have their Protestant version of Christianity tolerated and they, in their turn, had to tolerate Muslims, Jews, Lutherans and Catholics. It was an education for all concerned. In Antwerp, for example, the main trading centre of North-West Europe in the mid-16th century, religious freedom was granted to the London Merchant Adventurers by the authorities. This was extended, for practical reasons, not only to the merchants but to all English subjects living or working in the town. This created a problem for the English government. The Merchant Adventurers and their associates were not allowed to practise their own (often Lollard-like) religious beliefs in London but were allowed to do so in a foreign country. Worse, this base for the Merchant Adventurers, at first in Antwerp, later in Middelburg, became over the years a place of refuge for English dissenters. Chaplains in Middelburg abbreviated the English Prayer Book, imposed in England as a pragmatic compromise with Catholicism, and replaced it with the simpler services advocated by the radical critics of the Anglican Church.

Dutch Church

There was a further repercussion caused by foreign trade. As Antwerp and then Middelburg granted freedom of religion to English merchants, it followed logically that merchants from the Netherlands should be granted the same in London. This led to the development of 'stranger churches'. Foreigners were referred to as 'strangers' in England, and so their churches became 'stranger churches'. The first one in London was set up as early as 1547 by the Italian Protestant community (though it welcomed other nationals), but it had been quite informal. In 1550 the Dutch Church in Austin Friars was established and this was strikingly different. Under the Protestant king, Edward VI (1547-53), it was the first stranger church to receive official recognition, and so become the first 'nonconformist' chapel allowed in England. The Dutch Church was a historic breakthrough for English freedom.

Like its Italian forerunner, the Dutch Church was international: it was used by German and French Protestants as well as the Dutch; the founder and first Superintendent was Jan Laski, of Polish origin. English merchants of foreign origin attended the church. In the 1580s French refugees formed such a large proportion of the congregation they opened up their own stranger church in Threadneedle Street. However, unlike its Italian predecessor the Dutch Church had a congregational and democratic element, and it was this that made it a model for the church of the *Mayflower* Pilgrims.

Austin Friars was influenced more by the Protestant luminary Martin Bucer than by Martin Luther or John Calvin and (initially at least) it gave members the right to elect their own Pastors, Elders and Deacons. The Dutch Church was also a 'gathered church', just the type of church the *Mayflower* Pilgrims advocated. A gathered church was not confined to a local parish. It was an independent church that accepted as its members only those who made a profession of belief and a binding covenant with the church and such members could come, in theory, from all over the world.

The Dutch Church was not tolerated by the English government simply to cater for the needs of foreign merchants but it was also a tactic to nullify the impact of Anabaptist refugees flooding in from the Netherlands. The communistic Anabaptists were notorious for leading uprisings in Germany. The idea was that an official Dutch church, monitored closely by the English government, would be able to stem the tide of these heretics with their dangerous, radical ideas. The trouble was that the Dutch Church itself had a more democratic polity than the Church of England; it offered an alternative model perhaps more tempting than the Anabaptists; and it soon dawned upon the English authorities that they might have made a mistake. They had to take steps to try and restrict the freedom that the Dutch had been so imprudently granted, but it was too late. A tract in 1568 talked of the Dutch Church in Austin Friars and 'other Congregations which, in these days, do spring up'.[4] If foreigners could have democratic churches, then Londoners wanted them too.

Mary Tudor

All this was rudely interrupted by Edward VI's successor, Queen Mary (1553-58). A fervent Catholic, Mary launched five years of persecution against her Protestant subjects. Nearly 300 were burnt at the stake. Underground churches were organised by radicals as acts of resistance and to one of those clandestine churches in London the *Mayflower* Pilgrims traced the origin of their own church.

Mary did not respect status. In 1555 Hugh Latimer, Bishop of Worcester, and Nicholas Ridley, Bishop of London, were burnt at the stake. In 1556 Mary had Thomas Cranmer, the Archbishop of Canterbury, burnt to death. He was the last Archbishop of Canterbury to be burnt, though not the last to be executed. The result was emigration. Many found sanctuary with the help of merchants who not only had ships to transport them but commercial bases to transport them to. In all, in Mary's brief reign, about 800 refugees fled abroad, to France, Germany and Switzerland.

On the economic front the Merchant Adventurers in London and Thomas Gresham suddenly found themselves distinctly out of favour, because they had supported the previous (Protestant) king, Edward VI, and his designated successor, Lady Jane Grey, a teenage girl of scholarly gifts. Mary froze out the merchants (except Gresham was simply too clever and useful to discard) and Jane Grey was beheaded in 1554.

Mary's reign of terror had the opposite effect to that intended. The burning bishops, the innocent young girl, and the refugee families fleeing for their lives attracted the sympathy of the decent majority. There were many more Protestants at the end of her reign than at the beginning.

The London church regarded by the Pilgrims as their spiritual ancestor was a 'gathered church' like the Dutch Church at Austin Friars. That is to say, it was a church open to all 'true Christians', it elected its own officers, and it was held together by a sworn covenant, not by state power. In 1557 it elected its own Pastor, John Rough, a former monk from Scotland, who had fled to the Netherlands with Kate, his wife, but then boldly (some would say suicidally) returned to London. He was imprisoned in Newgate and, in December, at Smithfield, burnt at the stake.

Mary did not let matters rest there. In March 1558, three more members of the Rough church – John Devenish, Hugh Foxe and Cuthbert Simpson – were arrested at the Saracen's Head tavern in Islington. Simpson, a tailor but also a scholar, who had bravely become Deacon of the underground church, was horribly tortured on the rack in the Tower of London before being burnt at Smithfield, along with Devenish and Foxe.

In April 1558 forty more men and women were seized at a night-time meeting in an Islington field. Half of them were sent to Newgate Prison, and seven of these, not recanting, were burnt at Smithfield in June. It was wholly counter-productive. When the Sheriff of London read out a proclamation at Smithfield threatening the arrest and punishment of anyone who voiced support for the heretics, the sympathetic crowd, nonetheless, shouted out their protests as the hapless martyrs died in agony.

The burnings had no more impact on Rough's church than they did on the City of London crowds. They simply elected after Rough, in their democratic way, another pastor, Augustine Bernher, and then Thomas Bentham (later Bishop of Coventry and Lichfield). Behind the scenes they were backed by City of London merchants such as Nicholas Burton and Roger Holland, a member of the Company of Merchant Taylors.

For the *Mayflower* Pilgrims the burning of Rough and Simpson in particular was the founding moment of their movement. William Bradford, the Governor of New Plymouth who became its historian, and John Robinson, the eminent Pastor of the Pilgrim church in Leiden, both traced back the roots of their own church to the Rough church of 1557. It is not clear from the records what the followers of Rough precisely believed. What was decisive for the *Mayflower* Pilgrims, however, was the 'gathered' character of the church, its election of ministers, and its use of an agreed covenant. This was the polity the Pilgrims adopted themselves and tried to put it into practice first in Southwark, then in Holland and then in New Plymouth, America.

There was one other outcome of Mary's bloody reign that deeply affected the Pilgrims. In 1563 John Foxe's *Book of Martyrs* (as it was later called, against Foxe's wishes) was published. Foxe had intended a history of the Protestant church but his vivid accounts of the 'Marian Martyrs' made the book at one time the most widely read in England after the Bible.

According to Foxe England was the first Protestant country in the world ('country' as opposed to a city-state like Geneva); it had been targeted by the mighty Spanish Empire of Philip II; but little England had, miraculously, survived the onslaught. Foxe, following *Deuteronomy* (the first book of providential history, which traced the story of Josiah's Judah) concluded that the English were the Chosen People of modern history, as the Jews had been in ancient times.

Thus, at the start of Elizabeth's reign (1558-1603) there was already a widely held belief in England's special role in history: John Aylmer in 1558 ('God is English') and Archbishop Parker in 1573 both affirmed that the English were the new Chosen People. From this time on there is a patriotic component to English Protestantism. The defeat of the Spanish Armada (1588) and then the Gunpowder Plot (1605) confirmed God's special favour. By then even foreign Protestants felt England was a special nation unto God. The Pilgrims of the *Mayflower* absorbed this narrative with their mothers' milk. Bradford's history, *On Plimmoth Plantation,* begins with a proud declaration that 'our honourable nation of England' was the very first Protestant nation in the world, and it has been hounded 'ever since' by a vengeful Satan.

Elizabeth Tudor

On Mary's death the succession went to Elizabeth, daughter of Anne Boleyn. Immediately, Elizabeth put the 'Marian Revolution' into reverse and in effect restored, with some modifications, the Protestantism of Edward VI. The Acts of Supremacy and Uniformity in 1559 made Elizabeth the Governor of the Anglican church, imposed a Prayer Book similar to Edward's, and compelled attendance at church every week on penalty of a fine. The Book of Common Prayer laid down the liturgy to be used and set out the church's faith in 39 articles of essentially Calvinist belief. The problem was that the 800 exiles, flooding back from Germany and Switzerland, had been expecting something more radical than a return to the status quo.

At first the resistance to the 'Elizabethan Settlement' could be discounted because it had not coalesced around a definite group, but by *c.*1565 those reformers inside the Anglican Church who wanted to 'purify' the church of its Catholic remnants were identifiable and were being dubbed the 'puritans'.

The centre of resistance was London. As early as 1566 Archbishop Parker admitted there was a crisis in London, where the 'irritable precisionists', or 'puritans', were especially strong. He felt the London church was getting out of control.[5] He noticed that Catholic-style fonts were being quietly replaced in churches and brazen eagles on the lecterns melted down.

The reason London became the centre of resistance is not hard to find. As Gurney writes:

> ...manufacturers and traders were strongly represented in the capital and, although to a lesser extent, in south-east England. There can be little doubt that they and their contacts were the chief means by which the thought and teaching of Luther and Calvin, and those who followed after them, were brought from mainland Europe to the British Isles. These people were the entrepreneurs and capitalists of the period.[6]

They were also the people most hamstrung, in trade and in their beliefs, by Tudor state control.

The puritans were not the worst news for the Church establishment. As well as puritans inside the church there were others outside it, meeting separately, who were more radical. One of these, the Fitz Church (after its minister, Richard Fitz) was later recognised by Bradford and Robinson as the ancestor of the separatist churches in Amsterdam and Leiden. Robinson considered the Fitz Church as a direct predecessor of his Leiden church, since the Rough Church had dispersed at the end of Mary's reign.

In the 1560s there were many clandestine meetings in London, either in the private homes of wealthy merchants or in ships anchored in the Thames but the government hit back. In 1567 the Fitz Church had 77 attenders arrested on premises in the Savoy, London, the disreputable area between the Strand and the Thames.[7] Some underground groups, such as the one at Plumbers Hall, were probably not in the tradition of the *Mayflower* Pilgrims but Burrage says the Savoy church of Richard Fitz was. It was separated; it was a 'gathered church'; it had a covenant, and it was approved by both Bradford and Robinson as their church.[8]

The Fitz Church was duly suppressed but it was part of a movement against the 'Elizabethan settlement' that was to endure. From *c.*1571 on there was an outbreak across the country of so-called 'prophesyings': unauthorised talks and debates organised by puritans inside existing parish churches. For the government this was hard to combat; firstly because sympathiser Edmund Grindall, Bishop of London and then Archbishop of Canterbury, was happy to turn a blind eye to these unauthorised activities; secondly, because there was considerable merchant support for the radicals: thirdly, because the Dutch immigrants were with impunity constantly airing radical ideas at the Dutch Church in Austin Friars.

In 1571 Elizabeth had to pressure Austin Friars to ban the prophesying she was trying to ban in the rest of London. The Dutch Church was a persistent nuisance for the government. It was right in the heart of the City, not far from the Guildhall, and its presence posed the question for Londoners: if foreigners ('strangers') are allowed to have an independent church in London, then why were they not allowed to have one?[9]

There was a similar question raised in connection with Huguenot refugees. In 1572 came the Massacre of St Bartholomew's Day in France, when perhaps 30,000 French Protestants known as 'Huguenots' were massacred in a Catholic pogrom. Hundreds of Huguenot refugees poured into England. The arguments of Foxe seemed to be valid. The English were now acknowledged everywhere as the beacon of the Reformation: the Chosen People, the Elect of God, the new Israel. Even Cecil, Elizabeth's chief minister could comment proudly that it had 'brought honour to our kingdom to be accounted a refuge for distressed nations'. But the remnant of the Fitz Church (there was one) might have justly asked: if the Huguenots in France have independent churches, and their refugees are now protected by the English government, why are not we, English independents, granted freedom of worship here in London?

The problem was that in England religion was run in the same way as the economy. In 1534 Henry VIII, in founding the Anglican Church, had granted it a monopoly which bestowed a degree of autonomy but left ultimate control in the hands of the state. Like the trading monopolies, the Church was in charge of enforcing uniformity of belief across England and not allowing interlopers (dissenters). It had its own taxation (tithes), its own courts, its own police and its own network of well-paid informers. In return, the Church kept order for the king, conducted strict censorship, and promoted from the pulpit the policies of the government. As Charles I remarked: 'People are governed by the pulpit more than the sword in time of peace.'[10]

Robert Browne

From the midst of all the prophesying discussion groups set up in the 1570s emerged a highly controversial figure in the history of the *Mayflower* Pilgrims: Robert Browne, the founder of Brownism. He has been revered as the 'Father of the Pilgrim Fathers', denounced by others for his unstable character, and summarily dismissed by the chronicler, Bradford, as 'an apostate, like Judas'. A graduate of Corpus Christi, Cambridge, Browne was in trouble early on. In 1572 he was summoned before the dreaded ecclesiastical commissioners but slipped through their fingers, as his patron was none other than William Cecil, Elizabeth's chief minister. This fortuitous connection arose because his father, Anthony Browne, owned 900 acres at Tolethorpe, Rutland, and the Brownes together with the Cecils dominated land ownership in the Stamford area.

During the 1570s Browne was at first a schoolteacher in London but then returned to Cambridge. He was preaching in Islington in 1580 and it is likely he combined a house in Cambridge with a townhouse in St Nicholas Lane. It is understandable that London was his base, since Cecil's friends, the Earl and Duchess of Sussex, lived at the splendid Bermondsey House in Southwark. Stephen Bredwell, who wrote an account of Brownism, said that Brownists were most concentrated in London and the adjacent counties and that Browne's preaching in London had been very effective.[11] This may well have been because within his sermons Browne included an element of social protest: he denounced moneylenders, the 'undoers of the poore men', profiteers, and the clerics who lived off the fat of the land. Linebaugh and Rediker overstate the case when they say Robert Browne's theory of 'congregational churches governed from below, by mutual consent, rather than from above, by elder, king, or nation, and organised on principles of lawful debate, dispute, protest, and questioning ... had revolutionary implications, calling as it did for democratic covenants'[12] but they capture the essence of why church and state authorities were scared of Brownism.

Browne married Alice Allen in *c.*1580 and in 1581 founded a gathered church in Norwich with Robert Harrison, who was rich. If Browne was not separatist before, he was separatist now and he was arrested, though soon rescued by Cecil. The problem was that the followers Harrison had gathered in Norwich could not all be protected by Cecil and the church adherents soon decided that rather than be imprisoned they would emigrate to Middelburg, Holland, where the Merchant Adventurers were establishing themselves and where the Dutch government was granting toleration even to the pacifist and communist Anabaptists. Sprunger says Browne's group was the first radical group to emigrate from England 'as a church'.[13] It was a church because members were bound by a 'covenant'. The idea comes from the Old Testament and was first used to bind new members by Anabaptists in Germany. Browne described how new members would, firstly, give consent to the agreed laws and government of the church and then, secondly, agree to accept the authority of those elected to teach them and run the church. For Punchard, formalisation of a gathered church with a covenant was a historic moment: 'the beginning of the final and triumphant struggle of our English ancestors for religious freedom' was 'about the year 1580...'[14] Others say it was not a proper church because it had no Pastor and no Elders. In Middelburg Browne wrote two books, one of which was to become a classic of the Brownist movement: *A Treatise of Reformation without Tarrying for Anie* (1582). Not only did Browne call for the immediate formation of illegal gathered churches without 'tarrying' for permission but he urged separation of church and state, and 'insisted that church business be decided by the whole church and not just by its leaders'.[15] These radical books were smuggled from Middelburg into Norwich and London, but the Anglican Church immediately hit back. The books were banned. In 1583 in the town of Bury St Edmund, Suffolk, dozens were arrested, and a shoemaker called John Copping and a tailor, Elias Thacker, were hanged for distributing the books.

Browne's church soon fizzled out. There were only 30 or 40 in Middelburg and in 1583 there was an acrimonious split between him and Harrison, and as this was later blamed on 'Mrs Browne's pride', it might be deduced that the level of debate was not high. Harrison had an eye for returning to England with his dispirited followers, which meant some rapprochement with the Anglican Church, but Browne would not countenance any such compromise. Defeated by Harrison, Browne now retreated to Scotland (another place of refuge for English dissenters) but finding no support there, he returned to London where he faced imprisonment. He resolved this, in October 1585, by recanting, thus earning himself the contempt of all his former admirers, and soon afterwards he became the headmaster of St Olave's Grammar School in Southwark, presumably the school where he taught in the 1570s. Was he just disillusioned? Was he put under some personal pressure by the government? Or was he all along an agent of Cecil, flushing out extremists for him so they could be hunted down?

The Brownists who had revered his writings in 1582 now rushed to distance themselves from his name but it made no difference to his reputation. He had become part of popular consciousness as the man with radical social ideas who argued for immediate separation from the Church of England – right now, without waiting for anybody. This popular perception of 'Brownism' was to last for the next 60 years.

Richard Hakluyt

In the same year, 1582, when Browne was writing his inflammatory book, a Richard Hakluyt was publishing *Divers Voyages Touching the Discovery of America*. While at Oxford University Hakluyt had heard stories from sailors who had visited the Penguin Islands in Newfoundland. The sailors told him the conditions were very inhospitable but the island was rich in cod, bears and flightless great auks easily seized upon and eaten. After reflecting on the emigration of the Brownists to Middelburg, Hakluyt conceived the notion of using such settlers. Their steely determination and high work ethic would make a commercial success of any colony. In Ireland in 1583 there was an attempt along Hakluyt's lines. A Christopher Carleil had wanted to found a puritan colony in America so that 'the godly minded ... shall be at their free liberty of conscience,' but, unfortunately, in 1584 the expedition collapsed before it could sail out of Cork harbour.[16]

Hakluyt, of Welsh extraction, came from a merchant family and his father was a member of the Worshipful Company of Skinners whose business was skins and, significantly, furs. After being orphaned, Hakluyt entered Christ Church, Oxford, with financial support from the Skinners and the Clothworkers. There he studied to be a puritan clergyman but one day he came across a globe, at that time a marvellous novelty. He was enthralled, and developed an interest in cosmography. Adair writes that, 'Hakluyt's vocation as preacher and his avocation as cosmographer fitted together as two eyes are joined in sight.'[17] An English and Protestant nation could be established in the New World where the iron self-discipline of the puritan, with the grace of God, would overcome all adverse conditions.

Hakluyt emerged from the ranks of the same City merchants and politicians whose behind-the-scenes protection of puritans is glimpsed from time to time. They were campaigning in London for trade expansion and in particular for exploration of a possible North-West Passage into East Asia. Hakluyt's idea was that China and Japan were advanced countries which would be a market for English cloth. These puritan sympathisers (Burghley, Leicester, Sidney, Sussex, Walsingham) had backed Martin Frobisher's expedition of 1576 to discover a North-West Passage through Canada to the Pacific. They were political and cultural heavyweights: Lord Burghley (William Cecil) was chief minister to Elizabeth, Leicester was her favourite, and Sir Philip Sidney, with Hakluyt at Oxford, was a leading light of the Elizabethan intelligentsia. Their motive was primarily commercial, and they needed permanent settlements as bases for trade.

Elizabeth favoured an alternative model of overseas enterprise. Spain was still a major threat and in the 1570s English privateers had engaged in what was in practice state-sponsored piracy against Spanish possessions in the Americas. For privateers like Drake the purpose of colonies was to act as military bases for war against Spain. The aim of expeditions was to acquire treasure (silver and gold), seize land for England (or, at least, for the second sons of the aristocracy), take a share in the fast-growing slave trade, and of course (it was always dutifully added) to convert the heathen. The incentive for Elizabeth was the generous slice of looted treasure that privateers such as Drake brought back for the royal coffers.

This was the polar opposite of the motivation for City companies such as the Skinners. They wanted colonies for trading in furs and catching fish, which demanded co-operation with Americans, and a refuge from religious persecution. For them it was frustrating when Martin Frobisher's search for a North-West Passage in 1576, perhaps opening up trade with China, was then diverted into a fruitless search for gold in 1577-78.

England's first attempt to colonise North America, by Humphrey Gilbert in 1583, was backed by Merchant Adventurers but, as with Frobisher, seemed to have mixed motives and, therefore, confused objectives. Gilbert laid claim to Newfoundland for England and hoped to found a permanent settlement at St John's, which had long been visited by fishermen, but he was ultimately unsuccessful and Gilbert, on the return trip, was drowned.

In 1584, when some Brownists were threatened with banishment, Hakluyt saw an opportunity and asked the Queen to send the separatists to colonise America. They would cause less contention for Her Majesty on the other side of the Atlantic, he argued; they would convert savages to the Christian faith; and their colony would act as a refuge for those poor Huguenots, and other Protestants, 'forced to flee for the truth of God's word'. He was not heeded. The priorities at court were still the same old short-cuts to wealth and fortune: gold, silver, empire and slaves.

Instead, Elizabeth granted Walter Raleigh a charter to colonise America. In 1585 a colony was established on Roanoke Island off the coast of North Carolina. Raleigh's fellow-investors were hoping for quick returns from gold and silver and the government wanted a privateering base from which to harass Spain. Raleigh called the region 'Virginia' in honour of Elizabeth, the 'Virgin Queen'.

At first the colony looked as if it might succeed and in 1587 history was made when the first English child was born in North America, Virginia Dare, born to Ananaias Dare and Eleanor White of London. Alas, Roanoke, England's first settlement in America did not survive. War with Spain held up the sending of supplies and by 1590 Roanoke was abandoned. Nobody has ever found out for sure what happened to the remaining settlers.

Hakluyt persisted. In his *Principal Navigations* (1589), after the defeat of the Spanish Armada in 1588, he called on Protestant England to seize its chance and build an 'empire' to match that of Spain, but this was a spiritual message, he insisted, for trade and religion, for the good of the world. Hakluyt did live long enough to help develop the colony of Virginia, though not long enough to see his dream fulfilled: the day in 1620 when the Protestant *Mayflower*, bent on trade in fish and furs, not gold and slaves, reached New England.

The London (Johnson) Church

Meanwhile, the persecution of Brownists had not stopped with the executions in Bury St Edmond but intensified under John Whitgift, the new Archbishop of Canterbury. Evans describes him as: 'a man of conspicuous ostentation' who detested puritans. When he arrived at Canterbury Cathedral he brought with him 'a vast and flamboyant retinue'[18] on hundreds of horses. The Brownists' egalitarian critique of the 'hierarchy' was not to his liking.

In London many Brownists were arrested in October 1587 and imprisoned in the Clink Prison, Southwark. One of them was a brilliant Cambridge scholar, John Greenwood. He made good use of his time, writing pamphlets that were smuggled out to Dordrecht for publication. This feat was engineered by his wife, whose servant-girl, Cicely, apparently visited the prison and carried out the illicit manuscripts under her clothing.

Greenwood made an unexpected and welcome recruit while in the Clink. He was visited in November 1587 by a Henry Barrowe who was duly seized and imprisoned himself. Barrowe, a graduate from Clare Hall, Cambridge, had been a libertine in his youth, had attended court, had even known Cecil, but then had a conversion experience. Passing a church in the City of London, he heard some preacher declaiming loudly inside. From curiosity he opened the door and entered the church, and that decision changed his life. Overwhelmed by what he heard, he renounced his life of luxury and sinfulness and became a radical. Francis Bacon said the Brownists would never have become so well known had it not been for Browne's pamphlets and for Barrowe, 'a gentleman of a good house, but one that lived in London at ordinaries', who had leapt all of a sudden from 'a vain and libertine youth to a preciseness in the highest degree'.[19]

There was still a social edge to Brownism despite Browne's defection. Behind the earnest and melodious psalm-singing (sung with deep sincerity, 'not as the papists do') could always be heard a rumble of social discontent. Barrowe was a good example. A democrat before his time he held an egalitarian belief in education. Not just the Bible should be studied, he pleaded. The arts and sciences should be taught everywhere, and not just at universities but 'in all places', and at very least 'in everie citie'.[20]

Despite imprisonment, Barrowe and Greenwood managed to keep writing. Some of their output is so vituperative that it is in parts almost unreadable. For example, Greenwood wrote that the Church of England was 'the harlot sitting upon many waters' and 'the murdress of the saints'. In 1648 Bradford wrote that Barrowe and Greenwood were rigid and very intemperate in their language but this should be excused because the persecutions they suffered under Elizabeth filled them with indignation.[21] Their most significant work was the first 'manifesto' of the Brownist movement. Culpepper says the *True Description* (Dordrecht, 1589), although not as good as the later Brownist manifesto of 1596, is 'the first statement of faith written by the separatist congregation in London'.[22] In fact, Browne had never summarised Brownist beliefs in writing but Barrowe and Greenwood did.

Apart from the manifesto, their great achievement was to establish the first organised Brownist church in London, but this happened through a strange sequence of events. In 1589 a Francis Johnson had been expelled for puritan views from Cambridge University after a sermon in which he denounced the low standards of the Anglican clergy and called for the appointment of Elders, a Presbyterian device, to enforce discipline. When he was then sent to prison, demonstrations took place and 68 Cambridge Fellows and students signed a petition demanding his release. This had little immediate effect but in the end he was saved by the intervention of William Cecil and released in February 1590. He next appears as the chaplain of the church in Middelburg.

As Johnson was known to be strongly anti-Brownist, the English Ambassador to the United Provinces (as the liberated Dutch provinces in the Netherlands were known from 1581) now asked Johnson to purchase all copies of a treatise by Barrowe and Greenwood (*A Plaine Refutation*), and burn them. Johnson did as he requested but out of interest kept two copies back from the bonfire, one for himself and one for a friend. On reading the pamphlet later he found himself convinced by its arguments (he said), and after a stormy meeting in Middelburg around April 1592, he visited the Fleet Prison in London, where Barrowe and Greenwood were now confined, to discuss his conversion to Brownism. They agreed to form a Brownist church in London with Johnson, an ordained minister, as its Pastor. This appears to have been welcome to the authorities who thereupon released Greenwood and several others from prison. All his life Johnson was a collaborator with the authorities against the Anabaptists and perhaps Whitfgift felt that, with the uncompromising Barrowe kept in prison, Johnson could turn the Brownists in a more moderate direction. The proposed church was agreed by Brownist members at the house of Roger Rippon in Southwark, and in September 1592 at a meeting in Nicholas Lane, near London Bridge, Johnson was chosen as Pastor, Greenwood as Teacher, Studley and Kniveton as Elders, Lee and Bowman as Deacons. Barrowe was omitted as he was still in prison. It was the first fully organised church in England that was independent of the state: it was run under the supervision of Elders; it had a covenant; it had a trained minister as a Pastor; and it had a public manifesto in the *True Description* of 1589. It was a milestone in the history of religious freedom, and both Robinson in Leiden and Bradford in New Plymouth looked back on it with pride.

Persecution

This Southwark Church, in its first incarnation, did not last long. It provoked a fierce persecution and by the middle of 1593 had been virtually wiped out. No one is sure why this persecution erupted. The main reason was probably the end of the Catholic threat. Until the late 1580s the government had feared to go too far against radical Protestants because they were the most staunchly anti-Catholic sections of the population, but after the defeat of the Spanish Armada in 1588, the crushing of Catholic internal opposition by Walsingham, and the execution of Catholic Mary, Queen of Scots, the government was in no serious danger from Catholicism and therefore the puritans and Brownists were no longer needed as a bulwark against Rome and could safely be suppressed.

The Brownists also suffered from the death of Francis Walsingham in 1590. He had been in Paris at the time of the St Bartholomew Day massacre and was haunted all his life by the dreadful slaughter he had witnessed. Though in 21st-century terms a spymaster or even the head of the 'secret police', he was the protector of both puritans and Brownists and also a champion of maritime expansion to open up new trade routes. Hakluyt's *Principal Navigations, Voyages and Discoveries of the English Nation* was dedicated to Walsingham.

There was a third factor behind the persecution. The scathing *Marprelate* tracts of 1588-89 by author or authors unknown, satirising the Church leaders, drove those in authority into such a fury that a huge hunt was mounted by the Church to track down and arrest those responsible. There were two waves of arrests: firstly, in December 1592 when Johnson, Greenwood and many others were arrested in the house of Edward Boyes, a Fleet St haberdasher with a house in Ludgate Hill; and, secondly, in March 1593 when Johnson, Penry and others were arrested in Islington.

The details of the arrests can be viewed in the table on page 48. Analysis of the class composition shows the strong connection of Brownists with manufacture and trade: 29 were skilled artisans (shipwrights 5, tailors 3, purse makers 3, shoemakers 3, weavers 2 and then various trades such as cloth-worker, felt-maker, glover, goldsmith); the second largest category was professional workers (clergymen 4, schoolmasters 2, scriveners 2, and then others such as apothecary, lawyer, scholar, writer, physician); and finally the third category was traders (fishmonger 3, haberdasher 3, draper 1). All those interrogated refused to take the oath, which obliged them to tell the whole truth, thus incriminating families and friends. They also knew that taking the oath had problematic legal consequences. After the oath the interrogators could pounce on any inaccuracies and bring a charge of perjury, or contempt of court, for which punishments were very severe.

Johnson and Studley refused the oath but then spilled the beans anyway, naming names and offering details (as did two others). This leads one to the supposition that these four were either very frightened, or agents of the state. This did not mean that Johnson and Studley were simply informers. It was probably just that they were prepared to collaborate against a common enemy (the Anabaptists). Patrons such as Cecil, the Earl and Duchess of Sussex, and Robert Rich would expect no less. There was a tragic outcome – some of the comrades they helped to convict died in prison. The same thing was to happen again in 1618 when Johnson followers defended a similar betrayal as for the greater good.

Of the 52 Brownists interrogated by officers of the church nearly all could read. The transcripts show the interrogators assumed they were talking to literates. Literacy was suspect. An Act of Parliament in 1543 had, on pain of a month's imprisonment, banned artisans, husbandmen, labourers and women from reading Scripture, though pointedly an exception was made for 'noble and gentry women'.[23]

The dissenters, whether puritan insiders or radical outsiders, took pride in their literacy. Ability to read was a badge of true religion. Indeed, one of their grievances was that many parish priests were not literate, and some were incapable of delivering a sermon. In some places high numbers of the congregation had never heard a sermon for lack of a clergyman capable of delivering one. On Sundays some clergy did not turn up, often because a living was just a side-line. Occasionally, absentee ministers did bring colour to the Church. One musical vicar became a minstrel, while a John Beale of Juxta Fowey became the best wrestler in Cornwall.

The records of the interrogations give some illuminating insights. Margaret Maynard said she had not attended a service of the state church in 10 years. A separatist child was mentioned, aged 12 but still unbaptised for lack of a pastor. This suggests that a London congregation existed in *c*.1580, when Browne was still in and out of London. Robert Abraham, leather dresser and servant to Mr Rooks of Southwark, told interrogators that their meetings were at St Nicholas Lane or Roger Rippon's house, or Lee's house in Smithfield, in fields near Deptford, or woods near Islington (chosen because the Marian Martyrs met there).

It appears that George Johnson, a schoolteacher in St Nicholas Lane, was already active with London Brownists when his brother returned from Middelburg. In March 1593 George was delivering the sermon when 56 separatists were arrested. George said he had first been drawn to separatism by hearing Presbyterian Stephen Egerton, who had founded in Wandsworth, London, in *c*.1585 a congregation claimed later to be the first Presbyterian church in England. John Nicholas, a glover, said Nathaniel, his son, had been recently baptised by Francis Johnson at the age of five.

Reading through the interrogations as a whole one is struck by the contrast between the naivety of the Brownists and the realpolitik of their enemies. The followers of Browne, Greenwood and Barrowe opposed having parish-based churches because they could not abide having church members who were not believers. They could look along the pews of a parish church, they said, and spot atheists, papists, heretics, whores, adulterers and perjurers. They also disliked the Book of Common Prayer, which killed off all spontaneity. Prayers should come from the heart, they said, from the living spirit.

Brownist prisoners also stressed the orthodoxy of their beliefs. They were not heretics like Anabaptist or Arian separatists, they protested, and they differed from their persecutors only in respect of how the church was run. This was pure naivety. As Whitgift told Elizabeth, they had to be imprisoned for 'reasons of state'. People must all attend their parish churches so they heard government policies from the pulpit; the services must be strictly uniform to restrict deviation by incompetent clergy; and the income of the clergy had to be maximised to provide employment for the younger sons of the upper classes. The

Brownists treated the church as if its primary purpose was religious, which was not the case.

By 1592 the government of Elizabeth had lost patience with the Brownists and other 'sectaries'. There had already been 16 or 17 Brownists who had died in prison due to the poor conditions (especially in Newgate) but to little effect. In addition, London was in turmoil. In Southwark there were riots by artisans and in 1593 a devastating outbreak of plague which killed above 10,000 people and caused London public theatres to be closed until 1596, a blow to Shakespeare.

In October 1592 Penry had returned from Presbyterian Scotland, calling in on the way to dine with his father-in-law in Northampton. He then met his wife, Eleanor, at Stratford le Bow (now in London) before entering the capital. With catastrophic consequences, he now decided to join the Brownist church and in December he was at a garden house in Duke's Place, Aldgate, where both he and John Greenwood made speeches. This was probably Heneage House, a large tenement block in a dissenter area where in 1620 Pilgrim leaders met to negotiate the *Mayflower* expedition.

The second wave of arrests was not connected with Marprelate but more with the spread of disorder in London. In Southwark there were riots by artisans and everywhere there was open contempt for the bishops. In February 1593, as new legislation was being passed (the stern Conventicle Act allowing government to execute or banish separatists), the funeral of Roger Rippon was held. He had died in Newgate Prison, just inside the City on the corner of Newgate St and the Old Bailey. Newgate was notorious for its ill-treatment of prisoners and Rippon's funeral was rapidly turned by the populace into a demonstration against the Church. A placard was affixed to his coffin by person unknown declaring that Archbishop Whitgift was a 'great ennemye of God' and 'great ennemie of the saints'. This placard was taken to the house of the prosecutor and was the occasion, says Gurney, for the wave of arrests that followed.

In March there was a mass arrest of 56 Brownists at an illegal gathering in Islington Woods, near Finsbury. Penry was arrested but escaped. Johnson was despatched to Clink Prison, his brother George to the Fleet and Studley to Newgate with Barrowe and Greenwood. In April, Barrowe and Greenwood were taken to be hanged in Westminster at Tyburn (near Marble Arch), but this did not go according to plan. It had to be postponed because a great crowd of sympathisers assembled at Tyburn and they made their feelings known when Barrowe and Greenwood arrived. At first postponement seemed the sensible move but, the authorities noted glumly, it proved a serious mistake. The postponement was met with delight by 'the people' and all the way back to Newgate the streets were thronged with applauding crowds as Londoners flocked to express their joy at the apparent reprieve. Of course the authorities got their way in the end. The pair were hanged from Tyburn Tree, a device with which several persons could be executed at once. It was the latest technology. Victims were seated on a cart with nooses round their necks and the horse was then whipped. Strangulation could take ages and friends would often pull on the legs of the victims to strangle them quicker and shorten their agony. The crowds did not necessarily mean support for Brownism. Probably they knew nothing of 'double predestination', or 'prelapsarianism' but they did know that they hated the extravagance of the Bishops along the Strand, the corrupt practice of the monopolists who sold at high prices, the clergymen prying into their lives, the High Commission of the Church imprisoning and executing, the tithes and taxes, the compulsory church attendance, and the legion of informers restricting what they could say in public.

It should also be pointed out that some of the children who watched Barrowe and Greenwood dangle from the Tyburn Tree might have lived long enough to witness the time when they would be vindicated. They might one day watch the beheading of Archbishop Laud on Tower Hill, and the beheading of King Charles at Whitehall.

John Penry meanwhile had been arrested in Ratcliff, Stepney, at the house of Mr Lewes, along with Kniveton, Grave and Billet. He was imprisoned in the Poultry Comptoir. According to his biographer, he may have been living at the time in Long Lane, Bermondsey. In May he appeared before the King's Bench and was indicted under the Act of Uniformity. Though he appealed for help to William Cecil, who had often in the past protected Brownists, he was sentenced to death for sedition on evidence extracted from private papers found in his home. Cecil was powerless. Whitgift had convinced Elizabeth that the Brownists, however 'godly', had to die and Whitgift also believed Penry was the author of the Marprelate tracts, which satirised the bishops. The whole church hierarchy was up in arms. Being criticised was one thing but being laughed at was another.

Historians are now agreed that the author of the Marprelate Tracts was not Penry but probably a former MP, Job Throckmorton. Nevertheless on 29 May Penry was hanged from a gibbet at Thomas a Watering, where Albany Road joins the Old Kent Road, by the pond in what is now Burgess Park. He left behind a widow and four daughters. Aptly enough, considering that Penry was regarded as a martyr by the *Mayflower* Pilgrims, the site is called Thomas a Watering because it is where the pilgrims in Chaucer's *Canterbury Tales* met up to begin their pilgrimage to the shrine of Thomas a Becket in Canterbury.

In Penry's last letters written in April 1593 from his cell in the King's Bench Prison, then just to the north of St George church in Southwark, he names the 13 people he is most looking forward to meeting in Heaven, starting with 11 biblical figures (such as Adam and Moses) and ending with Henry and John, 'my two dear brethren'. He tells the remaining Brethren they should expect banishment and implores that they take his wife, Eleanor, and his four young daughters (named Sure-Hope, Safety, Comfort and Deliverance) with them: 'Take my poor and desolate widow' and my 'fatherless and friendless orphans, with you into exile, whithersoever you go.' The youngest daughter, Deliverance, was many years later living with Johnson in Amsterdam.

His main concern is with the 'remnant' of the Brownist church. The Bill of Coercion in 1592 against separatists said anyone who attended churches other than the state church could be imprisoned. Those arrested would be given three months to recant before banishment and, if found in the country after banishment was applied, they would be executed. As prisoners were released their banishment would come into effect, which meant that to avoid execution they must leave the country within three months, or recant. Penry could see that the only solution to this was mass emigration; but their options were limited. In 1592 they had petitioned Elizabeth to be allowed to emigrate to America but, given the three-month deadline, they clearly had to emigrate to Holland, either to Middelburg or Amsterdam. Penry urged his followers to communicate with the Brownists around the country (though he never uses the term, 'Brownist') to try and choose a place of banishment where they could all be together and not be dispersed. On 16 May he writes: 'The church is a Pilgrim here upon earth.' From that day on there was a recurring use of the term, 'Pilgrim', by those who survived the persecution.

Penry was also concerned with upholding morale. Referring to 'my beloved M. Barrowe and M. Greenwood', whose role he seems to have assumed, he urges: 'Be kind, loving, and tender-hearted, the one of you towards the other; labour to increase love... I would wish you earnestly to write, yea, to send, if you may, to comfort the brethren in the west and north countries, that they faint not in these troubles.' Above all, he wanted the movement to survive.

But the last word seemed to rest with the young Francis Bacon, a promising intellectual, who wrote in 1593 what he clearly believed was the epitaph of the Brownist movement:

And as for those which we call Brownists, being, when they were at the most, a very small number of very silly and base people, here and there in corners dispersed, they are now, thanks be to God, by the good remedies that have been used, suppressed and worn out.[24]

Little did he know.

2

The London Church

It looked at first as if Francis Bacon would be proved right and the Brownists were finished. Middelburg, solidly puritan, did not take them, just as it had not taken refugee Jews in 1591. Amsterdam would not take them either. Some of the Brownist refugees had arrived in Amsterdam even before July 1593. They were frightened by Elizabeth's stipulation that any found in the country after three months would be executed. As a travel incentive this was persuasive. On reaching Amsterdam, they met in the house of Israel Johnson, an English merchant, but were moved on by the intervention of Arminius, the founder of 'Arminianism'. Arminius believed in state control of religion for the sake of order (as did Elizabeth) and he put pressure on the local authorities to keep disorder out of Amsterdam.

In the end they found work in Kampen, in the eastern province of Overijssel, a centre of the woollen textile industry and desperate for cheap labour. Kampen had been advertising for immigrants 'of whatever nation' and offering easy terms of citizenship,[1] but the town was remote and after a while they looked for a refuge closer to Amsterdam and found Naarden. After independence from Spain the Dutch Protestants had a policy of handing over monasteries and convents they had seized to Walloon refugees (French-speaking Protestants from what is now Belgium). There was one such complex in Naarden and the Londoners were probably installed with the help of the Walloon community.

The Kampen-Naarden church was by now only about 40 strong and might have dwindled further but then, very probably through Walloon contacts, they received an offer of accommodation in Amsterdam from Jean de l'Ecluse, a printer from Rouen formerly living in London. After moving into Amsterdam in c.1596 their fortunes began to recover. There they met with Brownists who had arrived in

Amsterdam as individuals, unnoticed by Arminius, and one of them, Henry Ainsworth, was set to become their greatest asset. Ainsworth was already winning renown as an intellectual and he fitted with l'Ecluse like a hand in a glove: what he wrote, l'Ecluse, the radical printer, published.

Ainsworth had escaped from England to Ireland in 1593 before settling in Holland. According to Bradford he was 'modest, amiable and sociable' and had a 'meeke spirit and a Calme temper'.[2] He soon got a job as a porter to an Amsterdam bookseller who, impressed by his vast knowledge of Hebrew, encouraged his studies. It was not long, says Bradford, before Ainsworth was accounted better at Hebrew than any at Leiden University. Under Ainsworth's intellectual impetus the Londoners were now able to produce a document, the 1596 *True Confession of Faith*, which was to be the key to their success, and later an inspiration to the *Mayflower* Pilgrims.

The Confession

Amongst scholars there is a division of opinion about who was the author of the 1596 *Confession*. Some say it could not have been Ainsworth because much of it reads like Johnson, still housed in the Clink Prison, Southwark, but well able to communicate with his flock in Holland. Others say it must have been written by Ainsworth because the 1596 work, unlike the 1589 manifesto, *A True Description*, did not have the Presbyterian, centralist emphasis Barrowe and Johnson endorsed. The 1596 *Confession* has more checks on the power of the Elders: it is more bottom-up Congregationalist than top-down Presbyterian. But this authorship dispute does not seem intractable. Common sense suggests that Ainsworth in Amsterdam would have initiated the project, Johnson would have contributed, and then Ainsworth would have edited the final version. Ainsworth and George Kniveton, one the de facto leader of the church in Johnson's absence and the other a friend of John Penry, were on the spot and obviously they would have the final say.

The *Confession* of 1596 became well known all over Europe. The leaders of the *Mayflower* expedition took it to be one of their founding documents, and in 1610 John Robinson in Leiden refers to it as 'our Confession'. It starts by complaining that everybody 'falsely' calls them 'Brownists'. This was the routine disclaimer, dissociating themselves from the apostate. They do still endorse, nonetheless, Browne's fundamental principle that church members should be believers, 'true Christians', who enter a covenant of membership with their gathered church. Baptism of infants is allowed but does not signify membership of the church, which can be gained only through the covenant.

The 1596 *Confession* trusts the congregation more than the earlier work did. Each local church should elect its own Elders, accountable to the whole congregation. The Elders can excommunicate members only in exceptional circumstances. All authority should be by the command of God and by the agreement of men. The document stresses the division of power between church and state. This was radical then but is now one of the pillars of modern democracy: 'Render to God what is God's and what is Caesar's to Caesar.' This should lead to a general toleration but in 1596 they are still not radical enough for that. They make two exceptions: the state should suppress Catholics and heretics. A ban on Catholics was normal – they were the agents of a foreign (Spanish) invasion, bent on the conquest of England. The ban on heretics was aimed at the Anabaptists who, as the revolutionaries of the day, refused to recognise the authority of church or state: they believed in adult baptism; relied on their inner light, not the Bible; refused to bear arms; and refused to swear oaths. On this the Brownists agreed with the Church of England that if Anabaptist beliefs were tolerated the whole structure of society could collapse.

The Brownists now had a home, a church organisation, a printing-press, an agreed manifesto and even their own intellectual (Ainsworth). What they did not have was an agreed name. Despite the frequent usage of 'Pilgrims' by Penry, by Ainsworth ('in singleness of heart we sought God in the midst of our Pilgrimage...') and by the preface to the *Confession* ('We are but strangers and pilgrims, warring against manie and mightie adversaries'), yet the term 'Pilgrims' was too loose to be a name. Later on, the phrase 'strangers and pilgrims', taken from the *Confession*, was echoed by Cushman, Winslow and Cotton Mather but it was not a name they could use.

They also rejected 'Brownists', though that is what everybody called them. In popular parlance a 'Brownist' was a plain-speaking rebel who did not tarry for anybody. When Shakespeare used the term, 'Brownist', in this popular sense there was a tinge of admiration, but the Pilgrims did not want to remind others or even themselves of Browne's apostasy and instability of character. In any case, as Bradford said, they did not want to be associated with modern figures with all their foibles, but with Moses, the Prophets, and Paul.

Another option was to call themselves 'separatists' and sometimes they did. The trouble was that the suspect Anabaptists were also separatists, as were the Familists and Arians, so that usage had to be carefully judged. 'Church of the Separation' was sometimes used. Others called the church the 'Ancient Church' and this caught on to some extent because it did suggest that they were followers of the early Jewish and Christian 'churches' they were always trying to emulate.

It was left to Pastor Johnson to resolve the matter and his usage was: 'Exiled Church'. This cut through the above complexities and emphasised that they were still the same London church, unjustly banished from the country they loved.

Francis Johnson

Not only had the Exiled Church now been revived by Ainsworth, but suddenly in 1597 Francis Johnson appeared, out of the blue, with Daniel Studley. After four years (not forty) of 'wandering in the wilderness', the London Church now found itself, almost miraculously, reconstituted in Amsterdam. Johnson was their Pastor again; Ainsworth had replaced Greenwood as Teacher; and the former Elders of 1592, Studley and Kniveton, were back in place.

The reappearance of Francis Johnson requires some explanation. In 1593 he and Studley had been on death row, but they were never executed or even, as Penry had expected, banished. Instead they enjoyed privileged conditions in prison, especially in the case of Johnson, who was for most of the time kept in the Clink Prison, Southwark. There he wrote pamphlets in the company of Thomasina Boyes, widow of the rich merchant, Edward Boyes, and engaged in polemical correspondence with Anglican scholars such as Henry Jacob. In 1595 Johnson, while still in the Clink, even wrote his first full-length book. The well-off could always buy good accommodation in the privately run prisons and in addition Johnson, clearly, still had support from Cecil.

Francis had a brother, George, who did not receive such privileges and who was no doubt aware that, while Francis was enjoying almost a normal life, other Brownist prisoners were dying of pneumonia in freezing, windowless cells or, in the case of Bridewell Prison, were being beaten with cudgels for refusing to attend the prison chapel. In addition, George had a strong dislike for Thomasina's worldly ways and ostentatious dress and was shocked when he discovered that, just a few months after Edward Boyes died, Francis was about to marry what, in the idiom of the day, was called a 'warm widow'.

George wrote that Thomasina wore 'whalebones in the bodies of peticotes' to accentuate her figure and also 'the long white brest after the fashion of young dames, and so low she wore it, as the world call them codpeece brests', and withal an 'excess of lace'. In her mid-20s, she quaffed wine excessively, wore four or five gold rings and a 'copple crowned hatt with a twined band ... immodest and toyish in a Pastors wife.' Bradford later defended Thomasina. When he knew her personally in 1608, he said, she dressed soberly like a pastor's wife and she seemed 'godly'.[3]

For George, matters came to a head one day in 1594 when Thomasina and Francis visited him in the Fleet Prison. Francis had secured mobility around London in the company of a 'keeper' (an astonishing degree of licence) and they had come to ask for his blessing on their forthcoming marriage. Instead, his refusal deeply offended them, and it was the beginning of a breach that poisoned their relationship. Francis and Thomasina may have been genuinely surprised by George's reaction. For Brownists marriage was not a big deal. They did not regard it as a religious, but as a civil, matter and were happy to discover that in Holland civil marriage had been legalised in 1590. Similarly, while England was far less tolerant of divorce than other Protestant countries, the Brownists were more liberal, allowing any divorce for 'conscience'. Indeed, Johnson's church was later accused of immorality, so easy was it to obtain a divorce, and similarly the Brownist excusing of sex before marriage was often used against them by enemies.

In George's defence it should be mentioned that in 1586-92 there were 17 or 18 Brownists who had died in London prisons, as well as others elsewhere in the country, and of the 60 imprisoned in 1592 most were not allowed visitors, let alone outings and a girlfriend.

Newfoundland

Johnson's biggest outing was a visit to Canada. In 1597 the Brownists held in London (the 'Remnant'), and some exiles, petitioned Elizabeth for a licence to emigrate to America. They wrote:

> Whereas we, her majesty's natural born subjects, true and loyal, and now living many of us in other countries, as men exiled her highness' dominions, and the rest which remain within her grace's land greatly distressed through imprisonment and other great troubles sustained only for some matters of conscience – means is now offered for our being in a foreign and far country which lieth to the West from hence in the province of Canada where, by the Providence of the Almighty, we may not only worship God – but also do her Majesty good service and greatly annoy that bloody and persecuting Spaniard about the Bay of Mexico.

The petitioners were clearly weak on geography, but they did know that two London merchants, Hardwick and Leigh, had embarked on a project to settle Ramea Island, Newfoundland. When the merchants sailed from Gravesend they took with them Francis Johnson,

George Johnson, Daniel Studley, John Clarke and many others (according to Bradford). In addition, Charles Leigh, the captain of the *Hopewell* ship, was a secret member of the Brownists and a cousin of Thomasina. It looks as if Thomasina's family had sunk money into financing the enterprise.

George's relationship with his brother plunged to new depths on this voyage. At first they were kept apart, with George sailing on the *Chancewell* ship, but it was wrecked and George had to transfer to the *Hopewell*. After the failure of the expedition and its return to Southampton the Johnson brothers, Clarke and Studley travelled together to London but George was annoyed that the route was chosen so that Studley could call in on his contacts. In London George was further disturbed to learn that the authorities knew the four were in the city. When George was sent to Gravesend, alone, to be joined by the others later, he was affronted again. Francis seemed to be excluding George from important discussions.[4]

It has to be said that though Francis' conduct appears unreasonable, he did have a defence. George was a narrow sectarian who believed Anglicans were not true Christians and should be 'shunned' (not communicated with). George was no moderate. He took a dislike to Ainsworth for his mild manner and his willingness to debate. If Francis and Studley wanted to meet their Anglican or Presbyterian contacts, they would naturally not want George present. On the other hand, it might have been that Johnson and Studley were still working for Cecil against the Anabaptists and that was the reason for George's exclusion. It would explain why they moved about London with impunity.

In 1598 George openly opposed the election of two new Deacons backed by Francis and Studley. When, in 1599, an important debate with Henry Jacob was under way and George disapproved, Francis excommunicated his own brother. Their father, naturally enough, refused to 'shun' the excommunicated George, as members were expected to do, so Francis excommunicated him as well and had them both shunned. George returned to England, was soon apprehended, and died in Durham Prison. Bradford says Johnson took the extraordinary step of excommunicating his own father and brother because their opposition was relentless and insupportable.[5]

Scholars are still divided about Johnson. With Barrowe and the Barrowists, he had always preferred Presbyterian strong government and this episode had brought all his authoritarianism to the fore. What the *Confession* had striven to achieve – a reduction in the power of the Elders and the pastor – had been badly dented. Culpepper wrote: 'Francis Johnson angrily insisted on several occasions during his rift with George that the congregation abide by his wishes because they were not as educated as he.'[6] This is damaging, but perhaps in the context of justifying an academic debate with Henry Jacob there was a logic to it.

Henry Jacob

Henry Jacob was an Anglican living in London in the 1590s. In 1595, in the parish of Southwark St Saviour, he married Sara Dumaresq from a Jersey Huguenot family, several of whose members lived in London. The Channel Islands, of which Jersey is the largest, was a refuge for the English dissenters along with Germany, Ireland, Morocco, Scotland, Switzerland and the United Provinces of the Netherlands. In 1596 Jacob had visited Johnson in the Clink prison and begun a correspondence with him, as he did with the scholar, Thomas Bilson, Bishop of Winchester. The Clink was part of Winchester Palace. The church of Southwark St Saviour also seemed to have some sympathy with Jacob's radical puritanism. An Edward Phillips, minister there 1588-1602, expressed this sympathy in a sermon at the time.

In the 1590s Jacob had joined a group of Anglican intellectuals, the so-called 'quintumverate': William Ames, Paul Baynes, William Bradshaw, Robert Parker and himself. They looked at how the Church could be made more accountable (the word 'democratic' was rarely used in a favourable sense since Aristotle had apparently proved that democracy led to dictatorship), without embracing Presbyterianism (accountable only amongst Elders at the top) or Brownist separatism (accountable to the congregation at the bottom). Their view was that puritans such as themselves could stay in the Anglican Church if Anglican congregations were granted some autonomy. As all were respected scholars, it indicates the high esteem in which the Ainsworth-Johnson *Confession* was held that they now engaged Johnson in debate.

Jacob's movements at this time are obscure. At some time in the late 1590s he became chaplain to the Merchant Adventurer church in Middelburg, where Johnson had been chaplain in 1589-91. Most Middelburg records have been destroyed and exact details are hard to find but certainly Jacob was chaplain when in 1599 he decided to publish the debate with Johnson: *Against Master Francis Johnson and others of the Separation commonly called Brownists*. Johnson replied with his *Answer to Master Jacob* (1600). Jacob's line was that before Johnson took over Barrowe and Penry never denied that members of the Anglican Church were 'true Christians'. Johnson is insultingly putting the Anglican Church on the same level as pagans. The corruption in the Anglican Church and the oppressiveness of its hierarchy, which Jacob does not deny, should not cause the Church as a whole to be condemned. Johnson is exaggerating and he should name the 'abominations' he says the Church of England is guilty of.

Johnson was happy to oblige. He had plenty of abominations. He started by saying that the Brownists took as their model the ancient Jewish constitution at the time of the Prophets and then listed no fewer than 91 'abominations' including tithes; the lavish retinues of prelates (a dig at Whitgift); churching of women; kneeling for communion; non-resident ministers; saying children are damned if they die unbaptised; saying priests can forgive sins; and church courts with civil powers of arrest and imprisonment. Jacob replied that the 91 items were 'too small' to condemn 'us' (the whole church) and in any case many Anglicans agreed with Johnson on many of the 91. One is left with the feeling, however, that some of the 91 were not as 'small' as Jacob makes out and therefore on the whole it was Johnson who prevailed in the debate.

Bishop of Brownism

The Brownism of the Exiled Church now entered its period of greatest power and influence, mainly thanks to Ainsworth. In 1598 he had published the 1596 *Confession* in Latin. This may not strike the modern reader as a mighty step forward, but it was. Every scholar throughout Europe could now read it easily, instead of having to struggle with English, commonly regarded as an obscure and rather barbarous language. An international Brownist network emerged with members or supporters in France, Germany, Ireland, Scotland and the Netherlands. From 1599 Johnson had a branch in Africa. Islam did not have so much of a problem with religious toleration as Christianity did and there were Brownists employed by the Barbary Merchant Company in Morocco. Their leading light, Peter Fairlambe, regularly sent money from Morocco to Amsterdam. The Dutch authorities were impressed. They now yielded to this international endorsement and the London Exiled Church was recognised in 1601 as a fully-fledged church in Amsterdam, and not just the meeting-place of a sect.

This status was a spur to further consolidation of what scholars sometimes refer to as the 'London-Amsterdam Church'. As their Amsterdam membership rose from around 40 in 1595 to over 300 in 1608, they were able to acquire their own church building. They had ticked over hitherto on money left by Barrowe in his will to assist them with emigration, money from the London underground movement (the Remnant), money from Middelburg merchants and from Fairlambe in Morocco, but now with success they attracted other rich merchants to their cause. In 1607 the Exiled Church opened its own church building on the Lange Houtstraat in Vloomburg, the district where since 1596 they had been meeting in l'Ecluse's house. In Vloomburg, it was said, there were as many religions as houses and it was the centre of the Sephardi Jews, to which the Brownists were always close. As well as physical proximity, their admiration for the ancient Jewish church and Ainsworth's renown amongst Hebrew scholars meant constant interaction with the Jewish community. The main street was Jodenbreestraat (Jews' Broad St), where Rembrandt later had a house.

It was within Britain, however, that the spread of Brownism was most crucial. From 1601, the year of their recognition in Amsterdam, there were Brownists in Bristol, Kent, Lincolnshire, Norfolk, Nottinghamshire, Suffolk and Wiltshire. Even in London, where the Brownists had been crushed, Peter Fairlambe wrote: 'I doe heare that there be some increase of Brownists now in and about London.'[7] These were areas with a prominent middle class in the vicinity, often with strong trading connections to the Netherlands. Henoch Clapham, who joined the Exiled Church but then left, observing how widespread Johnson's influence became from 1601, called him the 'Bishop of Brownisme' since he 'exerciseth authoritie over some assemblies in England, which is a Bishoppricke of more length, by many hundred myles, then any Bishop in England hath...'.[8]

Apart from the geographical expansion at this time, there was an admiring and witty reference to the Brownists, apparently wiped out by Whitgift but now back, as it were, from the dead. In *c.*1600 Shakespeare's play, *Twelfth Night,* was first performed. In it Andrew Aguecheek is told to act either with courage or calculation, to which he replies: 'It must be with valour; for policy I hate: I had as lief be a Brownist as a politician.' Outspoken Brownists are contrasted favourably with calculating puritans represented by unsympathetic Malvolio. Puritans play down their dissent ('policy'), it is suggested, in order to remain inside the privileged Anglican Church. James I expressed something similar, writing in 1619: 'Our puritans are the founders and fathers of the Brownists: the latter onely boldly putting into practise what the former doe teach.'[9]

Shakespeare's reference also indicates that in his view his audience would be well acquainted with Brownists – they are no longer a tiny, obscure sect. At the time the Bishop of London estimated there were only about 200 London Brownists but the Spanish Ambassador thought 5000. Shakespeare's attitude implies that the Ambassador may have been nearer the mark.

James I

The miraculous spread of Brownism, which had so unexpectedly risen from the ashes of 1593, soon began to run into problems. In 1603 James I, son of Mary, Queen of Scots, was proclaimed the

King of England, a country whose previous ruler, Elizabeth, had executed his mother. Nonetheless he liked the Elizabethan Church Settlement. Having clashed as King of Scotland with the Scottish church, fairly independent of the Crown, he was looking forward to the English system which, through Elizabeth's Act of Supremacy, had put the monarch in full charge of both church and state.

James' accession was misinterpreted by both puritans and Brownists. They assumed that as Scotland had been one of their places of refuge, the arrival of a Scottish King would mean improvements, but James had never liked the religion in Scotland. When James called a conference at Hampton Court near London they took that to mean he was going to reform the Church of England along their lines. In fact, James preferred the existing Anglican system.

At first it did look good for the reformers. In 1603, Johnson and Ainsworth had immediately contacted the court on behalf of the Exiled London Church and were granted permission to travel to London and present a petition. Their petition incorporated the *Confession* of 1596, pointed out that nowhere in the Bible is marriage given as the business of a church (a plea for civil marriage in England as in Holland), stressed that they were loyal subjects of the king, and asked that their religion be tolerated 'as the French and Dutch churches are...'[10] They never received a reply.

Henry Jacob and his friends, as Anglicans, expected to do better at Hampton Court with their 'Millenary Petition' but instead received a devastating blow. The proclamation issued by James after the end of the conference, together with the subsequent church canons, demanded a strict adherence to the Elizabethan settlement. Clergy had to take an oath of loyalty not just to the king but to royal supremacy, the 39 Articles and the Book of Common Prayer. As radical puritans could not in all conscience accept these terms, they were faced with losing their livings.

Johnson took advantage of being in England and preached outside London. His preaching in Wiltshire must have been successful, since in 1604 a small Wiltshire group at Bradford-on-Avon emigrated to Amsterdam. Perhaps he or Ainsworth did something similar in Kent. In 1604 Robert Cushman, later to be closely associated with the *Mayflower*, was excommunicated in Canterbury and, again, there seems to have been emigration from Kent to Amsterdam. In 1604 in London four Brownists were obliged to leave the country under threat of hanging.[11] Johnson and Ainsworth could not have stayed for long as the atmosphere turned so poisonous, but they made sure their message was well publicised anyway by publishing *An apologie or defence of such true Christians as are commonly (but unjustly) called Brownists* (1604).

East Midlands

It is not known whether Johnson had time to visit his native Yorkshire, where several leading Brownists came from, including William Bradford. If he did, he would have passed through the East Midlands. There, a modest Brownist movement had started to grow. Its origins are unclear but it seems likely that William Brewster started to promote Brownism in Scrooby, Nottinghamshire, in 1598, the year after the Exiled Church in Amsterdam was reconstituted and in the same year the international edition of the *Confession* was published. His interest in the *Confession* may have been shared with Richard Clyfton in nearby Babworth. Brewster had studied at Cambridge University with Penry and Greenwood in 1580-81 and would have followed the tragic destiny of his fellow-students.

In 1585 Brewster had gone to the Netherlands with Thomas Davison, who was working for Walsingham, Secretary of State, and there mixed with such great figures as Sidney and Leicester, but on their return Davison was made the scapegoat for Elizabeth's unpopular execution of Mary, Queen of Scots. Eventually Brewster, suddenly brought down in the world through no fault of his own, left London and returned to his native Nottinghamshire to become Postmaster of Scrooby in succession to his father. When and where he was married is contested but a famous 19th-century editor passed on the printing trade belief (Brewster later became a printer) that Mary Brewster was raised in Duke St, Southwark, and that was where they married. As it happens this is just inside the parish of St Saviour, centre of the Brownist Church, which the editor would not have known, and the precise naming of the street also lends credence to his claim. It seems Brewster was permanently marked by this drastic change of fortunes in London. Bradford remarked later of Brewster: 'He was tenderhearted and compassionate of such as were in misery, but especially of such as had been of good estate and rank and were fallen into want and poverty.'[12]

It is clear that from 1598 onwards Brewster was Brownist in sympathy, if not a member. It is in that year that he is in trouble for sermon 'gadding' (listening only to sermons in the churches so as to avoid the rest of the service) and for 'publicly repeating' (not strictly preaching but repeating apparently by heart what an afternoon preacher has said). Both are Brownist practices and it may even have been that he was running by subterfuge a Brownist church, since in Scrooby he and his associates used a chapel, not the parish church, and guest speakers were brought in from outside,[13] which is also typical of the Brownist gathered churches.

The guest speakers were presumably the 'zealous preachers' who according to Bradford came to 'the North parts' around 1600.

In his chronology these preachers are placed between the period when William Perkins (a defender of Johnson) was popular, in the mid-1590s, and the accession of James I in 1603.[14] This fits with the expansion of the Amsterdam church from 1598, when Johnson and Ainsworth went into evangelical mode. From then onward Brewster and Clyfton, and then John Robinson, would have been well aware of Amsterdam as the centre of Brownism and a possible place of refuge.

Nathaniel Morton, the historian of New England, attached the foundation of the Brownist church in Scrooby to the year 1602, when the Nottinghamshire group headed by Brewster in Scrooby and Clyfton from Babworth 'entered into a covenant' and formed a gathered church. In 1606 there was a similar development to the east of Scrooby in Gainsborough, Lincolnshire, on the River Trent, when John Smyth also formed a gathered church with a Brownist character. In between, in 1604, the most important recruit of all was made to the Brownist cause – John Robinson.

John Robinson

Robinson, born around 1575, was educated in Cambridge at Corpus Christi College, where he became a Fellow in 1598 and was ordained. He took up a joint ministry in Norwich but was denounced by an informer for his radical opinions. However, he wrote that although he was mixing with Brownists in Norwich (perhaps with Francis Cooke and members of the Walloon church), he did not take the decisive step toward Brownism there, but only later in Cambridge.[15] He resigned his Fellowship in February 1604, it seems, and then returned to his native Nottinghamshire, where he married Bridget White.

Although taking the decisive steps was a gradual process, Robinson had clearly identified with the cause earlier. In his *Justification of the Separation* (1610) he wrote of 1598 that 'we published our confession' (the Ainsworth Latin version) and sent it to all the universities of Europe. He explains that, though in sympathy with the 'Brethren' (he never says 'Brownists' of course), he still lacked the self-confidence to join them for a long time because so many respected authorities spoke against them. He described the irritation he felt towards those he calls the 'reformists' in the Anglican Church (he doesn't say 'Puritans') who argued about trifles such as surplices and caps. He embraced the whole of the Brownist tradition, hailing the 1567 and 1592 churches and defending Barrowe, Greenwood, Johnson and Ainsworth, although he did admit he found Barrowe a little tricky to defend because of his 'railing'.

It was not, however, until 1605-07 that persecution by the Church authorities of those who did not accept the new Church canons drove

Brewster, Clyfton and Robinson to have serious thoughts about emigration to Amsterdam. It was in 1606 that a notable conference was organised in Coventry by Lady Isabel Bowes, an impressive organiser and intellectual, who had with Henry Jacob supported the Millenary Petition. She brought together the would-be separatists to debate with non-separatists like herself. Robinson was a very reluctant separatist. When in 1605 he was suspended for not conforming to the new requirements laid down after the Hampton Court conference, he said he really wanted to conform, and would have conformed, 'had not the truth been in my heart as a burning fire shut up in my bones'.[16] The die was now cast, and from 1606 on he was assisting Richard Clyfton with the Brownist congregation that met at Brewster's house in Scrooby.

Robinson knew the price he would have to pay. The authorities had already started arresting non-complying Brownists in the area. In 1607 a Gervase Neville at Scrooby was charged as being a member of 'one of the sects of Barrowists or Brownists, holding and maintaining erroneous opinions and doctrine repugnant to the Holy Scriptures and the Word of God' and on that basis imprisoned in York Castle. William Bradford later wrote of the historic decision by Brewster, Clyfton, Robinson, and Smyth in Gainsborough, to flee to Amsterdam and join the main Brownist body: 'Yet seeing themselves thus molested... they resolved to go in the Low Countries, where they heard was freedom of religion for all men; as also how sundry from London and other parts of the land had been exiled, and persecuted for the same cause, and were gone thither, and lived at Amsterdam and in other places of the land.'[17] The spreading persecution had left them no option but to join the London-Amsterdam church set up by those of 'the same cause'.

How did the East Midland Brownists get the money to organise emigration? Isabel Bowes seems to have been the main patron of Smyth but the funding for the emigration seems to have come from Thomas Helwys, a merchant in Gainsborough. Yet they could not just go to the Lincolnshire coast, hire a ship and cross the North Sea. Emigration was illegal without permission from the authorities. There were 'searchers' in every port and informers in every town. Any ships had to be Dutch and organised at the Dutch end. In addition, there had to be accommodation in Amsterdam. Jeremy Bangs says Johnson and Ainsworth probably helped the refugees who crossed over to Amsterdam in 1608.[18] Culpepper concluded that Johnson and Ainsworth initially moved Brewster, Clyfton and Smyth towards separatism and then in 1608 helped them to emigrate.[19]

John Smyth was rather a special case. He had been under the influence of Francis Johnson for some time. When in 1586 he went to study at Christ's College, Cambridge, Johnson was his tutor. He had resigned his Fellowship in 1598, at the time of the international *Confession,* and had then become a preacher in Lincoln. This was the same year that Brewster had apparently become a supporter of Brownism. Jason Lee has compared texts and shown how passages written by Smyth clearly show the influence of Johnson. Even Smyth's church covenant is very similar to the one drawn up by Johnson in Middelburg.[20] Yet, by the time he arrived in Amsterdam in 1608, probably after visiting Middelburg, Smyth was at odds with Johnson, at whose church he must initially have worshipped, and in 1609 he became an Anabaptist.

According to Brewster later on, in the 1630s, Smyth was a 'rigid' separatist, which meant he would not have countenanced any relations with the Anglican Church. As the Anabaptists were also absolute separatists, it was logical for Smyth to adhere to them – in Amsterdam the Mennonite Anabaptists (pacifist and egalitarian, forerunners of the Quakers) were very strong. Thus, though Robinson did not like Smyth's lack of self-discipline and Brewster disliked his rigidity against Anglicans, Smyth had virtues of his own. The libertarianism he and Helwys favoured was to produce eventually a commendable doctrine of toleration and Smyth's group was also much more favourable to women than either Helwys or the Brownists, allowing them to have a prominent role in his church.[21] This may have been the influence of Isabel Bowes.

Leiden

John Robinson also parted company with Johnson in 1609 but not as a result of some acrimonious row such as broke out between Johnson and Smyth. He simply moved out of Amsterdam and, with approaching a hundred followers, settled in the city of Leiden. Robinson applied first to the Leiden authorities for permission and by May 1609 the move was completed. Richard Clyfton, the Pastor of the Scrooby congregation ('a fatherly old man ... having a great white beard' said Bradford), was very loyal to Johnson, and he remained in Amsterdam with a remnant of his flock.

It is necessary to describe Robinson and the Leiden church because many of its members sailed on the *Mayflower* in 1620 and Robinson created an ethos in Leiden that carried over to the Plymouth Plantation. Until he died in 1625 Robinson was the Pastor of the Pilgrims, communicating to his congregation by letter across the Atlantic.

It is not exactly clear why Robinson and his supporters decided to move from Amsterdam to Leiden. Chiefly, it was because of the turmoil within the Exiled Church, gripped by its own internal divisions and now in a battle with the strict separatism of John Smyth. The Nottinghamshire congregation, many brought up amidst rural husbandry, also found it difficult to adapt to busy Amsterdam, at that time one of the most dynamic cities in the world. It was much easier for Smyth's congregation from Gainsborough, a busy town in Lincolnshire. De Baar wrote that the urban followers of Johnson in Amsterdam had even mocked Robinson's semi-rural group as 'ignorant idiots'.

Those were the negatives but there were also positive reasons for emigration to Leiden. The city itself was (and is) beautiful. On the Old Rhine, 25 miles south of Amsterdam, it was in 1609 a city of migrants. The lighter 'new draperies', so popular and profitable, developed in Walloon textile towns such as Lille, were brought into Leiden by Huguenot refugees fleeing north to Leiden and Middelburg and in the 17th century they made Leiden the most important industrial centre in Europe, challenged only by Lyon. From 1574 (the year of Leiden's liberation from Spain) to 1622 Leiden's population, by mass immigration, rose from 12,500 to over 40,000. By the time the Pilgrims arrived it had two Walloon churches, an English church and even, near the Peterskerk, a Catholic church, tolerated on condition its members kept themselves reasonably well hidden.

The second positive was the large English community in Leiden. It consisted of English students at the esteemed Leiden University, some refugees from Kent and East Anglia, and some well-off merchants close to the Brownists, such as John Carver. One of the main reasons for moving on to Leiden must have been the number of English sympathisers already there and therefore the possibility for Robinson's church to grow. On the *Mayflower* the majority of the Leiden contingent were not Pilgrims from the East Midlands (though they did supply such leading figures as Bradford and Brewster) but Pilgrims who had originally come from places such as Canterbury, Colchester, Norwich or Sandwich, some of whom were in Leiden before the East Midlands group arrived. A clothier in Leiden, Abraham Gray, was from London and several others had London connections.

John Carver was especially important since he played a leading role in the negotiations for the *Mayflower* expedition and was elected the first Governor of Plymouth Colony. It is not known how long he had lived in Leiden before Robinson's arrival in April but in February 1609 Carver had joined the main Walloon church. He had married a wealthy Walloon, Marie de Lannoy de L'Ecluse, who came from a distinguished family. Charles de l'Ecluse was the Professor at Leiden University famous for establishing the Dutch tulip industry in the botanical gardens of Leiden. Marie de l'Ecluse established 12 houses for refugees and it looks likely that it was she who arranged accommodation in Leiden for Robinson's 80 or 90 Pilgrims, just as Jean de l'Ecluse arranged accommodation for the Pilgrims in Amsterdam in 1596. This would certainly explain why Bradford says Carver was 'much approved' by the passengers on the *Mayflower*, and why they chose him as their first Governor.

Carver had joined the same Walloon community in Leiden as Francis Cooke, another *Mayflower* passenger, and his wife, Hester Mahieu. Although Francis probably had family in Norwich (where Robinson was a curate), it looks likely that they came to Leiden from the Walloon community in London, given that nearly all their *Mayflower* associates later on had London connections. That would be normal. The Walloon and French Huguenots in London were mostly in the textile trade and Leiden was the biggest textile centre in Europe. In 1600-1630 about 80 Walloons are known to have joined the Walloon community in Leiden from London.

The Mahieu family had moved to Leiden *c.*1590 and the Lannoy family had been rich merchants in Middelburg in the 1580s. Hester Mahieu, who married Cooke in the Vrouwekerk, Leiden, in 1603, had a nephew, Philippe de Lannoy who in 1621 sailed to New Plymouth as 'Delano' on the second Pilgrim ship, the *Fortune*. These were migrant families to whom America was just another frontier. The French Huguenot community in Leiden even had a tradition of attempted emigrations to America dating back to the 1560s and it was Leiden Huguenots led by Jessé de Forest who were the first to settle on Manhattan, thereby founding New Amsterdam, now New York.

Robinson's great achievement in Leiden, in contrast to Johnson's failure in Amsterdam, was to create a stable church without any splits or scandals that was able to earn respect and attract support. His Leiden church at its peak probably exceeded 400 members and was still around 300 in 1620. Partly this was down to his personal qualities: he was able, Bradford wrote, to head off any sharp disputes, nip them in the bud, or resolve them so that 'love, peace and communion' were restored. Only in very few cases did he have to take a firm line and excommunicate.[22] Just as important, however, was his belief in seeking as much agreement as was possible with alternative points of view, including those of other churches. Two of the pieces of advice he urged upon his congregation, and often quoted, are always be open to 'more truth'; and choose 'rather to study union than division'.

In Amsterdam relations between Johnson's church and the English, Dutch and French churches were always tense. In Leiden, by contrast, the relations between Robinson's church and the other English-speaking church in the city, the English Reformed Church (essentially Anglican) were amiable (although Robinson disagreed with some of its practices), while his relations with the Dutch and French churches were actually very warm. Members of the Dutch Reformed Church attended Robinson's church and received the sacraments. Members of Robinson's church attended the Dutch Church for sermons, if they understood the language, and Robinson intended to have his own son trained to be a minister in the Dutch Reformed Church.[23]

This closeness was much appreciated by the Leiden city authorities who, in 1620, on the eve of the *Mayflower* expedition, praised Robinson's church for its peaceableness and orderliness. When Robinson died Dutch professors attended his funeral, and after his death his wife, family and friends joined the Dutch Reformed Church. Thus John Robinson, a leading figure in Leiden and Pastor of the *Mayflower* Pilgrims ended his days on good terms with a Dutch Reformed Church which in the 1560s, at Austin Friars in London, had played a key role in the movement for churches independent of the state.

The 1592 Brownist Church

Bradford and Robinson recognised the church of Rough (1557) as the first 'true' church; the Fitz church (1567) as the direct ancestor of the Leiden and Plymouth churches; and the 1592 church of Greenwood and Johnson as their parent church, the first properly constituted church in their tradition. As none of these churches has left surviving records it is often difficult to be sure who was a member and who was just a supporter. The list below also understates the large number of women in the movement (Archbishop Grindal said there were 'more women than men') since women were usually not arrested and therefore had few prison records. The Brownist prisoners of 1587-93 are marked #.

Names	Background
#Abraham, Robert	Leather-dresser. Servant to Thomas Rookes of St Olave, Southwark. 1593 arrested, Islington, and d Newgate.
Ainsworth, Henry	1593 escaped to Ireland. c.1596 to Amsterdam. 1596 co-author of *Confession*. 1597 Teacher in Amsterdam. 1604 to London to petition the king. 1607 md Marjory Appleby. 1607 *Communion of saincts*. 1608 *Counterpoyson*. 1610 broke with Johnson. 1613 won control of Amsterdam church. 1622 d.
#Allen, Avis	1593 arrested, Islington.
Allen, Peter	1593 to Amsterdam
Bailey, Robert	1593 to Kampen and Amsterdam.

#Barnes, John	A tailor of Duck Lane, off Smithfield. 1593 arrested, Islington.
#Barrowe, Henry	1566 Clare Hall, Cambridge, then lawyer. 1587 arrested at Clink when visiting Greenwood. 1589 *A True Description*. 1591 *A Brief Discoverie*. 1593 hanged.
Beauchamp, John	1610 sided with Ainsworth in Amsterdam. 1613 Bought the Amsterdam church for Ainsworth from Blackwell. 1620 backed the *Mayflower* as an adventurer.
#Beche, John	1593 arrested, Islington.
Bennett, Edward	Elder, and patron, of Exiled Church. Wealthy merchant. 1610 backed Johnson and Studley against Ainsworth. 1612 interested in emigration to America. 1618 backed Blackwell. 1621 Virginia Co granted him patent for Isle of Wight county.
Bennett, Richard	1610 sided with Ainsworth.
#Billett, Arthur	1593 arrested in Stepney with Penry. A 'scholar', perhaps book distributor.
#Billett, Scipio	A 'gentleman'. d in Newgate.
Bischop, Thomas	1610 sided with Ainsworth.
Blackwell, Francis	1605 Elder of Exiled Church. 1612 after Dutch court ordered him to sell Lange Houtstraat, he moved to London with Bennett. 1615 went to buy ship in London. 1618 (Aug) sailed from Gravesend to Virginia but voyage a disaster.
#Bodkin, Anne	1593 arrested, Islington.
#Boull, Robert	Fishmonger, perhaps book distributor. 1596 d in Newgate.
#Bowman, Christopher	Goldsmith. 1588 Imprisoned for petition to Elizabeth asking for freedom of worship. 1592 elected Deacon. 1593 arrested in Islington. *c.*1596 In Kampen and Naarden. 1608-09 Deacon of Exiled Church. 1619 d on voyage of Franciscans to Virginia.
Bowman, Ellyn	Wife of Christopher
#Boyes, Edward	Rich haberdasher of Fleet St. 1592 Brownists arrested at his house. Imprisoned in Bridewell Prison and then the Clink where he d 1594.

Names	Background
#Boyes, Thomasina	1593 arrested, Islington. 1594 widowed, md Francis Johnson.
#Bray, Robert	1593 arrested, Islington.
Brewer, Thomas	1615 enrolled as student at Leiden University. With Brewster set up the 'Pilgrim Press' to publish books in Leiden. 1621 helped Sandys
Brewster, William	*c.*1567 b Nottinghamshire. 1580 to Peterhouse, Cambridge, at same time as John Penry. 1584 in Holland as secretary to William Davison, assistant to Walsingham. 1586-90 in London. *c.*1590 returned to Scrooby. 1594 made postmaster in Scrooby. 1608 to Amsterdam. 1609 to Leiden, as chief Elder. 1617 with Robinson co-signed Seven Articles. 1627 Undertaker.
#Bristow, David	Tailor in St Martin's le Grand. 1593 arrested, Islington.
#Buck, Daniel	Scrivener of Southwark. 1593 arrested, Islington. Named those attending the March meeting.
Bulward, Robert	Recanted, returned to Church of England.
#Bylson, Mr	Held meetings at his home in Cree Church, Aldgate.
#Chandler, Alyce	Imprisoned later than John. Had 8 children.
#Chandler, John	1587 arrested at Martin's house. d in Poultry Compter.
Clapham, Henoch	Brownist in Amsterdam who left the church in 1598.
#Clarke, John	Farmer from Walsoken, Norfolk, near Wisbech.
Cleyton, George	1593 to Kampen and Amsterdam.
Clyfton, Richard	1586 rector at Babworth near Retford & Scrooby. 1605 ejected. 1608 to Amsterdam 1609 stayed in Amsterdam with Johnson.
Cockey, Thomas	1597 'Prophet' of the Exiled Church, Amsterdam. In 1610 he backed Ainsworth.
#Collier, George	Haberdasher of St Martin Ludgate.
#Collins, William	1593 arrested, Islington.
Cooke, Nicholas	1593 to Kampen and Amsterdam.

#Crane, Nicholas	1566 minister in Deptford. Lecturer in the Minories, preacher at Plumbers Hall. 1587 arrested at Martin's house in St Andrew Wardrobe. d in Newgate.
Crumford, John	1610 sided with Ainsworth.
#Dalamore, John	Weaver.
#Darvall, Wm	Carpenter, Shoreditch.
#Daubin, Margery	1593 arrested, Islington.
#Denford, William	Schoolmaster. d in Gatehouse Prison, Westminster.
Dennis, William	Executed, Thetford.
Dicker, Thomas	1593 to Kampen and Amsterdam.
#Diggins, Christopher	Weaver, St Olave. 1593 arrested, Islington.
#Digson, Thomas	1593 arrested, Islington.
#Dore, John	1587 arrested.
#Drewet, Thomas	d in Newgate. Probably related to William Drewet, of the Fitz church.
#Edwards, John	Friend of Penry.
#Eyles, William	Tailor in Walbroke, near Mansion House.
Fairlambe, Peter	1588 became a Brownist. 1593 banished. Preacher to English merchants in Morocco. 1599 left Brownists. 1606 *Recantation of a Brownist*.
#Farland, Peter	1593 arrested, Islington.
#Farre, Edward	Likely related to Sybill Farre, wife of John Clarke.
#Farrer, Margaret	d in Newgate.
Fluet, Andrew	1593 to Amsterdam.
Fowler, John	Recanted.
#Fowrestier, James	A physician, but also possibly a book distributor.
#Fox, Mr	Held meetings at his home in St Nicholas Lane.
#Gamble, Clement	1587 arrested.
#Gilbert, Edward	Apprentice trunk maker of St Gregory's by St Paul. Survived to be founder member of Jacob's church in 1616.

Names	Background
Gilgate, William	Ordained Anglican minister, became Brownist.
#Grave, Edward	Fishmonger, St Botolph in Thomas St. 1593 arrested in Stepney with Penry.
#Greenwood, John	1577 at Corpus Christi, Cambridge. A clergyman. 1585 deprived of his benefice in Norfolk. 1587 arrested at Martin's house in St Andrew Wardrobe. 1587-92 Imprisoned in the Clink, then in the Fleet. 1592 elected Teacher of church. 1593 arrested, Islington. 1593 hung at Tyburn, bd at All Hallows Barking by the Tower.
Greenwood, Mrs	Sent servant, Cicely, to Clink prison to smuggle John's writings to Holland for publication.
Grove, David	1593 to Kampen and Amsterdam.
#Gwalter, John	d in Newgate. Incriminated by Studley as a distributor of books.
Hales, John	1610 sided with Ainsworth.
Helwys, Joan	Wife of Thomas. 1608 imprisoned in York Castle.
Helwys, Thomas	1593 admitted to Gray's Inn. 1595 md Joan Ashmore.1607 became a Brownist separatist. 1607-08 financially backed Brownist emigration from East Midlands. 1608 Dispute with Johnson. 1609 (Jan) became Anabaptist with Smyth. 1610 split with Smyth. 1612 his *Mystery of Iniquity* calls for toleration by the state to include Jews, Turks and even Catholics. 1613 returned to England and was imprisoned. d *c.*1615.
#Hewet, Thomas	Purse-maker in St Martin le Grand.
#Holmes, Ann	1593 arrested, Islington.
#Howton, William	d in Newgate
#Hulkes, John	Deptford shipwright.
#Jackson, Richard	1593 arrested, Islington. d in Newgate.

#Johnson, Francis	1562 bp Richmond, Yorkshire. 1570 to Christ's College, Cambridge. 1584 Fellowship. Ordained. 1589 puritan sermon at St Mary's: imprisoned. 1590 refused to accept control of Church by the state: expelled from Cambridge University. 1590 Pastor of Merchant adventurers at Middelburg. 1591 burnt Brownist books. 1592 to London, elected Pastor of Brownist church. 1592 (Dec) arrested at house of Edward Boyes in Fleet St. 1593 was arrested in Islington. 1593 (April) interrogated in prison. 1594 md Thomasina Boyes. 1596 Probably co-author with Ainsworth of *True Confession*. 1597 (April) to Newfoundland, and then to Amsterdam; *c.*1598 excommunicated his brother, George. 1600 *Answer to Henry Jacob*. 1604 to London to put case to the king. 1604 preached in Wiltshire. 1610 (Dec) split with Ainsworth over congregational supremacy. 1614 to Emden, Germany. 1617 his *Christian Plea.*1618 d in Amsterdam.
#Johnson, George	1563 bp Richmond, Yorkshire. Christ's College, Cambridge. *c.*1590 schoolmaster, St Nicholas Lane, London. 1593 arrested in Islington. 1593 imprisoned in the Fleet. 1599 excommunicated. 1603 In Durham Prison. d 1604.
Johnson, Jacob	1597 Prophet of Exiled Church, Amsterdam
Johnson, John	Father of George and Francis. 1602 excommunicated.
#Jones, (Francis?)	1593 arrested
#Kniveton, George	1592 Elected Elder. 1593 arrested, Stepney, with Penry. 1593 to Kampen. Elder of Exiled Church in Amsterdam.
Laune, Christopher	Recanted, returned to Church of England. 1612 *The Prophane Schisme of the Brownists*.
L' E(s)cluse, Jean de	Printer and teacher. In 1590s was living as a Walloon in London. 1596 Brownists from Naarden met at his house in Amsterdam. 1610 sided with Ainsworth. 1615 bought the Amsterdam church from Beauchamp for Ainsworth.

Names	Background
#Lee, Nicholas	Deacon of the 'remnant' that survived in London after 1593
#Mrs Lee, Nicholas	1593 arrested, Islington.
#Lee, Thomas	1593 arrested, Islington.
Leigh, Charles	1597 Captain of *Hopewell* ship. Cousin of Thomasina Johnson ('Widow Boyes', née Leigh).
#Leye, Nicholas	1593 arrested, Islington.
Lushe, John	1593 to Kampen and Amsterdam.
Mainestone, William	1593 to Kampen and Amsterdam.
#Maner, Mother	d in Newgate
#Manners, George	1593 arrested, Islington.
Mansfield, Richard	1612 with Studley accused of misdemeanours by Laune.
#Marshall, William	Wapping shipwright. 1593 arrested, Islington.
#Martin, George	1593 arrested, Islington.
#Martin, Henry	1587 arrested with others at his home in St Andrew Wardrobe.
#Mason, William	Wapping Shipwright. 1593 arrested, Islington.
May, Dorothy	1613 md William Bradford. Daughter of Elder of Exiled Church in Amsterdam.
May, Henry	1610 sided with Ainsworth.
#Maynard, Margaret	Said she had not attended church for 10 years. 1587 arrested at Martin's house. d in Newgate.
Mercer, Stanshal	1593 to Kampen and Amsterdam.
#Micklefield, Thomas	Joiner of Southwark St Saviour.
#Miller, Judith	d in Newgate.
#Mitchell, Thomas	Turner. 1593 arrested, Islington.
#Moore, Elizabeth	1593 arrested, Islington.
Morton, George	*c.*1585 b Bawtry, Yorkshire. In Leiden.
Neville, Jervaise	Imprisoned with Joane Helwys in York Castle, then banished.
#Nicholas, John	Glover. 1593 arrested, Islington.
Payne, John	1593 to Zeeland, then to Kampen, then Amsterdam. 1610 sided with Ainsworth.

#Parker, John	Clothworker of Doelittle Lane.
Penry, Deliverance	Daughter of John. 1597 in Amsterdam with Johnson. 1611 md Samuel Whitaker, a bombazine worker.
Penry, Eleanor	Wife of John.
#Penry, John	From Cefnbrith, Brecknockshire, Wales. 1580 to Peterhouse, Cambridge with William Brewster. 1589-92 in Scotland. 1592 became a Brownist. 1593 arrested Stepney. 1593 hung at Thomas a Watering, Old Kent Road, now Southwark.
#Pidder, Leonard	Blackfriars shoemaker.
Plater, Richard	Printer, Amsterdam.
#Pulbery, Abraham (c.1567-)	Purse maker. 1590 md Jane Cole, St Stephen Coleman Street. 1593 arrested, Islington. 1610 sided with Ainsworth.
#Pulbery, John	1593 arrested, Islington.
#Purdy, John	Died, Bridewell Prison.
#Raper, Christopher	1593 arrested, Islington.
#Rippon, Roger	1592 bd son, Ezekiel, Southwark St Saviour. 1593 arrested, Islington. d in Newgate.
Robinson, John	c.1575 b Sturton, Nottinghamshire. 1592 to Corpus Christi, Cambridge, 1598 Fellowship. Ordained. 1603. In Norwich was denounced by an informer for his criticisms of the Church. 1604 (Feb) resigned his Cambridge Fellowship, returned to Notts. and md Bridget White. 1606 attended Coventry conference. 1608 emigrated to Amsterdam. 1609 Pastor of Leiden church. 1610 *A Justification of Separation*. 1610 Debate with Ames, Jacob and Parker. 1612 defeated Episcopius in Leiden University debate. 1615 (Sept) enrolled at Leiden University. 1617 approved the Seven Articles. 1620 'Farewell Sermon'. 1625 d in Leiden.
#Rowe, Ellyn	1593 arrested, Islington. d in Newgate. 'Mother Roe'.
Sanders, Clement	Recanted, returned to Church of England.
Sedgwick, Richard	c.1601 In Hamburg

Names	Background
#Settle, Thomas	*c.*1570 Queen's College, Cambridge. Anglican minister. 1586 Imprisoned. 1592 lived in Cowe Lane, Smithfield St, London. 1592 arrested. 1593 arrested, Islington. Somehow stayed in England after release from prison.
#Settle, Mrs	1593 arrested, Islington.
#Sheppard, William	1593 arrested, Islington. 1610 sided with Ainsworth.
#Simkins, Christopher	Coppersmith, Aldersgate St. 1593 arrested, Islington.
Slade, Matthew	From Dorset, a graduate, a mason. 1598 elected Elder of Exiled Church but later excommunicated. 1605 asked Dutch Reformed Church to establish an English-speaking church in Amsterdam.
#Smells, George	Tailor of Finche Lane, Cornhill. 1593 arrested in Islington. 1640 buried St George the Martyr, Southwark.
#Smyth, Quinton	Southwark felt-maker. 1589 arrested for distributing pamphlets.
Smyth, John	1586 to Christ's College, Cambridge, with Johnson as his tutor. 1594 Fellowship. 1598 resigned Fellowship. 1600-1602 Lecturer in Lincoln. 1606 formed Brownist group in Gainsborough. 1608 to Johnson in Amsterdam. 1609 (Jan) became Anabaptist.
Smyth, William	1597 imprisoned in Marshalsea Prison. Anglican minister from Wiltshire. Elected Preacher for Exiled Church, Amsterdam.
#Snape, Mr	1592 prisoner according to Waddington. Snape a minister of St Peter, Northampton, turned Brownist.
#Sparewe, John	Feltmaker or fishmonger. Probably related to the two Sparrowes in the 1567 church. In White Lion prison, Southwark.
#Stamford, Barbara	1593 arrested, Islington.
#Stevens, Thomas	d in Newgate.

#Stokes, Robert	Of St Saviour, Southwark. In 1589-90 he financed the printing of writings by Barrowe and Greenwood. Yet in 1593 under interrogation he gave full information, as did Buck, Johnson and Studley.
Stuart, John	1593 to Amsterdam.
#Studley, Daniel	Draper and girdler. 1592 elected Elder. 1592 arrested. 1593 in Bridewell prison. Sentenced to death but sentence commuted. Gave information about distribution of books incriminating Smith, Forester, Barrowe, Billett, Gwalter and himself. 1597 went to Newfoundland with Johnson. 1604 accused of gross immorality. 1612 expelled from the Exiled Church.
Sutherland, John	1593 to Amsterdam.
#Tailour, Anne	d in Newgate.
Taylor, Henry	1593 to Kampen and Amsterdam.
#Thompson, Edmund	1593 arrested, Islington.
Thorpe, Giles	1604 elected Elder of Exiled Church. In charge of the church's printing press, closed down in 1619. 1610 sided with Ainsworth.
#Unwin, Katherine	Widow. 1593 arrested, Islington.
#Waterer, Roger	Haberdasher of St Martin Ludgate. Servant to Robert Pavey. 1610 buried child, Bathshua, at St Botolph Aldgate.
#Weaver, William	Shoe maker, Gray's Inn Lane, Holborn.
#Weber, William	1593 arrested, Islington.
White, Thomas	From Slaughterford, Wiltshire. 1604 Took his Brownist church to Amsterdam. 1605 he recanted, and attacked the Exiled Church in *Discoverie of Brownisme*.
Witcomb, Samuel	1593 to Kampen and Amsterdam.
Witcomb, William	1593 to Kampen and Amsterdam.
#Withers, Henry	Deptford shipwright. 1593 arrested, Islington.
Yonge, (John?)	1592 held meeting of Brownist church in St Nicholas Lane, probably in the tenement block Walsingham was buying in 1587.

Decline in Amsterdam

The situation in Amsterdam deteriorated even further after Robinson left, as he had suspected it would. In 1603 brother George had denounced Daniel Studley, Johnson's right-hand man, but his accusations carried no weight until in 1606 Studley was charged with committing incest with his wife's daughter and beating his wife when she protested. In 1612 a former member who had recanted, the rich ship-owner, Christopher Laune, published *The Prophane Schisme of the Brownists, with the Impietie, Dissensions, Lewd, and Abominable Vices of that Impure Sect*. This revealed Studley had disclosed confidential details of his Eldership to a certain Marie May, to whom he had granted sanction for sex before marriage; that he had taken part with a Judith Holder in a 'knowne evil'; and that he was also discovered in bed with her, though she was a married woman. As accusations came in from different sources it did not look good for Studley, and Jeremy Bangs says the evidence is against him. Johnson did not defend Studley's 'sins' but asserted that he did a good job as an Elder: his sins were 'personal sinnes and not the sinnes of his administration'. The critics really should take a broader view, Johnson argued: Studley was 'indued with the Spirit of God', whatever his personal lapses, and he had been given a death sentence (deferred) for his beliefs. The last part may not, of course, have sounded so impressive had the critics known that both Studley and Johnson had collaborated with the authorities during their interrogations in 1593. They lived, but Barrowe, Greenwood and Penry died.

The Exiled Church was also under attack from London (or Westminster, to be precise). James had taken note of Brownism's rising appeal and instructed the British Ambassador in the United Provinces to counteract its influence in the Netherlands. In 1605 Matthew Slade, a former Elder excommunicated by Johnson, filed a complaint about the Exiled Church to the Dutch Reformed Church. He implored them to establish an English-speaking Dutch Reformed Church in Amsterdam. As a result, in February 1607, the Amsterdam City Council allowed English Presbyterians use of the former Begijnhof church. The first sermon was preached by John Paget, a devout Presbyterian who believed Presbyterianism was 'appointed by God'. Paget worked together with Matthew Slade to destroy the Brownists, and they were in constant touch with James via the Ambassador.

Paget's church, due to the large number of Scottish and Presbyterian soldiers and merchants in Holland, proved a great success. It was soon followed, to the satisfaction of London, by the formation of an English Reformed Church in the university city of Leiden to combat separatist influence there (Anabaptist as well as Brownist), although this church did not have a pastor until 1609. It, too, was an English-speaking Dutch Reformed Church financed by the Dutch government. In 1612, a third such church was set up to combat separatism in Veere (near Middelburg), the main centre for Scottish soldiers still stationed in Holland as a precaution against an unexpected invasion by Spain.

There were other attacks on Johnson's church. In 1605 Hugh Broughton, an anti-Semitic opponent of the Brownists, highlighted the known closeness of the Brownists to the Jews by denouncing the Exiled Church as 'a synagogue of Satan'. Broughton said Brownist sectaries 'have no fellows in the world but Mohammedans and Jews'.[24] This was probably aimed at Ainsworth, currently being hailed by lecturers at Leiden University as the best Hebrew scholar of the day, but it also applied to Brownists in general, since the Brownists made no secret of their opinion that Jews and Muslims were closer to true religion than Catholics and some Anglicans.

It was just as well that Robinson made such a success of the Leiden church since in Amsterdam Johnson continued to lose ground in 1610. His defence of Studley's sexual adventures had proved unconvincing. He was still losing members to Paget's Presbyterian church, backed as he was by the British Ambassador, and he was still failing to contain the Anabaptism of Smyth and Helwys. Culpepper argued it was mainly this war against Anabaptism that led Johnson to crack, since he had always made the defeat of the Anabaptists his main objective. It had been the basis of his collaboration with Cecil. In any event, the crisis within the church brought Johnson's authoritarianism to the fore and, in 1610, to regain some control, he tried to strengthen the power of the pastor and the Elders against the congregation. Although he disliked the conservative practices of the Presbyterians in many respects, he had always admired strong Presbyterian government by Elders elected for life. They were able at will to admit members and expel them. Indeed, his brother, George Johnson, claimed Francis never accepted the 1596 *Confession* – another argument in favour of Ainsworth as the author – but had no choice but to go along with it, given its popularity.

Johnson's proposed concentration of power into his own hands was all too much for the mild, long-suffering Ainsworth who was a doughty defender of Brownist democracy. For Ainsworth it was the democratic polity of the church, not any doctrine, which made the Brownists rightly distinctive. He may also have bridled at this sudden seizure of power by the Elders given that Studley now stood accused of sexually abusing Ainsworth's own daughter. Whatever the truth, in December 1610 the 'London-Amsterdam church' was split between Johnson and Ainsworth. Ainsworth won over the congregation, but Johnson and Studley, as officers, kept legal control of the church building. The result was a stalemate. The church was paralysed.

Francis Johnson defended himself in *Tell the Church* (1611) by appealing to the revered puritans of the previous generation. As Lee put it: 'Johnson cites Thomas Cartwright and Dudley Fenner as witnesses to the fact that power is with the Elders, contradicting the views of Smyth, Ainsworth, John Robinson and Henry Jacob.'[25]

Ainsworth, backed by the majority of the congregation and by Robinson in Leiden, went to court to get control of the church building and won his case in 1613. The court ruled that his group were the legal owners of the Lange Houtstraat church on the grounds that they were the legitimate continuation of the original congregation. Johnson and Studley packed their bags and left for Emden in Germany.

Paget was the main beneficiary of all this mayhem. He gleefully pointed out that his argument against Brownism had always been that it opened the door to other separatists (Anabaptists, Arians, atheists) and now they had paid the price for it. Indeed, it was an irony. Historically, it was the great contribution of the Brownists that their stubborn insistence on separation from the state opened the door to freedom for everybody else, but in the short term it had brought them down. Paget was also delighted, it seems, that Ainsworth, when ejected from Lange Houtstraat, had moved his congregation to a former meeting-house of the Jews. This showed that Brownists and Jews were hand in hand. Ainsworth had always been pro-Jewish and, to the great annoyance of Paget (a Hebrew scholar himself), he had even expressed admiration for Talmudists; especially for the mediaeval Jewish scholar, Maimonides. Worse, Paget discovered, Ainsworth did not list as a motive for his philo-semitism a desire to convert the Jews, which every good Christian was supposed to do.

The Amsterdam church had not completely collapsed, but what Ainsworth retrieved had considerably shrunk. In Holland they had found their freedom, but with freedom came stiff competition. The Anabaptists and Presbyterians were equally free. The Brownists had survived English intolerance, but Dutch tolerance had proved too much for them to handle.

How did all the turmoil leave relations between the Leiden and Amsterdam churches? The answer is that they remained close throughout. This was due to the warm relationship between Robinson and Ainsworth, who consulted with each other, wrote Bradford, 'in all matters of weight'. The events in 1610 had brought to light that it was not simply 'turmoil' that had caused Robinson to move on to Leiden in 1609 but also a lack of confidence in Johnson. When Helwys and Smyth said Johnson was in love with hierarchy, Robinson merely replied that Johnson was 'immoderately jealous for the officers' dignity'. His position was awkward. The overall attitude towards the Amsterdam church by Robinson, and later Bradford, was one of veneration. To the London churches of 1567 and 1592 they traced back the ancestry of their own Leiden church. To them, Johnson, whatever his personal faults, was the Pastor of 1592, the church of the Brownist martyrs. As Bradford put it: Johnson was 'the Pastor of the Church of God.' It was to join up with him that they had left the shores of Lincolnshire, and the church in Lange Houtstraat was where they worshipped when they arrived. As late as the 1640s Bradford was still defending the good name of Johnson though admitting Johnson, like Browne, had fallen away in the end. The warm relations with Ainsworth were therefore of the greatest value, maintaining Leiden's link with the 'Church of God'.

For certain English merchants in Amsterdam, Leiden and London the downfall of Johnson and the vindication of Ainsworth and Robinson seemed to offer a chance of reconciliation between the Brownist churches and radical puritans like Henry Jacob. Their motive was probably to bring the Brownists back into the ranks of the radical puritanism which they represented and the Brownists had forsaken, but there was also a commercial motive. In 1609-10 there was a reinvigoration of the London Virginia Company, and it was now no longer looking for swashbuckling privateers but for hardworking, conscientious types who would establish settlements in North America. The evidence for these motives is only circumstantial but what definitely happened was that in 1610 some English merchants went to considerable lengths to assemble in Leiden for a conference with John Robinson and William Brewster, three of the most eminent puritan theologians: William Ames, Henry Jacob and Robert Parker.

Ames, Jacob and Parker

In 1603, with the accession of James, Jacob had turned away from further polemics against Johnson and focussed on the radical puritan movement, but this led to his imprisonment in 1603-4. Whitgift called him 'very insolent', and the conference at Hampton Court Jacob had planned to influence proved a disaster for the puritan cause. In 1609, after further imprisonment, he returned to the fray and boldly sent to King James *An Humble Supplication for Toleration and Liberty*. Though there was a similar plea for toleration by the Mennonite, Peter Twisck, also in 1609, this is reckoned to be the first plea for general toleration in English, pre-empting the Anabaptist, Thomas Helwys, who published a tract on similar lines *c.*1613, and also Leonard Busher in 1614.[26] Jacob's limited toleration did exclude Catholics (because they would support the invasion of Britain by a foreign power) but he was still way ahead of his time. His arguments were sufficiently powerful for James to take his pamphlet seriously, as is proved by the hand-written notes in the margin of the royal copy still held at Lambeth Palace in London.

The London merchants also appreciated this pamphlet, since Jacob had this time couched his argument not in terms of religion but in terms of 'reason'. As previously explained, the arguments of 'reason' against state interference in the freedom of religion could also be used to combat state interference in freedom of trade. One of the merchants interested in Jacob's pamphlet was Edward Bennett, Elder of the Exiled Church in Amsterdam, wealthy shipping merchant, and ally of Robert Rich, Earl of Warwick, prominent in the Virginia Company. If Henry Jacob could convince Robinson in Leiden of the need for rapprochement with the Anglican Church, then the London Virginia Company might have the supply of settlers it was seeking.

Jacob faced no easy task. Robinson and Brewster were still uncompromising separatists who believed that gaining the right to form churches independent of the state was the only way forward. Jacob, like Ames and Parker, wanted to see autonomous congregations inside the Church and believed there was therefore no need for separatism. Jacob had referred to congregational polity in his *Humble Supplication to his Majesty King James* (1605) where he said: 'Each Church of Christ should be so independent as it should have ye full Power of all ye Church affairs entire within itselfe.' He had reassured James that he still rejected Brownist separatism, despite the corruption in the church, because many Anglicans were still 'true Christians nonetheless'.

In Leiden the trio told Robinson that although they were all members of the Church of England, they believed just as much as he did in elected ministers and agreed covenants. If they could stay in the Church with their views, then so could he. For Robinson and Brewster, however, this did not deal with the main problems: the Anglican church was a 'national' church enforcing state conformity and permitting no others to exist outside its monopoly and it was also a 'hierarchy', with corrupt bishops parroting government policies and exercising police powers to censor and imprison.

Nonetheless, the trio were partly successful. Robinson did modify his views after the debates with Ames, Jacob and Parker but did not agree to share in full public worship with the Anglican Church, as they wished he would. He did agree that Brownists should stay as close as possible to 'godly' Anglicans, but did not believe that, as it stood, Anglicanism as a whole was godly. He agreed to halt wholesale denunciation of Anglican bishops, out of respect for those who were 'true Christians', but he did not rein in his attacks on the others. As for Ames, Jacob, and Parker, they reacted differently. Ames mellowed and later became friendly with Robinson. Parker, to Jacob's disappointment, moved sharply away from Robinson's Leiden church, which he said was too 'democraticall', and in Amsterdam took a job with Paget.

Jacob, on the other hand, became a Brownist himself after the 1610 debate and in 1612 he is citing the Latin motto, 'Quod omnes attingit, ab omnibus approbari debet' ('What toucheth all, ought to be approved by all'). This is as close the 17th century could get to calling for a democracy. He expressed this in religious form (also 1612): 'Where each ordinary congregation giveth their free consent in their own government, there certainly each congregation is... indued with power immediately under and from Christ...'[27] He says that 'we' are 'heartily sorry' for the offensive language deployed against the Anglican bishops by some of 'the Brethren' in the past. He is confident that Brownists will not let that happen again (though, in the late 1620s, they did).

Bradford described the meeting with Ames and Parker in Leiden (they lodged with Jacob, he says) and sums up what happened by writing that Robinson met Jacob 'half-way'. This 'half-way' was to be of great significance in the negotiations for the *Mayflower* voyage. The 'semi-separatism' Robinson and Jacob had hammered out would play a crucial role in winning over the king.

3

The London Company

By 1613, when Ainsworth won his legal battle, the organisation that was the main engine of emigration to America was the London Company or, more precisely, the London Virginia Company. The Virginia Company originated, significantly, not with government or a monopoly but with the initiative of a private individual, Bartholomew Gosnold. His expedition in 1602 was for trade and settlement not for plunder or land-grabbing and it visited the same places as the *Mayflower* Pilgrims did, in what became New England, and with similar peaceful objectives, though in the end no settlement came out of it.

Backed by the knowledgeable Richard Hakluyt, Gosnold left Falmouth on the *Concord*. Instead of sailing south to the Canary Islands, he steered south and then west from Cornwall and was the first to accomplish a direct voyage to America from England. He aimed at the stretch of coast between Raleigh's patent in Virginia, where the Roanoke colony had failed, and Newfoundland, opened up by Cabot and frequently visited by fishermen. Gosnold's aim was to assess trading opportunities. He started in Maine where he found Indians well acquainted with European fishermen, mainly Basques. Further south he came across a strip of coast teeming with fish and he named it 'Cape Cod'. Further south still, he named Martha's Vineyard after the vines and after his daughter, Martha. An uninhabited island was named 'Elizabeth's Isle' and it was decided to make a settlement there, having observed its plentiful supply of fish and fresh water. There they peeled off sassafras bark, prized in Europe for its almost magical medicinal powers, and collected some sassafras twigs, used in London as toothbrushes and as a dental anaesthetic. Sassafras, they believed, whether served hot or cold, would remedy any minor ailment, from fever to gout. Often they dined out with the Indians, drinking beer and eating dried fish, but eventually they loaded the ship with furs, skins, cedar logs and precious sassafras before abandoning the settlement, not leaving any men behind for fear of the winter.

In 1606 Gosnold founded the Virginia Company by obtaining from James letters patent setting up two joint-stock companies whose shares could be traded. Again, his backers included Richard Hakluyt. The stated aim was to establish colonies in North America, find a passage to the Pacific and find precious metals. As this was no longer a private venture but a state-backed company, it reflected the interests of the state, not just commercial interests. The territories granted were named in this first Virginia Company charter as the 'first colony' (in the south) for London investors, and 'second colony' (in the north) for investors from west of England ports such as Plymouth, Bristol and Exeter. These two groupings became the London Virginia Company and the Plymouth Virginia Company.

The Virginia companies fell into one disaster after another but, while Gosnold was still involved, they did score one historic success: the London Company founded Jamestown, Virginia. This was the first permanent English settlement in America (little remains of it today). The problem for both companies was the conflicting motives of investors and passengers on the one hand and the state, with its court interests, on the other. The latter ensured that Captain Newport was in charge of the *Susan Constant* (1606), the *John and Francis* (1607), the *Mary Margaret* (1608) and the *Sea Venture* (1609). Newport had been a 'privateer' (a state-backed pirate), plundering gold from Spain under Elizabeth I; his main objective still was obtaining gold; and he regarded John Martin, a London goldsmith, as a key passenger on the *Susan Constant*. Nonetheless, the involvement of Gosnold did preserve a commercial motive and Newport did establish Jamestown in May 1607, a turning-point for British colonisation. In the 17th century an estimated 380,000 emigrants crossed the Atlantic from England to America and creating Jamestown was an indispensable first step.

John Smith

It was on the *Susan Constant,* flagship of the fleet that left London under the command of Newport in December 1606, that a strong personality emerged who was to influence considerably the destiny of the *Mayflower*. John Smith wrote indignantly a withering account of the expedition. Half the passengers, he noted, were gentry expecting to find gold lying on the ground and not do any work farming, hunting or building fortifications. When they started to run short of food they sent Smith out to hunt, or to obtain food from the Indians whose language he had learnt. One foray went wrong, and he would have been executed by the leader of the Powhatan, Wahunsenacawh, but for the intervention of his 10-year-old daughter, later known as Pocahontas.

Smith's criticisms were bitterly resented and back at Jamestown he received two more death sentences, but this time from his own side, before managing to escape those as well. Smith was a down-to-earth realist appalled by the rampant incompetence he witnessed in both London and Virginia. When he judged it to be the right moment, he sent what he called a 'rude answer' to the London Company, telling them to take a long-term view of settlements in future rather than simply look for short-term profits. He added, 'When you send againe I entreat you rather send but thirty Carpenters, husbandmen, gardiners, fishermen, blacksmiths, masons and diggers up of trees, roots, well provided; than a thousand of such as wee have...'

In 1609 the London Virginia Company was totally revamped. The Plymouth Company had fallen by the wayside after the failure of its Popham Colony in Maine, and that left the London Company as the only organisation capable of planting settlements in America. In May Edwin Sandys, now increasingly prominent, tried to take Smith's remarks into account when he drew up the second charter of the London Company and the new Treasurer, Thomas Smythe, also placed the great fleet sent out in June on a more realistic basis. The fleet comprised nine vessels, sailed from Plymouth, and was led by the flagship, *Sea Venture*. For the first time it included women settlers (100 out of the 600 passengers), which signalled that the aim was trade and a permanent settlement, not just a gold rush or a military base.

The new company had a good reception in the City of London. It attracted 650 members including notables such as Francis Bacon, Richard Hakluyt, the Earl of Southampton, Captain John Smith, Christopher Nicholls (part-owner of the *Mayflower*), Edwin Sandys and John Wolstenholme. The last two were later to help the Pilgrims in organising the *Mayflower* expedition.

Stephen Hopkins

On the *Sea Venture* was Stephen Hopkins from London who in 1620 was to be a passenger on the *Mayflower*. It is often forgotten that the first *Mayflower* passenger to set foot on American soil landed there in 1610. Hopkins should have landed in 1609 but was entangled in a dramatic series of events before he reached Virginia. The *Sea Venture*, caught in a storm, was shipwrecked off the uninhabited island of Bermuda. This was a strange island with mysterious sounds that struck fear into the hearts of the superstitious but it nonetheless had everything the 150 castaways could desire in terms of food, fresh water and security, with the result that many wished to stay there rather than build pinnaces to transport them to their original destination of Jamestown. Six of the men (one of whom, John Want, was a 'suspected Brownist') went on strike rather than build the pinnaces but this rebellion was defeated.[1] Later, Hopkins, who was so well-versed in the Bible he used to assist the chaplain, also encouraged the castaways to remain in Bermuda. He was arrested for mutiny, sentenced to death and reprieved only after a high-level delegation had repeatedly pleaded for his life with the governor, Thomas Gates.

Linebaugh and Rediker say Hopkins was a Brownist: 'Stephen Hopkins was a learned puritan and follower of Robert Browne, who advocated the creation of separate, congregational churches in which governance was based on mutual consent rather than on deference to elder, king, or nation.'[2] They portray Hopkins as a radical who went along with the rebels' opinion that they were better off on Bermuda in freedom, amid plenty, than labouring for seven years under indentured servitude in Jamestown. They also suggest that in 1620 Hopkins probably made a mutinous speech on the *Mayflower* – and this led to the writing of the Mayflower Compact. This is all speculation but it does capture the challenge to established authority that Brownists and radical puritans continuously presented.

The castaways did eventually make it back to Jamestown, where one of the passengers, William Strachey, a poet who in London had once held shares in the Blackfriars theatre, wrote an account of the Bermuda shipwreck in a letter to 'an excellent lady'. This circulated in manuscript in London and is thought from evidence in the text to have inspired Shakespeare's play, *The Tempest*. Shakespeare's patron was the Earl of Southampton, a key supporter of the London Virginia Company, of which Strachey was also a member.

Rolfe and Smith

In 1612 there was a breakthrough for those like Smith who wanted colonies based on profit-making activities such as farming, fishing, hunting and trade. In Virginia a John Rolfe began planting tobacco. Rolfe had been marooned on Bermuda for nine months with Stephen Hopkins and back in Jamestown he would have worked with John Smith. In 1614, after experimenting with the tobacco plant, he sent a tentative shipment of a 'sweet' variety of tobacco to England and in 1615 sales of this 'sweeter' tobacco began to take off rapidly in London. This would eventually be the economic salvation of Virginia.

While Rolfe was establishing his tobacco plantation, the teenage daughter of Wahunsenacawh, Pocahontas, who had saved Smith's life, was kidnapped by the English. She was held hostage near Jamestown until the Powhatan showed them where the gold mines were (though no gold mines existed). It was there that she met John Rolfe, a dedicated man 'unmoved by the search for gold, and who instead busily tended some seedlings…' In 1614, after a swift conversion to Christianity and baptism with the new name of 'Rebecca', she and Rolfe were married.[3] Smith expressed delight at this marriage and its historic character: Pocahontas, he wrote, was 'the first Christian ever of that nation, the first Virginian [who] ever spake English, or had a child in marriage by an Englishman.'[4]

Although Rolfe's tobacco crop was a big economic breakthrough for Virginia, it was to be some years before it took effect. Meanwhile there were two other developments that made migration to North America sound more attractive. In 1614 the first indentured servants to complete their seven-year contracts gained their freedom and received from the company plots of land to cultivate as they saw fit. This was a positive benefit of emigration the London Company could trumpet. Land ownership was a prime aspiration in Britain. In 1616 there was a similar step forward when, as the Company could not afford cash dividends, they granted stockholders plots of land for their own use. They introduced at the same time the 'head-right' system, granting 50 acres of land to whoever financed their own, or another's, passage to Virginia. The London Virginia Company was making these concessions only because it was desperate for volunteers, but they did influence future migrants, including the *Mayflower* passengers. As Davis quite rightly says: 'In the long run, the possibility of becoming an independent cultivator with a secure freehold title to land was found to be the lasting attraction that would bring migrants to America.'[5]

This evolution in Virginia was very useful for John Smith's crusade on behalf of peaceful trading settlements. He wanted to resume where Gosnold had left off and open up territory north of Virginia (the boundary of which already stretched as far north as the Hudson River). In 1614-15 Smith led three expeditions to a region he named 'New England'; and in 1614 the place-name of 'Plimouth' appears on a map of New England that he drew. His first attempt was a two-ship expedition to Maine. His targets were fish and fur and he succeeded in bringing a large cargo back to England, where he then met with Ferdinando Gorges, Governor of the Fort at Plymouth in Devon (and who had a house in Clerkenwell, London) to discuss the next steps for founding a colony sustained primarily by fish caught by Devon fishermen.

In March 1615 Smith set sail again but this time he was captured by French pirates and held hostage for three months before pulling off another of his daring escapes. While in captivity he wrote *A Description of New England* (1616), arguing passionately for the commercial promise of 'New England', if only some migrants could be found to settle there. He emphasised the similarity in vegetation and climate to England, and he included the map he had drawn, together with a portrait of himself.

Smith was well aware that his trade-and-settlement concept had still not fully triumphed over those who regarded America as a hunting-ground for slaves, gold and plunder. Not long after the kidnap of Pocahontas to extort gold, a Captain Hunt arrived in the area designated on Smith's map as Plymouth. Hunt captured 27 young Indians and transported them to Malaga in Spain to sell them off as slaves for a handsome profit. Smith was absolutely furious: at one stroke Hunt had made the Indian population in New England so hostile Smith would not be able for years to return and hold a discussion about trade. William Bradford was also disgusted by Thomas Hunt: 'a wretched man that cares not what mischiefe he doth for his profit.'[6]

Smith's plan for trading settlements in New England also had to overcome the plans of rival bodies. Not only was he in competition with those in the London Virginia Company focussed on sending ships out to Jamestown, and those who still pushed for a settlement in Guiana, but in 1611 the City of London livery companies began to 'plant' in Ulster, Northern Ireland, and by 1619 the Ulster plantations had at least 8,000 men of English Protestant stock. Ulster colonisation was backed by the government for political reasons (they wanted to counter-balance the large Catholic majority in Ireland) and would continue for decades. As a consequence both Smith-Gorges and the London Virginia Company had to intensify their publicity and promotional campaigns to find recruits for North American emigration.

Publicity and Propaganda

Colonialist literature had started with Richard Hakluyt in the 1580s. Later, a new commercial genre appeared, the 'promotion tract', whose themes were backed by merchants (for trade), by social reformers (for reduction of unemployment and poverty) and by a debt-ridden court (for gold, silver and empire). Promotional material had to appeal to three quite different constituencies: the government, would-be investors and potential emigrants. The government was told that American colonies would damage the Spanish Catholic Empire, discover gold and silver mines, establish military bases, damage commercial rivals, skim off excess population, reduce unemployment, increase national wealth, secure the supply of raw materials and, it was always added (given that the church was a department of the state), achieve the conversion of the natives. Promotional pamphlets had to start by convincing the king because the court controlled trade through monopoly companies that first of all had to pay bribes and then later had to pay compulsory 'loans'. Investors had to play along with this system. Few were ready to accept the notion that business might be best left to the business community and trade might be best left to traders.[7]

In 1609 Thomas Smythe, governor of the London Virginia Company, already had the backing of the government and therefore his priority was to win over more potential investors and emigrants. He commissioned Robert Johnson of the Grocers' Company in the City (his son-in-law) to write a promotional pamphlet (*Nova Britannia,* 1609). Johnson decided to ground his appeal to investors upon patriotism and religion – investors would help make Britain a great power and convert North America to Christianity. The Indians, whom he compared to wild animals, would benefit, and he added some reference to the relief by emigration of the social problems in London. The Church hammered his message home in the London pulpits. Colonisation was for Britain and for God. In the City Smythe applied pressure on the livery companies through the Lord Mayor, offering them shares at the bargain price of 12 pounds and 10 shillings. This worked like a charm. The first Virginia charter had attracted only 8 subscribers but now, despite all the failures, the second charter in 1609 listed 659 individuals and 56 livery companies. The Mercers, Clothworkers, Goldsmiths and Haberdashers all signed up while individual investors ranged from aristocrats to a shoemaker. Given the xenophobia of the campaign, the Spanish Ambassador was deeply alarmed.

For the would-be emigrants, *Nova Britannia* (1609) painted a very rosy picture of North America. Johnson depicted beautiful landscapes: the rivers swarmed with fish, the Indians were loving and gentle, the climate was healthy and the woods bursting with luscious fruits. Furs, sturgeon and caviar could be found on all sides, the presence of gold and silver was hinted at, while magic herbs – sassafras and tobacco – were on hand to cure most diseases. These claims, he pointed out, were not excessive but backed by original sources. Thomas Harriot, for example, in *A Briefe and True Report of the New Found Land of Virginia* (1588) had shown that tobacco would purge phlegm, cure ague and gout, and open up all bodily passages. He added a direct economic benefit. A settler would receive a share in the enterprise at no extra cost to themselves, and after working for only five (perhaps seven) years would be in possession of his own land and property – the aspiration of so many ordinary Londoners.

The contents of the pro-colonialist sermons ordered by the government to be preached in all the pulpits of the capital are not known but in February 1610 a William Crashaw preached a sermon before the Virginia Company Council in London, probably at the Company's headquarters in Philpott Lane, just north-east of London Bridge, which was also Thomas Smythe's house. Crashaw gave the Christian perspective, starting with the moot question of whether it was right to occupy land belonging to the Indians and he concluded it was justified because America had so much surplus land they would not miss it. In addition, the Indians were very friendly and were welcoming the settlers. At home he believed opposition to colonisation had been stirred up by actors in the London theatres who had mistakenly taken against the Virginia Company. These actors did not understand the benefits of colonisation: the conversion of the heathen, the advance of England's power in the world, and remedying the social problems of London caused by over-population. He disdained trade and private profit. Colonisation should be for loftier reasons than that. Alluding to some recent problems in Virginia, he called for stronger government from now on. Order must be imposed. The Church of England should be rigorously upheld, 'blasphemers' (heretics) should be executed, and any Brownists, or similar types, should be expelled.

This sermon ran directly counter to the views of John Smith, who thought that colonisation would be successful only through private profit, not any so-called loftier reasons. Smith said of America: 'I am not so simple to think that ever any motive than wealth will ever erect there a Commonwealth.' In the early 1620s a Christopher Levett (who was trying to found a colony in Maine based on fishing and had won the backing of Ferdinando Gorges, always interested in boosting West Country fishermen) echoed Smith in rejecting the campaign of propaganda. Like the London theatres before him, and fearing that settlers would arrive in America with false expectations, he parodied Robert Johnson by promising: 'I will not tell you... that corne doth grow naturally (or on trees), nor will the Deare come when they are called, or stand still and look on man till he shoot him ... nor the fish leap into a kettle...'[8]

In 1616 Smith, fortified perhaps by Rolfe's vindication of his philosophy in Virginia, decided he would promote the settlement of New England in his own way and break with the delusions of Smythe and the Virginia Company. His chosen method of promotion was the lecture tour. Starting in London, he toured England (visiting, among other places, Bristol, Exeter, Barnstaple and Dartmouth), giving lectures illustrated by his books and maps (for sale) and specifying exact details of cost (an expedition would cost £5000, he said). His plans were never grand enough for the court and the politicians but he found much enthusiasm in the West Country for a fishing settlement and so he joined the Plymouth Council of Ferdinando de Gorges.

This was no endorsement of Gorges. Smith was always a maverick, a voice from the wilderness who was consistently ignored, but who – one suspects from his books – much enjoyed always being proved right.

Pocahontas in London

The London Virginia Company did have a big success in 1616. They brought Pocahontas to London, where she was a social sensation. They paid the fare not only for Pocahontas and John Rolfe but also for a dozen other Powhatans to come over. They also paid the famous engraver, Simon van de Passe, to portray Pocahontas sporting a beaver hat – the same type of hat worn by the Queen, Anne of Denmark, wife of James I.

The Rolfes arrived at the port of Plymouth in June and journeyed to London by coach. They stayed at the Bell Savage Inn, a theatre-pub off Ludgate Hill, and in a house in Brentford. Afterwards Rolfe took his wife to his family home, Heacham Hall in Norfolk. John Smith, in London at the time, wrote to Queen Anne, urging that Pocahontas be treated with all due respect as a royal visitor. Accordingly, in January 1617, she was brought before the king in the Palace of Whitehall at a performance of Ben Jonson's masque *The Vision of Delight*. However, according to Smith, the informal James was so unprepossessing Pocahontas did not realise she had met him until it was explained to her later. She would not have been introduced as 'Pocahontas' of course (only a nickname) but as Matoaka, alias Rebecca, daughter of the most powerful prince of the Powhatan Empire (as it says on the engraving). Samuel Purchas, the travel writer, met her and describes her as impressive because she 'carried her selfe as the daughter of a king'.

In early 1617, Smith met Pocahontas in London and he later wrote that when Pocahontas saw him, 'without any words, she turned about, obscured her face, as not seeming well contented.' She had to be left alone for two or three hours. Later, she spoke to him, but with bitterness. She reminded him of the 'courtesies she had done' and added, 'you did promise Powhatan what was yours would be his, and he the like to you.' She then discomforted him by calling him 'father', explaining Smith had called Powhatan 'father' in Virginia, 'and by the same reason so must I do you'. Smith declined to accept such a form of address, he wrote, since she outranked him as a king's daughter. Pocahontas, then, 'with a well-set countenance' said: 'were you not afraid to come into my father's country and caused fear in him and all his people (but me) and fear you here I should call you "father"? I tell you then I will, and you shall call me child...' Smith does not explain the reason for this antagonism from the woman who saved his life, but simply records it.

In March 1617 Rolfe and Pocahontas boarded a ship at Gravesend bound for Virginia. Gravesend, which had a dock, a customs house and searchers, was often used by passengers to America who would travel down there from the City of London. Before the ship could leave port Pocahontas became ill and had to be taken ashore, where she died at the approximate age of 21.

A New World Proposed

In 1610 the Leiden church was not yet contemplating emigration. They had only just arrived. In 1611 John Robinson, with the help of the wealthy Randall Thickens, William Jepson and Henry Wood, bought the 'Groene Poort' on Bell Alley (Kloksteeg) in which they built 21 one-room houses. It included space for worship, though it must have been low-key, since Dutch toleration did not extend to allowing public worship by sects. In 1611 Leiden looked solid while the church in Amsterdam was in turmoil; Robinson had largely beaten off his Anabaptist and Presbyterian competitors in the 'religion market'; and above all he had kept his congregation united.

Nonetheless, the Leiden church was not spared discontent. This was mainly due to an economic recession *c.*1612. At first new refugees are grateful for any job, whatever the rates but, once established, they become conscious of their exploited status, and then in a recession their disadvantage becomes all too obvious. In Leiden, for most immigrants the hours they worked were long, the work intensive, and the pay negligible. Leiden was one of the first major manufacturing centres in Europe and early industrial capitalism had conditions akin to those common in the 19th century. Haley says of the beautiful city of Leiden: '... industrial growth was won at the price of terrible conditions for those who laboured. Hours were long, indirect taxation bore heavily, housing was inadequate, and it was said that in Leiden there were more beggars than in the whole of the rest of Holland.' In 1622 one quarter of the Leiden population was excused payment of poll-tax for reasons of poverty and in 1634 some 20,000 received a free distribution of bread.[9] Dutch cities were proud that they gave more relief to the poor than elsewhere in Europe – but the reason they had to do it was not so flattering.

For those weighed down by the relentless burden of labour it seemed as if Leiden was not after all the Promised Land for which they had left Kent, East Anglia or the East Midlands. In such circumstances one dazzling prospect aroused great interest: Robert Harcourt's *Relation of a Voyage to Guiana* (1613). It recalled the dreams of a 'New World' in South America inspired earlier by Walter Raleigh's *Discoverie of the Large, Rich and Bewtifull Empyre of Guiana* (1596). Here was a short-cut to paradise. Nor was that all. Straight after Harcourt's publication came three important developments in 1614: firstly, the Dutch set up the New Netherland Company, of special interest in Leiden because it was the Leiden Walloons who were leading the way for a Dutch settlement on the Hudson River; secondly, news came of the first awards of land ownership by the London Virginia Company to settlers in Virginia; and thirdly, in one year, 1614-15, three expeditions were organised by John Smith to the country he named 'New England'.

There had long been indications that the Brownists might be candidates for emigration to America. They were not heretics. All they wanted was enough freedom to run their own churches and Hakluyt had nominated them as ideal settlers in the 1580s. London merchants had backed Francis Johnson in an attempt to colonise Newfoundland in 1597. The Brownists themselves had twice asked Elizabeth for permission to colonise North America, and they had raised the question again in 1606. Not only that, but both the Amsterdam and Leiden churches had prominent members interested in emigration.

In Amsterdam was Edward Bennett, a ship-owner also operating in Delft and London, himself a member of the London Virginia Company, where he was an ally of the Earl of Warwick, and in Virginia records is described as 'a wealthy merchant of London'.[10] An Elder of the Exiled Church and a patron of Francis Johnson, Bennett backed fellow-Elder, Francis Blackwell, in seeking migration to America for the 'Franciscans' after their defeat. Boddie said that as early as 1612 the Amsterdam Elders, Bennett and Blackwell, had moved to London 'probably in the hope of being able to settle in Virginia'[11] and in 1615 Blackwell was in London buying a ship.[12]

In Leiden there was William Brewster, who had close ties with the family of Sir Edwin Sandys, a founder of the Virginia Company and a rising star in the company's ranks. It was Sandys who had in May 1609 in London drawn up the second charter of the London Company. Although very anti-Brownist early in his career, Sandys became radicalised by his experience with the Virginia Company (which was described by the Spanish Ambassador as a 'seminary of sedition'), to the extent that later he was accused of lending the *Mayflower* Pilgrims £300 without interest, in some plot to make New England a 'Brownist Republic'. On the board of the Virginia Company Sandys was an ally of the Earl of Southampton, rival to the Earl of Warwick, so there may have been an element of competition between him and Bennett as to who might pull off the first successful Brownist emigration to America.

Thomas Brewer

It is not known for sure when in Leiden a real interest in emigration took hold, but a decisive change in mood seems to have taken place in 1615.

Leiden had been hit badly by the economic recession and the Leiden church, which had apparently been growing in 1610-12, perhaps reaching 400 members, lost many members who left for economic reasons. They were not allowed to evangelise in Holland and so replenish their numbers; instead, they decided to publish pamphlets and export them to Britain. As Bennett and Blackwell in Amsterdam were seeking emigration to America for the Franciscan Remnant in 1615, this was probably the moment when the Leiden church began to look at emigration seriously.

In 1615 Thomas Weston, the London merchant who would later organise the *Mayflower* expedition, arrived in Leiden. He worked with the London-Leiden merchant, Edward Pickering, on the export and distribution of the pamphlets. Pickering (of the notable Northamptonshire family, and perhaps father of the William Pickering arrested in 1632) kept shops in London and Amsterdam, and had been involved with Weston as an 'interloper' in various trades. As he left money in his will to help the Pilgrims, he may have been a Brownist member.

Weston and Pickering, despite their role in distributing the pamphlets, were not the main inspiration behind the 1615 'expansionism'. The key player was Thomas Brewer, a wealthy Brownist merchant in Leiden who teamed up with William Brewster. In 1616 they set up their own press, the 'Pilgrim Press', and had pamphlets printed which Weston then distributed in Britain. These pamphlets were aimed at winning over opinion in England without offending the authorities, so they were not inherently dangerous.

The key importance of Brewer was his array of contacts. He was a friend of Edwin Sandys, just rising to the top of the London Virginia Company, and in 1621 Brewer's wealth secured the election of Sandys as the MP for Sandwich in Kent. Brewer's own base seems to have been in Canterbury and Sandwich, which were from *c.*1611 strongly represented in the Leiden and London churches: Cushman and his wife, Hester Cooke, Richard Masterson, the Chilton family, and Moses Fletcher are just some of the Kent names.

Brewer's will in 1618 shows his important contacts in London and Leiden: he left money not just to his relatives but to the Leiden church, the Leiden library, to Carver, Brewster, Robinson, John Dod, Henry Jacob and Richard Lee in England, Ainsworth and Ainsworth's church in Amsterdam – and to a special fund for the publishing of books forbidden by bishops! In his person, therefore, he united the Brownist churches in Amsterdam (Ainsworth), Leiden (Robinson), London (Jacob) and Wolverhampton (Lee) and was a friend of Dod, the radical-puritan closest in sympathy to the Brownists.

On a personal level, Sprunger says Thomas Brewer was a merchant trading in saltpetre and a member of the Leiden congregation.

He enrolled in 1615 at Leiden University along with next-door neighbour, John Robinson, which at least conferred on them the benefit of protection from extradition. In 1616 he was married to an Anna Offley and had three children but by 1618 Anna and two of his children were dead, leaving only a daughter, Mercie. This is the catastrophe which in 1618 necessitated the writing of a new will. In 1619 Sir Dudley Carleton, the British Ambassador, described Brewer as 'a Gentleman of good house' as opposed to the majority of the Leiden congregation which, he reported, consisted of 'inferior persons'.

Unfortunately, the publishing project then went awry. Brewer and Brewster began to print books by David Calderwood, who James had banished from Scotland. They knew the dangers because these books were sent as contraband across the North Sea at the end of 1618. Carleton, the British Ambassador, reacted immediately and in December persuaded the Dutch authorities to ban English exiles from printing books and sending them to Britain. By July 1619 Carleton's network of informers had discovered that the publisher of Calderwood was 'one William Brewster, a Brownist' and a hunt for Brewster thereupon began. Brewster stayed underground until 1620, somehow, and managed to get to America on the *Mayflower,* but Brewer was apprehended. Enrolment at Leiden University now came in useful and he was able to stave off extradition until favourable terms had been agreed.

Reasons for Emigration

If a significant proportion of the Leiden Pilgrims, though not necessarily a majority, were in favour of emigration from around 1615, why? The promotion tracts from 1609 onwards from the London Virginia Company, the promotion of Guiana in 1613 mentioned by Bradford, and the promotion of New England by John Smith after 1614 had combined with the economic discontent in the recession after 1612 to awaken keen interest in emigration, but neither interest in the company promotions nor economic distress were sufficient reasons. Faith in emigration propaganda was dissipated by news of tragic failures and economic distress was reduced by Leiden's economic recovery, even prosperity, from 1616 to 1620.

The underlying reason for emigration is clear from the histories written later by Bradford and Winslow and it has already been stated: faced by a decline in church membership and the ban by the Dutch authorities on evangelising in Holland, the Pilgrims wanted to preserve their religious identity and, what to them was the same thing, their English identity. It is the same reason given by John Robinson, except he expresses himself more positively than Bradford and less politically than Winslow.

According to Robert Ashton, John Robinson thought the main reason for emigration was a desire to spread their beliefs and enlarge their membership, restricted in Holland by the language barrier (their services were in English) and by the authorities' ban on proselytising by foreigners.[13] Bradford says the same thing, but with his usual melancholy, by saying that if they had not spread their wings they would have died out; it was expand or die. Winslow, trying to play down the separatism of the Brownists to fit the politics of the 1640s, plays up their fears about losing their English language and English customs while they stayed in the 'United States' (the contemporary name for the United Provinces of the Netherlands). All three agreed on the fundamental reason for emigrating: it was self-preservation.

Bradford's views are mainly recorded in *On Plimmoth Plantation*. He makes the point early on that they were not motivated by economic factors but by the survival and unity of their group. Economic considerations would have kept them in, or taken them back to, Amsterdam.[14] In his main account he says that after the Brownists had lived in Leiden for 11 or 12 years they 'began' to consider emigration. Here he may be looking back, roughly from the year 1615, to the first Brownists, who migrated to Leiden in 1603 or 1604 from Essex, Kent and Norfolk, before the arrival of the East Midlanders in 1609. Bradford then says the question of emigration arose from 'their present dangers' as the Elders foresaw that the older generation was beginning to die out. They did not consider the question vaguely, he says, but analysed 'solid reasons' for their declining numbers. First was economic hardship, which meant 'few would come to them' and few who came stayed the course. Enthusiasts did come eagerly from England but when they discovered how many hours they had to work, returned to England despondent ('as it were weeping'). Similarly, some already in Leiden found the work too much and went home, preferring 'prisons in England' to 'liberty in Holland'. Pastor Robinson expressed the same point but differently: if they could find a land where they 'might have liberty' but 'live comfortably' then everyone would want to join them and live as they did.[15]

Secondly, though the existing congregation bore economic hardship 'very cheerfully', they too would die out or succumb to old age. Third was concern for their children who, oppressed by labours, rebelled and left home, some becoming soldiers, sailors or falling into licentious ways, 'to the danger of their souls'. Fourth, 'though not least', was the opportunity to spread the Christian faith in 'remote parts of the world'.

Bradford gave a summary of the final debate between the Elders and the congregation, where the decision was made. The congregation expressed many legitimate doubts and fears, he said. The Elders answered firstly that their purpose was 'honourable'; secondly, that they 'lived here but as men in exile, and in a poor condition'; thirdly, that the years of truce 'were now out, and there was nothing but beating of drums and preparing for war'. After that the congregation decided by a majority vote ('the major part') to endorse the plan, though it was left to individuals who would volunteer.[16]

Edward Winslow, writing much later in *Hypocrisie Unmasked*, said the idea of emigration came from the Elders for approval by the congregation. Most did approve. The reasons were, wrote Winslow: 1) decline in numbers as many returned to England for economic reasons; 2) fear of losing their Englishness as children became Dutch; 3) persistence of their original motivation, the desire to live somewhere 'exemplarily', so other English settlers would be attracted to 'enjoy the like liberties with us' and live in a truly Christian society; 4) their ultimate desire to 'enlarge' the 'Church of Christ'.

Some points that neither Bradford nor Winslow deal with should be taken into account. Firstly, Bradford refers to the 'truce' but takes it as given that all along, since they first arrived, their stay in Holland was viewed as temporary because war with Spain would be renewed and they would be prime targets. It is not listed as a reason for emigration but it is always there as a backdrop. At one point he says they have been warned about some savage Indians in America but 'the Spaniard might prove as cruel'.

Secondly, what became very evident after they settled in America was that many Leiden Pilgrims, presumably the poorer ones, hankered after a solution the richer ones rarely mentioned: if they owned their own land they would be free from harsh exploitation. For them a major reason for emigration was the aspiration to land ownership.

Thirdly, Bradford does not mention the embarrassing fact that the children not only adopted the customs and language of the country, but then 'married out' to Dutch or Walloon spouses. Worse still, some joined the English Reformed Church of Hugh Goodyear, or even the Mennonite Anabaptists. Such choices were also a drain on their church numbers.

There was another unmentioned problem. Their Dutch neighbours in Leiden expressed the view that Brownist children did not run away from home by reason of economic exploitation but because their parents were too strict. A particular issue was the Sabbath. The Dutch regarded Sunday as a day of relaxation once church had finished, but the Pilgrims regarded Sunday as a day of worship, both morning and afternoon. Sermons had to be preached, then debated. Brownist children, understandably, found Sunday afternoons in Holland very difficult as it was the time when Dutch children played.

There is one last point. It is often made out by those who wish to puncture the reputation of the Pilgrims that they were not refugees, since in Holland they were never persecuted. This is not how they saw it.

Bradford said: 'We live as men in exile.' Elizabeth had refused them permission to settle in America and warned them that if they did not leave England within three months she would execute them. The East Midlanders would have been imprisoned by James if they had returned. In Holland the British Ambassador harried them, constantly pressurising the Dutch to restrict their activities. He destroyed their publishing business and had their members hunted down and arrested, well aware that the Dutch needed British support in the impending war. Nor were the Dutch themselves in that period completely tolerant but placed many conditions on foreigners, such as the ban on evangelising, which for the ultimate survival of the Pilgrim church was essential. In addition, relentlessly hanging over the Pilgrims was the threat of a Spanish invasion, when they would have had to flee for their lives. History shows that refugees remain refugees until they find a permanent home, and Holland was intended only as a temporary residence. Their dearest wish was to return to England in freedom, as was demonstrated in the 1640s, when they did return. In 1646 Edward Winslow (who returned) made it clear that the Pilgrims thought of themselves as refugees. He wrote that the *Mayflower* Pilgrims were 'a poor persecuted people that went into the wilderness to avoid the tyrannical Government of the late Hierarchy'.[17]

Henry Jacob and the London Church

The talk of emigration in 1615, both in Amsterdam and Leiden, was only talk because at that stage it could not be translated into action. Virginia and New England were British territories and neither King James nor the Archbishop of Canterbury would allow Brownists to settle there. The merchants' attempt in 1610 to bring back the Pilgrims into the Anglican Church as radical-puritans had failed. Indeed, it had backfired since Robinson had won over Jacob, not the other way around. There was, however, a new possibility. Robinson had met Jacob 'half-way' and if that half-way had convinced Jacob it might also convince others in London, perhaps in the government, that the Brownists were now acceptable. Accordingly, at some stage in 1615 it was decided to send Jacob back to London to found a Brownist church there and see what happened. If they were not closed down, then the next step would be to obtain permission for emigration to America from the king.

In 1616 Jacob established his church in London, using the Brownist method of asking each would-be member for a statement of personal faith followed by agreement to the church covenant. To found the church he and eight others 'met together in a private house at Southwark on the southern bank of the Thames...'[18] Unsurprisingly, Jacob was chosen as Pastor. This was almost certainly in Bankside, in the parish of St Saviour, Southwark, where Jacob married Sarah, where Brewster probably married Mary, and where the Brownist martyrs of 1592 were kept in the Clink. Jacob said his church was modelled on Leiden, just as Leiden was modelled on the international *Confession* of 1598.

Murray Tolmie has hailed the foundation of the London (Jacob) Church as a historic moment, declaring it the model for the great Nonconformist churches of the future; and indeed a church met in Southwark, claiming to be the successor of the Jacob Church, until the late 20th century. It was able to function because it was a 'semi-separatist' church, not a fully separatist one. As agreed between Jacob and Robinson in 1610, the church recognised 'true Christians' inside the Anglican Church, did not publicly denounce the Anglican Church and encouraged its members to attend their parish church, if only to hear the sermon.

There were nine founding members, including Henry Jacob, and at least one of them, an Edward Gilbert, had been a member of the 1592 Church. He had stayed in London as part of the underground 'Remnant'. It was disappointing for Jacob, no doubt, that many of the Remnant did not join, preferring either Johnson or full-blooded separatism, but the influx of new members from the radical-puritan ranks must have been encouraging. Indeed, Jacob's church was quite a success and, though harassed by the authorities, it was never closed down.

The names below are not all known definitely to be members taking the covenant, but they were at least strong sympathisers or supporters. Edward Gilbert was an old survivor from 1592 and there were others. The dates show when names are mentioned in texts. The nine founder members are marked #.

The 1616 Brownist (Jacob) Church

Name	Background
#Allen, John	1616. Of Southwark. 1636 To Gatehouse Prison as a Brownist.
Allen, Mrs	1632
Allen, Thomas	1633
#Almey, Andrew	Founder member.
Arnold, Brother	1632
Arundell, Thomas	1632 arrested. Of Southwark St Olave.
Atkin, Mary	1633
Atwood, William	1632 arrested.
Barebone, Praise-God	1632 arrested. 1640 had Brownist church in Fleet St. 1653 The Barebones Parliament was named after him.

Barebone, Sarah	1632 arrested. Wife of Praise-God.
Barnard, Humphrey	1632 arrested. Joined church while in prison.
Barnet, Humphrey	*c.*1632 his house was raided and 42 arrested.
Bates, Mr	1632 to Amsterdam.
Batty, William	1634 to the Gatehouse.
Bellamy, John	1616 As an apprentice joined the Jacob church. Successful bookseller. 1623 published *Mourt's Relation*. 1626 left Jacob church. 1642 was still the publisher of the Brownists.
Blunt, Richard	After 1633.
Boye, Rice	1630 supported Duppa. Of Coleman Street but from Wiltshire. Like Traske, he was a philo-semite.
Brown, David	1616. 1630 supported Duppa. Scottish writing master who moved to London and taught adults to read. Bought summer house in Greenwich.
Browne, Richard	1610 As a London wherryman he rescued the radical puritans, William Ames and Robert Parker, from imminent arrest.
Canne, John	1623 'Teacher' at Hubbard's Brownist church after return from Ireland. 1630 emigrated to Amsterdam, took over the Lange Houtstraat church. 1634 *A Necessity of Separation*. In 1647 returned to England after 17 years banishment. A Leveller.
Chidley, Daniel	1630 supported Duppa. 1632 Freeman in Haberdashers Co.
Chidley, Katherine	1630 supported Duppa.
Chidley, Samuel	1630 supported Duppa.
Clayton, John	1624 mentioned in Amsterdam correspondence. Had church in Shad Thames, Bermondsey.
Collier, William	To New Plymouth. Probably church member. *See* investors.
Cudworth, James	1634 'Lathrop our Pastor'.

Name	Background
Denne, Elizabeth	1632 arrested.
Digby, Mrs	1636
Dod, Henry	1632 arrested. Famous translator of Psalms. d in prison.
Duppa, John	1630 led strictly separatist breakaway from Lothrop. 1647 listed as a 'tub preacher'. Of Colchester, led church in London.
Dyer, Thomas	1630, of Colchester.
Eaton, Samuel	1630 supported Duppa. 1632 arrested, button-maker in St Giles without Cripplegate. 1633 Maiden Lane and Gatehouse prisons. 1639 d Newgate, bd Bunhill Fields.
Egge, John	1632 arrested.
#Farre, Edward	1616 Founder member.
Fenner, John	1636
Ferne, Joan (widow)	1630. 1632 arrested.
Flower, John	1630
Gibbs, Mr	1616
#Gilbert, Edward	1592 Church. The only one known to have survived until 1616.
#Goodal, Henry	1616
Goodson, William	1630 supported Duppa. Later, a Vice-Admiral for Cromwell.
Grafton, Ralph	1630 supported Duppa. 1632-38 in prison. Wealthy upholsterer in Cornhill.
Granger, William	1632 arrested. Of St Margaret, Westminster. 1634 Gatehouse.
Green, Brother	1633
Greenway, Mary	1633
Hammond, Mrs	1634 to New England.
Harris, Jane	1632-33 member of Lothrop's church in Southwark.
Harris, Thomas	1632-33 member of Lothrop's church in Southwark.
Harris, William	1610 b Northbourne, Kent. 1628 took seven-year apprenticeship as a needle-maker to Thomas Wilson of the

	Drapers Company in Eastcheap, London. 1633 in London. 1632 was member of John Lothrop's church in Southwark along with his brother, Thomas, and sister, Jane. In *c.*1634 he md Susan Hyde. 1635 emigrated from Dartmouth. 1638 bought Pawtuxet from Roger Williams.
Harvey, Widow	1633
Hatherley, Timothy	To New Plymouth. *See* investors.
Howes, Penina	1632 arrested. Sister-in-law of Lothrop.
Howes, Samuel	1632 arrested. Brother-in-law of Lothrop. To New England.
Hubbard	1621 There was a second congregational church formed in Southwark by Hubbard. But they soon after left for Ireland. Canne took over the congregation.
Ireland, John	1632 arrested. Of St Mary Magdalen, Bermondsey.
Jackson, William	1632 arrested.
#Jacob, Henry	1563 b Cheriton, near Folkestone, Kent. 1581 to St Mary's Hall, Oxford, then Corpus Christi, Cambridge. 1595 (Sept) md at St Saviour, Southwark, London, to Sara 'Dimericke', sister of John Dumaresq of Jersey. 1596-97 debate with Johnson. *c.*1599 probably Pastor at Middelburg, where his pamphlets against Bilson were published. 1599 defence of the Anglican Church. 1603 in London campaigning for Millenary Petition. 1603 was imprisoned after campaign in Sussex. 1603-08 living in London. 1604 a London representative at Hampton Court Conference. 1605 imprisoned in Clink. 1609 His *Humble Supplication* urged toleration. 1610 in Leiden. 1611 to Amsterdam. 1616 to London, setting up by covenant a semi-separatist church in Southwark. 1622 he emigrated to Virginia, founding Jacobopolis. 1624 d in parish of St Andrew Hubbard, London.

Name	Background
Jacob, Sarah	1595 md Henry in Southwark. 1622 did not accompany Henry to Virginia but stayed in London. 1632 arrested.
January, Henry	1630, of Colchester.
Jennings, William	1633
Jerrow, John	1630 supported Duppa.
Jones, Sarah	1632 arrested. Of Lambeth. See Jessey Church.
Jones, Thomas	1632 arrested. Of Lambeth. Was a dyer with a business on London Bridge. 1606 md Sarah Hayes, St Mary Aldermanbury.
Kempton, Menasseh	1590 (Feb) Berwick, Northumberland. To Colchester, then London. Member of Jacob Church. 1623 On the *Anne*. 1623 Land List. 1626 Purchaser. 1627 Cattle List.
Kiffen, William	1630
Knight	1630 supported Duppa. Of Cheapside. Fled to Amsterdam.
Laberton, Mr	1634 to New England.
Laberton, Mrs	1634 to New England.
Lee, Richard	Preacher in Wolverhampton. 1618 Brewer bequeathed him and Jacob money, as if they were in the same church.
Lemar, Abigail de	1632
Lemar, Mr	1632 arrested.
Linnell, Robert	1634 to New England.
Linnell, Mrs	1634 to New England.
Lothrop, John	1584 (Dec) bp Etton, Yorkshire. *c.*1601 to university. 1610 md Hannah Howse. 1611-23 Vicar of Egerton, Kent. 1619 (Ap) son, 'Joan' Lothrop. bp, St John Hackney. 1624 succeeded Jacob as Pastor of Brownist church, London. 1632 imprisoned. 1634 to Boston on *Griffin*. Was a founder of Scituate and Barnstable, New England. 1639-53 minister in Barnstable.

Lucar, Mark	1632 arrested.
Masterson, Mary	Née Goodal. May have been related to Henry Goodal, above.
Masterson, Richard	Wool-carder from Sandwich. md Mary Goodal of Leicester. With Sabine Staresmore of Leicestershire during raid in 1618 but escaped to Leiden.
Melbourne, Elizabeth	1632 arrested.
Melbourne, John	1632 arrested.
Melbourne, Mabel	1632 arrested.
Morton, Brother	1630
Morton, Sister	1630
Norton, Widow	1634 to New England
Parker, Henry	1632 arrested.
Pickering, William	1632 arrested. Probably related to Edward Pickering.
Plater, Richard	Printer. 1621 he renounced Brownism.
Price, Edward	1635
Price, Mary	1635
Pride, Thomas	1630 supported Duppa. Colonel who led 'Pride's Purge'.
#Prior, David	Founder member.
Puckle, Stephen	1630, of Colchester.
Ravenscroft, John	1633
Reynolds, John	1618 London printer who moved to Leiden in 1619.
Reynolds, Robert	1632 arrested. Of Isleworth.
Sargent, Elizabeth	1632 arrested.
Sargent, Mr	1632 arrested.
Southworth, Alice	1619-20 London. 1613 md Edward. 1623 md Bradford.
Southworth, Edward	1613 md Alice Carpenter in Leiden but lived in Aldgate, London.
Spilsbury, John	Of Aldersgate, London. 1633 left Brownists. 1638 formed Baptist church in Ratclff, Stepney.

Name	Background
#Staresmore, Sabine (Saben or Sabine a Leicestershire name)	1599 'Sabeon' Staresmore bd, St Dunstan Stepney, London. 1616 (Dec) md Sarah Rawlinson, St Mary Whitechapel. 1618 negotiated with Privy Council on behalf of Leiden.1618 (Sept) betrayed by Blackwell and sent to Wood St Counter. In 1622 *Notes on Ainsworth's Last Sermon.* 1623 published his *Loving Tender.* 1624 rejected by L'Ecluse in Amsterdam but accepted by Robinson in Leiden. 1630 supported Duppa's breakaway. In *c.* 1631 bp child in London (Lothrop's church). 1636 son, John, bd St Botolph Aldgate. 1644 met with Jessey. 1647 defended Roger Williams against Cotton. Merchant and printer. From Frolesworth, Leicestershire. Cousin to Francis Staresmore, MP.
Staresmore, Sabrina	1635 in prison.
Swinerton, Mrs	1634 to New England.
Talbot, Tony	1632 arrested.
Thickens, Randall	Draper, brother-in-law of Carver, land in Stepney. Investor in M.
#Throughton, Robert	1600 (Nov) md St Giles Cripplegate to Amy Ownsted. 1611 (May) Judith Throughton md St Giles Cripplegate to John Yonge.
Traske, John	1618 whipped and branded. 1636. Philosemite and Judaiser. 1637 Joined the Jessey Church.
Treadwell, Katherine	1633
Treadwell, Richard	1633
Trimber, John	1633
Vessey, Hugh	1630
Warren, Joshua	1630, of Colchester.
White, Widow	1633
Wiffield, George	1633
Wilkins, Benjamin	1630 supported Duppa.

Williams, Mary	1629 md Roger.
Williams, Roger	c.1603 b London. Educated Charterhouse and Pembroke College, Cambridge. 1630 Brownist opinions in London. 1630 emigrated to Massachusetts Bay. 1631-33 Brownist in Plymouth. 1635 condemned by Boston Court. 1636 founded Providence, later Rhode Island. 1644 published *Bloody Tenent of Persecution*.
Wilson, Phyllis	1632 arrested.
Wilson, Susan	1632 arrested.
Wilson, Thomas	1632 arrested. Draper in Eastcheap, London.
Wincop, John	1619 took patent for Pilgrims with intention of emigrating.
Wincop, Alice	1632 arrested.
Wincop, Elizabeth	1632 arrested.
Wincop, Rebecca	1632 arrested.
Wing, John	1616 backed formation of Jacob's Church.
Woodwynne, John Sr	1632 arrested. 1634 to New England.
Woodwynne, John Jr	1634 to New England

Staresmore

In 1616 the member of the Jacob church deputed to help the Leiden church achieve religious toleration was a Sabine Staresmore. By origin Staresmore was a merchant from Leicestershire, where Sabine was a not uncommon name. He had a cousin, Francis, who was MP for Leicestershire in 1626. In London he traded in exotic items such as pepper, indigo and silk. He was suitable for holding the talks in 1617 because as a wealthy merchant he had contacts with possible investors and in addition he wanted to emigrate to America himself and so had a vested interest in success.

Staresmore was to have a long history with the Jacob Church. In the 1620s, after Jacob died, the church was run by Pastor John Lothrop, who emigrated to America in the 1630s and there founded a church in Barnstable which to this day celebrates his name. In the late 1630s the Pastor was Henry Jessey, so the church is sometimes referred to as the Jacob-Lothrop-Jessey Church. Staresmore knew all three of them, as well as Robinson in Leiden.

Staresmore was one of those members whose separatism was undimmed and he maintained that the resolutely separatist membership in the Jacob Church was always a majority. John Bellamy, a member of the church who ran a bookshop in Cornhill, confirmed this opinion, saying that after Jacob died in 1624, few 'Jacobites' took communion at their parish church. For this reason Bellamy ceased to be a member.

It was the opposite for Staresmore; Jacob's church was too Anglican for him and sometimes the puritans who joined from the Anglican Church were not really Brownist. For example, when a puritan, Richard Mansell, joined he was shocked to find that Brownists allowed into their church women who had not received their husband's consent, and servants who had not received their master's.[19] Tolmie says this proved Whitgift and Abbott were right about the subversive nature of the Brownists for it 'demonstrated the socially explosive nature of the gathered church: it could cut through social barriers and through institutions like the family to pose a threat to the whole social order.'[20]

For Staresmore to conduct the negotiations as one of Leiden's agents, it did of course have to be made clear that the Jacob Church represented Leiden. Walter Burgess wrote that the crucial point was that Leiden and the London (Jacob) Church had the same covenant. Robinson was still confirming this as late as 1624. In reply to a question from London on whether Jacob's church was a 'true church or no', Robinson replied: 'We have so judged ... and so do we judge still.'[21] He sent to London papers that had dealt with this question over the years. Ainsworth in Amsterdam also recognised the Jacob Church. Not only did the Jacob Church model itself on Leiden and represent Leiden, but it counted as a sister church to Amsterdam. This recognition, however, did not survive the demise of Ainsworth. When Staresmore and his wife arrived in Amsterdam in 1622 they were refused membership of the Amsterdam church though accepted into the Leiden church immediately, without being asked for a covenant, since the covenant they had sworn in London was automatically valid in Leiden. Tolmie adds that it was just the same in New England. Any member of the Jacob church in London was immediately recognised as a 'true Christian' and no new covenant was needed.[22]

1617-20 Summary of London Negotiations

Negotiation 1 (1617-18) with James for toleration. James agreed to 'connive'.
Negotiation 2 (1618-19) with Virginia Co for patent granted to Wincop (June 1619).
Negotiation 3 (1619) with Virginia Co for an expedition. No success.

| Negotiation 4 (1619-20) with New Netherlands Co. No success. |
| Negotiation 5 (1620) with Thomas Weston. *Mayflower* ship (July 1620). |

The approach to the London Virginia Company must have been worked out in the summer of 1617. As well as Staresmore and Jacob in London linking up with Robinson and Brewster in Leiden two emissaries were appointed at the Leiden end, John Carver and Robert Cushman. Thus, until Staresmore was arrested, the London negotiations were run by a team of six. Bradford in his history does not mention the barely legal Jacob Church but that was because he always avoids mention of anything remotely illegal – he does not even mention the name of the *Mayflower* ship, which had its illegal elements (such as having on board at least one wanted man, Brewster, who is said to have travelled under a pseudonym).

On their visits to London where did Carver and Cushman worship? Sprunger believes they worshipped at the Dutch Church in Austin Friars. They probably attended the Jacob church in the afternoon since this is the pattern the 'semi-separatist' Jacob church is known to have observed in later years: the local Anglican Church, at least for the sermon, in the morning and then a gathered church later. Winslow says the Leiden church members who lived in London would, if they knew Dutch, take communion with the Dutch Church and Bangs takes this to mean that those like Winslow preferred to attend at Austin Friars over any Anglican Church.[23] Since the Dutch Church in Austin Friars was the first recognised independent church in London, this was apt. To be sure, by 1620 the church was not so radical as in its youth. Some of the Austin Friars congregation were now merchants with English names and some were not even members of the church: for example, Daniel Mytens, the portrait painter; Samuel Hartlib, the educationalist; Philip Burlamachi, the wealthiest financier in London; and Thomas Weston, the organiser of the *Mayflower* expedition. All of these are known to have attended since they donated books to the Austin Friars Library. Interestingly, the book donated by Weston was the Works of St Basil, the saint renowned for helping the poor and underprivileged. This may shed light on why Weston helped the Pilgrims with their publications (risky for him) and why he helped organise the voyage of the *Mayflower*.

In the afternoon it is not known where Carver and Cushman worshipped as the Jacob Church did not own a building until the 1640s. They probably met in the parish of Southwark St Saviour. Both the 1592 church and the Jacob church are sometimes described as the 'Southwark churches'. As at Duke's Place there was a Dutch element and in 1618 there were potteries making Delftware in Montague Close and at the Pickle Herring site (now known as Potters Fields).

According to Waddington, the 19th-century church historian who drew on the 18th-century traditions handed down to him, the Jacob Church met in Bankside, Southwark, and 'When messengers came from Leiden to London to arrange for the voyage to America they met the brethren of this church for united prayer.'[24]

Since the Jacob Church in Southwark used Leiden as its model, a picture can be drawn of their style of worship: non-set prayers standing up; psalms sung with beautiful melodies but without musical instruments; readings from the Bible; sermons with some audience participation after the sermon; simple rituals; no Christmas Day, no Easter, but several feasts of Thanksgiving.

Seven Articles

The negotiations initiated by Staresmore and Jacob were based on Seven Articles setting out the basic position of the church. They read like Henry Jacob but were signed off in Leiden by Robinson and Brewster and then communicated to Edwin Sandys of the London Virginia Company by Carver and Cushman. In a letter of 12 November Robinson and Brewster received warm approval from Sandys, keen to tap this rich new seam of potential settlers. Nonetheless, Sandys was problematical for them. Though there was a family link in Scrooby with Brewster, Sandys had, like Bacon, heartily approved the persecutions and executions of 1592-93. Since then Sandys had become far more radical, especially since 1614, but that was causing another problem because by 1617 Sandys and his ally in the London Virginia Company, the Earl of Southampton, were fast becoming the leaders of the opposition to James and the Pilgrims were aware it was the government they needed to convince. The patent from the London Virginia Company was useless if James did not allow them to settle in North America.

The Seven Articles were the starting point of the negotiations. They promise passive obedience to the king even if they feel the king is wrong and respect for all officers appointed by the king, including Bishops. They were able to do this because they regarded the Church of England as a state organisation not a religious one and therefore they could abide by the Church on civil matters while reserving their own position on spiritual matters. They believed in the division between church and state: 'Give unto Caesar what is Caesar's and unto God what is God's.' In addition, Jacob and Robinson tried in general to stay as close as possible to the French Huguenot church as well as close to the Dutch Reformed Church. It is sometimes thought this was a clever tactic, since James could not afford to offend either the Dutch or French Protestants, but in fact the closeness was genuine. Jacob had married a Huguenot wife; several Leiden Pilgrims, including Carver, had married French Walloon wives; and relations with the Walloon church in Leiden were good.

In December 1617 there was a meeting of the king's Privy Council which considered the Pilgrims' request for religious toleration and then emigration. Those present were quite hostile, some referring to the 'lewd' Brownists (in reference to their recognition of civil marriage and indulgence of sex before marriage) and the Council as a whole demanding further concessions by Robinson in religious conformity. Robinson and Brewster wrote to Sandys on 15 December that they were sending Deacon Carver back to London with another representative, Robert Cushman, and they took the opportunity to impress upon Sandys their suitability as settlers in northern Virginia, due to their industriousness, frugality and experience. They added a pledge, often quoted as an illustration of their steely determination: 'Lastly, it is not with us as with other men, whom small things can discourage, or small discontentments cause to wish themselves at home again.'[25]

Staresmore contacted a financier in London called John Wolstenholme to find out how best to steer the Pilgrims' case through government. Wolstenholme offered constructive criticisms; for example, in the Seven Articles Leiden had conceded the Anglican Church had true features and true Christian members but failed to condemn those who would separate themselves off. Something might be done there. Another serious difficulty Wolstenholme spotted was over the ordination of ministers. In January 1618 Staresmore delivered a reply from Robinson which tried to address these issues.

Wolstenholme was not doing this because of sympathy with Brownism (far from it) but because he was among those who still believed there might be a North-West Passage to China through New England or Canada. In addition, he and Fulke Greville were helping the Duke of Buckingham, who had just taken power at court, to overhaul the navy. It was thought the Hudson River (in Virginia in those days) and New England, rich in timber and materials for rigging, could provide a naval base to deal with North African pirates currently inflicting terrible damage on British ships in the Atlantic. Ships bound for America were regularly captured by African ships from Sallee (now Rabat, Morocco) even though close to Land's End. The Africans sold passengers and crew into slavery. White women were highly prized as 'they bought high prices in the Mediterranean slave markets'.[26]

Once he had dealt with Wolstenholme, Staresmore was able to make contact with Fulke Greville, the Chancellor, and Robert Naunton, Secretary of State. Greville, poet and playwright, had wanted in his youth to emigrate with Sidney to Virginia and was a member of the Virginia Company. Naunton was head of the secret service and a radical puritan (so another Walsingham), and it was he who made the crucial breakthrough with King James, something Sandys, as an oppositionist, could never do. Later, it was to Naunton that the Pilgrims awarded most gratitude. His breakthrough was to persuade James, who was scared of causing a row with Abbott, the Archbishop of Canterbury, if he granted toleration, to turn a blind eye to what the Pilgrims were doing and 'connive at them'. Naunton convinced James the Pilgrims were harmless and would cost him nothing since they would pay their own way by fishing. James cracked a joke in reply: fishing was just right for them, as it was 'the Apostles' trade'. Thus it was that by having a laugh with the king, during a conversation about how to bamboozle the Archbishop of Canterbury, Naunton secured the go-ahead for the *Mayflower* expedition.

In Leiden there was deep disappointment that the king would only turn a blind eye and not grant them the religious toleration they had requested. They felt that was more damaging for them than if they had not asked in the first place. Their enemies could now say their request for toleration had been refused. In a way that was true, but Naunton foresaw that if they now went to the Hudson and James wanted to persecute them, he would find it very difficult to do so. That Naunton had actually won took some time to sink in.

Blackwell

Meanwhile the Jacob Church, and therefore Leiden, suffered a complete catastrophe. Francis Johnson, the discredited Pastor of Amsterdam, had in early 1618 died in Amsterdam after returning from Emden. The year before he died he had published a book in which, to the horror of most Brownists and puritans, he had recognised as a 'true church' not only the Anglican Church but also the Catholic Church. Some denounced him as an apostate like Browne but Jeremy Bangs has pointed out that he did not recant but merely 'broadened his reach',[27] just as Robinson had been doing with Jacob since 1610. With Johnson dead, an Elder of the 'Franciscan' church in Amsterdam, Francis Blackwell, crossed from Holland to London, just as Jacob had done, founded a legal church in London for the Remnant loyal to Johnson and then applied to emigrate to America. Blackwell thus achieved in a few months what had taken Jacob eight years. He was clearly reaping the rewards of Johnson's partial endorsement of the Anglican and Catholic Churches and receiving some backing from the authorities.

It so happened that in the spring of 1618 there was a secret meeting of the separatist groups – illegal of course – which Blackwell and his supporters duly attended. Unwisely, Sabine Staresmore also attended. There was a police raid (church police) and many were arrested. Staresmore managed to make his escape along with another 'Jacobite', Richard Masterson, and obviously they believed they were safe. Unfortunately, Francis Blackwell was arrested but he did a deal with the Church listing the names of all the separatists at the meeting, including the names of Staresmore and Masterson. In return for his loyalty, Blackwell and the London 'Franciscans' (named after Johnson) were given permission to emigrate to America.

The Pilgrims were bitter. Sabine Staresmore, the London agent of the Leiden Pilgrims, was now in prison while Masterson had to go on the run to escape arrest. Bradford wrote scathingly that Blackwell, by betraying Staresmore and others, 'won the favour of the bishops (but lost the Lord's)'. He complained that 'in open court, the archbishop gave him great applause and his solemn blessing to proceed on his voyage.'[28] It is no wonder that Archbishop Abbot was delighted. Not only did he round up most of the separatists in London but by netting Staresmore and his friends he was able to classify Staresmore as an outright separatist and eliminate him from the Leiden negotiations. In fact, as Staresmore went to prison and became a marked man, it meant he and others in the Jacob Church were unable to sail on the *Mayflower* in 1620. Blackwell was unrepentant, to the fury of the Pilgrims. He said he acted for the greater good. By striking a deal with the Archbishop he had enabled his group at least to emigrate. It would have been absurd for neither group to go.

Reaping their reward, Blackwell and his group sailed out on the *William and Thomas* from Gravesend on 24 August 1618, but Blackwell made a mistake. He agreed, no doubt for financial reasons, to take 180 of them into a small ship. They were 'packed together like herrings', wrote Robert Cushman, and when they hit a storm the blessing of the Archbishop of Canterbury did not suffice to save them. Overladen, the ship was driven off course. They could not withstand, given the low supply of water, an outbreak of the 'bloody flux' – dysentery induced by parasites in which faeces are ejected along with such a stream of fluid, blood and mucus that fatal dehydration is the consequence. Blackwell died of it, and with him 130 out of the 180 or so on board.

The imprisoned Staresmore was in quite a fix – 'my wife great with child' – and his business incurring debts due to his absence. Despite calling on the radical lawyer, Edward Coke, he did not obtain a release from imprisonment in the Wood Street Counter (or Compter) until 1619. He did secure, as the well-off could, a study in prison where he could write and correspond but as far as helping the Pilgrims was concerned his name had become a liability, not an asset. The king could not 'connive' with the Jacob Church now Abbot and the Church officers were in full possession of the names and had them all under surveillance. The result was that there were few, if any, from the Jacob Church on the *Mayflower* in 1620. The church had been thrown into total disarray and in 1622 Jacob himself emigrated to Virginia. He is said to have formed what sounds like a commune of semi-separatists at a place called 'Jacobopolis' – but this may not be Henry Jacob's eponym or be a misunderstanding, since 'Jacobopolis' is Greek for 'Jamestown'.

Wincop Patent

There was equal disarray inside the London Virginia Company. From 1617 faction-fighting engulfed the company and the crux of it was the struggle for control between the head (Treasurer) of the Company, Thomas Smythe, and the Assistant Treasurer, Edwin Sandys, who was backed by the majority on the governing body. Smythe belonged to the 'merchant-court' faction – those merchants close to the courtiers and the king.

This struggle impacted on the Pilgrims because Smythe also had support from Robert Rich, the Earl of Warwick, whose ally was the merchant Edward Bennett, patron of Francis Blackwell and Francis Johnson. Edwin Sandys, on the other hand, allied with the Earl of Southampton, was the patron of William Brewster and John Robinson in Leiden. Thus the downfall and imprisonment of Staresmore, followed swiftly by the grant of a patent to Blackwell, seem very likely to have been a consequence of the struggle inside the Company.

Certainly, the Pilgrims were held up after the arrest of Staresmore and it may have looked as if their chance of emigration had gone forever. This would explain why Brewster and Brewer so blithely published a book that was likely to make James I angry: *The Perth Assembly* (1618). James was so furious (as it dealt with church matters in Scotland about which he was very sensitive) he ordered Naunton and the British Ambassador in the United Provinces to hunt down Brewer and Brewster. It looked as if the Robinson church in Leiden and the Jacob Church in London had now offended the king so much there was no hope of their ever crossing the Atlantic.

What resolved the situation in their favour was the victory of Sandys in April 1618. He was elected Treasurer of the London Virginia Company in place of Smythe, even though Smythe was supported by the king. Two consequences flowed from this. Firstly, Sandys was able in May to set up a committee that would draw up a constitution for Virginia. By this a House of Burgesses was set up in the colony, the first legislative body in America. In June the laws of Virginia were revised and in July the first representative assembly in colonial America met.

Although all this had been under consideration under Smythe, the arrival of Sandys had broken the logjam. Suddenly Virginia and also America had made a significant political step forward.

Secondly, Sandys was able to cut through what was blocking the Pilgrims, mainly the king and the Church. The patent for Leiden was agreed fairly soon and finally sealed and delivered in June 1619. Unfortunately, no copy survives but apparently it was for an area of North Virginia around the Hudson River. The signing had been delayed until June 1619 because a manoeuvre regarding the signature was deemed advisable. The Pilgrims were told that it would be best if the patent was not made out in the name of any prominent Brownist who might scare off potential investors. Staresmore's arrest, the warrant for Brewster's arrest, the king's refusal to grant outright toleration, only 'connive' – none of it had been good publicity. After searching for an obscure Brownist they found, says Bradford, John Wincop, 'a religious gentleman then belonging to the Countess of Lincoln' who desired to emigrate to Virginia. From all angles he was a perfect choice. The Wincop family were Brownists or Brownist sympathisers living in London (Alice, Elizabeth and Rebecca Wincop were members of the Jacob church under Lothrop) and Wincop was employed by the Countess of Lincoln, whose husband, the Earl of Lincoln, was a member of the London Virginia Company.

The Wincop Patent was, as Bradford in his mournful way pointed out, never used. It is sometimes claimed that this was because Wincop in the end could not go (if he ever could) but patents and other documents do not depend on the signatory. The Warwick Patent did not end with the death of the Earl of Warwick. It was never used because the Virginia Company was in turmoil and could not organise or finance the voyage. Did the Wincop Patent, then, as Bradford said, just vanish? Not at all. Jacob and Staresmore had engineered acceptance of the Seven Articles. They had prompted the 'conniving' without which nothing else could have happened and the *Mayflower* could never have sailed. It was bitter for them that Blackwell benefited from that 'conniving' and not them, but at least Blackwell proved that Brownists could now sail to America.

Thomas Dermer

As soon as they had their patent, the Leiden church was energised again and they started selecting who should go. As the majority seemed to be staying, it was decided Pastor Robinson should stay in Leiden with them and Brewster accompany the settlers to America. Robinson and the others would join them later. It was also decided that the church in America would, like the Jacob Church in London, be regarded as a distinct church and yet a sister church. Any member of either church would be a member of the other automatically.

They also started looking for shipping. The problem was that they could no longer expect much support from the Virginia Company, which was incapacitated by factionalism, and therefore they could not look for a ship since the Virginia Company investors were not going to back anything until the confrontation between Sandys and the king was resolved.

A new wave of optimism suddenly came from an unexpected quarter, not from Virginia but from New England, where the indefatigable John Smith was still pressing to establish a settlement. Smith had published a book in 1616 full of enthusiasm for the stretch of coast he dubbed 'New England'. The book had a chart; it included places named 'Plymouth' and 'Cape Cod'; and it told tales of fish, fur and timber. A young man called Thomas Dermer had been with Smith in 1614-15 and had then stayed for a long time in Newfoundland, an established centre for fishing but judged too inhospitable for a pioneering settlement. There he met an Indian, Tisquantum (sometimes called Squanto) who had lived a while in London and was fluent in English. Squanto had been one of the Indians kidnapped by Thomas Hunt in 1614 and taken to Malaga to be sold into slavery. He had been lucky enough to be helped by Spanish friars who bought him out of slavery and enabled him to reach London, where he was looked after by John Slaney, the Treasurer of the Newfoundland Company.

Although Squanto had enjoyed good fortune, the incident had, to Smith's annoyance, put the whole of the New England coast off limits to any idea of a settlement, since any English or French ships that sailed there were now met with immediate, extreme and justified hostility from the native population.

Dermer now resolved the situation by restoring relations with the Indians and thus paving the way for the *Mayflower* Pilgrims to settle in New England in 1620. He did this by taking Squanto back to England to meet Gorges, who thereupon commissioned Dermer to be the commander of a new expedition to New England in which Squanto would act not only as his interpreter but as his intermediary with the Native Americans.

In May 1619 Dermer's ship reached Monhegan Island in Maine and in June he sailed south into New England. Dermer was shocked as they sailed along the coast to find so little sign of human life. Since 1616 there had been huge depopulation as epidemics (of smallpox and other diseases brought in by the Europeans to which the natives had no immunity) had swept through village after village. To Squanto's distress, he found his home village of Patuxer had also been abandoned.

Nonetheless Squanto was able (although not without difficulty, so deep was the distrust caused by Hunt's behaviour) to arrange a meeting between Dermer and the local leader of the Wampanoag, Massasoit. A workable friendship was established and Dermer then went on to explore every detail of the New England coast, using John Smith's map, as he sailed south to Jamestown in Virginia.

The encouraging news from Dermer in 1619 had a great influence upon the voyage of the *Mayflower*. The news he sent to London was of a New England where the Indians were no longer intractably hostile, if intermediaries were available, and where there now existed vast depopulated spaces ready for colonisation. Indeed, Dermer sent a celebrated letter, dated 30 June 1620, in which, drawing upon his reports of the previous year, he recommended for a future settlement one area in particular, the area marked on Smith's map as 'Plimouth'. Dermer wrote: 'I would that the first plantation might here be seated, if there come to the number of fifty persons or upwards...' There was also a direct link between Thomas Dermer and the Pilgrims. One of Dermer's mariners in 1619 was William Trevor, and he was to be chosen in London not only to be one of the *Mayflower* passengers but one hired to stay on for a year and help establish their settlement. Trevor would have known Plymouth well and probably shared Dermer's enthusiasm for it.

The Defeat of Sandys and the End of the London Company

The granting of the patent and positive reports reaching London from Dermer could not outweigh for the Pilgrims the decline and fall of their champion in the London Company, Edwin Sandys. Although Sandys had successfully pushed through two projects held up by royal and clerical interference, the London Company remained a monopoly ultimately under royal dispensation. The battle between Sandys and Smythe now became a direct battle between Sandys and the king and it was a battle Sandys could never win.

In the autumn of 1619 Sandys proposed sending out young women to be wives for the men in Virginia, and also some cattle, but the king wanted to send out ships of convicts. Sandys was keen to address London's social problems by sending out the unemployed and the orphans from the streets, with the guarantee of a plot of land at the end of the seven years of indentured labour, but the king's priority was a naval base. The king also was averse to tobacco planting, Virginia's most profitable crop, while Smythe had left a pile of debts and these had to be paid off. Smythe himself was still active and had been forced to advocate an expansion of tobacco planting (despite the king) to pay off the debts, to which he now added a brand new policy of rooting out Indians and taking their land instead of the previous policy of converting them to Christianity, which necessitated treating them well. Sandys in turn accused Smythe of enriching himself at the company's expense – the most obvious explanation for the huge debts the company had incurred.

In May 1620 the Company was going to re-elect Sandys, but the king simply vetoed his election. Unfortunately for James, this peevish intervention made little difference since the removal of Sandys still left Southampton a majority on the company Council. In 1620 Sandys and Southampton were engaged in a battle with Ferdinando Gorges over New England fishing rights. The king once again backed Gorges' New England Company, which claimed monopoly rights over New England fisheries worth £100,000 per annum. Sandys was defeated again.

Sandys decided to turn towards politics in the hope he could effect change by that route. In 1621 he won election as the MP for Sandwich with the help of Thomas Brewer, who enlisted the help of local radicals. The Brownists had always been strong in Sandwich and in Leiden there were several families from the Sandwich-Canterbury area. In Parliament Sandys presented himself as the defender of free trade against monopoly and the East India Company. He also presented a detailed analysis of the new economic recession and the accompanying unemployment. He blamed the recession on monopolies and restrictions on free trade but he also demanded practical attention to crops and to economic diversification – such as founding an iron industry in Virginia.

Soon Sandys was leading the opposition in the House of Commons while Southampton was the leading critic of the king in the Lords and all the time, to the fury of the king, the Sandys-Southampton group still held a majority of votes on the London Virginia Company Council. But in 1623, after a massacre of settlers in Virginia by the Powhatan Indians, James seized his opportunity. He was able to make use of the massacre to take over the Company and force its dissolution. By then there were only 1000 settlers left alive in Virginia from all the many thousands who had been sent out; 8000 had been killed, either by disease, malnutrition or fighting with the Indians. In 1624 James made Virginia a Crown colony under his direct rule while New England was handed over to the control of Warwick and Gorges. The defeat of Edwin Sandys and Southampton, who spent some time in prison, was complete.

Although Sandys was defeated, he was to be proved right in the long term. Running the country through financial monopolies that restricted enterprise and a church monopoly that restricted freedom of speech and assembly was not sustainable, especially in booming London where trade and diversity of opinion were expanding at a phenomenal rate. The country was now heading towards a possible revolution since the system of constant royal and church interference no longer worked, though it had been appropriate when Britain's economy had initially been taking off. As has been pointed out, if this system of state control of the economy had not been overthrown by revolution in the 1640s, then Britain's historic Industrial Revolution in the 19th century would have been impossible.[29]

Looking back, it may be difficult to imagine now why 'monopoly' should lead to a revolution until it is appreciated how far monopolies bit into everyday life. Describing the typical life of a London merchant, Christopher Hill wrote:

> His walls were lined with monopoly tapestries. He slept on monopoly feathers, did his hair with monopoly brushes and monopoly combs. He washed himself with monopoly soap, his clothes in monopoly starch. He dressed in monopoly lace, monopoly linen, monopoly leather, monopoly gold thread. His hat was of monopoly beaver, with a monopoly band. His clothes were held up by monopoly belts, monopoly buttons, monopoly pins. They were dyed with monopoly dyes. He ate monopoly butter, monopoly currants, monopoly red herrings, monopoly salmon, and monopoly lobsters. His food was seasoned with monopoly salt, monopoly pepper, monopoly vinegar. Out of monopoly glasses he drank monopoly wines...[30]

No area of ordinary life was free from economic restriction by a state monopoly. On Sundays there was the church monopoly. Originally, it made sense in a largely illiterate society for the state to communicate to the population via the church but, as literacy spread enlightenment through the printing-presses, it became problematic. The clergy announced government measures in Sunday services; they organised military training in the churchyard; and they were expected to discipline social behaviour. Thus in 1620 James I ordered the London churches to denounce 'the insolency and impudency of women'. It transpired that women were wearing, quite shamelessly, out in the streets, broad-brimmed hats and pointed doublets. Thomas Platter, a German visitor, was shocked to find that England was 'a women's paradise'. Women had far more liberty than in other countries and in London, for example, 'they often stroll out [of the house] or drive by coach in very gorgeous clothes' and 'the men put up with such ways'.[31] The church called on London men to get their women under control. The Dean of Westminster set an example by barring entrance to his church to women carrying yellow muffs. The church was in danger of becoming a laughing stock, in some ways much more dangerous for its existence than the gruesome execution of dissidents. Hill wrote: 'In the forties the radicals attacked, in the same breath, the Merchant adventurers' export monopoly, the Stationers' printing monopoly, and the Church's monopoly of preaching.'[32]

The defeat of Sandys was a crushing blow for the Pilgrims. Sandys had been their mainstay. In the long run, however, it was the king, the Church and the monopolies that would be demolished and the Pilgrims in New England would play a signal part in bringing them down.

4

The *Mayflower* in London

By the autumn of 1619 it seemed that all Leiden's hopes for emigration had been exhausted. In the winter, however, the Dutch suddenly came up with not one but two offers for the Pilgrims: they could move from Leiden to Middelburg in Zeeland, or move from Leiden to the Hudson River in America. There were good arguments for Middelburg: the town had a long history of connection with the Pilgrims, dating back to Browne, Johnson and Jacob; the Merchant adventurers were moving their operations from Middelburg to Delft, and no doubt vacating their accommodation there (which is probably how this offer arose); Middelburg had a history of religious toleration; and there was a textile industry where they could find work. Nonetheless, the Middelburg offer was rejected. The Pilgrims were probably frightened by the war being prepared on all sides and Middelburg was further south, nearer to any Spanish invasion, which was perhaps why the Merchant Adventurers were moving out.

The other offer was in any case more attractive. The Dutch New Netherland Company, founded in 1614 for American colonisation, had enjoyed very little success. Dermer had found only a Dutch trading-post. They now offered to take the Pilgrims to the Hudson River, just outside the Virginia Company's territory. Transportation to America would be free, they would be provided with cattle free of charge and, as the Dutch emigrants who wanted to settle around the Hudson were chiefly Walloons from Leiden, they would have an instant rapport with their neighbours. Crucially, they would be beyond any persecution by the authorities in London (which even Middelburg was not immune to) and have their own community, their own language and their own local government.

The Dutch offer seemed ideal for the Pilgrims and the company told Prince Maurice enthusiastically that Robinson had 400 families 'from these lands and from England'. It sounds as if Robinson had succeeded Johnson as the 'Bishop of Brownisme'. Unfortunately, Maurice, Prince of Orange, effective leader of the Dutch United Provinces, opposed it and a petition from the New Netherland Company was rejected in April 1620 by the States General. It was felt that a settlement near the Hudson would be too close to Virginia and the last thing Maurice wanted was friction with Britain while he was on the verge of a war with Spain, in which it was hoped Britain would be their ally. There was already friction between the British East India Company and the Dutch in Asia. In one dispute, in October 1620, the Dutch sank two EIC ships off Java. Nearer home there was tension with the Dutch over cloth exports and even in London James was in hot dispute with the Dutch Church in Austin Friars over the trading done by the merchants who worshipped there. The Pilgrims were keen on the Dutch offer, nonetheless, and they would have persisted in trying to find a solution acceptable to Maurice if there had not been another offer, apparently even better than the Dutch one.

Weston's Offer

It was Thomas Weston who now arrived in Leiden with a confident offer from some London merchants, telling the Pilgrims that there was no need for them to consider offers from the Dutch or to wait for the London Company. He told them that 'sundry Honourable Lords' (a resurrection of the Plymouth Virginia Company led by Fernandino Gorges) had obtained a large grant from the king for the area lying north of Virginia, called 'New England'.[1] Weston managed to enthuse the majority in Leiden for a settlement in New England rather than Virginia, in particular because the good fishing in New England would guarantee a regular food supply.

Weston was born in 1584 in Rugeley, Staffordshire. In 1609 he had been admitted as a member of the Ironmongers Company, presumably after an apprenticeship in London. He then became a trader with the Netherlands, with an interest in iron-related goods, dodging round the various monopolies. At one stage he and his business partner, Philomen Powell, were importing tons of alum from Holland without paying custom duties, presumably to avoid being picked up as outside the alum monopoly. Alum, like iron and copperas, was a mordant, or dye fixative, used in the dyeing of woollen cloth, preventing the colour from being washed out. In London, iron (which enhanced alum and copperas) came from industrial Blackwall; copperas was obtained from the copperas farms in Blackwall, Deptford and Rotherhithe; but the alum had to come either from the Netherlands or from Yorkshire. Dutch alum was nearer, and no doubt of higher quality, and the chief source of Dutch alum was Leiden, the centre of the Dutch textile industry. Thus it was that Weston and Powell were active in Leiden. As alum was also used in printing, this also explains his link with Brewer's pamphlets and the Leiden church.

In 1619 Weston and others were brought before the Privy Council and told to cease their trade with the Netherlands. Like many other merchants he was an 'interloper', breaking the monopoly of the Stationers Company (printing for Brewer), and of the Merchant Adventurers (treating cloth). Weston seems to have abided by the Privy Council ruling – he turned to organising the *Mayflower* instead – but in 1621, bankrupted by lack of quick returns from the *Mayflower*, he was tempted into ignoring the Privy Council and resumed his suspect trading in alum. Betrayed by an informer, he fled the country and ended up in America. As Nick Bunker noted, sympathetically: 'The fraud, if that is what it was, arose because of the way in which the Crown had riddled the economy with perverse regulations and monopolies, creating incentives for cheating.'[2]

According to Bradford, Weston told the Pilgrims, 'They should make ready, and neither fear want of shipping, nor money; for what they wanted should be provided.'[3] This was a compelling message. On Weston's recommendation, they immediately broke off the stalled talks with the London Virginia Company and the New Netherlands Company. Both of those suitors had asked that the Pilgrims settle near the mouth of the Hudson, though for opposite reasons. The London Company wanted them at the Hudson to establish an English colony, while the Dutch wanted them there to start a Dutch colony. Weston assured them that, instead, he could sign up investors in London, soon form a joint-stock company and soon find them a ship. A contract between the Pilgrims and the putative investors was outlined. The Pilgrims would work for about five years and each Pilgrim would be given shares in the colony. At the end of the term all property would be divided up according to the number of shares held. Every adult settler would be guaranteed at least one share (in effect, a plot of land). The investors would buy shares but they would have no vote in the colony's affairs and the Pilgrims would therefore have, at last, the self-government and freedom of religion they had always craved.

To try and entice the Pilgrims away from New England, which Weston was discussing with them, and attract them to the Hudson River, inside London Virginia Company territory, the Company gave the Pilgrims a new patent, known later as the Peirce Patent, accompanied by a declaration (which the Wincop Patent did not have) that guaranteed them considerable autonomy. They would be as free as if they were in untrammelled New England but at the same time they would be legal. This generous patent was dubbed the Peirce Patent because it had been quickly arranged by a wealthy London Clothworker, John Peirce.

The result was chaos, according to Bradford's account. The Leiden Pilgrims were split between those who wanted to go to Virginia, those who still wanted to go to Guiana, and those (including those they 'most relied on', suggesting Brewster) who felt strongly that they should settle in New England. In March 1620 the Leiden leaders 'struck hands' with Weston but it is not very clear what they 'struck hands' on. In the same month Gorges petitioned for a new charter for his Council of New England but this charter would be held up for months by a row over the fishing monopoly Gorges wanted. It looked as if the Pilgrims might be heading for New England without any legal entitlement, since the Peirce Patent was for the Hudson River in what was then Virginia. All this was caused by the battle raging at the highest level, way above the head of Weston, let alone above the heads of the baffled Pilgrims. Bradford does not even mention a Peirce Patent for Virginia. Everyone was in great distress – some in Leiden had prematurely given up their jobs and sold their houses – while Sandys and Gorges slogged it out, somewhere up in the political clouds.

James was backing Gorges, as were the 'imperialists' who wanted military bases in New England (and still hankered after the discovery of gold). From James' point of view, if Weston could divert the Pilgrims away from Virginia to New England then this would have the double benefit of helping Gorges and damaging Sandys and Southampton, his enemies at the Virginia Company. Gorges wanted the voyage of the Pilgrims to be delayed as long as possible to give time for his Council of New England to be formalised and his fishing monopoly to be granted. As a result, to the despair of the Pilgrims (and of Weston) two months (April and May) were frittered away by this policy of delays without anything happening.

The extra time did allow Weston, probably helped by Carver, to recruit more investors ('adventurers'). He drummed up about 70 in the end, according to John Smith. He wrote later that they were a mixture of gentlemen, merchants and traders, and most were 'of London'. They invested about £7,000, says Smith, which was a great deal of money – comparative values are notoriously difficult to assess over centuries, but something like £900,000 today. The names are known of only about 50 of them and by 1628 these had dwindled to only four, but by then the colony was well established and success had been secured.

The Mayflower Investors

In the table below the 1626 letter referred to lists the names of 42 investors (41 male and 1 female). The symbol § marks the four investors left in 1628, the so-called 'undertakers' (who did not bury the colony, but saved it).

Allden, Robert	1626 Letter
Altham, Emmanuel	1626 Letter. Master of pinnace, Little James.
§Andrews, Richard	1626 Letter. Undertaker in 1628. Haberdasher of Cheapside. Alderman. Brother of Thomas.
Andrews, Thomas	1626 Letter. 1629 invested in Massachusetts Bay Company. Financial supporter of Cromwell. involved in execution of King Charles I. Leather-seller. Lord Mayor of London.
Anthony, Laurence	1626 Letter
Bass, Edward	1626 Letter. 1627 representative of the adventurers. Gave them loan.
§ Beauchamp, John (note there was an uncle, John Sr, and a John Jr)	1610 Follower of Ainsworth in Amsterdam. In 1626 Letter. 1627 representative of the adventurers. 1628 Purchaser. Fur trader of Clapham with Sherley. A Salter. In London was an importer and exporter trading with Amsterdam. An interloper.
Brewer, Thomas	1626 Letter
Browning, Henry	1626 Letter
Collier, William	1626 Letter. A brewer. Active in government of New Plymouth, so probably a Brownist church member.
Coulson, Christopher	Known prior to 1626.
Coventry, Thomas	1626 Letter
Cushman, Robert	Known prior to 1626.
Fletcher, Thomas	1626 Letter. Owned Little James.
Gibbs, Mr	Known prior to 1626.
Goffe, Thomas	1626 Letter. 1629 invested in Massachusetts Bay Company. Ship-owner. Friend of Winthrop.

Greene, William	Known prior to 1626. Partner of Edward Pickering.
Gudburn, Peter	1626 Letter
§ Hatherley, Timothy	1614 md Alice Collard in St Olave Southwark. 1623 Passenger on *Anne-LJ*. 1626 Letter. 1626-32 back in Southwark. 1628 taxed in Southwark. 1628 Undertaker. 1632 emigrated to New Plymouth on *William and Mary*. In Feltmakers' Company. Assistant Governor.
Heath, Thomas	1626 Letter
Hobson, William	1626 Letter
Holland, Robert	1626 Letter
Hudson, Thomas	1626 Letter
Keayne, Robert	1626 Letter. 1627 representative of the adventurers. A Merchant Taylor. To Boston with Winthrop. Prominent in Massachusetts.
Knight, Eliza	1626 Letter. Only woman.
Knight, John	1626 Letter. Probably of Cheapside.
Knowles, Myles	1626 Letter
Ling, John	1626 Letter. Lost his property and ended in poverty.
Millsop, Thomas	1626 Letter
Mott, Thomas	1626 Letter
Newbald, Fria.	1626 Letter
Penington, William	1626 Letter
Penrin, William	1626 Letter
Pickering, Edward	Known prior to 1626. 1612 md Mary Stubbs as a 'merchant of London'. 1615 worked with Weston on smuggling pamphlets. 1619 with Weston travelled to Leiden.
Peirce, John	Known prior to 1626. Clothworker. 1620 granted the first Peirce Patent. 1621 second Patent. His ship, the *Paragon*, intended to supply Plymouth Colony, met with disaster.

Peirce, William	Known prior to 1626. Brother of John. Master of the *Anne* 1623.
Pocock, John	Known prior to 1626. Merchant Taylor, religious, lived off Bread St, a puritan area. 1619 joined Artillerymen set up to defend London against Spanish invasion. Perhaps recruited Myles Standish to M. 1626 letter. 1627 representative of the adventurers. 1629 invested in Massachusetts Bay Company. In 1644 at Independent church of Henry Burton in Stepney.
Poynton, Daniel	1626 Letter
Quarles, William	1626 Letter
Revell, John	1626 Letter. 1629 invested in Massachusetts Bay Company and migrated to New England. Ship-owner.
Rookes, Newman	1626 Letter
Sharpe, Samuel	1626 Letter. 1629 invested in Massachusetts Bay Company. 1629 to New England (Salem).
§Sherley, James	1587 bp St Magnus the Martyr. Supporter of Ainsworth. Partner of Beauchamp. Treasurer for New Plymouth adventurers. Fur trader. His town house was in Crooked Lane, his goldsmith shop was the Golden Horseshoe on London Bridge and his out-of-town house was in Clapham. Was md to a Mary Mott of Colchester. 1626 Letter. 1627 representative of the adventurers. 1628 Purchaser.
Thickens, Randall	Draper, brother-in-law of Carver, with land in Stepney, London.
Tilden, Joseph	1626 Letter. Of London but from Kent. Brother of Thomas Tilden.
Thomas, William	Known prior to 1626. Was a colonist in 1630s.
Thornell, John	1626 Letter
Thornhill, Matthew	1626 Letter
Ward, Thomas	1626 Letter

Weston, Thomas	1584 b. Rugeley, Staffordshire. 1609 admitted as a member of the Ironmongers Company. 1615 began helping Brewer distribute publications in Britain. 1620 Found about 70 adventurers to invest in the *Mayflower* expedition. 1620 (May) struck deal with Pilgrims. 1620 (June) Chartered *Mayflower*. 1620 (Aug) in Southampton.
White, John	1626 Letter. 1629 invested in Massachusetts Bay Company.
Wright, Richard	1626 Letter. Settler in New England.

Who were these investors, or 'adventurers'? They are hard to envisage, as they lived 400 years ago, but, as they were responsible for the *Mayflower* expedition, and no less indispensable than passengers and crew, it is worth examining who they were and what interests they had.

In terms of their commercial interests, the *Mayflower* investors are hard to pin down. Only for about a dozen of the 50 do we have information about which livery company, if any, they belonged to. The extreme variety of the dozen indicates that a religious motive was at work and not just a commercial one. On the other hand, analysis does show a bias towards fur and those livery companies involved in the fur trade: the Skinners; the Haberdashers (who sold beaver hats); the Feltmakers (a City company but not yet liveried); the Merchant Taylors (users of fur); and the Leather-sellers Company (fur boots). There are no Fishmongers in these dozen names, as might be expected, but this may be just chance, and there is a Salter, closely linked to Fishmongers in this historical period before the advent of refrigeration.

What sort of London did these Mayflower investors live in? In 1620 London was a city built almost entirely of wood, with around 300,000 people. It was a boom town, densely packed, with great disparities of wealth. People poured into London, where wages might easily be 50% higher than in the provinces and where there were many opportunities for self-advancement. On the other hand, the capital was regularly swept by epidemics, especially in the summer months. In 1625 plague killed 41,000 in London and the average expectation of life has been estimated as no more than 35 years. One quarter of babies were dead before they were ten. This meant the population needed to be constantly replenished by more and more immigrants, either from the rest of England or from France and the Netherlands.

The City consisted of narrow alleys rather than streets. To fit in all the people a typical house in London (usually half-timbered with a clay or plaster filling) had a very narrow front and some rose as high as five or six storeys. Houses on the opposite side of an alley almost met and in some places one could lean out of an upstairs window and shake hands with the householder across the way. There was a constant stench from sewage and from foul streams like the so-called 'river' Fleet. The streets were piled high with rotting refuse and a multitude of flies swarmed in the summer months. Rats were common (including those that spread Bubonic Plague). Personal hygiene was lacking, even pungent, and passers-by might carry on their faces the scars of smallpox.

One sight that would particularly offend modern taste was the row of heads on poles displayed above the Great Stone Gateway on the Southwark side of London Bridge. The heads were all of 'noble' men (or at least of 'notable' men like Cromwell), since only upper-class men and women had the privilege of being decapitated. A passing descendant might be proud that their ancestor had their head stuck on a pole and was not, like the common people, hanged, tortured or disembowelled.

The contemporary writer, Stowe, also complained about the smokiness of London. This, caused by the burning of coal (mostly from Newcastle), was the first augury of the 19th-century Industrial Revolution. He was saddened by the contrast between the beautiful London of his youth and the ugly commercial centre at the beginning of the 17th century. He recalled his life as a young boy, buying milk from a farm just outside Aldgate, before the days of this smoky London covered in 'mean cottages and tenements'.

Amid all the ugliness, London was also beautiful. A German visiting Wapping in 1609 wrote: 'Here for almost two miles we saw an infinite number of ships on the river, gallant in their beauty and loftiness.' Some waited to unload at the Legal Quays, between London Bridge and St Katherine, where smaller ships were checked, while others waited on wind and tide. The goods these ships disgorged could also have beautiful effects. In this period every London street 'from the Tower to Westminster alonge' was full of French and Italian shops displaying colourful goods 'able to make any temperate man to gaze on them and to buy somewhat, though it serve no purpose necessary'.[4] This was the dawn of the consumer society.

The houses, in which some of the adventurers lived, could also be beautiful. The grandest housing lay in the west of the City (Aldersgate, Cripplegate, Ludgate, Newgate) on the way to Whitehall and the court. Further west, the Strand was lined with impressive residences, home to the aristocracy and the courtiers. It was in the west too that

London's greatest church, the old St Paul's Cathedral dominated the skyline. For these well-off inhabitants there were solutions to all of London's problems. Fresh water was delivered to their homes in wooden churns by professional water-carriers. They could retreat in the summer to their country estates to avoid the epidemics. Carriages were on hand to transport them swiftly across the City to wholesome destinations. Most of the adventurers would have lived comfortably enough in streets off Cheapside, such as Bread Street, would have employed servants and would have had country houses as well as their town houses.

Puritans

In terms of identifying the religion of the adventurers, it can certainly be said that few of them would be Brownists. The majority would be puritans, since the City of London at that time was largely puritan. The word 'puritan' should not, however, be taken as in any way the opposite of commercial. One of the proofs of God's blessing was success in business. Equally, it would be quite a mistake to believe 'puritans' were merely a sect of sour killjoys (Macaulay's stereotype). A puritan was merely somebody inside the Calvinist Church of England who wanted to 'purify' it of corruption. It did not necessarily follow that they were grim, severe and sententious, though some were.

What sort of life would a puritan family in London lead? Typically, they were middle class, had a humanist as well as a religious education, read books, played music and wore an array of clothes. Inventories show that male and female puritans often owned outfits of silk and satin in a fashionable range of bright colours. Magistrates and ministers wore black, but black was a mark of social status and importance. In general, puritan clothing was not restricted except by the requirements of work, but low-cut bodices and exaggerated male codpieces were frowned upon as sexually provocative (as in the case of Thomasina Boyes). Nonetheless, puritans had far less attachment to sexual repression than Catholics. Luther enjoyed the nude paintings of Cranach and rejected the Catholic notion that celibacy was a superior moral state.

The puritan approach to marriage may be disconcerting to modern taste but in a world where upper-class marriages were arranged by parents, or at least had to receive the parents' blessing, there was in any case little romance. If a marriage was not for property it was for sex: the temptations of extra-marital sex had to be defused by swift and frequent marriages. Puritan men stuck to the accepted age norms for marriage (a boy must be 14 and a girl must be 12) but they would commonly marry another wife within a year of one wife's death (in childbirth all too often). They did not wait for love. If there was a degree of friendship then it was assumed that, once sexual relations had begun, love would follow. This approach was quite usual amongst middle- and upper-class people in general, not just puritans.

The puritans were famously against plays, because they were connected to the court, were usually performed on the Sabbath, and were often lewd and disreputable. They did not oppose plays in themselves. On sports there was a similar distinction. The puritans opposed bearbaiting and cockfighting for their odious cruelty to animals and they opposed boxing and football since, having few rules at that time, they were both characterised by bloody violence; but tennis and bowling were approved. For their other leisure activities, puritans loved music and dancing (though the dances must not involve close contact between the sexes). They did not allow musical instruments inside church (though singing was allowed) but outside church it was quite different. Milton and Cromwell liked paintings, wine, music and dance. Cromwell is said to have promoted the first opera. The puritans, and the Brownists too, often threw parties and enjoyed good food, wine, beer, skilled storytelling, card-playing, music and song. The Leiden congregation had excellent musicians, said Winslow, who was moved to tears by their music, and Robert Browne, founder of Brownism, was a skilled musician, expert on the lute.

Aldgate

In 1632 the Bishop of London referred to the Aldgate ward as a 'nest of Non-conformists' but it was mostly the area known as Duke's Place that attracted the radical elements. Duke's Place was in the former parish of the Holy Trinity Priory, dissolved in 1531. As no parish church had replaced the Priory, Duke's Place was not subject to the Act of Uniformity, which said that everyone had to attend their parish church. There was no parish church to attend so you could not be compelled to attend it. For years this anomaly was tolerated – Francis Walsingham, head of state security for Elizabeth, even lived in the Place – but finally in 1622 an exasperated Archbishop Abbot ended its privileged status by having a new church built inside the parish boundaries.

Before that, the radicalism of Duke's Place had been compounded by the arrival of refugees. The Duke of Norfolk and the Heneage family, who had acquired the former church buildings, which were made of stone, converted the properties into tenements. As craftsmen who needed to use fire in the manufacture of their products delighted in stone masonry buildings, skilled Dutch and Huguenot refugees poured into the area. London's first Delftware pottery was made by Jacob Jensen of Antwerp in Aldgate and his house, The Rose, was in Duke's Place. In 1586 a survey of the shell of Holy Trinity Priory found houses built inside it and the precinct inhabited by Dutchmen, probably refugees, some of whom were firing Delftware vessels and tiles.

The most important building for the history of the *Mayflower* in what was then Duke's Place (more extensive than now) was Heneage House. This building was formerly the town palace of the Abbot of Bury St Edmonds and it stood at the western end of Duke's Place, which the Duke of Norfolk had owned but sold off to a Thomas Heneage. Heneage House itself abutted three streets: Heneage Lane, Bevis Marks and Berry (Bury) Street. Part of this site is now occupied by the Bevis Marks synagogue. Samuel Morison wrote: 'Heneage House, Duke's Place, was a sort of rabbit warren of tenements in Aldgate where many dissenters lived. Ironmongers Hall, to which Weston belonged, was nearby [in Fenchurch St].'[5]

Leon Hills has written: 'It is apparent that a number of Robinson's followers (separatists) resided in London much of the time, probably for business reasons. This they could do safely at Heneage House in Duke's Place, Aldgate Ward... Rogers, Fuller, Cushman, Southworth, Allerton, Martin, Hopkins and many other separatists and puritans made Duke's Place their London headquarters, and many of Sir Edwin Sandys' closest friends resided there.'[6] In 1620 Robert Cushman addressed a letter to Edward Southworth at Heneage House. Hills speculates that the rabbit-warren of Heneage House must have been where William Brewster hid away in 1619-20 when he was on the run from arrest. Hills and Banks both concluded that William Bradford would have visited Heneage House after he sold his house in Leiden in 1619, as the name, William Bradford, is on a tax return. When Edward Southworth died, after the *Mayflower* sailed, his wife, Alice, at the next opportunity set sail for New Plymouth, where she and Bradford immediately married.

Historian Charles Banks was impressed with the importance of Heneage House and wrote that, though Heneage House is long demolished and 'not a vestige now remains of that "great house large of rooms" where once these Pilgrim leaders – Bradford, Cushman, Mitchell and Southworth – lived and planned with Weston and Sherley (probably in Ironmongers Hall) the details and prospects of their epochal venture', it should be remembered. He said the Jewish synagogue of Bevis Marks which stands on part of the site where Heneage House once stood 'may well be designated as the only Pilgrim shrine in London'. He added: 'It is more worthy of remembrance than the quays at Southampton and Plymouth, England, where brief stops were made, the last named port being an unintended anchorage...' The site of Heneage House 'should receive at least equal commemorative notice'.[7]

Banks was the first to understand the central importance of London to the voyage of the *Mayflower*. It was where the investors lived, where the crew lived, where half the passengers lived, where the ship came from, where the Pilgrim church came from, and where the final negotiations took place.

Faction-fighting

The frustration for the Pilgrims was that, although they knew negotiations were going on in London they could not find out from Weston, or their other contacts, what was happening. They pressed on with selling their properties and making arrangements for their families but all the while having to trust that Weston would hire them a ship. They even bought a small ship of their own, the *Speedwell,* impressed by Weston's argument that fishing would guarantee them a food supply. In May they sent a Thomas Nash to London to recruit a pilot, and he returned with a man called Reynolds. They purchased the ship in Holland (probably through the Merchant Adventurers in Delft), but they had to have a pilot approved by Trinity House in London if they were to navigate, legally, the English and American coasts. The idea of buying a small ship, and not just hiring, was to keep the *Speedwell* in America for a year and use it for fishing. Robinson was cross with Weston because he ridiculed this idea, but perhaps Weston knew about negotiations to award Gorges a fishing monopoly and this made him nervous. Maybe Robinson would have been nervous if he had known what Weston knew.

June was chaos. Behind the scenes investors in Holland who wanted a Dutch colony on the Hudson were desperate for the Pilgrims to be pushed north into New England. Maurice would have concurred since he wanted no quarrels with Britain over territory around the Hudson. Gorges also wanted to have the Pilgrims to the north as he wished to develop New England and gain a fishing monopoly for the West Country fishermen. As he was not likely to be granted a fully constituted Council and a fishing patent for months, his policy was to delay the Pilgrims' voyage until the autumn. On the opposite side, Sandys and the Virginia Company wanted the Pilgrims to set off for the Hudson immediately, on their patent, and to their territory.

Weston was only a go-between and, as Robinson mentioned in a letter with some irritation, Weston was even asking George Morton, when he went to London from Leiden, whether he had any news about what was happening. Suddenly all came to a head, as shown in a letter from Allerton, Bradford, Fuller and Winslow to Carver and Cushman. They said they were shocked to have heard from Thomas Nash the news that Cushman has gone beyond his brief (which had been set down in writing to him) and agreed new terms with the adventurers, disregarding the March agreement. The politics are obscure, but this drastic change cannot have been unconnected with James' removal of Sandys in May from the leadership of the Virginia Company. James still did not command a majority, but removing Sandys was a psychological blow to Sandys' supporters.

The Pilgrims were known to rely heavily on Sandys; his removal may have exposed the Pilgrims to a feeling amongst the adventurers that the risk was now higher and they therefore needed to tighten up the terms more in their favour. The new terms agreed by Cushman on 1 July, without consulting Leiden, were that the joint stock company would last seven years, not five, and therefore no land (including houses and gardens) would be distributed until 1627. The Pilgrims would work for the company every day of the week for two more years. Some denounced this as 'servitude', but Jeremy Bangs is clear that the main bone of contention, which caused such anger, was not the work but the fact that they would not own their own houses and gardens for seven years. He also makes the distinction that it was not the 'servitude' of indentured labour. Although they were working non-stop for the company for seven years, they were still shareholders in the company and could not be treated as slaves. Nonetheless, it probably felt like servitude, whatever the legalities, if only because it had been imposed at the last minute.

Robinson was appalled. Those committed to undertaking the voyage had all been recruited on the basis of the terms agreed in March. Several had sold their property and many had handed over their money. They were incensed they would not be getting their own land for seven years. Robinson wrote to John Carver: 'Neither do I think is there a man here who would pay anything if he had again his money in his purse.' Robinson says Leiden would have continued to try for a deal with Maurice if Weston had not offered them terms superior to anything the Dutch could offer. Robinson felt they had been deceived. As for Weston's failure to arrange a ship after three months, he condemns that as 'inexcusable'. It would have been obvious to Robinson, as indeed to anyone else, that a ship needed to reach America in early autumn, before winter set in. He must have realised that Weston and the adventurers were not in control of events because he places most blame on Cushman, whom he judged 'unfit to deal with other men'.

Rotherhithe

Soon afterwards Weston and Cushman announced that they had hired a ship in Rotherhithe. It was the *Mayflower* and its Master was Christopher Jones.

It was not explained how they had suddenly hired a ship in just a few days; nor why they had chosen a Master who usually sailed to Europe and possessed no relevant experience, except perhaps some whaling in Greenland; nor why they had looked to a wine-ship from Rotherhithe instead of a big ship from the vicinity of Blackwall or Wapping more accustomed to long-distance voyages. Rotherhithe was not authorised by the Port of London (it had no Customs House) to take passengers or cargoes out of the country but Blackwall, Gravesend and Wapping were. To understand this, it is useful to examine the background of Rotherhithe, the home of the *Mayflower*. The adventurers and the Dutch merchants, after the king's move against Sandys and the triumph of Gorges, were looking for a ship that could take the Pilgrims to New England instead of taking them to Virginia, and Rotherhithe was the key to this plan.

Since the 14th century, Rotherhithe, a peninsula on the south bank of the Thames just east of Southwark, had been an important area for shipbuilding, ship-repair, ship-breaking and ship-refitting. At the start of the 17th century, with London needing more ships, Rotherhithe prospered, as did Deptford, a centre for British naval ships just to the south. Rotherhithe and Deptford also benefited from incipient industrialisation. Both had small rivers: in Deptford the River Ravensbourne and in Rotherhithe the rapid stream called Earl's Sluice flowed through creeks into the Thames. Such creeks were ideal for industries that depended on fresh water.

One of the industries on Earl's Creek, as on Deptford Creek, was copperas. Although little known now, exploitation of copperas stones was once a major business and perhaps Britain's first highly capitalised industry. The copperas farms in Rotherhithe were not new. The monks of Bermondsey Abbey had built them by the Mill Ponds in western Rotherhithe to make into gunpowder by the admixture of saltpetre. With the demise of the monasteries the first private gunpowder mills in England were opened in 1544, and they opened in Rotherhithe. In 1566 an Act of Parliament gave the manufacture of copperas official encouragement by the state. This was for national security because England at that time was dependent on Catholic states for supplies of alum and copperas, upon which the manufacture of gunpowder, chemicals and dye fixatives for cloth (Britain's main industry) depended.

Copperas stones were heavy dark pebbles found on shore-lines and were used to make sulphuric acid, gunpowder, printers' ink and dye fixatives. The stones were left for many years in trenches, in pools of water, until the water was pitch black. It was then used as a black dye or, strongly heated, it could produce sulphuric acid. The trenches could be 100 feet long and 12 feet deep with layers of stones. The stones could stay there for five years to 'ripen by the sun and rain'. The bottom of the beds was solid clay so the rainwater did not leak. From each trench a channel led into a boiler house with a lead boiler. An alternative to boiling was mixing the copperas with scraps of iron, bought in large quantities from ironmongers such as Thomas Weston. The 'copperas-farms' were dangerous – anyone who fell in a copperas pit suffered an agonising death – and in addition the blackened land was permanently contaminated. Earl's Sluice in Rotherhithe was called 'Black Ditch'.

The huge surge in demand for copperas was driven chiefly by a need to use copperas as a mordant to fix dyes in fabric, leather or even bricks. It was especially in demand for the finishing of woollen cloth. Boosted by growth in demand for ship-repair and for copperas Rotherhithe became attractive both to investors and to middle-class residents looking for property that would rise in price. In 1605, even Robert Cecil, the king's chief minister, bought some land on the edge of Rotherhithe. It was in this context that two new well-off residents appeared in Rotherhithe at roughly the same time, *c.*1611. One was Thomas Gataker, who became rector of St Mary's, the parish church for the whole Rotherhithe peninsula, and the other was Christopher Jones, the Master of the *Mayflower*.

Jones came from Harwich, one of the biggest sources of copperas in the country, and Gataker was a friend of the Crispe family, the owners of the Rotherhithe copperas farms. The second of Gataker's four wives (they married in 1612) was a member of the Crispe family and the family would have had a big say in who became rector of Rotherhithe St Mary.

Ellis Crispe was an Alderman in the City and also a member of the Salters Company, which had diversified from salt into chemicals. Another activity of the family was building houses – the copperas was used to darken the bricks and so make bricks of all shapes and colours look uniform and impressive. The politics of Ellis are unclear but young Nicholas Crispe, who took over the business in 1625, was an enemy of Sandys and everything he stood for. He made incursions into Ghana and pioneered the slave trade in West Africa. If he could make a small contribution to stopping Sandys and destroying his hold on the Virginia Company, he would.

Thomas Gataker

Gataker, at St Mary's, was not necessarily an opponent of Sandys but he was heavily committed to the Dutch and to the Dutch Church in Austin Friars. His motive for finding a ship that could take the Pilgrims would have been to help the Dutch merchants.

Gataker was certainly no friend of the Brownists or of any separatists. His brand of puritanism ('episcopalian Presbyterianism') belonged to the most moderate variety: bishops should be kept but should be accountable, though not to the congregation. On the other hand, he was definitely a puritan and sided with Parliament against the king in the Civil War. He was a good City man, active in the Haberdashers Company. In his youth he was esteemed by even radical puritans, and at the time he became rector of Rotherhithe it was being proposed by William Bradshaw and Henry Jacob that he should instead become chaplain to Prince Henry, the heir to the throne, of whom the puritans had high hopes. Gataker, who said he disliked politics, chose to be rector of Rotherhithe rather than chaplain of the heir apparent.

Gataker was a brilliant scholar whose sermons are still readable now, and his edition of Marcus Aurelius endured for centuries. He aimed to establish in booming Rotherhithe an academy for all students, including foreign students from the Netherlands. Oxford and Cambridge had a monopoly on university education, but he would break that monopoly with a 'university of Rotherhithe' that would assist the puritan cause.

When he arrived in Rotherhithe Gataker found the broken-down old rectory 'wilfully much neglected and defaced by the late incumbent's widow and the wharf before it ready to drop down'.[8] It was thatched with reeds, and since it was to be not just a rectory but also his academy, he had to replace the reeds with tiles in order to protect against fire. He also enlarged it to twice the size so he could teach his students there. Backed by rich local shipowners and the Crispe family, all keen to develop Rotherhithe and enhance its status, he was provided with funds and with an assistant, a scribe and a curate.

Gataker's academy was a success and it has been acclaimed as the first of the great Nonconformist academies that were to educate the British middle class in later centuries. His assistant, Thomas Young, became tutor to John Milton. Gataker represented the new middle class, an intellectual who was engaged though his pamphlets with the topics of the day, and he even possessed a typical 'house in town' (not his own but lent by a friend) since he regarded Rotherhithe as 'too remote' from London.

Despite these progressive ideas, Gataker was poles apart from the Brownists because he had a typically puritan love of 'hierarchy'. For example, in *God's Eye on his Israel* (1645) he complained that he was living in a time of 'liberty' when many are seduced by new ideas, but especially the lower classes and women. In his *Marriage Duties* he warned against allowing women to become the masters. Women were on the rise, he cautioned, and he was clear that they 'seek to rule'. The institution of marriage was in danger, and the worst evil that could blight a marriage, he thought, was 'a contentious woman'.

Gataker had a close relationship with the Dutch Church in Austin Friars and in Middelburg, both of whom sent students to his academy.

Willem Teelinck, minister at Middelburg 1613-29, was a personal friend of Gataker. When the much-esteemed Simon Ruytinck, a minister of the Austin Friars church, died in 1621 his successor was Wilhelm Thylein, another student of Gataker's academy in Rotherhithe. Needless to say, Gataker was a stout champion of the Dutch merchants in London and defended them, for example, during the Star Chamber case in 1619 that seriously threatened the economic security of the Austin Friars Church.

It seems very likely that Gataker had a hand in the choice of Jones and the *Mayflower*. Once the Pilgrims had rejected the Dutch offer to be part of New Netherland on the Hudson River, the Dutch merchants, Dutch Ambassador and Dutch government wanted the Pilgrims to land as far away as possible from the Hudson. Gorges did not want them on the Hudson either. Gataker knew all the factions – the Popham family, friends of Gorges, were friends of the Gatakers and he had married into the Crispes – but his primary alignment was with the Dutch Church.

In London the Dutch Church was the natural place for the Dutch plan to be discussed in April-June 1620. The Church was attended by Dutch merchants from Amsterdam, by several Pilgrims from Duke's Place, and by Weston. The staff at the church would have been taught by Gataker, at least in English if not other subjects, and probably all would have visited Rotherhithe. Weston would know Rotherhithe through the alum and copperas trade. Although there is no way of proving Gataker introduced Jones to Weston, the circumstantial evidence is strong. The destination of the *Mayflower* was likely altered, and no doubt with the king's 'connivance', before the ship sailed. The last thing James wanted was a successful settlement in Virginia credited to Sandys.

Gataker did have one problem. As a minister it was his job to report to the Church on the activities of his congregation. Parish ministers were the nodal points in the Church's network of informers. He knew that Jones would be meeting the *Speedwell*, full of Brownists, in Southampton and it was possible that some passengers who boarded the *Mayflower* in London would be illicit. Moreover, Christopher Jones (approved by Gorges, the Dutch and the king) was, if an opportunity presented itself, going to break the patent in America. Given this, Gataker left Rotherhithe for exactly the days when the *Mayflower* was due to sail, thus clearing himself of any obligation to report. He was away in the Netherlands from 13 July until 14 August and the *Mayflower* sailed at the end of July. He visited many friends over there and delivered a lecture in Middelburg. It sounds like an informal trip put together at the last moment.

There was an interesting postscript to this manoeuvre. When Gataker died in 1654 the funeral sermon by Simeon Ashe included a biography of Gataker (published in 1655). Ashe claimed Gataker for the Presbyterian Church but 1654 was the exact moment when New Englanders, including Winslow, were in the Cromwell government. In his attempt to prove Gataker never had any radical connections but was always a solid Presbyterian, Ashe picked out two events from all of Gataker's life: firstly, his support for the Presbyterians in the Westminster Assembly in the 1640s; and secondly, his absence from Rotherhithe on a tour of the Netherlands for a month from July 13, 1620.

Christopher Jones

Christopher Jones, Master of the *Mayflower*, must have attended St Mary's church in Rotherhithe every Sunday when not abroad, and listened to the acclaimed sermons of Gataker, full of wisdom culled from the Bible and from Roman literature. Jones was born in Harwich, Essex, in about 1570 and in 1593 he married a Sarah Twitt. He prospered, and in 1601 became a freeman of Harwich and then in 1604 one of the town's 'capital burgesses'. When Sarah died in May 1603 he married six months later Josian, widow of Richard Grey. Soon after, in 1605, he fell victim to what the Brownists called 'hierarchy' since, despite his progress, he was still only middle class and he was charged with keeping hunting dogs, allowed only to 'gentlemen'. In the same year Jones had built a brand-new 240-ton ship (named the *Josian* after his new wife) and in 1607 it is known that he sailed her to Bordeaux. In the next 14 years the wine trade with Bordeaux and La Rochelle seems to have been the bedrock of his business, and, as those towns were strongholds of the Huguenots, and Jones is known to have visited Spain only once, it seems that, like Gataker, he had puritan sympathies.

Jones sold the *Josian* and bought the *Mayflower* around 1609. The *Mayflower* was considerably smaller at 180 tons but Jones seems to have set his sights on the booming trade in London and a smaller ship enabled easier access to narrowing rivers such as at Wapping. In August 1609 the ship left London for Trondheim in Norway, hired by a London merchant, Andrew Pawling, and it is Jones' first *Mayflower* voyage on record. It was a disaster and in December 1609 the *Mayflower*, severely battered by storms, limped into London and anchored off Ratcliff. The hamlet of Ratcliff, Stepney, had by the early 17th century grown to 3,500 inhabitants, mainly sailors. Ships approaching the City anchored there while waiting for cargoes to be checked in at Wapping.

In 1610 Jones played safe, turned to the profitable wine trade, and brought into London on the *Mayflower* wine from the Charente coast. This prefaced his move to Rotherhithe, nearer to London, in 1611. In 1609-11 the *Mayflower* was listed as 'of Harwich' but in 1611-21 it was listed as 'of London' and from then on Jones is recorded as having children buried and baptised by Gataker at St Mary's church in Rotherhithe. Though Rotherhithe was not in London, it was supervised by the Port of London and was therefore 'of London'.

As well as access to the London wine trade, Jones may have been attracted to Rotherhithe because it was close to Wapping and Blackwall, both of which had docks authorised by the Port of London for the checking of passengers and cargoes; because Rotherhithe was booming on account of copperas; and because of the increased demand in general for shipping and ship repair. The number of Master Mariners in both Ratcliff and Rotherhithe was soaring and in 1612 Rotherhithe shipwrights were awarded a royal charter of their own.

Jones' normal pattern of exchanging English cloth for Huguenot wine was disrupted in 1614-15 when he sailed twice to Hamburg and then to Malaga. This was probably connected with the 'Cockayne episode'. In 1614 the king summarily ended the monopoly of all English cloth exports to northern Europe enjoyed by the Merchant Adventurers and handed it to Alderman Cockayne, a London merchant who argued that, since London now had its own copperas supplies, plus alum from Yorkshire, the English could now 'finish' (treat and dye) their own cloth instead of sending it to Holland first. He promised James that huge increases in customs duties would accrue to the Crown. Instead, in 1614-17 there was massive disruption of the cloth export trade since, though England had copperas and alum, it did not have Dutch expertise. Finally, in 1617 James had to hand back the monopoly to the Merchant Adventurers.

By 1620 Jones had re-established his routine and was returning with wine from France in January and then again in May. He could not therefore have heard before May from Gataker that the Dutch were concerned to avert a Brownist settlement on the Hudson and that Weston was looking for a ship.

5

The *Mayflower* Sails from London

Nobody knows for sure where the *Mayflower* was built. Harwich, Leigh-on-Sea and Aldeburgh have all staked their claims but Harwich, also the home of Christopher Jones, is usually awarded the accolade. The ship was a Dutch-style *fluyt*, rated at 180 tons, the most sophisticated cargo ship of its day, designed to maximise cargo space. It is thought to have been about 110 feet long and about 26 feet wide but the only sure thing known about its size is the tonnage – the dimensions have all been deduced from similar ships.

The *Mayflower* had three masts – mizzen (aft), main (midship) and fore – plus a spritsail, and it was square-rigged, with high castle-like structures fore and aft, and a 'beak'. There were four decks: a main deck, a gun deck, a cargo hold, and an extra 'poop' deck above the 'captain's cabin' at the stern. The ample cargo hold would have contained supplies for two months and passengers would have slept on the gun deck: 50 feet long, 25 feet wide, only 5 feet high.

In 1609 records show that the *Mayflower* was owned by Christopher Jones, Christopher Nicholls, Robert Childs and Thomas Short, with Jones as the Master. The ownership of ships was commonly a partnership in the early 17th century because insurance cover did not develop until late in the century and there was therefore a need to spread liability by allotting shares in a ship. Partnerships in ships usually had one Master who sailed the ship and sold its cargo while the others contributed goods and capital and shared in the profit or loss. By being part-owner in a number of ships the owner could spread the risk. Normally, partnerships in ships were made for just one voyage.[1] Charles Banks says that in 1620 Thomas Weston and Robert Cushman chartered the *Mayflower* from Jones and Childe.

When Cushman and Weston came to Rotherhithe in early June to see the *Mayflower* and meet Jones, as mentioned by Cushman in a letter, they would have had to go to where the ship was berthed. Ships could not remain long on the river, where they would be in danger from high winds and in any case would impede other ships, and they could not be kept near the shore for long because the Thames is tidal, so they were berthed in harbours or creeks. As Rotherhithe had no harbour and was not a port until the 18th century, the ship would have had to be berthed in an inlet or creek. As there was no inlet and only one creek on the Rotherhithe peninsula, Cushman and Weston must have gone to Earl's Creek, close to where Greenland Dock stands now. At Earl's Close a small river came down from Camberwell, bringing non-tidal water into the Thames. The north side of the creek was part of Rotherhithe, in Surrey, and its parish church was St Mary, while the south side was part of Deptford in Kent. As Jones must have lived on the Rotherhithe side, the *Mayflower* must have been berthed on the north side of Earl's Creek.

Embarkation

It was at the end of July that about 65 out of the 102 *Mayflower* passengers, (as calculated by the historian, Charles Banks) embarked at either Blackwall or Wapping in London. He allowed for the possibility that a couple of the 65 London passengers may have boarded in Southampton and allowed for the possibility that a few from Leiden might have been among the 65 boarding in London. There is a distinction between where they hailed from and where they boarded. Since Banks' pioneering work, it has also been felt that Gravesend, also approved by the Port of London, should be added to Blackwall and Wapping as possible embarkation points, since in the 1610s Gravesend was increasingly used. Boats, as in the case of Pocahontas, could transfer passengers from the City down to Gravesend, provided they could produce the necessary documents at the Gravesend Custom House. It is also not clear what Banks meant by 'Wapping'. In those days Wapping was quite a small patch of land to the east of the Tower, where St Katharine Dock is now, and he must be assuming that passengers embarked there after having been checked by officers from the Custom House to the west of the Tower.

It is sometimes asked why the number of possible embarkation points is so few. This is because just as Trinity House was very strict on navigation in the Thames so the Port of London was strict on checking all cargoes and passengers coming into the country and going out. Everything and everyone had to be checked in by 'searchers' at Customs Houses in docks where ships could be held for many hours. Each passenger and each item of cargo had to be documented. The searchers made their money from finding discrepancies, and networks of paid informers deterred any ship's master from trying to evade the rules. A master like Jones could forfeit his ship if found to be smuggling either cargo or passengers. In this period, apart from the Legal Quays in the City set up by Elizabeth I (which a generation of larger ships later found difficult to access) only 'Wapping', Blackwall and Gravesend had the custom houses, docks and searchers required.

Naturally, the searchers were private monopolists and varied their routines. 'The searchers at Gravesend, for example, charged sixpence apiece to issue the clearance licences.'[2] Nonetheless, the system was usually very effective. Already in 1586 Mendoza had sent a report to Philip of Spain explaining that none of his spies could enter an English port because the 'arrival of a man, or even of a fly' would be noticed. It was no easier later. Charles I in 1633-34 launched a big tightening up on who was leaving and entering the country. He wanted all Masters of ships not only to have licences for all their passengers but to swear an oath on the Bible. He also proposed that Church of England services be held on all ships so as to flush out the Brownists and other separatists. Trinity House scoffed at all this, as they felt the nationwide network of customs houses and searchers was already very strict: 'In every port and creek of the realm, the customs house is like the eyes of Argus, ever vigilant and prying'.[3]

Sometimes it is mentioned that in 1606 a 14th-century statute which forbade leaving the country to all but great lords, great merchants and soldiers, was repealed and this is confusing since certainly after 1606 the monitoring was just as tight as before, if not tighter, as the Pilgrims trying to emigrate from Lincolnshire knew to their cost. McKechnie has now explained convincingly that it was done following the union of the crowns of England and Scotland, since the statute as it stood was inimical to Scottish interests, but it made little practical difference since the king could still prevent any of his subjects from leaving the realm.[4] A proclamation of 1607 mentioned that anyone wishing to emigrate needed a licence signed by four Privy Councillors, so it is clear that control over freedom of movement persisted.

Is there any way of deciding whether the *Mayflower* passengers embarked at Blackwall, Gravesend or Wapping? There can be no definitive answer to this question since the Port of London records are incomplete. Banks seemed to prefer the idea of Wapping (he imagined the passengers walking down from Duke's Place in Aldgate to the waterfront). Nor would Gravesend have been easy to organise for over 60 people and their belongings, in small boats and with paperwork prepared (and Bradford would hardly have said they sailed 'from London' if they sailed from Gravesend in Kent). Blackwall is far more likely.

At Blackwall there were the East India Company docks, well-equipped for long-haul travel. Already Blackwall had been the departure-point for several ships that sailed to America (including the Jamestown fleet of 1606-07). It had a good connection by road to the City of London (and one into Essex). From Rotherhithe the *Mayflower* would have found Blackwall 'on its way' to America whereas Wapping meant going in the opposite direction. Most importantly, it was on the border with Essex which, Bradford observed, was the source for 'sundry' *Mayflower* passengers. Blackwall itself may even have served up a passenger or two: In 1619 the East India Company shipyard in Blackwall was employing about 400 workers and about 2,500 seamen.

It is sometimes suggested that some passengers were embarked in Rotherhithe but this would be illegal. As explained, there had to be a dock for loading, or embarking, with a Custom House for officials. There is no record of anything like that in Rotherhithe. Indeed, the Port of London records, held at Maidstone, register no ships sailing from Rotherhithe in the first half of the 17th century. There are naval ships in the second half of the century, but their personnel were not really 'passengers'. Furthermore, access to Rotherhithe was dire (it was 'remote' said Gataker) since to reach it from London Bridge a trek across the marshes was required along tracks only ten feet wide. In addition, the *Mayflower* was listed as belonging to the Port of London and Rotherhithe was not recognised by the Port of London, as were Blackwall, Gravesend and Wapping. Indeed, Rotherhithe was not listed as a 'port' until the 18th century (though then its Greenland Dock became one of the greatest and most beautiful docks in London).

Delfshaven

At the end of July, while the *Mayflower* (180 tons) was preparing to sail from Earl's Creek in Rotherhithe, the *Speedwell* (60 tons) was, at the same time, preparing to sail from Delfshaven in Holland. The two ships planned to meet in Southampton and travel across the Atlantic together.

Delfshaven, 24 miles from Leiden, was the port for Delft though it now lies in West Rotterdam. The Pilgrims were leaving from Delft probably because the ship they had bought, the *Speedwell,* was a Merchant Adventurer ship and in 1620 the Merchant Adventurers were transferring their headquarters to Delft from Middelburg. The switch had been confirmed by James in the January of 1620 and the transfer to Delft was well under way.

There were probably fewer than 50 Pilgrims sailing on the *Speedwell* out of about 300 living in Leiden. Many more, including Robinson, had promised to travel later. Before they left Leiden itself, Robinson threw a farewell party (a 'feast') at his house at which there was much singing, 'there being many of the congregation very expert in music'.

When it came to the moment of departure there were emotional scenes, first in Leiden and even more so in Delfshaven. Some had been living in Leiden for eleven years, since arriving there in 1609 with Robinson from Amsterdam, while a few had lived in Leiden even longer. Bradford wrote: 'So they lefte that goodly and pleasante city which had been their resting place near twelve years; but they knew they were pilgrimes, and looked not much on those things, but lift up their eyes to the heavens, their dearest countrie; and quieted their spirits.'[5] He was referring to the book of *Hebrews*, chapter 11, which narrates the moves by the people of faith from country to country, and their sacrifices, ever since the first move by Abraham.

In Delfshaven relatives and friends accompanied the emigrants to the ship, and some came down from Amsterdam to see them off, but they were barely able to speak to each other for sobbing and tears. Robinson gave a farewell sermon full of insight and advice. Its theme of a flexible interpretation of the Bible and openness to new ideas ('progressive revelation' in Christian terms) has drawn much commentary since, for it implied a wider toleration than the Robinson of 1608 would have ventured to suggest. He had grown in Holland and learnt from engagement with the French and Dutch churches and then with Henry Jacob. Although the sermon as it is reported may not be exactly word for word, Robinson's message opens the way to a rational interpretation of Scripture:

> I am verily persuaded the Lord hath more truth yet to break forth out of His holy word... I beseech you remember it is an article of your church covenant that you be ready to receive whatever truth shall be made known to you from the written word of God... It is not possible that the Christian world should come so lately out of such thick Anti-christian darkness and that perfection of knowledge should break forth at once.[6]

These parting words by Robinson were of great significance for the future of the Pilgrims. Robert Browne's covenant had been very basic. It had merely bound the new member, firstly, to the laws and government of the church and, secondly, to acceptance of those elected to run the church. Robinson is now saying that openness to 'more truth' and 'knowledge' is an article of Leiden's church covenant, which means that all members are bound to seek the truth and be open-minded towards new ideas.

Robinson also wrote a long letter to those departing and it is thought this was probably read out on the deck of the *Speedwell* at some point. No doubt the Pastor anticipated that his flock would be encountering many sorts of different people, from 'profane' Londoners to 'heathen' Indians and he wanted them to proceed not with dogmatism but with an open mind.

Southampton

When they arrived in Southampton they found the *Mayflower* had already arrived there seven days before. The two sets of passengers met each other with 'joyful welcome and mutual congratulation'. They soon assigned families to each ship, and chose a Governor for each, to supervise fair distribution of the food and drink that had been bought in Kent and transported to Southampton for loading. To Bradford it seemed that the main preparations for the voyage were made in Southampton and he regarded the voyage of the *Mayflower* as not from London to America nor from Plymouth to America but from Southampton to America.

Unfortunately, a blazing row broke out almost immediately when Weston tried to justify the new conditions the adventurers had imposed. Weston was 'much offended' by accusations of duplicity on his part and by their refusal to sign the altered contract. In retaliation he refused to hand over some money they were owed. Cushman received an even worse reception than he did, since it was he who had accepted the revised conditions without reference back to Leiden. A letter was now written by the passengers to the adventurers in London rejecting the new terms and protesting that Weston and Cushman had acted without their knowledge. Ownership of land was by no means the only reason they were emigrating to America, they said, but it was a 'special' one.

There was also squabbling in Southampton over food and drink supplies. Weston and Cushman had wanted the supplies bought and loaded in London but then Christopher Martin, from Billericay in Essex who worked and had a house in London, was designated the representative of the London group, and he had different ideas. He insisted on buying food in Kent and loading it in Southampton. In addition, he and Carver hired a cooper, either in London or Southampton, called John Alden, who would look after the barrels and casks. Weston and Cushman were worried about the purchase of food being taken outside London.

Their concern turned into fury when it was found in Southampton that £700 of the money assigned to food had disappeared and Martin refused to give an account of it. When questioned, he responded very arrogantly and aggressively.

By this time some of the Pilgrims were beginning to panic and regret they had signed up. Bradford reveals that some passengers would have now run away if they had been allowed to leave the ship. They were virtually imprisoned on the ship, with their working conditions apparently changeable at will by the investors, with an uncertain food supply controlled by an apparent dictator, and with the prospect of living in a desolate wasteland with an acrimonious, feuding group for the rest of their lives.

The two ships set sail from Southampton for America but the *Speedwell* soon sprang a leak and they had to put in to Dartmouth for repairs. The *Speedwell* was a solid ship with a distinguished history – it was said to have been one of the ships that defeated the Spanish Armada in 1588 – but apparently it had been 'over-masted' in Delfshaven, perhaps to carry more passengers, and now the weight of the masts was forcing the ship down into the water and causing repeated leaks to occur.

As it happens there exists, thanks to Bradford, a letter sent by Cushman in Dartmouth to Heneage House in Duke's Place, Aldgate.[7] Cushman's style varied from cocksureness to righteous indignation and self-pity, and this letter is abject self-pity, but some facts emerge. He says the *Speedwell* was already leaky at Southampton but near Dartmouth it almost sank; that Weston did not realise Leiden had not confirmed the conditions but imagined Cushman had full authority; that Martin despised the adventurers and called them 'bloodsuckers' for imposing the new conditions but despised the Pilgrims even more for their stupidity. Martin had been telling off the sailors (presumably for not dealing properly with the leaks), thus alienating them as well as the Pilgrims.

In Dartmouth, as soon as the *Speedwell* was repaired, the ships resumed the voyage, perhaps with about 90 passengers on the *Mayflower* and about 30 on the *Speedwell*. This time they sailed a long distance before the *Speedwell* sprang a new leak and they had to turn back. Bradford suspected that the leaks could have been dealt with by the crew but Reynolds, the Master of the *Speedwell*, had decided he no longer wanted to proceed. There may be some truth to this. He was supposed to stay for a year in Virginia, fishing from the Speedwell to supplement the diet of the settlers, but it is easy to see from his point of view that the constant leaks from over-masting, plus the prospect of spending a year with these feuding factions, was not attractive.

This time the ships turned back to Plymouth, Devon. They had decided to abandon the *Speedwell*, send it back to London, and have it auctioned off. They would reduce the 120 passengers by about 20 and cram the 100 or so remaining onto the *Mayflower*. The 20 who returned to London with Reynolds on the *Speedwell* included several who were totally demoralised, some with young children, plus the unpopular Cushman, blaming everyone but himself. The *Mayflower* sailed on with 102 passengers plus 20 to 30 crew. This time, unimpeded by the *Speedwell*, they did cross the Atlantic, though it has been suggested that the ship first called in at Newlyn in Cornwall to replace some contaminated water.

The London Connection

The voyage of the Mayflower was organised and financed in London and it was a London ship with a London crew, but the passengers were not just chosen in London but also in Leiden. The (mostly) London adventurers were keen on using the Leiden Brownists because their aim was a permanent settlement based on trade along the lines advocated by John Smith. Their reward would be fish and fur, perhaps tobacco and sassafras – not gold, loot and slaves – and it was felt, from Hakluyt onwards, that conscientious, hard-working Brownists would be able to build up a profitable settlement that would bring enduring commercial success. This ethos was reflected in the make-up of the passengers: the *Mayflower* was very unusual in having a substantial number of women and children on board (over 40). This included 19 adult women. This testified to the pacific, and economic, character of their mission.

The exact size of the London contingent on the *Mayflower* cannot be known but it is usually thought to be around 50. This is not to be confused with the number embarking in London, which was surely higher. A figure often cited is that 65 out of 102 *Mayflower* passengers embarked from London and only 37 from Leiden. This is the classic assessment by historian, Charles Banks, but he assumed the merchants among the passengers moved between London and Leiden all the time. It can be argued too that nearly all of the 18-20 who dropped out at Plymouth would have been from Leiden, which means that the original passenger list (about 120) could have had many more from Leiden than from London. On the other hand, some argue as far as embarkation is concerned that the size of the two ships is decisive: in London the 180-ton *Mayflower* was hired but in Leiden only the 60-ton *Speedwell*. The size that was chosen must have had a relationship to the number of passengers.

Bradford says that when starting to disembark at the beginning of 1621 they divided the passengers into 19 families (not counting those travelling alone who had families back home) so that the size of the houses they were about to build could be roughly estimated. The 19 families would have been the Allertons, Billingtons, Brewsters, Carvers, Chiltons, Cookes, Crackstones, Eatons, Fullers, Hopkinses, Martins, Mullinses, Rigsdales, Standishes, Tilleys, Tinkers, Turners, Whites, and Winslows. Of these about seven might be designated as of London and twelve of Leiden. If the members of the 19 families are totalled they amount to 63 persons (62 without James Chilton who was already dead). Bradford (who did not himself count as a family since his wife had just died) says the 'single' men (though not really single since some had left wives at home) were assigned to the houses of these families. Of those 'single' men most embarked in London.

In the debate about which passengers were living in Leiden and which were in London it is not easy to be sure. That, for example, a Brownist passenger was betrothed, or married, in Holland proves nothing. Brownists, being outside the church, had great difficulty getting married in England, but they could travel to Holland, where civil marriage was permitted by law, and then return. A civil marriage in Holland did not demand a long-term residency and was simply solemnised by a friendly Leiden Alderman. Even acquisition of 'citizenship' in Leiden did not prove residency since acquiring 'citizenship', like a 'freedom' in London, was connected not with government but with the membership of guilds.

An example of a London marriage in Leiden given by Banks is that of Edward Southworth, who went to Holland, married Alice Carpenter, and then returned with his bride to Aldgate. An example of just how misleading a civil marriage in Holland can be is the betrothal in 1613 of Willem Katford (William Bradford) and Dorothea May. Neither of them was present at their betrothal. Instead, an attestation was delivered to Leiden on their behalf. Bradford, too young to be on the list of marked men, could travel back and forth without being arrested, and was probably in England at the time, dealing with financial matters after he had received his inheritance the year before.

There has long been a debate (since the 1930s) about whether Bradford was in London in 1619-20. This arouses particular interest because Bradford was elected Governor of Plymouth Colony in most years, 1621-57, and his history of New Plymouth, *Of Plimmoth Plantation*, has been hailed as both the first American history book and the first great work of American literature. In his book (unpublished at his death) he does not mention being in London but on the other hand everything he wrote was meticulously impersonal, and very guarded.

He does not, for example, mention the ship's name, the *Mayflower,* or the *Speedwell,* or the tragic death of his own wife.

Bradford, from a family of wealthy farmers in Austerfield, Yorkshire, very close to the Brownist triangle of Scrooby, Babworth and Gainsborough, had hardly any connection to London. He joined the emigration from Lincolnshire in 1608 and proceeded, with some difficulty, to Amsterdam and then Leiden. In 1613 he married Dorothy May in Amsterdam but she was drowned in 1620, either accidentally or by suicide, and in 1623 he married Alice Southworth, who in 1620 had been living at Heneage House, Aldgate, London, with her husband, Edward. She is Bradford's only known connection to London but it was partly because of her that Banks felt sure Bradford had visited London in 1619-20.

There were three links: firstly, he had found the name of a William Bradford, right after Bradford had sold his house in Leiden in 1619, listed as a taxpayer in Duke's Place, Aldgate (the area of Heneage House, which was where the Southworths lived); secondly, Alice, straight after the death of her husband, Edward, sailed unaccompanied on the *Anne* to New England, and married Bradford immediately after landing; and thirdly, in 1617 the Elders in Leiden had made Bradford a member of the group which was organising the emigration and he would therefore be likely, as he could travel freely, to visit London. The counter arguments are that Alice could have met Bradford on her visits to Leiden, and the name of William Bradford is fairly common.

Some Leiden church members were in Leiden before the arrival of Robinson and these may be from families that fled London in the 1590s. John Turner was definitely a Leiden passenger but he seems to have been in Leiden before the East Midlands contingent arrived. Francis Cooke was also residing in Leiden well before the arrival of Robinson, as was John Carver. Both men married Walloon women: Marie de Lannoy de l'Ecluse and Hester Mahieu.

Other passengers are tricky to pin down since they were merchants or traders in both Leiden and London. Thus Thomas Rogers had London connections early on but then operated later in Leiden as a merchant. The same applies to Isaac Allerton (London blacksmith), Degory Priest (London hatter), Samuel Fuller (London serge maker) and Edward Winslow (London printer). Others are clear enough. Bradford says outright that the 'London merchants' were John Billington, Stephen Hopkins, Christopher Martin, William Mullins, Richard Warren and William White. Similarly, Banks says: 'With the exception of Bradford and Brewster, the principal leaders of the Pilgrim Colony were of London origin and association.' He lists Allerton, Hopkins, Warren, Winslow and 'probably Standish' as constituting that London connection.[8]

These problems are not just due to a deficit in 17th-century information. There is also an additional problem with London, which suffers simultaneously from too many names in the records and too many gaps in the records. Even more than elsewhere the parish records often make little sense: more die than are born, and those who marry in Holborn this year are next year baptising a child in York. The Brownists and other separatists caused some significant gaps since they rejected marriage in an Anglican Church and avoided, if possible, Anglican ceremonies of baptism and burial. In 1609 *Mayflower* passengers, Mrs Chilton and Moses Fletcher, were excommunicated after performing a secret burial in Sandwich and being caught. More serious gaps in the records are of course caused by shifting populations and by epidemics in a city that is doubling its size.

None of this is helped by a natural prejudice against London, which boasts much history already, in favour of small towns whose only claim to fame may be a connection with a *Mayflower* passenger. The latter have their records minutely ransacked whereas London's are often passed over. Even Charles Banks admitted he did not consult the South London records and others have admitted the same subsequently. In the past it has also been easy to overlook records for areas of Essex, Kent, Middlesex and Surrey that are now part of London. Expert genealogists do not fall into these traps but the burden of past research still weighs upon the assumptions of the present.

A common misunderstanding is about town houses. The practice of owning a house in town as well as one in the country started with the Norman lords. Around 1600 this practice spread to the City of London's prosperous middle class and it became normal to stay in London during the winter and then return to Devon or Herefordshire, say, in the warm summer months when London was subject to epidemics, including smallpox and plague. In some cases the town houses were owned by the person concerned but perhaps more often they were owned by the richest family member. This meant Staresmore could be in Stepney and in Leicestershire at the same time; Ferdinando de Gorges could be in Clerkenwell and Devon; and the Winslows could be in Holborn and Worcestershire. The young John Winthrop, living at the manor of Groton in Suffolk, went up to town regularly either by coach or on horseback, lodging with his brother-in-law in Fleet Street. Even Thomas Gataker who lived only across the river in Rotherhithe used the town house of a friend in the City.

It is because of the town-house phenomenon that it is safe to start from the assumption that all those who boarded the *Mayflower* in London in 1620 lived the whole time, or part of their time, in London. The burden of proof lies with those who believe that this passenger or that travelled in for the embarkation; just as in Leiden the burden of proof must be on those who believe that some travelled in to Delfshaven from Amsterdam. Otherwise it is not unreasonable to assume that those who embarked in Leiden were from the Leiden area and those who embarked in London were from the London area. Take the case of William Mullins about whom it is sometimes asked how on earth he travelled to the *Mayflower* from Dorking, where he is known to have lived. Yet, as a rich man (he held shares in the adventurers company), he would surely have had either access to a town house or else he would have owned a shop in London to sell the shoes and boots he manufactured. Dorking was on the Roman Road from Chichester to the City, which passed through Southwark to London Bridge. It would probably be in Southwark that Mullins had his shop, close to his fellow-investor, Timothy Hatherley, the feltmaker.

James I and Charles I struggled with the phenomenon of town houses, which was causing neglect of country estates. In 1615 James had felt obliged to issue a proclamation requiring that noblemen and gentry stay in their country mansions for at least nine months of the year and not live in town (exceptions were made for businessmen, in which category the *Mayflower* leadership tended to fall) but in 1623 this proclamation was rescinded when the City complained of the big drop in house prices it had caused. In 1632 when Charles I revived the proclamation in a more severe form (as was his way), the Venetian Ambassador reported that the City of London swiftly became 'empty'. The gentry, he wrote, were disgusted as they had been accustomed to staying in London throughout the winter of every year.[9]

The More Children

Four London passengers on the *Mayflower* that actually were brought in from outside London were the More children, all said to be orphans: Ellen aged eight, Jasper six, Richard five and Mary four. On the *Mayflower* there were seven children who travelled without their parents. It was the policy of the City of London at that time to try and solve the problem of orphans astray on the London streets by exporting them to Ireland or America, where, it was argued, they would have an opportunity to get on in life instead of being social outcasts in Britain. The *Mayflower* would have been expected to make a contribution to this policy, especially as one of its enthusiastic advocates on the board of the Virginia Company was Edwin Sandys, patron of the Pilgrims. The promise was that each child, on reaching adulthood, would receive a plot of land and would therefore be better off than if they had stayed as beggars in London.

The trouble was that the four More children were not orphans. Their mother (and perhaps their father) was very much alive but she had no knowledge, until too late, that her children were being transported across the Atlantic. The children had initially been taken away from the mother, Katherine More, in 1616 after a battle in court with her husband, Samuel, who had discovered he was not the father of the children. He subsequently took the children from their home in Larden Hall, Shipton, Shropshire, and deposited them with a tenant of his in Linley. Katherine, having failed legally, appeared in Linley, and tried to take back her children by force, assaulting her husband's tenants in the process.

The origin of the tragedy was back in 1611 when Katherine, aged about 25, was married off by her parents to her cousin, Samuel, aged about 17. It was not a marriage for sex and children, nor a love match, but a property match. The aim of Katherine More's parents was to unite the estates of Larden Hall with the estates of Samuel's father at Linley. After marriage the couple then lived at Larden Hall with Katherine's parents. What the parents did not know, or underestimated, was that Katherine was in love with Jacob Blakeway, 'a fellow of mean parentage and condition' who she could, for social reasons, never marry. According to Samuel in court, he and others knew the four children were Blakeway's, since the majority resembled Blakeway in 'their visages and lineaments'. Katherine's defence was that she was not legally Samuel's wife since she had married Blakeway 'informally' before she married Samuel. She relied on English law's recognition of common marriage but, unfortunately for her, had no proof of the chronology she claimed.

Katherine had little chance in the courts. Samuel was the eldest son of a respected parliamentarian and had several connections to high society. In 1656 his portrait was to be painted by Sir Peter Lely, no less. Nonetheless, Samuel found Katherine and Jacob Blakeway 'impenitent and incorrigible'. Even after he had proved them guilty of adultery, and they had been fined, Katherine continued to 'accompany' Jacob 'in secret and obscure places'.

In 1619 Samuel sought a judicial separation which would place all the four children under his legal control. The case was heard in the Court of Audience at Paul's Cathedral, London, where, despite fierce opposition from Katherine, he won the case. Katherine would not give up and went to appeal at the High Court of Delegates, the final court of appeal for ecclesiastical causes. Samuel won there too on 8 July 1620 and now he could legally dispose of her children as he liked.[10]

Samuel was Secretary to Edward Lord Zouche, who had himself discarded a wife who did not please him. Zouche, an influential man who had entertained King James at a mansion he had built in Bramhill, Hampshire, was also a Commissioner of the Virginia Company, which in 1618 had started collecting up vagrant children from the streets of

London (with the blessing of the Lord Mayor) and sending them to Virginia. Zouche saw in the *Mayflower* expedition an opportunity to help his Secretary, help the More children and help the Virginia Company. The children were therefore transferred to Thomas Weston in London; he handed them over to his-fellow alum dealer, Philomen Powell; and he passed them on to John Peirce, the representative of the Mayflower adventurers. According to Samuel's account, they stayed at Peirce's home until the *Mayflower* was due to depart, at which point they were placed in the care of Winslow (Ellen), Carver (Jasper) and Brewster (Richard and Mary). This can be taken as evidence that Winslow, Carver and Brewster must have departed from London. The searchers at customs in Blackwall or Wapping would have wanted to know who was responsible for the children.

Financially, everything was set up for the children's good. On the *Mayflower,* passengers had to buy either a £10 share or a £20 double-share. Samuel paid Weston £80 for four double-shares and then added another £20 as an 'adventure', making £100, a large sum of money. It was the annual salary of a highly paid state official. This £20 would eventually go to the children, he said, not to him. As the children would each receive the allotted acres of land from the adventurers after seven years he must have felt that their prospects for the future were secure. Thus everyone did what they thought was best for the children. Yet in a year Ellen, Jasper and Mary were all dead – buried furtively, on a wintry coast, in unmarked graves.

Passengers and Crew

The table that follows does not claim to be definitive. Alternative versions should be consulted. Too little is known about the passengers and crew, and even what is known is often the subject of dispute. The main sources used here are, apart from the original records themselves, Jeremy Bangs, Charles Banks and Caleb Johnson. The number of passengers is listed as 102, a number often chosen but which can be slightly tweaked up or down depending on who is defined as a 'passenger' and who 'crew'. The number stayed at 102 because on the voyage one person died but another was born. Of the 102, there were 50 men, 19 women (three pregnant), 14 young adults and 19 children (aged 12 or under). Of the pregnancies, one baby was born during the voyage (Oceanus Hopkins) and then, after arrival, Peregrine White was born. Mary Allerton had a still-born son.

There is ongoing dispute about which passengers embarked in Delfshaven and which in London. Most can be safely deduced but it is complicated: great merchants like Allerton and Carver probably slipped in and out of London and Leiden all the time, and they had 'servants' in both cities. A few from Leiden, especially Brewster, who was in hiding, may well have embarked in London. There is also dispute about which passengers hailed from Leiden and which from London – with 'hailed from' meaning where they worked and lived their lives. London seems to have had only a small majority, if any. Finally, there is dispute about where the passengers originated (were born and brought up). This again is partly speculative, since hard information is lacking, but it does seem to be the case that passengers originated more in London (as it is now) and East Anglia than in any other areas. Few of the passengers originated in Leiden or the East Midlands, even though those places contributed the great names of Bradford, Brewster and Robinson.

Who were the many who greeted each other at Southampton with such joy? The possibilities are that Brewster met Mary again, and Bradford met Dorothy; Samuel Fuller met Edward; John Carver met Katherine; Gilbert Winslow met Edward; Anne Tilley and Edward, with Humility Cooper and Henry Sampson, were reunited with John and Joan. If these encounters happened, they would illustrate why, according to Bradford, there was such widespread rejoicing in Southampton. One thing, however, is certain: nobody welcomed Weston and Cushman in Southampton.

One big unknown factor is the composition of the crew. The *Mayflower* could have had a crew of perhaps as many as 30, but the names are known only of a few and there is some confusion about who should count as 'crew'. Should it include the doctor (Heale), the cooper who stayed in America (Alden), the mariners, Trevor and Ely, and the mysterious 'Master Leaver' mentioned in passing by John Smith? Decisions on such borderline cases often cause the number of passengers to be listed as 101, 102 or 103. It is not just the crew numbers which are unclear, but also the question of locality.

The *Mayflower*'s crew would have been recruited mostly from the area of Rotherhithe-Deptford where Jones and the ship were based but some would have come from across the river in Ratcliff, the sailors' end of Stepney. In the table below it is indicated that Christopher Jones, John Clarke and John Parker were from Rotherhithe-Deptford and that two passengers, Richard Clarke and Richard Gardiner, were probably from that locality. The two Richards were probably from the Deptford side of Earl's Creek, which is in Kent, and that is why they may have been overlooked by researchers. The rare names of Britteridge, Margesson and Ely may, perhaps, be added to the same geographical group on the border of Kent and Surrey. Just as the More children may have been last-minute recommendations in July to Carver and Weston, there may also have been such recommendations by Jones for Rotherhithe-Deptford and by Martin for Essex. The Billingtons, who Bradford knew nothing about, lived on the border with Rotherhithe and were probably recruited by crew members.

Christopher Jones, his crew and the suggested passengers in Rotherhithe-Deptford do have an interesting feature in common with other names in South London: they are apparently not religious. The dearth of religious passengers in Southwark, Bermondsey and around London Bridge was almost certainly due to the treachery of Blackwell and the downfall of Staresmore. Staresmore and the other members of the Jacob Church who wanted to emigrate were blocked by Archbishop Abbot who, unlike King James, had no commitment to 'connive'. That meant the Southwark contingent (Doty and the Billingtons) were 'profane'.

Other passengers may have worked in Southwark and Bermondsey, though not living there or originating there. The Mullinses, and the associated Peter Browne, together with George Soule, are likely to have had shops or town houses in Southwark and Bermondsey because those areas were the centre for leather, boots and shoes and for chemicals used in treatment of leather, such as would be provided by salters such as the Soule family.

Those marked with a § (41) signed the Mayflower Compact; CJ = Caleb Johnson. CB = Charles Banks. JB = Jeremy Bangs. WB = William Bradford; M = Mayflower; b = born; bp = baptised; bt = betrothed; md = married; d = died; bd = buried. It should be borne in mind that a betrothal or civil marriage in Leiden does not prove the couple were living there permanently. A witness did not have to be present. 'London' refers to London borders as they are now; and so with other towns.

The Mayflower *Passengers and Crew*

Name	Background
The Passengers	
§ Alden, John	*c.*1598 b, possibly in Harwich or, if he pretended to be a year or two older than he was, bp 1600 (July) Hackney St John, London. Bradford says he was ambitious ('hopeful'). Might have been hired in Southampton (JB). A cooper by trade.
Allerton, Bartholomew	*c.*1613 b.
§ Allerton, Isaac	*c.*1587 b Ipswich, Suffolk, to Bartholomew Allerton, a tailor. 1609 apprentice to Blacksmith Company, London. 1611 md Mary, Leiden. 1614 Leiden citizen. 1615 guarantor, Leiden. 1618 betrothal witness, Leiden. 1619 marriage witness, Leiden. 1620 bd child, Pieterskerk, Leiden.

§ Allerton, John (d 1621)	1580 (Aug) bp St Andrew Undershaft, London. 1613 (Oct) bp son, John, at St Dunstan, Stepney, 'church of the sailors'. 1616 bd child, Leiden. Associate of Thomas English. Due to return on M to help others to emigrate. WB: 1620 in Leiden.
Allerton, Mary Jr	*c.*1617 b. In 1699 d. She was the last surviving passenger of the *Mayflower*.
Allerton, Mary Sr (d 1621)	Wife of Isaac. 1592 bp Mary Norris, Welford, Berks. 1611 md Leiden. 1617 at marriage, Leiden. 1618 at betrothal, Leiden. 1618 at marriage of Edward Winslow, Leiden. 1620 pregnant. 1621 her still-born child d.
Allerton, Remember	*c.*1615 b.
Billington, Eleanor	WB: 'from London'.
Billington, Francis	WB: 'from London'. *c.*1608 b.
Billington, John Jr	WB: 'from London'. *c.*1605 b.
§ Billington, John Sr	*c.*1580 d. WB: 'London merchant'. 1613 (Jan) John Billington bd Edward Billington at St Olave Southwark, London. This is the only John Billington in the London records.
Bradford, Dorothy (d 1620)	*c.*1597, b Dorothy May. In 1613 (Dec), aged 16, md Bradford in Amsterdam. 1620 drowned at New Plymouth. Dter of an Elder of the Exiled Church in Amsterdam.
§ Bradford, William	1590 b Austerfield, Yorkshire. 1590s both father and mother d. *c.*1602 came under the influence of Clyfton in Babworth, Nottinghamshire. 1608 to Amsterdam. 1609 to Leiden. 1612 received his inheritance. 1613 md Dorothy May, Amsterdam. 1617 loan, Leiden. 1619 sold house, Leiden. 1619 taxpayer, London. 1621 elected Governor of New Plymouth. 1630-50 wrote his history.
Brewster, Love	Son of Mary.
Brewster, Mary	*c.*1590 md. Probably lived at Duke's Hill, Southwark St Saviour, London.

Name	Background
§ Brewster, William	*c.*1566 b. 1580 at Peterhouse College, Cambridge. 1585-*c.*1588 in Netherlands as secretary to Davison. 1588-90 in London. 1590 father d in Scrooby. *c.*1590 md Mary, probably in Southwark. 1593 Jonathan b Scrooby. 1600 Patience b Scrooby. 1606 Fear b Scrooby. 1608 in Amsterdam. 1609-20 'Ruling Elder' of the Leiden Church (second to Robinson).
Brewster, Wrestling	Son of Mary.
§ Britteridge, Richard (d 1621)	CB: 'probably from London'. Quite unusual name. There was a Britteridge family in St Nicholas Deptford, London, in 1614, though a Richard is not recorded, and also one in Essex.
§ Browne, Peter	1595 bp Dorking, Surrey. Probably associated with Mullins.
Butten, William (d 1620)	1620 d at sea. Servant to Samuel Fuller.
Carter, Robert (d 1621)	CB: 'probably came from London or vicinity'. Servant of William Mullins.
§ Carver, John (d 1621)	*c.*1584 b. 1609 (Feb) joined Walloon church in Leiden and md Walloon wife, Marie de Lannoy de L'Ecluse. 1609 (July) bd child, Leiden 1610-15 Marie d and he md Katherine White. 1616 betrothal witness, Leiden. 1617-20 Emissary with Cushman. 1619-20 recruited many adventurers and recruited Martin and the Essex contingent. 1621 (April) chosen first Governor of New Plymouth.
Carver, Katherine (d 1621)	CB: from Sturton-le-Steeple, Nottinghamshire. 1615 betrothal witness, Leiden. 1617 betrothal witness, Leiden.
§ Chilton, James (d 1620)	*c.*1556 b. CB: 'citizen and tailor of Canterbury'. *c.*1585 md. 1587 dter Isabella bp. Canterbury. 1589-1600 other children bp, Canterbury. 1601 dter Christina bp, Sandwich. 1603 son James bp Sandwich. 1607 dter Mary bp, Sandwich. 1615 dter Isabella md, Leiden. 1619 deposition, Leiden, after being struck by an anti-Arminian stone.

Chilton, Mary	Dter of James. Md John Winslow.
Chilton, Mrs (d 1621)	*c.*1586 md. 1609 excommunicated with Moses Fletcher, Sandwich, for secret burial. Wife of James.
§ Clarke, Richard (d 1621)	1601 (Aug) Richard Clarke had son, Richard, bp St Nicholas Deptford, London.
§ Cooke, Francis	*c.*1582 Cooke b. 1603 betrothal witness, Leiden. In 1603 Hester betrothed to 'Franchois Couck'. 1603 baptism witness, Leiden, for Philip de Lannoy ('Delano'). 1603 (July) md Hester in Vrouwekerk. *c.*1604 dter Jane b. 1606 they visited Norwich so not a 'marked man'. 1607 son John bp, Leiden. 1608 bd child, Leiden. 1611 dter Elizabeth bp, Leiden. *c.*1612 joined Pilgrim church, Leiden. 1627 In Plymouth with Hester and his children sharing cattle with Philip Delano. Wool-comber.
Cooke, John	1607 bp Leiden. Son.
Cooper, Humility	1619 (March) bp at Holy Trinity the Minories London. Niece of Anne Tilley, b Cooper.
§ Crackstone, John Sr (d 1621)	1594 md Colchester, Essex. 1616 betrothal witness, Leiden. 1617 betrothal witness, Leiden. 1618 marriage witness, Leiden. Crackstone (Craxton) family also in Southwark.
Crackstone, John Jr	Son of John.
§ Doty, Edward	CB: 'was from London and came as a servant of Stephen Hopkins'. WB: 1620 in London. 1621 Duel with Edward Leister. 1623 received 1 acre. 1626 one of 27 Purchasers. 1627 not in New Plymouth. 1629 Edward 'Dowtie' juror in Southwark.
§ Eaton, Francis	1596 bp Bristol. 1615 carpenter in Bristol. *c.*1619 md Sarah. *c.* 1621 md Dorothy. Was a Brownist Eaton family in St Giles Without Cripplegate, London.
Eaton, Samuel	1620 b.
Eaton, Sarah (d 1621)	Wife.
Ely, Mr	A mariner like Trevore hired to stay with settlers for one year. Possibly the 'Elle' bp 1594 in Deptford St Nicholas, London. In 1621 he returned to England.

Name	Background
§ English, Thomas (d 1621)	Master of the schallop. Associate of John Allerton, so may have been from Stepney, London. WB: 1620 in Leiden.
§ Fletcher, Moses (d 1621)	c.1564 Sandwich. CB: 'a blacksmith by occupation'. 1589 md, Sandwich. 1602 Moses, son, bp. In 1609 excommunicated, Sandwich. 1613 md Sarah Denby, Leiden. 1616 betrothal witness, Leiden.
§ Fuller, Edward (d 1621)	1575 (Sept) bp Redenhall, Norfolk. CB was sure he was 'of London' but JB did find a mention of the name in Leiden.
Fuller, Mrs (d 1621)	Wife of Edward.
Fuller, Samuel	c.1608 b. Son of Edward,
§ Fuller, Dr Samuel	1581 bp Redenhall, Norfolk. CB: 'a serge maker of London'. Md Alice Glasscock. 1612 betrothal witness, Leiden. 1613 md Agnes, Leiden. 1613 betrothal witness for Alice Carpenter to Edward Southworth, Leiden 1614 betrothal witness, Leiden. 1615 Agnes d. 1617 md Bridget Lee. Deacon at Leiden. Amateur doctor. Took custody of Edward's son, Samuel.
§ Gardiner, Richard	1582 b Harwich, Essex. 1610 (June) md to Joane Marr at St Nicholas Deptford, London. 1623 one share in land division. 1624 crew member on *Little James*. Seaman.
§ Goodman, John (d 1621)	CB: 'from Leiden'. May have originally come from Everdon in Northamptonshire (CJ).
Holbeck, William (d 1621)	CB: Servant to William White.
Hooke, John (d 1621)	Disputed. CJ: c.1607 was b. Norwich. CB: in 1600 in St Giles Cripplegate, London, a servant to Isaac Allerton, 'one of the London contingent'. CJ: 1619 an apprentice, Leiden. CB: in 1620 was a taxpayer in St Bartholomew the Great, London.
Hopkins, Constance	1606 bp Hursley, Hampshire.
Hopkins, Damaris	1619 Daughter, b Whitechapel, Middlesex.
Hopkins, Elizabeth	c.1585 b. Elizabeth Fisher. 1618 md Stephen at St Mary Whitechapel, London. 1620 pregnant: gave birth to Oceanus at sea.

Hopkins, Giles	1608 bp Hursley, Hampshire
Hopkins, Oceanus	1620 b Atlantic Ocean.
§ Hopkins, Stephen	1581 bp Upper Clatford, Hampshire. 1604 dter Elizabeth bp Hursley, Hampshire. 1606 dter Constance bp Hursley. 1608 Giles bp Hursley. 1609 shipwrecked on Bermuda, then to Jamestown, Virginia, with John Smith and Rolfe. 1618 (Feb) md Elizabeth Fisher, St Mary Matfelon, Whitechapel, London. 1623 received six acres. WB: a 'London merchant'. CB: in 1620 in parish of St Katherine Coleman, London.
§ Howland, John	CJ: *c.*1599 b Huntingdonshire. CB: *c.*1594 b London. 1596 a JH in St Mary Whitechapel, London. 1600 a JH, St Botolph Billingsgate. 1646 will of Humphrey Howland, St Swithin, mentions brother, John. Was 'servant' (secretary) to Carver. CB: 'Carver was in England for some considerable time before the sailing of the Mayflower and undoubtedly obtained the services of Howland in that city...' WB: 1620 in Leiden.
Langmore, John (d 1621)	CB: 'of the London contingent'. Servant of Christopher Martin. May have worked for Martin in London.
Latham, Wm	Servant to Carver, a 'boy'. Early 1640s: returned to England.
§ Leister, Edward	CB: 'Edward Lester, Leicester, or Litster, came from London as servant of Stephen Hopkins.' 1598 bp St Michael Wood St, Cripplegate, London. 1621 Duel with Edward Dowty.
§ Margesson, Edmund (d 1621)	Very unusual name. 1620 was a Margesson family in St Nicholas Deptford, London, though an Edmund not recorded. CJ: 1586 Edmund Margetson bp Swannington, Norfolk.
§ Martin, Christopher (d 1621)	Governor of Mayflower. WB: a 'London merchant' who 'came from Billirike in Essex, from which partes came sundrie others to goe with them'. 1607 md Marie Prower, Great Burstead, Essex. Worked in London. In 1620 in trouble with C of E.

Name	Background
Martin, Mary (d 1621)	Was b Prower. 1607 md Great Burstead, Essex
Minter, Desire	WB: went with Carver's family but returned to England.
More, Ellenor (d 1621)	1612 bp Shipton, Shropshire. 1620 (July) to London. In care of Edward Winslow on board.
More, Jasper (d 1620)	1613 bp Shipton, Shropshire. 1620 (July) to London. In care of John Carver on board.
More, Mary (d 1621)	1616 bp Shipton, Shropshire. 1620 (July) to London. In care of William Brewster on board.
More, Richard	1614 (Nov) bp Shipton, Shropshire 1620 (July) to London. In care of William Brewster on board. 1645 md bigamously, St Dunstan, Stepney, London. 1688 was censured by Salem magistrates for 'gross unchastity'. *c.*1695 d. Last surviving male passenger of the *Mayflower.*
Mullins, Alice (d 1621)	*c.*1580 b. Wife.
Mullins, Joseph (d 1621)	*c.*1605 b Dorking, Surrey? Son of Alice.
Mullins, Priscilla	*c.*1603 b Dorking, Surrey? Dter of Alice. Md John Alden with their romance becoming the basis of the Longfellow poem.
§ Mullins, William (d 1621)	*c.*1572 b. WB: 'London merchant'. CB: Will shows he held 9 shares in the adventurers Company and his estate consisted chiefly of a stock of boots and shoes. 1604 elected, Dorking. 1605 fined in Dorking. 1612 a will witness in Dorking. 1616 warrant, London: called before the Privy Council. 1619 sold his Dorking manor holding to Ephraim Bothell in London.
§ Priest, Degory (d 1621)	*c.*1579 b. CB: 'called a hatter from London in the Leiden records". 1590 (May) dter, Phillipa, bp at St Mary Islington, London. 1611 his own betrothal, Leiden. 1611 md Sarah Vincent (b Allerton), widow 'of London', Leiden. 1615 became Leiden citizen. 1617-19 depositions in Leiden, with his age.

Prower, Solomon (d 1621)	From Billericay, Essex, in family of Christopher Martin. 1620 before archdeacon court at Chelmsford, Essex.
Rigsdale, Alice (d 1621)	Wife of John.
§ Rigsdale, John (d 1621)	CB: 'undoubtedly from London'. There was a large family of Rigsdales in Stepney, London.
Rogers, Joseph	1602 b. Watford, Northants. 1626 Allegation. Son of Thomas.
§ Rogers, Thomas (d 1621)	*c.*1572 was b. 1597 md in Watford, Northants. CB: Names of Christopher Martin, Thomas Rogers and John Hooke found in 1620 as taxpayers in parish of St Bartholomew the Great, London. 1616 bought house, Leiden 1618 Leiden citizen. 1620 sold house, Leiden.
Sampson, Henry	1604 (Jan) bp Henlow, Bedfordshire. CB: 'of the London contingent'. Nephew of Anne Tilley. Tilley family at St Andrew Undershaft, London. Perhaps related to Stephen Hopkins.
§ Soule, George	*c.*1597 b. CB: London servant to Winslow. The Soule family in London were salters and Droitwich was a salt-mining area. In 1590s Soule couples were living in Aldgate and Southwark.
§ Standish, Myles	*c.*1584 b. Probably on Isle of Man. 1623 (March) pre-emptive strike against Massachusset Indians who Massasoit said were planning to wipe out Wessagusset and then attack New Plymouth. 1623 md Barbara.1625 sailed to London to negotiate with adventurers. Was one of 8 Undertakers. 1628 led expedition against Thomas Morton who was ruining relations with Indians. Was often Assistant Governor. Widely read. Was 5' 7" (grave).
Standish, Rose (d 1621)	Wife.
Story, Elias (d 1621)	Was fellow-servant with George Soule to Edward Winslow.
Thompson, Edward (d 1620)	Servant to William White.

Name	Background
Tilley, Ann (d 1621)	1585 bp Henlow, Bedfordshire. 1614 md Edward in Henlow. 1616 in Leiden. Took nephew, Henry Sampson, probably of St Andrew Undershaft, London, and niece, Humility Cooper of Minories, London on M.
§ Tilley, Edward (d 1621)	1588 bp Henlow. 1614 md Anne in Henlow. 1616 in Leiden. Brother of John. CB: 'from London'. WB: in Leiden, 1620.
Tilley, Elizabeth	*c.* 1607 b. Daughter of John. 1621 taken in by Carver family. 1623 md John Howland and had 10 children.
Tilley, Joan (d 1621)	Wife of John. 1596 md John, Henlow.
§ Tilley, John (d 1621)	1571 bp Henlow. 1596 md Joan Rogers in Henlow (CJ). 1605 Tilley family in parish of St Andrew Undershaft, London (CB). WB: in Leiden 1620.
Tinker, Mrs	Wife.
§ Tinker, Thomas (d 1621)	CB: 'credited to the Leiden contingent'. A wood sawyer. 1617 became citizen in Leiden, guaranteed by Abraham Gray, a London clothier living in Leiden.
Tinker, X (d 1621)	Son.
Trevor, William	Mariner employed to remain with the settlers for one year. Visited New England in 1619 on Thomas Dermer's ship. 1621 returned to England.
§ Turner, John (d 1621)	CB: with Leiden contingent. 1610 a merchant, he became a citizen of Leiden. 1620 in London as emissary from Leiden.
Turner, X (d 1621)	Son
Turner, Y (d 1621)	Son
§ Warren, Richard	*c.*1578 b. WB: 'London merchant'. 1606 md Marjorie Jordan at St Martin in the Field, London (CB). 1610 md Elizabeth at Great Amwell, Hertfordshire (CJ). 1612 admitted as member of Artillery Co. 1623 Elizabeth, wife, came on the *Anne*. 1623 received two acres. 1628 nominated as Purchaser but d.
White, Resolved	*c.*1615 b.

White, Susanna	1620 (July) pregnant. 1620 (Dec) gave birth to Peregrine, first English child b in New England. 1621 (Feb) William d. 1621 (May) md Edward Winslow. Wife.
§ White, William (d 1621)	His identity has been much disputed. Caleb Johnson says that: 'William White should actually be counted as one of the London merchants, and that neither of the two William Whites living in Leiden was the Mayflower passenger of the same name.' (TMAHP, p.247).
Wilder, Roger (d 1621)	A servant to John Carver.
§ Williams, Thomas	1582 bp Great Yarmouth, Norfolk. CJ: 1616 possible betrothal witness, Leiden, but the name is common.
§ Winslow, Edward	1595 (Oct) bp Droitwich, Worcs. 1594 (Nov) his parents, Edward and Magdalen, md at St Bride Fleet St, London. 1606-11 at school Worcester. 1613-17 apprentice, Fleet St, London. 1615 btd to Elizabeth Barker in Leiden. 1618 (May) md Elizabeth Barker in Leiden, identifying himself as a 'printer of London'. 1620 took £60 of stock in M venture. 1620 sailed from Delfshaven. 1621 Elizabeth d. 1621 (May) md Susanna White, first marriage in New England. 1623 received 4 acres. 1627 an Undertaker, 1633, 1636, 1644 elected Governor. 1635 travelled to London to represent all of New England. Laud imprisoned him. 1646 again sent to London to represent Massachusetts Bay. 1646 in Hypocrisie Unmasked he attacked ideas of toleration. In 1649 he issued a new version entitled *The Danger of Tolerating Levellers*. Keen on conversion of Indians.
Winslow, Elizabeth (d 1621)	Was b Elizabeth Barker. 1618 md Edward in Leiden with Mary Allerton and Jonathan Brewster present.
§ Winslow, Gilbert	Brother of Edward. 1600 bp Droitwich, Worcs.
X, Dorothy	*c.* 1621 md Francis Eaton (CJ). Servant of John Carver.

Name	Background
The Crew	
Clarke, John (d 1623)	Master's Mate, Pilot. 1575 (March) bp St Mary Rotherhithe, London. 1610 (Ap) md Sibill Farr. 1611-16 captive of Spanish. Probably came from family in Deptford St Nicholas, London. Had twice visited Virginia. WB: 1620 (June) hired as pilot by Cushman and Weston in Rotherhithe.
Coppin, Robert	Master's Mate, pilot. 1609 an early investor (one share of £12-10s) in Virginia Co, and had visited New England before. Was b 1563, md Elizabeth Barrone at St Swithin Cannon St, London. Likely related to Christopher Barron, supporter of Thomas Smythe of Virginia Co, in anti-Sandys faction.
Heale, Dr Giles	1619 Freeman of Company of Barber Surgeons in London. 1620 In Drury Lane, parish of St Giles in the Fields, London. 1621 probably returned to London with Jones.
Jones, Christopher (who spelt his name as 'Joanes')	Master and Part-Owner of Mayflower. 1570 b Harwich, Essex. 1593 md Sarah Twitt of Harwich. 1601 became a freeman of Harwich. 1603 (May) Sarah bd. 1603 (Nov) md Josian. 1604 Jones listed as one of 24 'capital burgesses' of Harwich. 1605 Jones had 240-ton ship, *Josian*, built. 1607 sailed *Josian* to Bordeaux. 1609 Master of the M. 1610 M returned to London with wine from France. 1611 M for last time M listed as 'of Harwich'. *c.*1611 moved to Rotherhithe, London. 1612 M now 'of London'. 1614 (Feb) Christopher, son, bd Rotherhithe St Mary, London. 1614 (March) son, Christopher, bp St Mary. 1614 M sailed to Hamburg. 1615 M sailed to Malaga. In 1620 (Jan) and in 1620 (May) M returned with wine from France WB: 1620 (June) Cushman and Weston inspected the M in Rotherhithe. 1620 (July) sailed M from Rotherhithe to embark passengers probably in Blackwall. 1621 child bp in Harwich while in America. 1621 (May) returned to London.

	1622 bd in Rotherhithe. 1995 memorial to Jones erected, St Mary. In 2004 blue plaque on wall of St Mary commemorated M.
Leaver, Master?	Referred to by John Smith in his *General Historie* (1624) but otherwise unknown.
Parker, John	Master's Mate. 1594 (Ap) md Rose Curton, St Nicholas Deptford. 1599 (Aug) md Elizabeth Newe, St Nicholas. 1601 (Ap) son, John, bp St Nicholas.
Williamson, Andrew	Master's Mate.
Boatswain	In charge of rigging, sails and anchor. Supervising others.
Carpenter	General repairman: hull, masts, interiors. Supervising others.
Cook	Supervising others.
Master Gunner	Supervising others.
Quartermasters (4)	In charge of ship's cargoes.
Swabbers	Cleaners, the unskilled level of crew.

Atlantic Crossing

Out on the open sea the Pilgrims were finally free of political shenanigans, commercial trickery and state control, but they had other problems on their hands. One of them was Londoners, foul-mouthed, lewd and blasphemous. It turned out that not all Londoners were of a 'profane' character, and some were even religious, but the first encounter seems to have been troubling. On their voyage (September-November 1620) they had to adapt themselves to living with these strangers, some of whom they might be living with for many years to come.

A far worse problem was the conditions on ship. Passengers lived in semi-darkness below decks, with no portholes and with headroom only five feet high (only four feet where the beams crossed). As this was the gun deck the ship's guns were stored amongst them; a hundred passengers, including children, confined within a space only about 50 feet long, and only about 25 feet wide (about 12 square feet per passenger). Washing was done with buckets of sea water, using the same buckets as were used for sanitary purposes. Despite this, only one passenger died at sea and only one crew member. These two losses were compensated for by the birth of two babies on board the ship. The first, named Oceanus by its parents,

Elizabeth and Stephen Hopkins, was born at sea; the second baby, named Peregrinus or Peregrine (meaning 'Pilgrim'), was born to Susanna and William White a while after the ship had anchored in America. Both the fathers were London merchants and both of them were familiar with the Latin language, the sign of a classical education.

The passengers would have brought at least one chest for their belongings and these would take up part of their space. From later voyages it is known that passengers brought along salted beef, pork or fish, butter, cheese, beer, lemon juice against scurvy and some 'good wine to burn', but in the case of the *Mayflower* all the food had been bought beforehand by Christopher Martin and John Alden and stored in the cargo hold below. This would have saved some space, but passengers had to bring their own bedding, their own long coats against the weather, and their own cooking pans.[11] These items would have been stored in their chests.

The route the ship took after leaving Plymouth (or Newlyn) is not known for sure but it is thought that Jones would have headed south from Cornwall towards the Azores and then turned west towards America along the 40th parallel, picking up the winds that would speed him towards his destination.

Having left Plymouth on 16 September, the *Mayflower* first caught sight of land on 19 November (9 November, Old Calendar). The land was Cape Cod, about 250 miles north from the mouth of the Hudson River in Virginia, their supposed destination. In 1612 the London Virginia Company had received a new patent extending their latitude to 41° N, near what is now New York, and this therefore included the mouth of the Hudson. There are now two versions of events. In the version related by Bradford the ship was driven far to the north by a storm and there was debate 'amongst themselves' and with Jones about what to do. It was decided to head south for the Hudson River but then Jones informed them they were confronted by 'dangerous shoals'. This meant they had no choice but return to Cape Cod and so accordingly on 21 November they anchored at what is now Provincetown on Cape Cod and decided to explore the coast from there. A second version of events, very different to Bradford's, will be discussed later.

The Mayflower Compact

Once anchored at what is now Provincetown Harbour, an important decision was taken. Before anyone set foot ashore the settlers agreed a 'combination' (an association) amongst themselves. The Pilgrim leaders took the view that some provision should be made for the government of the colony and this should be cleared up before anybody disembarked. Bradford says this was deemed necessary for two reasons. The first reason was because 'some' of the Londoners were discontented and were making mutinous speeches. They were claiming that once on land they could do as they wished 'for none had power to command them, the patent they had being for Virginia, and not for New England'. This was the line Stephen Hopkins had taken in Bermuda, which had nearly led to his execution. Secondly, says Bradford, the Pilgrims wanted in any case to make an agreement 'as firm as any patent; and in some respects more sure'. They were laying 'the first foundation of their government', he said. This had been recommended to them by Robinson before they left Leiden.

They therefore drew up a short document which all adult males were asked to sign, and 41 of the 102 passengers signed it on 21 November 1620. The text said the signatories had undertaken a voyage 'to plant the first colony in the northern parts of Virginia' and were now coming together 'in the presence of God, and one of another [to] covenant, and combine ourselves together into a civil body politic'. The signatories promised to make 'just and equal laws ... for the general good', which everyone would then obey. After the signing the 41 elected John Carver as Governor for one year and vowed to meet again once they had unloaded the ship and built their cottages.[12]

This peaceful outcome was quite an achievement in the circumstances. Of the 41 who signed what was later celebrated as the 'Mayflower Compact' the Pilgrims had a majority and there seems to have been no problem about electing Carver as the first Governor. The division within the settlers was less between Leiden and London, although that was very real, as between Pilgrim and Profane. As Jeremy Bangs has argued, there were among the London passengers some who were religious. Candidates, for example, could be the Whites, Hopkins, Martin, Warren and the possibly Brownist Eatons. Even if they were puritans rather than Brownists, they would be accustomed to the idea of covenants and combinations and would have preferred a religious leadership rather than a profane one.

It was not until 1793 that the agreement drawn up on the *Mayflower* in 1620 was dubbed the 'Mayflower Compact'. No one at the time used such a term. Bradford used 'covenant' or 'combination' but by the end of the 18th century those terms had to be ruled out: 'covenant' was associated with rebels, and 'combinations' were trade unions, just then in the process of being banned.

Even so, the 'Mayflower Compact' became the subject of hot debate. Was it a harbinger of liberal democracy in America? This debate started in 1802 when John Quincy Adams, educated in Leiden, then President of the US, hailed the Compact as an example of state formation by voluntary association from below and not imposition from above. Later, in the 20th century, the Compact was talked about as a harbinger of democracy.

To the modern observer, such claims to democracy seem at first easy to dismiss. Of the 41 entitled to vote and decide the laws, all were men; yet there were 29 female passengers on the *Mayflower* as well as 73 male. Equally odd to a modern democrat may be a list of signatories apparently in order of income or wealth. Yet to judge in this way would be a failure of historical imagination. Women had no economic power unless they were widows (as proved by Elizabeth Warren who, after Richard's death, inherited his property and then took up government duties) and most women were illiterate and constantly engaged in childcare and childbirth. The equality of women was not yet on the agenda. As for ranking signatories by income, this was at that time meritocratic, since the alternative was to rank people not alphabetically but by social status in a 'hierarchy'.

There were elements of democracy and liberalism in the Mayflower Compact but they should not be exaggerated. The puritan, Robert Parker, disliked the Leiden church of John Robinson because it was too 'democraticall' and yet Robinson himself was careful to say it was not democratic but a mixture of democracy (votes by the congregation) and aristocracy (the Elders), to which he might have added monarchy (the Pastor). He said that though the institution of Elders was the aristocratic element ('rule of the best'), they were also democratic socially in that they were drawn from social equals and not from a line of hereditary landowners. There was voting, but it was only by those admitted to church membership after careful scrutiny. Jeremy Bangs believes Robinson was being cautious. Although Adams was too grand in his assertions, the Compact was in fact a meaningful statement of democratic principles, Bangs argues. Robinson played down the democratic element because he did not want the Brownists associated with the Anabaptists.[13] Lord Acton was sure the Brownists were democrats, quoting Robinson's maxim, 'We are not over one another but one with another.'[14]

There were clearly many in the 20th century who, as Parker bridled in Leiden, bridled at the Compact for being too 'democraticall'. The idea that a band of relatively poor Brownists in the 17th century practising a limited democracy in their churches, backed by a group of merchants and financiers in the City of London allowing a limited democracy in their guilds and councils, should pioneer modern democracy was not welcome in some quarters. Typical of this approach was that of the historian Samuel Morison. He thought the Compact was not much more than a reaction to 'missing' Virginia: the Pilgrims found themselves in New England without a patent so were obliged to improvise. The Compact was not democratic since the 41 signatories ruled the colony; it was in any case superseded by the second Peirce Patent; and there was no separation of powers as in modern democracy.[15]

The problem, again, is one of historical imagination – taking care not to judge the settlers by modern standards. They simply promised to bind themselves together, voluntarily, into 'a civil body politic' to make 'just and equal laws ... for the general good'. Four hundred years later this sounds pedestrian but at the time, in a land ruled by kings and archbishops, it was radical. Not long afterwards Bradford explained their aim in these words: to 'combine together' to form such government and governors, 'as we should by common consent agree to make'.[16] This is not democracy, but it is government by consent.

As for Morison's point, that the Compact was superseded by later patents, this may be true legally, but on content Bangs pointed out that the second Peirce Patent in 1621 and the Warwick Patent in 1630 did not supersede but 'augmented' the Compact, by increasing the element of self-government.[17] Bangs also pointed out that the Compact was modelled on the covenant of the Brownist churches (a point Morison accepted) and Robinson had advised such a covenant in the letter he gave the Pilgrims to be read out on board the ship. Robinson said they should choose their governors themselves and draw up a 'solemn combination' (i.e. an agreement of association). It was just that, with the outbreak of mutinous disputes on board and the threat of disorder if they landed, they decided to form the 'combination' before disembarking instead of afterwards.[18] Morison was wrong, therefore, to dismiss the agreed compact as mere improvisation. The idea of government by consent was part of the Pilgrims' outlook and ethos.

More recently there has been a critique of the Compact from a different angle. The claim is that since in 1619 Jamestown in Virginia set up a representative assembly (the House of Burgesses), it was Virginia that set America on the path to democracy, not the Pilgrims' Mayflower Compact. Bemiss has even claimed the new House of Burgesses as 'the first freely elected parliament of a self-governing people in the Western World'.[19] Furthermore, this parliament was 'the logical extension' of a large increase in the offer to shareholders (50 acres per share) that was turning Virginia into 'a thriving private enterprise'.[20] Thus Virginia can be portrayed as the embryo of capitalist democracy.

The problem with Virginia's assembly is that the movement for it was not from below and therefore cannot really be called self-government. A representative assembly is definitely an element of modern democracy but only one, and it is not unusual for dictatorships to have representative assemblies. The House of Burgesses was set up by the Virginia Company and approved by the king. They needed it to standardise the price of tobacco. Magna Carta can stake a claim in the emergence of democracy only because the king did not want it. Under James I, the parliaments of 1624 and 1628, inspired partly by Edwin Sandys, represented freedom simply because in neither year did the king want the legislation they passed. Bangs believed the 1619 arrangements in Virginia were imposed by the companies in London for their own purposes. The Mayflower Compact on the other hand was derived from the culture of the Pilgrims themselves, a congregationalist group that was accustomed to setting up with covenants their own 'gathered churches'.

On the other hand, it should be said that the House of Burgesses was not nothing. It emerged because the population of Virginia reached a certain level of size and dispersal. The same thing happened in Plymouth Colony in the late 1630s. A representative form of government was a sign of progress. It was Edwin Sandys who promoted the representative body in Virginia and it was his ally, George Yeardley, appointed Governor in late 1618, who in 1619 established the House of Burgesses. Yeardley, baptised in Southwark St Saviour (centre of the Jacob Church), had been sailing on the *Sea Venture* in 1609 with *Mayflower* passenger Stephen Hopkins, when it was shipwrecked on Bermuda, but both of them managed to reach safety in Virginia. Since 1609 Virginia had come a long way.

Explorations

Once the Mayflower Compact had been signed on 21 November the settlers could review their situation. They had been on board the *Mayflower* for four months, since the end of July when they left London and Leiden. They had been at sea for 65 days since leaving Plymouth. In that time a baby had been born and one passenger, William Butten, servant to Samuel Fuller, had died. This meant the number of settlers at the end of the journey (102) was the same as at the beginning. Now, with a form of government agreed and a Governor elected by consent, they could begin to explore the coast and look for a place to settle.

They undertook three expeditions before they decided finally where they should settle, although where they settled, at the abandoned Indian village of Patuxet, could have been predicted without the wasting of so many weeks in freezing conditions. John Smith put it down to a stubborn pride. It was part of their general outlook, he thought. They had to decide everything themselves and would not take anybody's advice.

The first exploration, on 25 November, was led by Myles Standish, the military commander, and with him 'for counsel and advice' were William Bradford, Stephen Hopkins and Edward Tilley. They reconnoitred inland on Cape Cod but without much incident. They did find a European kettle while foraging and a cache of Indian corn. Bradford says the corn was needed, so they took it, but resolved that 'if we could find any of the [Indian] people and come to parley with them, we would give them the Ketle againe, and satisfy them for their Corne.'[21] Six months later they were able to make this restitution.

The second exploration party on 7 December was also of Cape Cod, but this time Christopher Jones and some of the crew came with them on the shallop, making a party of 34 altogether. This tour was also without incident except that, on their return, they found that Susanna White had given birth to a son, Peregrine, the first British baby, and the first London baby, to be born in New England. This happy news was nearly followed by catastrophe when another London passenger, young Francis Billington from Southwark, aged 12, took some gunpowder, fired some guns and set fire to his father's cabin, where a barrel of gunpowder was stored and could have been ignited.

It was the third exploration on 16 December that was decisive. They had a first encounter with some Indians and received a volley of arrows (without anyone being hurt). Despite this difficulty, their exploration was a success. They entered Plymouth Harbour and stepped ashore on 21 December (11 December, Old Calendar), a historic moment in the history of New England, remembered now as 'Forefathers Day'. This landing was from the shallop and they did not land from the *Mayflower* until 28 December, as it was difficult to approach the shore, the water being so shallow in Plymouth Harbour a ship the size of the *Mayflower* needed to anchor a long way out. When the *Mayflower* did drop anchor on 26 December it was at Goose Point, a mile and a half from the site they eventually chose for their town on 30 December.

Before then William Bradford would have heard the news that while he was away on the third exploration his wife, Dorothy, had drowned in Provincetown Harbour. It has been suggested that Dorothy may have committed suicide by throwing herself overboard after arrival. Bradford does not mention his wife's death in his narrative. This may be due to the impersonality of writing in that period or to Bradford's wise disinclination to mention anything tendentious or dubious in the ranks of the Pilgrims.

Bridenbaugh has written about the strange phenomenon of suicide amongst emigrants to America after they have safely arrived. It seems that some were shocked because, deceived by colonialist propaganda, they had expected to see towns and cornfields, while others were shocked simply by the daunting task ahead of them. Bradford himself, though not mentioning his wife, offers a possible explanation for this paradoxical trauma: 'Being thus passed the vast ocean ... they had now no friends to welcome them nor inns to entertain or refresh their weather-beaten bodies, no houses or much less towns to repair to... Besides. What could they see but a hideous and desolate wilderness, full of wild beasts and wild men...'[22]

The area where they chose to settle had already been called 'Plymouth' on John Smith's map. They decided to keep the same name for their settlement. Bradford wrote that they kept the name 'because Plymouth in old England was the last town they left in their native country and for that they received many kindnesses from some Christians there'. He does not say who these 'Christians' were but the use of that term (everyone was a Christian officially) implies they were Plymouth Brownists, or radical-puritans. That still may not have been the main reason for keeping 'Plymouth', which is likely to have been chosen to please Gorges, whom Jones had met, and who was likely to have an influence on the future of the colony.

All through the winter and into the spring the settlers buried their dead. Tragic was the case of the More children who, all but one, Richard, died in a distant land, torn from their mother's side. They died as 'orphans' yet with a mother still alive, who loved them and in England still trying to get them back. Whole families were wiped out in the first months of 1621; whether Pilgrim, puritan or Profane, it made no difference. Nobody is sure what was killing them but the candidates are scurvy, amoebic dysentery, pneumonia and insufficient food.

The winter was not severe by local standards but it was severe compared to London and Leiden. Bradford described how wet clothes frozen to his body felt like 'coats of iron'. Jones shot geese to feed the sick and Standish shot an eagle, which tasted like mutton. By August about half the *Mayflower* passengers had died.

It was not until March 1621 that enough housing was built on land for all the goods and passengers to be fully disembarked so Jones and the *Mayflower* could depart. The problem was that the ship was so far from the settlement. It was not until March that six cannons were brought ashore, after modifying the shallop to hold them, and mounted on the hill above the settlement in order to defend themselves from any attacks. Slowly they laid out a main street (now called Leydon St) with their cottages, having cast lots for choice of location. Occupying their cottages was the first fruit for the settlers. Their properties were freehold and they did not have to pay rent. For some of the passengers, who had endured oppressive landlords in England, this in itself would have been a source of great satisfaction.

Samoset and Tisquantum

It was in March too that the settlers received an unexpected visitor. All this time the Indians had kept their distance, apart from the initial skirmish, but now an Indian strolled nonchalantly along the beach and, as they picked up their guns, greeted them, explained who he was, and asked for a beer. This was Samoset, the first Indian they had encountered who spoke English; he knew that in London most water was contaminated by human and animal waste, making it the beverage of last resort, and the settlers would probably have brought with them a large supply of beer. The early 17th century was just before tea and coffee, made by boiling water, introduced Europeans to the benefits of healthy drinking.

Samoset had come down to Plymouth from Moneghan in Maine, presumably alerted to their arrival by a message from Gorges on one of the fishing-boats that plied between Maine and Barnstaple or Plymouth. Although his English was limited, he was a mine of information for the settlers. He knew the names of the masters, captains and commanders that usually came to New England and he had been on Dermer's ship when in 1620 it rescued Frenchmen still alive but held hostage at Cape Cod. That meant he knew William Trevor, but either he and Trevor did not reveal this, or Bradford chose not to record it.

Samoset introduced the settlers to another Indian, Tisquantum, who had a much better command of English than he did. Tisquantum was a native of the village of Patuxet, the abandoned Indian village which the settlers had chosen to be their home. He had been kidnapped by the infamous Thomas Hunt in 1614, taken to Malaga in Spain and sold into slavery. With the help of some Spanish friars he managed to escape Spain and reach London, where he learnt good English while staying with a John Slaney who lived at Cornhill in the City. In 1610 Slaney had become the Treasurer of the Newfoundland Company and in 1619 he became Master of the Merchant Taylor Company, the largest of the London livery companies. He had made friendliness toward native Americans a policy of his company in Newfoundland and had taken Tisquantum under his wing. Thanks to Slaney, Tisquantum was eventually able to return to his village, only to find that the entire population had been wiped out by an epidemic, probably smallpox. He may have felt an interest in the resurrection of Patuxet by the *Mayflower* settlers, even though they were not Americans but foreigners.

John Slaney was at the centre of a web of contacts in London, all of whom had an interest in the success of an English colony in New England rather than on the Hudson River. Slaney lived near the Dutch Church in Austin Friars and, when he became Master of the Merchant Taylors in 1619, the Dutch Ambassador attended the ceremony. He would certainly have known or known of, Christopher Jones. His brother, Humphrey Slaney, had imported wine on the *Mayflower* as recently as in the winter of 1619-20 and William Speight, who had also traded with Jones, was on the governing body of the Merchant Taylors. In addition, Slaney knew John Pocock, the *Mayflower* adventurer, who was also a Merchant Taylor. In London Tisquantum and Jones would have moved in the same circles and an Indian in the City was still exotic enough to attract attention. As Bunker rightly says, the appearance of Tisquantum in Plymouth was hardly likely to have been a coincidence. It is very likely that Jones was expecting this contact and may have waited until Tisquantum arrived before sailing the *Mayflower* back to London.

Tisquantum's purpose was to help the settlers, first of all by introducing them to Massasoit, the Indian 'king' of the Wampanoag and the dominant force in the area. A few days after Tisquantum's visit Massasoit duly arrived with 60 warriors and held a meeting with John Carver, as a result of which an alliance was struck up, on 1 April 1621, between the Wampanoag and the Plymouth settlers. This agreement was to keep the peace them for well over 50 years, and it was ended not by the settlers but by Massasoit's son, 'King Philip'. The alliance had practical benefits: Tisquantum acted as guide and mentor to the settlers and showed them how to grow beans and 'Indian corn' (maize), and how to catch eels with their feet.

The Mayflower Returns and a Judgement on Jones

The day after the treaty the settlers agreed various laws and directives that needed to be put in place and then elected John Carver as Governor for the coming year. Everything now seemed under control and Christopher Jones was now ready to embark on his return trip to London. The *Mayflower* sailed on 5 April 1621 and the voyage back to London took only half the outward voyage, as was to be expected with the winds now behind the ship, and he was back in London at the beginning of May.

Jones found on his return that Josian had given birth back in Harwich to a son, John, but Jones did not live long afterwards and was buried at St Mary Rotherhithe in March 1622. Nor did the

Mayflower ship survive for long. An inventory was done in May 1624 for Josian and the other co-owners and it is assumed that this was prior to the breaking-up of the ship. Josian was given a valuation of £128 8s 4d and it is very likely that the *Mayflower* was broken up in 1624-25, probably in Rotherhithe, famous for its breaking and ship-repair yards. It is possible that the timbers of the ship may have been bought by the owner of Jordans farm, Buckinghamshire, who is said to have used them to build the 'Mayflower Barn'. Jordans does lie in a Brownist district, Chiltern, and the barn could have been named 'Mayflower' in the 1640s, at the time when New England was feted. The only evidence is oral tradition, but oral tradition is sometimes valid. Certainly, Rotherhithe's breaking yards were still famous in the 19th century. The breaking up of the famous *Temeraire* ship in Rotherhithe was immortalised in Turner's painting.

Jones has been depicted down the centuries as either a villain or a saint. If he, through the Dutch Church, Gataker and the Dutch Ambassador, agreed to take the ship north to Cape Cod, in breach of the Peirce Patent, and this led to the deaths of half of the passengers and half of his own crew, then he does bear a heavy responsibility. His supporters point to all the good he did, fondly attested by Bradford himself, who praised his 'kindness and forwardness'. He participated in the risky explorations: the Jones River is named after him and Clarke's Island is named after his first mate; he foraged for food and lent his crew for labour; above all, he stayed on until April 1621, allowing the ship to be used as a refuge until the cottages were built, although he could have died himself. He did not leave the settlement until an Indian guide and a Governor were both in place. That was just his guilty conscience at work, replied his critics, and a desperate attempt to salvage what had become a total disaster so that he had something positive to report back in London.

In a booklet by Gorges, *A Brief Relation* (1658 edition) there is a footnote on page 47 asking whether it was Ferdinando Gorges who persuaded Jones to take the *Mayflower* northwards or whether it was the Dutch. That was the debate for contemporaries. Nathaniel Morton, the first historian of the *Mayflower* (as Bradford was not published until the 19th century), says it was certainly the Dutch who persuaded the 'infamous' Jones to follow such a plan. He wrote at a time of hostility to the Dutch following the second Anglo-Dutch War of 1665-67 but claimed the facts of the case were correct.

Morton's *New Englands Memoriall* (1669) was the first published history of the New England colony and the first account to mention the *Speedwell* as well as the *Mayflower*. After the death of his father, George Morton, in 1624 Nathaniel was brought up by his uncle, William Bradford, and therefore had ready access to Bradford's papers. He makes extensive use of Bradford's unpublished manuscript. What is more, his book is an official history written at the request of the Plymouth Colony government and he dedicates the book to Thomas Prence, a *Mayflower* passenger and many times Governor of the colony since 1634. He says that Prence, and other *Mayflower* witnesses still alive, will verify the truth of the facts he has presented.

In the *Memoriall*, Morton wrote of Jones and the *Mayflower* expedition that, whilst 'their Intention ... and his Engagement was to Hudsons River', some Dutchmen who wished to locate there themselves induced him, first 'by delayes whilst they were in *England*, and now under pretence of the danger of the Sholes, etc., to disappoint them in their going thither'.[23] Morton says arriving at Cape Cod was, therefore, partly due to a storm but more due to 'the fraudulency and contrivance' of Christopher Jones. Given the tragic outcome of so many deaths he describes the role of Jones, 'hired' by the Dutch, as 'satanic'. There is no doubt, he says, that the Dutch persuaded Jones to sail to Cape Cod, not the Hudson. Of this Morton says he 'had late and certain Intelligence' from a contact of his who had read the Dutch state archive in Holland. He is therefore appealing to a primary source and, though this archive no longer exists, it is extremely unlikely that Morton would make up what could be checked by contemporaries. In addition, he is saying that the *Mayflower* passengers still alive – living witnesses – are making no objection to the facts he is presenting.

It is important in reading Morton's *Memoriall* always to distinguish fact from interpretation. He is heavily biased in his interpretation in favour of a puritan view against any separatist view, yet the actual content is factual enough. He is, for example, rather vague about the move from the East Midlands to Leiden. Like his uncle, William Bradford, he minimises any mention of persecution or illegality at every point so as to produce a respectable account of Plymouth's origins. Thus he says the Pilgrims settled in Leiden in 1610, which may well be true in terms of finishing the move, but thereby passes over all the contention in Amsterdam before their initial arrival in 1609. Similarly, he says that in the East Midlands their congregation was formed in 1602 ('they entered into a covenant'), which may formally be true, but avoids mention of their Brownism or their persecution. They emigrated, he says mildly, because they held some different opinions on religion and did not want to cause offence to others. He creates the impression that they were just being very considerate.

In the case of Jones, the same applies. He wants to present the Pilgrims as law-abiding and respectable. Any disastrous change of course had nothing to do with them. He is correct that officially the ship left London in 1620 heading for the Hudson River in Virginia. That was what the Peirce Patent said. In this they were backed by

Sandys and the London Virginia Company. John Pory in 1622 says the Pilgrims carried with them letters of introduction from Sir Edwin Sandys and John Ferrar, Treasurer and Secretary of the Virginia Company, to Sir George Yeardley, Governor of the Jamestown colony, 'that he should give them the best advice he could for trading in Hudson's River'.

The assertion in the Dutch state archive that Jones deliberately took the ship to Cape Cod also fits the facts, though not Morton's interpretation. It seems that Jones and the pilots and Martin, with the probable knowledge of Carver, had intended to arrive either at Cape Cod or nearby all along, but this had to be disguised since any destination in New England was in breach of their patent, which was issued only for Virginia. However, in London Gorges was setting up his Council of New England and trying for a fishing monopoly. If he were successful (which was highly likely since he was backed by King James), a breach of the patent caused by the ship's arrival in New England could then be corrected retrospectively and no harm would be done. This is a far more convincing explanation of what happened than the 'naive' one from Bradford. It is implausible that Jones and two experienced pilots, Clarke and Coppin, could have missed the Hudson by 250 miles, even with a storm, and there is no reason why they could not have gone back after the storm, despite the difficult (but well known) shoals, if they had wished. Clarke and Coppin knew the coast well and on board they had William Trevor, another experienced mariner, who had sailed that very coast with Thomas Dermer, using John Smith's maps, only the year before.

The Dutch explanation also fits the facts in Southampton. Christopher Martin, put in charge of the food supply over the heads of the furious Cushman and Weston, apparently overspent. If the true destination was New England, not Virginia, and the money was spent on buying extra supplies to allow for the ship's sailing north to Cape Cod and searching for a settlement site, then that would have been reasonable. It explains why Martin kept the amount of food under such strict control and responded aggressively when asked questions about it. It is revealing that when Weston, angry about their refusal to sign the new contract, withheld money needed to pay bills in Southampton, and the settlers were forced to sell some of the provisions Martin had bought, it turned out that there was an 'overstocking' of butter sufficient to pay off all the debt. It was therefore likely that Martin had not been cheating them but had spent £700 on 'overstocking' the food in order to get them safely to New England.

The Dutch archive also explains so many other mysterious issues. Thus, the *Speedwell*'s over-masting could have been managed,

Bradford suggests, if Reynolds, the Master, had not wanted to turn back. He was dismayed over Martin's control of the food supply. He needed to know how much of the food on the *Mayflower* would be available to the *Speedwell,* and he may well have worked out that the destination had been changed. Again, even after settling in Plymouth, the 'miraculous' appearance of Samoset and Tisquantum can be explained if the pro-Dutch, anti-Sandys alliance in London was expecting the *Mayflower* to arrive in New England, perhaps even in Patuxet. It would have been natural for Slaney, head of the Newfoundland Company, and the adventurers, who had big money at stake, to send a message on a fishing-boat to Samoset in Maine. It otherwise strains all credulity that Samoset, an Abenaki (a people living in Maine and Quebec), and Tisquantum, who was in constant demand as an English-speaking guide and always moving around on various ships, should both be at hand by sheer coincidence.

The virtue of the information in the Dutch archive is that it fits so well with so much. As well as explaining the behaviour of Martin, Reynolds and Samoset, it explains the apparent coincidence that St Mary Rotherhithe was a language school for staff at the Dutch Church; it explains why Gataker hightailed it out of the country in July; and it explains why Jones had Robert Coppin and William Trevor (New England experts) on the *Mayflower.* It also explains the fiercely mutinous Londoners at Plymouth. For them there had been no question of going to New England and, if Jones had not been under instructions, the ship would surely have taken them back to the Hudson. The narrative offered by William Bradford – that Weston, Martin, Reynolds and the Londoners all had weird or suspect personalities – is not credible. None of this means that Carver, Jones and Martin were 'satanic'. The trouble with Morton is that, however true his facts, his puritan interpretation colours them. In 1669 he was also caught up in the torrent of anti-Dutch propaganda. What Jones did was in fact perfectly reasonable. He would have been offered good reasons for going to New England and he would understand that, because of the patent, the true destination would have to be concealed. Gorges and King James would be correcting this anomaly as soon as possible, he would have been told. The majority of the Leiden Pilgrims had in any case wanted to go to New England, not Virginia, so they would be pleased when they arrived at Cape Cod. He would probably have been reassured that the plan was in the best interest of the colonists. Indeed, if the plan had not gone wrong, it might have been regarded as astute.

One last point. It must be remembered in *Mayflower* discussions that Jones, like Weston and Martin, were merely pawns in the game.

Above left: Dutch Church, in Austin Friars, London. (Author's collection)

Above right: The entrance to the site of Bridewell hospital, orphanage and prison, off New Bridge St, London. (Courtesy David Sankey on Flickr/Creative Commons)

Right: William Shakespeare, head-and-shoulders portrait by Samuel Cousins, engraver 1801–1867, published 1849. (Courtesy of Library of Congress)

Memorial to John Robinson in the Pieterskerke, Leiden. (Author's collection)

A window at the Dutch Church in honour of Jan Laski (Johannes a Lasco), its founder and first Superintendent. (Author's collection)

Above: Bevis Marks Synagogue, London. (Courtesy of Emmanuel Dyan on Flickr/Creative Commons)

Right: Christopher Jones statue in Rotherhithe. (Courtesy of Robert Scarth on Flickr/Creative Commons)

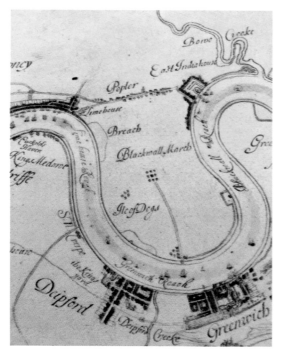

The Hollar Map of 1662 shows Rotherhithe (Redriffe), Deptford, the stream known as 'Earl Sluice' and, in the north-east corner of the Isle of Dogs, is Blackwall, where the *Mayflower* most probably embarked its passengers and had them checked. Note the main road connecting Blackwall with Aldgate. (Courtesy of the British Library)

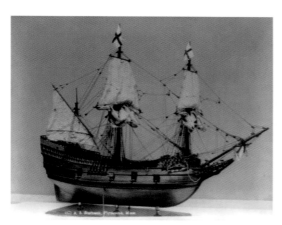

Left: The *Mayflower*, a 'fine ship', said Weston. Model of the ship at Pilgrim Hall, photographic print, c.1905. (Courtesy Library of Congress)

Below: This cut-away section of the *Mayflower* shows its interior and how little space there was for 130 people. (Courtesy mayflowersteps.co.uk)

Right: The bust at St Bride's Church of Virginia Dare, the first English child born in America (Author's collection)

Below: The reredos at St Bride's Church in honour of Edward Winslow. (Courtesy of Tony Hisgett on Flickr/Creative Commons)

Above left: The Chapel Yard in Union St, Southwark, where the 'Pilgrim Church' stood in the eighteenth century. The yard has original features. (Author's collection)

Above right: The Pilgrim Fathers Memorial Church in Great Dover Street, Southwark. The building is still there but is no longer used as a church. There is a video of its opening ceremony on YouTube. (Author's collection)

Mayflower Approaching Land, print. (Courtesy of Library of Congress)

Edward Winslow.
(Courtesy of New York
Public Library)

Captain John Smith.
(Courtesy of New York
Public Library)

The planting of the 'Mayflower (Jessey) Tree' at St George the Martyr Church, in Southwark, in 2018, in honour of Henry Jessey, a member of the 'Pilgrim Church' and advocate of toleration for Jews and Muslims. The event was attended by two Rabbis, an Imam, a Zoroastrian, Quakers, Anglicans and a minister of the United Reformed Church. (Author's collection)

The 'Pilgrim's Pocket' statue in Rotherhithe. The ancient Pilgrim is shown a magazine by a modern schoolboy and is astonished, and perhaps dismayed, by what he sees of modern life. (Author's collection)

They did not have enough power to be satanic. All three probably tried their best. The investors too, said Robinson, were 'mostly honest and loving'. Problems came from the machinations above them and the ignorance, or naivety, below.

John Smith's Verdict

In 1621 it was not Jones who was thought to be the villain but Carver. In the autumn letters arrived in Plymouth on the *Fortune* from London investors angrily blaming Carver for the two months delay in deciding on a settlement. He had not only caused the death of over 60 people but he had ruined their chances of an early return on their investments. Carver was by then beyond their reproach, having died the previous April.

When Smith wrote about this later, he said that before the Pilgrims left London he had offered to guide them round the New England coast. Therefore he, an associate of Gorges, must have known before they departed that they were heading for Plymouth, not the Hudson River. Smith spoke of all the sufferings endured by the Pilgrims in 1620-21 and blamed 'their obstinacy in not having employed him as a guide'.[24] They endured miseries for a year unnecessarily because of their 'humorous ignorances'. He wrote that they landed at Cape Cod and 'thinking to find all things better than I advised them, spent six or seven weekes in wandering up and downe, in frost and snow, wind and raine, among the woods, cricks and swamps' until 40 of them died. They did not die because of the winter, a relatively mild one, but simply because of ignorance of the geography, conditions and terrain. Their fault was 'pretending onely Religion their governour, and frugality their counsell, when indeed it was onely their pride, and singularity, and contempt of authority; because they could not be equals, they would have no superiors...' They lived their lives in a 'fooles Paradise'. Such Pilgrims aim to be 'Lords and kings of themselves', which is 'to the great disparagement of the general businesse.'

As usual, Smith judged everything in a hard-headed way, valuing competence above all else. He may also have been defending his current patron, Gorges, whose faction-fighting with Sandys was the real cause of the tragedy. Later, Smith was to tone down this scathing judgement on the Pilgrims, recognising perhaps that his severity arose out of frustration at the thought that he could have saved all those 60 lives, had he been given the chance.

In April 1621 John Carver died and his wife, Katherine, died soon after. As Christopher Martin was already dead, there was no one left in New Plymouth who knew for sure the truth about the change of course by Jones. The young William Bradford was chosen to replace

Carver as Governor. He had been on the committee that organised the voyage at the Leiden end and he seems to have been respected for his considered judgements and his diplomatic skills, necessary in appeasing the mutinous Londoners.

The Second Peirce Patent

As soon as Jones had arrived back in London in May and told everyone the *Mayflower* had landed in New England, there was a scramble to legalise the position. There had to be another patent. In June a second Peirce Patent set out legal terms for Plymouth retrospectively. The first patent had applied for land in the Delaware region near the Hudson River, where the Pilgrims were supposed to settle, but instead they had sailed north. The new patent now regularised the position, set out terms of land ownership and granted them the right to set up a government and elect a Governor. There was one crucial difference. This second patent was not granted to John Peirce by the Virginia Company but was between Peirce and a new monopoly called the 'Council of New England', approved by the king.

The Council for New England had been launched on November 1620. It held sway over everything from the 40th parallel to the 48th, from Philadelphia to the St Lawrence River in Canada. It was really a relaunch of the old Plymouth Virginia Company (1606) and it was led by Ferdinando de Gorges, based in Plymouth, Devon. It had a similar ethos to that prevalent in the early days of the Virginia Company. Gorges spoke in the military language of empire and his Council was packed with aristocrats looking for land. He aimed to set up a military base and distribute land as manors, at the same time ensuring the supremacy of the Church of England. The big difference was that he and his associates now accepted John Smith's emphasis on trade as the true basis for settlements and had integrated this into their approach. They would raise funds for their garrisons and forts by taxing the West Country fishermen and the London settlers they expected to recruit. It was they who now 'legalised' (they thought) the Plymouth settlement by granting the settlers the land they had already occupied, already legalised (so the settlers thought) by the agreement struck with Massasoit and the Wampanoag. Later, both of those alleged legalisations were to be challenged.

Wampanoag

In the summer there were a couple of incidents in August but most of the time the settlers were tending the land and seeking food. In the first incident young John Billington from Southwark became lost in the woods and a search party of ten men had to be sent out to Nauset (now Eastham), on Cape Cod, to find him. They slept overnight in Cummaquid (now Barnstable), later to be famous in London for its Brownist church, a twin church to the 'Pilgrim Church' in Southwark founded by John Lothrop.

The second incident was far more serious. It was reported in August that Tisquantum had been taken prisoner, or even killed, by an Indian sachem, Corbitant, who, disaffected with Massasoit, had become friendly with the rival Narragansetts and had opposed Massasoit's treaty with the foreigners. The ever-combative Standish and a handful of settlers embarked on a rescue mission to save Tisquantum. They launched an attack on Corbitant's house, but the colonists found Tisquantum unharmed and they brought him back to Plymouth. It had all been rather a misunderstanding and later, in September, Corbitant, along with eight other previously reluctant sachems, made a treaty with Plymouth. Subsequently, Corbitant became an enthusiastic friend, and even an ally, of the settlers.

Slowly, a widening network of peace was being established, thanks to the able assistance of Tisquantum, the wisdom of Bradford and Massasoit, and Robinson's commitment to a policy of friendship with native peoples. Another factor was that the Wampanoag Indians were not a hunter-gatherer people such as Columbus had found on the Caribbean islands, or were found in some parts of North America, but semi-agricultural. They knew how to grow maize and tobacco; they manufactured small items; and they were able to teach the settlers so much about husbandry, climate and the local environment. Behind it all, of course, there were more basic motives. The settlers needed friendly Indians to help them get hold of beaver skins and the Indians were terrified of the settlers with their infectious diseases and their death-dealing guns (at one stage Bradford described Massasoit as 'trembling with fear').

Did the British colonisers have the right to invade and take over other people's land? The question exercised Robert Cushman and he tried to answer it in his essay, *Reasons and Considerations touching the lawfulnesse of removing out of England into the parts of America*, which was published as part of *Mourt's Relation* in 1622. Cushman says that exception is being taken 'daily' in England to the emigration to America. He claims that as far as he knows his is the first attempt ever made by a coloniser to defend 'forraine plantations'.[25]

Cushman argues that since the famous emigrations by Abraham and Moses into Canaan the world has changed. Nowadays every part of the world is full of immigrants, so 'now we are in all places strangers and Pilgrims, travellers and sojourners...'[26] We cannot really say any more that where we live is our home and this leaves us with a responsibility: '...a man must not respect only to live, and doe good to himselfe, but he should see where he can live to doe most good to others: for as one saith, *He whose living is but for himselfe, it is time he were dead.*'[27]

He foresees a counter-argument: 'But some will say, 'what right have I to goe live in the heathens countrie?' Firstly, he says because we need to bring the heathen to Christ; secondly, because our land is full and their land is empty; thirdly, because they lack the art, science or skill to develop the land and it is lawful 'to take a land which none useth, and make use of it'. He adds another reason taken from the case of Plymouth: Massasoit and other sachems have acknowledged James I to be their 'Master and Commander' and this not by force but 'by friendly usage, love, peace, honest and just cariages'; and then, finally, because Massasoit and the other kings have agreed to grant their land to settlers and are welcoming new arrivals.[28]

It is hard to estimate how serious the first argument was taken (conversion to Christianity) since the Church supervised censorship and book publication via the Stationers Company. The second argument, however, may not be just a formality and it is one often made in connection with New England. Winslow and others describe walking, or sailing, for miles past abandoned villages and fields once used for crops. The land had been emptied by smallpox, plague, fever and other infectious diseases imported by the Europeans and which had spread like wildfire among native populations whose immunity to these infections was low. In 1614 the Wampanoag had been decimated by some epidemic, and Plymouth itself was built on the site of an abandoned village, Patuxet, to which no Indian dared return.

Nonetheless, although this empty land was used as a general argument in London to justify colonisation, the view of Robinson and Bradford was that all Indian land had to be paid for. This was the view in all Brownist settlements: Plymouth, Rhode Island, Scituate, Barnstable. Sometimes this is overlooked and Plymouth is lumped together with Virginia and Massachusetts Bay. In *Indian Deeds* (2002) Bangs attacked the tendentious views of Willison and Francis Jennings (*The Invasion of America*, 1975). Bangs said that until King Philip's War in 1675-76, 'Plymouth Colony did not pursue a policy of land conquest or overt usurpation. The colony received a gift [from Massasoit] of land that had been emptied by epidemic, but Plymouth did not consider land inhabited by Indians to be vacant...'[29]. They continued to buy land from the Indians after the 1621 treaty. As late as 1667 Plymouth was still insisting that land be purchased. Nor did Bangs accept that in the Pequot War (1637) there was seizure of land by Plymouth. For one thing, Plymouth did not participate in any war against the Indians until the King Philip War and in any case the Pequot War did not take place on Plymouth's territory.

For the Brownists and some other dissenters treating Indians well was part of English patriotism: England, the first Protestant country, had overcome Mary and the Spanish Armada and were a Chosen People like the Jews. They had been brought up from childhood on horror stories of how Spanish Catholics had introduced the slave trade and mistreated the Indians in South America. This explains why Bradford was careful about adherence to the spirit of the covenant with the Indians and tried to apply it to dealings with Indians other than Wampanoags. When three British settlers murdered a Narraganset, they were apprehended. Narraganset observers attended their executions and declared themselves satisfied that justice had been done. The settlers did everything they could to conciliate the Indians. They not only made amends for the corn they had taken when they arrived on Cape Cod but they helped the Indians (the 'savages') protect their own corn by shooting down with their muskets the crows raiding the Indian cornfields.

Plymouth's pursuit of friendship with the Indians was proactive. Everywhere they went they asked for an alliance: in exchange for military assistance from Plymouth the sachems had to avow submission to King James, which meant they would never support the Dutch or the French against the English. It was not always easy. Samoset warned them about the Nauset Indians. They were extremely hostile to the English because of Captain Hunt. On their way to the Nauset they encountered an old woman in a 'great passion, weeping and crying excessively'.[30] The English captain, Hunt, had tricked her three sons into going on his ship and then had taken them away to be sold as slaves in Spain (as was Tisquantum). Now she had no one to look after her in her old age. They made their view of slave-trading clear, telling her that 'Hunt was a bad man, and that all the English that heard of it condemned him for the same,' affirming that 'we would not offer them any such injury, though it would gaine us all the [beaver] skins in the Countrey'. Bradford wrote about Hunt: 'a wretched man that cares not what mischiefe he doth for his profit'.[31] For Brownists, slave-trading and land-stealing were ideologically impossible.

Sometimes it was the settlers who had to restrain the Indians. On a mission to Massachusetts to 'truck' (barter) Tisquantum wanted Winslow to seize all the goods, including skins, from the women of a village because 'they are a bad people, and have oft threatened you' but Winslow replied that 'were they never so bad, we would not wrong them, or give them any just occasion against us: for their words we little weighed them, but if they once attempted any thing against us, then we would deale far worse then he desired.'[32]

In the early days Winslow was very interested in Indian culture and language. In his *Good Newes* he said London was misinformed in believing that Indian religion was primitive. They do not just worship spirits but have a supreme God called Kiehtan, akin to the Christian God, who created the world and judges men after their death. Winslow was enthusiastic about his discovery and keen to show that Indian religion was similar to Christianity. The Indians were also impressed by the Christian religion. He did not, however, succeed in winning their full approval for the Ten Commandments. They approved nine of them but would not accept the one about adultery, which they regarded as unrealistic.

As early as the summer of 1621 relations with the Indians were so friendly the plantation had to ask Massasoit to limit the number of Indians flocking to the settlement with their wives and children for sight-seeing. The settlement had become a tourist attraction. There was also bonding with individual Indians, and not just Samoset, Tisquantum and Massasoit (Winslow saved his life). They became friendly with a Wampanoag war-captain called Hobomok, much beloved of Massasoit, and influential in preserving peace. When they divided the land in Plymouth the settlers gave a plot to Hobomok and in the 1630s he came to live in the settlement as a professed Christian. Winslow wrote:

Wee have found the Indians very faithful in their Covenant of Peace with us; very loving and ready to pleasure us: we often goe to them, and they come to us ... there is now great peace amongst the Indians themselves, which was not formerly, neither would have been but for us; and we for our parts walke as peaceably and safely in the wood, as in the hie-ways in England ... we entertaine them familiarly in our houses, and they as friendly bestowing their venison on us.[33]

Thanksgiving

There were practical benefits. In 1621 the Indians showed them how to sow Indian corn (maize) and fertilise the ground with 'shads' (actually alewives), which were in great abundance. This proved a great success. The harvest in 1621 yielded good crops of corn and of barley (though peas were a failure) and, as they always had an abundant supply of fish, lobster, eels and fowl, they were able to celebrate in style, inviting Massasoit and some 90 of his men to join them for a harvest feast that lasted three days, with the Indians contributing some deer.[34]

In 1621 Edward Winslow in a letter to friends mentioned the celebration by the settlers of their first successful harvest. There were more Indians present than settlers (about 50). This celebration, now known as the

'First Thanksgiving' would have taken place at the end of September or the beginning of October.

For the Brownists thanksgiving was special but not very unusual. They were schooled in the Old Testament and knew Psalm 107 which, Ainsworth had found in Maimonides, had given rise to the Jewish rite of thanksgiving. This was practised after recovery from sickness, the release of prisoners, the end of a voyage or the safe arrival of travellers at their destination. For the Leiden Pilgrims the first thanksgiving in America would have been on arrival, 'at the moment on Cape Cod when the Pilgrims fell on their knees to say the Jewish prayer.'[35] The event Winslow described would be familiar to all the settlers and in England would be called a 'harvest festival', except for one feature: its strikingly interracial and peaceful character. That caught the imagination of future generations. As de Baar wrote, the *Mayflower* group was 'practically the only group of colonists in American history which did not misbehave itself immediately towards the original inhabitants.'[36] This was perhaps a greater achievement than surviving the winter of death.

1620 Mayflower Chronology

This guide gives Old Style (Julian) dates first and modern (Gregorian) dates second.

February	First Peirce Patent.
June	Cushman and Weston hired the *Mayflower*.
01/11 July	Contract between adventurers and settlers ('planters') agreed.
End of July	*Mayflower* left London (probably Blackwall or Wapping).
End of July	Settlers left Rotterdam (Delfshaven).
05/15 August	*Mayflower* left Southampton.
23/02 September	*Mayflower* left Dartmouth
06/16 September	*Mayflower* left Plymouth.
09/19 November	Cape Cod sighted.
11/21 November	*Mayflower* anchored in Provincetown.
11/21 November	*Mayflower* Compact signed.
15/25 November	First exploration.
27/07 December	Second exploration.
06/16 December	Third exploration.

08/18 December	First Encounter with Indians.
16/26 December	*Mayflower* anchored near Plymouth.
18/30 December	Decided where to settle: Plymouth.
28/07 January	Company divided into 19 families.
14/24 January	Majority now on shore.
February	Peak month for deaths (17).
21/03 March	Cannon brought ashore.
16/26 March	Samoset arrived from Moneghan, Maine.
21/31 March	Transport of goods by shallop to the land.
22/01 April	Arrival of Samoset, Squanto and Massasoit. Treaty agreed.
23/02 April	Carver confirmed as Governor for a year (but d soon after).
05/15 April	*Mayflower* left Plymouth.
06/16 May	*Mayflower* arrived back 'in England' (Smith).
1621 June	Second Peirce Patent.

6

Family and Friends

The transportation of the London and Leiden settlers to New England took four ships, not one. The hundred or so who crossed the Atlantic in 1620 left behind family and friends who also wanted to emigrate. They sailed later, on board the *Fortune* (1621), and then the *Anne* with the *Little James* (1623). It was acknowledged at the time that all were part of the same expedition and the passengers on these four ships were even given a collective name: the 'Old Comers' or 'First Comers'.

It had always been planned to transport the rest of the would-be settlers, including John Robinson and his family, but in the original contract between Weston's adventurers and the Pilgrims there had been no mention of support or supply for any colony established. It had been characteristic of previous voyages to found new settlements that supply was considered in advance, but in the case of the *Mayflower*, everything was improvised. It had to be turned into an expedition after the event, primarily because the hiring of the ship was rushed through so quickly, but also because over the years the Pilgrims had wavered repeatedly over their exact destination.

When all four ships are considered, the predominance of London in all the arrangements becomes clearer, and certainly clearer than it is represented in Bradford's inevitably one-sided history. Everything is directed from London and the whole colony is dependent on London. It is London that sends out the supplies and it is London that is responsible for most of the mess-ups. It was not until 1627 that the settlement of the colony was completed, and settlers were no longer beholden to the London merchant financiers.

The *Mayflower* was not therefore representative of the expedition as a whole, firstly because the potentially large number of Brownist passengers living in London had been virtually eliminated by the treachery of the Franciscans and the raid launched by the

Archbishop, no doubt supplemented by associated arrests. The king connived but the Church did not. Indeed, it is not possible to say with certainty that any of the London passengers was Brownist. Blackwell probably gave the Church a full list of names. In addition, recruitment of the passengers in London had been very last-minute, whereas Leiden had drawn up their list of potential passengers in advance. This explains why there were far more London recruits amongst the Old Comers than on the *Mayflower*. Banks says that 'the large majority of the "Passengers" of the first four ships never lived in Leyden at all and ... most of them came from the great city of London where they had lived in its vast network of lanes and alleys.'[1]

The Fortune

In July 1621 Thomas Weston sent the *Fortune* from London to New England with 35 more settlers. The 'Misfortune' might have been a better name. It was only 55 tons and it struggled from the beginning, unable to reach Plymouth, Devon, before the end of August. It did reach Cape Cod on 19 November but, like the *Mayflower*, stayed there some time, presumably weighing up the best way to approach.

Bradford said there were 35 passengers on board, but not all of them have been identified. Perhaps the most important was Robert Cushman, who had come to get the new contract signed and was then going back. This was for the second Peirce Patent issued in June by the recently constituted Council for New England. Cushman left his son Thomas behind, in Bradford's care. Cushman's visit was important in another way: he took back to London the documents known as *Mourt's Relation or Iournal*, giving a narrative of events in Plymouth Colony by Winslow, Bradford and himself. Cushman dedicates it to his 'respected Friend', John Peirce, the Clothworker of London who had helped Leiden secure their patent. It was no doubt intended to be circulated in London but 1620-21 was another period of colonialist literature and when in 1622 it was printed by Bellamy and published by 'G. Mourt' (possibly George Morton), its aim was clearly promotional, to drum up new immigrants. It is not clear what was altered but Winslow, for one, was not at all happy about the commercial use of his letters. He said the letters 'came to the press against my will and knowledge'.[2] Perry Westbrook wrote that some parts of it are merely 'sales talk'.[3]

Another important arrival was Thomas Prence, the son of a carriage maker (who had a coat of arms), in the parish of All Hallows Barking, close to the Tower of London. He would marry Patience Brewster in 1624 and in 1634 be chosen as Governor of Plymouth Colony. Edward Winslow's brother was also on board, and so was Jonathan Brewster, William's son.

This time there was a strong representation from Southwark, which would have been the area worst affected by the Archbishop's raid and subsequent round-up. On the *Mayflower* they sent only the Billington family and probably Doty, none of them much of an asset to the Colony. Now there was Clement Briggs, a fellmonger, no doubt an associate of Timothy Hatherley, feltmaker and adventurer from Southwark and stalwart supporter of Plymouth Colony. There was Martha Ford (widow in all probability of leather-dresser William Ford); Robert Hicks (dealer in hides); Stephen Deane (a miller); and Thomas Flavel, who had married Elizabeth Hayward in 1610 at St Saviour. More from Southwark came over on the *Anne* and *Little James*.

Such practical recruits as these, as well as the religious diversity from Leiden (the Huguenot, Philip Delano, and the Dutch Reformed, Moses Simonson), were all very welcome, but otherwise the *Fortune* was a disaster – it had not brought any supplies. Plymouth entered a new crisis. With the new mouths to feed, the colony had to cut rations in half. They were able to send back on the *Fortune* a reasonable number of animal skins and wrote plaintively: 'We hope the Marchants will accept of it, and be incouraged to furnish us with things needful for further employment...'[4] Even this did not work out. During its return the *Fortune* strayed into French territorial waters, was seized by a French warship and had its cargo confiscated. It reached London empty-handed in February 1622.

1621 Fortune Passengers and Crew

Not all the passengers are known. Of the ones known, only two were women. Sixteen were from London, three from Leiden, while the origins of ten have not been determined. Again, 'London' refers to modern boundaries.

Name	Background
Austen, Nicolas	1623 land list.
Adams, John	From Wapping, Stepney, London. Carpenter. 1623 land list. 1626 Purchaser. 1627 cattle list.
Barton, Thomas	Master of the ship.
Bassett, William	From Bethnal Green, Stepney, London. 1623 Land List. 1626 Purchaser. 1627 cattle list.

Name	Background
Bassett, Elizabeth	1627 cattle list.
Beale, William	1623 land list, sharing with Thomas Cushman.
Bompasse (or Bumpas), Edward	1623 land list. 1626 Purchaser. 1627 cattle list. From St Bartholomew, London.
Brewster, Jonathan	1593 (Aug) b Scrooby. 1618 marriage witness for Edward Winslow and Elizabeth Barker, Leiden. 1623 land list. 1624 md Lucretia Oldham. 1626 purchaser. 1627 cattle list. By trade a ribbon-maker.
Briggs, Clement	Fellmonger. 1616 resident in Southwark. 1623 land list. 1626 Purchaser. 1627 cattle list.
Cannon, John	1623 land list.
Conner (or Coner), William	1623 land list.
Cushman, Robert	1577 b Rolvendon, Kent. 1597 apprentice grocer in Canterbury, Kent. 1604 excommunicated for spreading libels. 1608 (Feb) son, Thomas, bp Canterbury. 1617 md widow Mary Singleton of Sandwich. 1617 (autumn) is in London with Carver as an emissary for Leiden Church. 1617 (Dec) returned to London. In 1620 he and Carver back in London again.
Cushman, Thomas	1608 b Canterbury, Kent. Son of Robert. 1623 land list, sharing with William Beale. 1626 Purchaser. 1627 cattle list with Bradford family. Md Mary Allerton.
Deane, Stephen	1623 land list. 1626 Purchaser. 1627 cattle list. Miller 'probably from Southwark' (CB).
Delano, Philip (or Phillipe de la Noye)	1603 bp in Vrouwekerk, Leiden. 1623 land list, sharing with Moses Simonson. 1626 Purchaser. 1627 cattle list, with Cooke family.
Flavel, Thomas	1610 md Elizabeth Hayward at Southwark St Saviour, London. 1623 land list. From Stepney, London.
Flavel, X	1623 land list. Son.
Ford, John	1621 (Nov) b day of arrival.

Ford, Martha	1623 land list. 1626 md Peter Browne. 1627 cattle list.
Ford, Martha	*c.*1619. Daughter.
Ford, William	1623 land list. From Southwark St Olave.
Ford, William	1623 land list. Son.
Hicks (or Hix), Robert	*c.*1570 b. 1604-07 had children bp in St Mary Magdalen, Bermondsey: Thomas (1604), John (1605), Sarah (1607). 1616 Fellmonger in Southwark. 1623 land list. 1626 Purchaser. 1627 cattle list.
Hilton, William	Native of Northwich, Chester. 1620 London resident. 1623 land list.
Morgan, Benedict (or Benet)	1597 b. Sailor. 1619 md Agnes Porter. Resident of St James, Clerkenwell, London. 1623 land list.
Morton, Thomas	*c.*1589 b. Brother of George Morton. 1623 land list. 1626 Purchaser.
Palmer, William	Nailer. 1623 land list. 1626 Purchaser. 1627 cattle list. From Stepney, London.
Pitt, William	1623 land list, sharing with William Wright. From St Peter, London.
Prence (or Prince), Thomas	From All Hallows Barking, London. 1620 Ratcliff, Stepney. 1623 land list. 1624 md Patience Brewster. 1626 One of 8 Undertakers. 1627 cattle list. In 1634, 1638 and 1657-73 Governor of Plymouth Colony.
Simonson, Moses	1623 land list, sharing with Philip de la Noye. 1626 Purchaser. 1627 cattle list with Phillipe de la Noye.
Stacie, Hugh	1623 land list.
Steward, James	1623 land list.
Tench, William	1623 land list, sharing with John Cannon.
Winslow, John	*c.*1597 b. Brother of Edward. 1623 land list. Md Mary Chilton. 1626 Purchaser. 1627 cattle list with Adams, Bassetts and Spragues.
Wright, William	*c.*1588 b. 1623 land list, sharing with William Pitt. 1626 Purchaser. 1627 cattle list with Howland.

A Pre-emptive Strike

There was a crisis in the relations between the settlers and the Indians in March 1623. The background was the Jamestown Massacre of the previous year when the Powhatan Indians (to which Pocahontas belonged) had killed a quarter of the European population of Virginia. It had political consequences as well as humanitarian ones. It was the final blow to the tottering London Virginia Company. By 1624 it had ceased to exist, and Virginia had become a royal colony, a development not unwelcome to James and Gorges. The wider consequence, however, was deep tensions all along the North America coast between European settlers and the native populations.

What occasioned the crisis was the attempt by Thomas Weston to establish a second colony in the region at Wessagusett, now Weymouth, using settlers who had none of the anti-racist commitment of the Pilgrims. It was not long before there was serious conflict between the Wessagussett and the local Massachusetts. The Plymouth settlers were allied with Massasoit, leader of the Pauquunaukit (Pokanoket) branch of the Wampanoag nation, and he was himself in conflict with the Massachusetts. He told Winslow that the coastal Indians had decided to drive the foreigners back into the sea, wiping out both Weston's colony at Wessagussett and also Plymouth. Massasoit had gained much benefit from his alliance with the English settlers and he warned that, if the English did not attack the Massachusetts, he would. As allies, Plymouth would then be involved anyway. Remembering what happened last time, with the false information about Corbitant, Plymouth checked the story and received some confirmation, but this was all in the atmosphere of fear after what had happened in Virginia.

After much debate Plymouth decided to mount an expedition for the relief of Wessagussett, though it was acknowledged that the Wessagussett settlers were in the wrong. Relying on Standish for military expertise, they chose to take the offensive but with a strictly limited aim: they would kill Wituwamat, the Indian leader, cut off his head and bring it back to Plymouth as a warning to others. Standish was despatched with a small party of men to carry out what was essentially an assassination. Under pretence of friendship Standish was able to lure into a room Wituwamat and Pecksuot, the ringleaders, and kill them. In the fighting five other Indians also died. Two English settlers who happened to be nearby were killed by the Indians in retaliation, bringing the death toll to nine. Wituwamat's head was duly brought back to Plymouth and displayed on a spike atop the fort.

Back in Leiden, when Robinson read Winslow's account of this pre-emptive strike, he did not conceal his anger. He reminded Bradford that Leiden and Plymouth were still one church (though distinct) and he was still their Pastor. Standish was not a Brownist (and therefore not a 'Pilgrim') but Bradford and the other Plymouth leaders should have known that all men are 'made after God's image'. They should be converting Indians to Christianity, not killing them. It is shameful, he said, 'to be a terror to poore barbarian people...' In addition, there was no justification for such an attack: the Wessagussett men were clearly in the wrong; there was no need to kill as many as nine; and the argument of self-defence could not be used since the attack was conducted outside of Plymouth's territory.

Despite Robinson's ethical strictures, the effect was not too damaging. As it was an action done in concert with Indian allies there was no racial element as such and the number of Indians supporting Plymouth actually increased. However, in the long run, it meant Brownists had acted out of expediency rather than principle and Robinson, who distrusted Standish's aggressive attitude and worried about Winslow, was aware how corrosive this could be.

Anne and Little James

Not long after the controversial Wituwamat incident, in April 1623, about 90 passengers embarked in London on the ships, *Anne* (140 tons) and *Little James* (44 tons). They were sent by the same group of London investors who had sent the *Mayflower* and the *Fortune*. They count, therefore, as two of the four ships in the '*Mayflower* expedition'. Indeed, they were the last of the 'First Comers'. The *Anne* reached New Plymouth on 10 July 1623, with the *Little James* arriving a week or so later.

The passengers on the *Anne* and *Little James* in 1623 seem to have tried to cross in 1622 aboard the *Paragon,* a ship fitted out by John Peirce. The ship sailed from London but after two attempts leaks and storms forced Peirce to give up. That was the reason for the long gap since the arrival of the *Fortune.*

The passengers on these two ships were a mixed bag. Some were described as 'weak' and unable to withstand hardship and they seem to have been sent back, or they returned voluntarily. Others, belonging to a group around John Oldham, were to prove a disruptive force. The majority, however, consisted of families linked with previous settlers, including settlers from the *Mayflower*, or else they were capable additions in their own right.

It must have been a joyous occasion for the many being reunited with their families and friends. George Morton, the agent for the *Mayflower* in London in 1620, arrived on the *Anne* with his wife, Juliana, and five children: Nathaniel, Patience, John, Sarah, and Ephraim. George and Juliana would have been known to most of the *Mayflower* leadership. After George died in 1624, his eldest son, Nathaniel – raised by William Bradford, his uncle – was to write the first published history of Plymouth Plantation, *New England's Memoriall*.

As well as George Morton, there were several other reunions. For example, William Brewster was reunited after three years with his teenage daughters, Fear and Patience. Elizabeth Flavel was reunited with her son and husband, who had come on the *Fortune*; Hester Cooke brought her son Jacob and daughter Jane, to be reunited with *Mayflower* passenger Francis Cooke, her husband and their father. Margaret Hicks, wife of Robert, was reunited with her husband, who had sailed on the *Fortune*. The capable Elizabeth Warren was reunited with Richard. Unusually for a woman, she became prominent in the public life of the colony. Upon Richard's death in 1628, she inherited his property, took over his administrative work, and this led her on to assuming some government duties.

There were several Brownist arrivals. Menasseh Kemp was definitely of the Jacob Church. Experience Mitchell, possibly son of Thomas Mitchell, 1592 prisoner, was from Duke's Place in Aldgate, and was no doubt the travelling companion of Alice Southworth from nearby Heneage House. She married William Bradford shortly after arrival. There was a strong contingent, probably of a Brownist hue, from Southwark: not only Margaret Hicks, but the family of Edward Bangs and, above all, Timothy Hatherley, stalwart supporter of the Pilgrims who was to be an Assistant Governor of Plymouth Colony until the 1650s. There was an 'elderly' couple from Southwark, Mr and Mrs Burcher, who clearly enjoyed the trip. Captain Altham of the *Little James* wrote: 'Father Birrtcher and his wife wear as hartey as the youngest in the ship.'

The *Anne* did not stay long. It was urgent to impress the London adventurers and she was sent back immediately to London laden with timber and beaver skins. With them went Edward Winslow, to supervise sales, report to the investors, and find out why they were not sending appropriate supplies.

The *Little James* had been sent with the specific purpose of trading with the Indians for furs, but the crew soon discovered that the Indians did not want what they had brought. The Dutch traders simply had more attractive goods to offer. The London idea of what Indians wanted (sparkly things) did not match with what the Indians wanted (knives with a good cutting edge, well-made clothes, solid ornaments).

There was a contradiction. The *Little James*, though expected to trade, was outfitted for military service and authorised to operate as a privateer. The *Anne* had a Master, William Peirce, brother of John Peirce, the adventurer, but the *Little James* had a Captain,

Emmanuel Altham, a well-meaning young military man of little experience. Unable to trade successfully in New England because of his inappropriate supplies, Altham took the ship up to Maine, but the disillusioned crew mutinied and the ship had to return to England with not much to show. There had been divided counsels in London, with John Smith preaching friendly trade and Gorges wanting empire and military action. The *Little James* had fallen between two stools.

The *Little James* 'of London' had a further adventure in 1624. Sailing back to New England it was captured by a pirate warship from Sallee (now Rabat, Morocco). Michael Fletcher, the Master, was taken to Sallee and kept captive in miserable conditions. His wife, Thomasin, was asked for £300 in ransom. Fletcher must had a connection with Rotherhithe, the home of the *Mayflower*, because when Thomasin, unable to pay such a large amount, appealed to Trinity House, her plea was backed by Thomas Gataker, and the certificate she obtained was endorsed by, among others, Robert Bell, a founder of the charity school in Rotherhithe.[5]

1623 Anne and Little James Passengers and Crew

The names of the passengers and crew are sometimes recorded but are often deduced from the 1623 division of Land.

Name	Background
Altham, Emmanuel	A *Mayflower* adventurer. Captain of *Little James*. Wrote letter about New Plymouth. Disapproved of the adventurer faction that tried to impose Lyford on Plymouth.
Annable, Anthony	1626 Purchaser
Annable, Jane	1627 on Cattle List with Brownes, Fullers, Fords and Damaris Hopkins.
Annable, Hannah	Daughter
Annable, Sarah	Daughter
Bangs, Edward	1591, bp. Panfield, Essex. Shipwright. 1616 md Lydia Hicks in Southwark. 1622 (Oct-Dec) was on *Paragon* ship with 109 passengers sent by John Peirce that twice failed to cross the Atlantic. Was probably one of 60 passengers transferred to the *Anne*. 1626 Purchaser. 1627 on Cattle List with Hicks, Stephen Deane and Jennneys (Jenes).

Name	Background
Bangs, Lydia	Daughter of Margaret Hicks, 1616 md Edward Bangs. 1623 Land List. 1627 Cattle List. Probably living in Southwark.
Bangs, X (child)	
Bangs, Y (child)	
Bartlett, Robert	*c.*1603 b Devon. A cooper. 1623 land list.
Brewster, Fear	1606 b Scrooby. Daughter of William. 1623 Land List.1625 md Isaac Allerton.
Brewster, Patience	1600 b Scrooby. Daughter of William. 1623 Land List, with Fear Brewster and Robert Long. Md Thomas Prence.
Bridges, John	Master, *Little James*
Bridges, Wm	Possible relative of John Bridges. Md Mary Oldham.
Buckett (or Beckett), Mary	1605 bp Watford St Mary. 1623 Land List ('Marie Buckett'). Md George Soule. 1627 Cattle List.
Burcher (or Birrtcher), Edward	CB: St Saviour, Southwark, London. From Horselydown. 1623 Land List.
Burcher, Mrs	1623 Land List. Of St Saviour Southwark.
Clarke, Thomas	*c.*1600 b, Stepney, London. 1623 Land List. 1626 Purchaser. 1627 Cattle List. Md Susanna Ring.
Conant, Christopher	1598 bp East Budleigh, Devon. 1609 Moved to London. 1609-16 in parish of St Laurence Jewry. 1616 Freeman of London. 1623 Land List.
Cooke, Hester	1593 Huguenot Mahieu family, originally of Lille, left Canterbury for Leiden. 1603 Hester Mahieu admitted to Walloon Church, Leiden. 1603 Hester btd to Franchois Couck. 1603 (July) Hester Mahieu md Francis Cooke in Vrouwekerk, Leiden. In 1611 Francoise Mahieu, sister of Hester, md Daniel Cricket from Sandwich. *c.*1611 joined Robinson church, Leiden. 1623 Land List. 1627 Cattle List.
Cooke, Jacob	Son
Cooke, Jane	Daughter
Dix(e), Anthony	Mariner. 1623 Land List.

Faunce (or Fance), John	1623 Land List. 1626 Purchaser. 1627 Cattle List. Md Patience Morton.
Flavel, Elizabeth (wife of Thomas)	1610 md in Southwark St Saviour. 1623 Land List. 1623 Land List.
Fletcher, Michael	Mariner of Rotherhithe. Master of the Little James 'of London'. 1624 captured by Sallee (Rabat) pirates.
Flood, Edmund	1623 Land List.
Fuller, Mrs Bridget	1623 Land List. Third wife of Samuel Fuller.
Godbertson, Godbert (or Cuthbertson, Cuthbert)	Probably from Gdansk, Poland. Hatmaker of Leiden. 1623 Land List. 1626 Purchaser. 1627 Cattle LIst, along with Allertons, Priests, Edward Bumpasse and John Crackstone.
Godbertson, Sarah	Wife
Godbertson, Samuel	Son
Hatherley, Timothy	See list of adventurers. 1626 Purchaser. 1626-32 back in Southwark. 1628 Undertaker. 1628 taxed in Southwark. 1632 emigrated to Plymouth on *William and Mary*. Founded Scituate. Assistant Governor of Plymouth Colony.
Heard, William	1623 Land List.
Hicks, Margaret	Wife of Robert Hicks. 1623 Land List. 1627 Cattle List.
Hicks, Samuel	1623 Land List. 1627 Cattle List.
Hilton, Mary	Daughter of William Hilton. 1623 Land List.
Hilton, Mrs	Wife. 1623 Land List.
Hilton, William	Son of William Hilton. 1623 Land List.
Holman, Edward	CB: 'of Surrey' 1623 Land List. 1626 Purchaser. 1627 Cattle List.
Jenney (or Jennings or Jene), John	A cooper. Was a 'brewer man' from Norwich. 1623 Land List. 1626 Purchaser. 1627 Cattle List with Hicks family.
Jenney, Sarah Sr	1613 md John, Leiden. 1623 Land List. 1627 Cattle List.
Jenney, Abigail	Daughter.

Name	Background
Jenney, Samuel	1623 b Atlantic Ocean.
Jenney, Sarah Jr	Daughter.
Kempton, Menasseh	1590 (Feb) bp Berwick, Northumberland. To Colchester, then to Jacob Church, London (CB). 1623 Land List. 1626 Purchaser. 1627 Cattle List.
Long, Robert	1623 Land List. Brother of Fear and Patience Brewster.
Mitchell, Experience	CB: 1620 in Duke's Place, Aldgate, London with Southworths. 1623 Land List with Morton family. 1626 Purchaser. 1627 Md Jane Cooke. Cattle List with 7 members of Cooke family. Perhaps son of Thomas Mitchell, the 1592 prisoner.
Morton, Ephraim	Son of George.
Morton, George	1585 b Bawtry, Yorkshire. 1612 md Juliann(a) Carpenter in Leiden but may have been living in London. 1619-20 was the Pilgrims' agent in London, probably instead of Staresmore. Some believe he published *Mourt's Relation*. 1624 d.
Morton, John	Son.
Morton, Julian(a)	1584 bp Bath, Somerset (CB). 1624 Md Mennaseh Kempton. 1627 Cattle List.
Morton, Nathaniel	1616 son of George Morton and Juliana Carpenter. 1669 *New England's Memoriall*.
Morton, Patience	Daughter.
Morton, Sarah	Daughter.
Morton, Thomas Jr	Son of Thomas Morton Sr., nephew of George. 1623 Land List. 1627 Cattle List with John Howland.
Newton, Mrs Elinor	1623 Land List. 1627 Cattle List. Md John Adams.
Oldham. John (Jack)	1592 bp Derby. 1623 Land List. Led about 30 of the 90 passengers. Follower of clergyman, John Lyford.
Oldham, Lucretia	Sister of John, md Jonathan Brewster.
Oldham, Mary	Daughter. Md William Bridges.
Oldham, Mrs	Wife
Palmer, Frances	Wife of William Palmer. 1623 Land List. 1627 Cattle List

Penn, Christian(a)	1623 Land List. *c.*1625 md Francis Eaton. 1627 Cattle List. 1634 md Francis Billington.
Peirce, Abraham	1623 Land List. 1626 Purchaser. 1627 Cattle List.
Peirce, servant X	
Peirce, servant Y	
Peirce, William	Master, the *Anne*.
Pratt, Joshua	Brother of Phineas Pratt (*Sparrow* 1622). 1623 Land List. 1626 Purchaser. 1627 Cattle List
Priest, Mary	Daughter of Degory. Md Phineas Pratt.
Priest, Sarah	Daughter of Degory. Md John Coombe.
Rande, James	Possibly of St George the Martyr, Southwark. 1623 Land List.
Ratcliffe, Robert	Native of Cheshire. 1623 Land List.
Ratcliffe, Mrs	1623 Land List.
Snow, Nicolas	CB: from Hoxton, London. 1600 bp St Leonard, Shoreditch, London. 1623 Land List. *c.*1625 md Constance Hopkins. 1626 Purchaser. 1627 Cattle List.
Southworth, Mrs Alice	*c.*1591, b Wrington, Somerset. Widow of Edward. Sister of Juliana Morton, wife of George. 1623 md William Bradford. 1623 Land List. 1626 Purchaser. 1627 Cattle List.
Sprague, Francis	1623 Land List. 1626 Purchaser. 1627 Cattle List
Sprague, Anna	CB: daughter. 1623 Land List.
Sprague, Mercy	CB: daughter. 1623 Land List.
Standish, Barbara	1623 md Myles. 1623 Land List. 1626 Purchaser. 1627 Cattle List, along with Winslow and White families.
Tilden, Thomas	1593 bp Tinterden, Kent (CB). 1623 Land List. Brother of Joseph, the adventurer.
Tilden, Mrs	
Tilden, X (child)	
Tracey, Stephen	1596 bp Great Yarmouth, Norfolk. Say cloth weaver, Leiden. 1623 Land List. 1626 Purchaser. 1627 Cattle List.
Tracey, Tryphosa	Wife. 1623 Land List. 1627 Cattle List.

Name	Background
Tracey, Sarah	Daughter. 1623 Land List. 1627 Cattle List.
Wallen, Ralph	1623 Land List. 1626 Purchaser. 1627 Cattle List.
Wallen, Joyce	1627 Cattle List.
Warren, Elizabeth Sr	1583 bp Baldock. Wife of Richard. 1623 Land List. 1627 Cattle List, with John Billington and 3 Soules. 1626 she signed the charter. 1628 Richard d. 1628 Purchaser. 1673, d aged 90.
Warren, Abigail	Daughter.
Warren, Anna	Daughter.
Warren, Elizabeth Jr	Daughter.
Warren, Mary	Daughter
Warren, Sarah	Daughter. Md John Cooke, son of Francis?.

Land Division

The most important event in 1623, certainly as far as the original *Mayflower* settlers were concerned, was the division of land. In the first year the settlers had worked according to the 'common course': everyone put what they had produced from the land into a warehouse and settlers then received from it what they needed to live on. It is what Marx would have called 'primitive communism', as recommended by Plato and practised by the early Christians. The latter was undoubtedly the Brownist model when they tried to run Plymouth as a self-governing commune in 1620-23, though Bradford was to blame Plato when it failed.

There seem to have been three reasons for its failure: the ongoing discontent with the seven-year rule, which postponed land ownership for so long, a dire lack of success in producing enough food, and the arrival of new settlers who did not pull their weight. For these reasons they abandoned 'communism' and turned to private ownership. Each settler was allotted one acre of land where they could plant their own crops and trade the surplus. They got around the seven-year rule by designating the land distribution as only 'temporary'. All would be confirmed, or otherwise, after seven years.

Most of the settlers would have felt this reform to be so important because of the strong desire in developing economies to possess land of one's own. It was the ultimate aspiration for the rural poor and for the urban middle class. It may have been the main motive for emigration. When John Smith made his list of motives for emigration he placed it top of the list: first of all, he said, the dignity of owning and tilling one's own land; then, conversion of the 'savages' to Christianity; then extending human knowledge; building a new civilisation in a new continent; creating social justice; educating England to the benefits of virtue and gain; solving unemployment; and bringing praiseworthy fame to all those who undertook this work.[6] There are two subsidiary points of interest here: Smith makes the obligatory obeisance to conversion but usually this was supposed to go first and he puts it second; and he makes the typical 17th-century equation of 'virtue' and 'gain' (prosperity was the reward of goodness) which was to lead in the 18th century to 'enlightened self-interest'.

Robert Cushman also stresses land ownership in his account of emigration, though he looks at it from an opposite angle. He believed the main reason for emigration was poverty, and he says poor people emigrated from England on account of the oppressive landlords there, and so a desire for their own land overseas. He says economic competition in England has become cut-throat, with much 'oppressing' and 'multitudes' forced to get their living by 'prating' or begging, while spacious, empty land beckons from across the sea. He does not mince words: 'The rent taker lives on sweet morsels, but the rent payer eats a drie crust often with watery eies ... the land groaneth under so many close-fisted and unmercifull men'.[7]

Incidentally, the 'Allotment of Lands' document of March 1623 has the first mention of the *Mayflower*. The name of the *Mayflower* was not mentioned in *Mourt's Relation*, and neither do Bradford, Cushman or Winslow mention it elsewhere. The Allotment document itself was not public, so it was unknown outside Plymouth. As for the *Speedwell,* that was not mentioned until 1669.

The reason for keeping the names of the two ships under wraps for so long was probably to do with certain irregularities, such as the presence on board of law-breakers wanted by the authorities (such as Brewster, or any who fled as adults from East Anglia, Lincolnshire or Kent) and also because, when checked at the customs houses in London and Delfshaven, they would have given Virginia as their intended destination.

The land reform was a success but although it did initiate a period of rising production, the plight of the settlers was still pretty grim at the end of 1623. In a letter of 1624 Emmanuel Altham says Patuxet (Plymouth) is in a bad way after being devastated by a fire in November 1623. The settlers are no good at fishing and cannot get beaver skins from the Indians because the Dutch have far more attractive items to exchange. The worst is that the company in London has let them down badly by not sending good quality settlers and not sending items for barter the Indians want. Many settlers have been forced to return to England (on fishing-boats). He can only praise the 'wise' Bradford.

It was to try and overcome the problems identified by Altham that in 1624 Edward Winslow wrote *Good Newes from New England.* Winslow's target audience was the investors in the City of London. He asks them to keep faith. Plymouth Plantation was their creation, he points out, and they must not give up now. He knows they are disappointed by 'the small profits returned' but the plantation is now well established so future profits can be expected: 'no man expecteth fruit before the tree be grown.' He is weary of the deception in the colonialist literature and promises to give them a truthful account. He says the crisis the previous year was not altogether the fault of those who sent no supplies on the *Fortune* but partly of those who sent optimistic reports back to London, saying the colony had plenty. Fortunately, about 100 miles north-east of Plymouth there were about 30 fishing boats who helped them out with food when they were desperate. The reports received in London were not wholly untrue. They do have plenty of fowl they can shoot, but only from October to March and they do see plenty of fish in summer, but they have no fishing-tackle for their shallops and their nets are broken. It was just as well for the settlers last August that the *Discovery* called in and Thomas Weston's ship, the *Sparrow*. The Master of the *Discovery* not only sold them food but gave them goods they could trade with the Indians, and they made a useful trade agreement with Weston's colony. They do therefore really need supplies and he urges the investors, from their own self-interest, to think long-term and not to rely on quick-profit solutions.

Winslow's return from London on the *Charity* in March 1624 pointed up the mixed fortunes of the settlement. He brought with him three heifers and a bull, which were the first cattle in the colony, and a patent for a fishing centre at Cape Ann. The cattle were a great success and helped the faltering economy no end, but the Cape Ann project was a total disaster.

All was not gloom, even though Winslow was clear the colony was hanging by a thread. Though the repeated setbacks were terrible, outsiders could see how impressive what they had, against all the odds, achieved. John Pory, on his way back to England from Virginia, called in briefly at Plymouth. In a letter of January 1623, to the Earl of Southampton, Pory explained that the Plymouth settlers had been initially recommended by Sir Edwin Sandys to start trading on the Hudson River, but by chance they had ended up at Cape Cod outside Virginian territory. Yet now they had worked wonders. He was full of praise for the industry of the settlers in making the settlement viable, and for the way they had established peaceful relations with the local Indians: 'So they both quietly and justly sate down without either dispossessing any of the natives, or being resisted by them, and without shedding so much as one drop of blood.' He said the Indians themselves acknowledged the settlers' ownership of Patuxet, 'so that the right of those planters to it is altogether unquestionable – a favor which, since the first discovery of America, God hath not vouchsafed, so far as ever I could learn, upon any Christian nation within that continent.'[8] Pory compared New England favourably to Virginia: the 'planters' are more industrious and relations with the Indians more friendly. He felt the settlers had gained such respect among the Indian nations because, though always friendly with them, they put up with no injury at their hands.

In late 1624 John Smith paid a visit to Plymouth and the settlers received the ultimate accolade – they won the approval, even admiration, of John Smith. He reported that he found about 180 people, some cattle, some goats, many pigs, and much poultry. He counted 32 houses stretching about half a mile. Above the town on the hill was a fort containing cannon. The colonists had also made a saltworks, so as to salt and preserve the fish they were sending to London. He was impressed: discipline, hard work, practical projects. This was just up his street. This time he seems to have uncovered a different side to the Pilgrims – they did not just waffle on about religion but cracked on with 'the general businese'. In 1630, looking back, Smith (though still scathing about their religion) was able to acknowledge the role of the Pilgrims he had once scoffed at. The Virginia Company had always failed, he mused. Nobody had been able to make a colony in New England until 'some hundred of your Brownists of England, Amsterdam and Leiden went to New Plymouth.'[9]

7

The *Mayflower* Hanging by a Thread

John Robinson in his letters of 1623 says he is being prevented from coming to New England by the small group that made 'the covenants betwixt us'. In his first letter he said it was 'the adventurers' who were blocking any further emigration from Leiden, but then his second letter is more analytic. He says most of the adventurers in London are 'honestly minded, and lovingly also', while five or six are bitterly hostile, and another five or six are 'absolutely bent for us'; however, there is a small but dominant group above the adventurers, the driving force behind the scenes, the 'forward preachers' of the enterprise, and this group is telling the honest majority that if Robinson joined the colony it would spoil 'their market' and they would lose their money. The Pilgrims are to this group only 'accessories' to a greater design, leaving Leiden and New Plymouth as 'strangers' to the course of events.[1] In code he is referring to Gorges and the court, and the problem was even more serious than Robinson thought.

The conventional wisdom is that the Leiden Pilgrims and the City of London investors brought about the voyage of the *Mayflower* and the settlement of New England – Winslow told the City of London adventurers that they created New Plymouth – but that is only half the story. All over the world, from Java to Jamaica, European states were sending ships, soldiers and colonists as part of an imperialist expansion. Powerful interests at the royal court were making use of City investors and Leiden Pilgrims in the conduct of realpolitik. From their point of view the adventurers and Brownists had established a British base in North America; they had served their turn and now was the time for the state to take control in New England, which meant subjecting it to direct rule by Whitehall and the Anglican Church.

The campaign to stop Robinson was orchestrated by Sir Ferdinando Gorges who wanted New England to be Anglican, not Brownist.

It may already have been agreed in 1621 that the Council of New England would grant the Peirce Patent only on condition no more Brownists crossed the Atlantic. As Gorges was backed by the king, who by 1624 had completely defeated the faction led by Sandys and Southampton, it looked certain the Brownist leadership in Plymouth would soon be overthrown.

On the *Anne* and *Little James* came a group led by John Oldham which had been promised a separate settlement near New Plymouth. He was a follower of John Lyford, a Pastor from Armagh in Ireland and educated at Oxford, who had become the first ordained minister to arrive at New Plymouth when he arrived on the *Charity* in 1624. While pretending to be a sympathiser of the Pilgrims, Lyford wrote secretly to London, denouncing the Pilgrims from an Anglican point of view. At secret meetings he stirred up discontent against the Plymouth government and administered Anglican sacraments to members of Oldham's group. Together, they were trying to establish the Anglican Church in Plymouth. Lyford's aim was to get enough votes in Plymouth to outvote the Bradford regime. It was ironic. On the other side of the Atlantic, the Anglican Church was now the underground church in Plymouth just as the Brownists had been the underground church in London.

Bradford intercepted some of Lyford's letters but, like Shakespeare's Hamlet in dealing with the treacherous Rosencrantz and Guildenstern, he resealed the envelopes as if they had not been opened, biding his time until he had an overwhelming case for expulsion. In the letters Lyford warned London against William Peirce, the Master of the *Anne*, who favoured taking more Brownists to Plymouth, and he also mentioned a dangerous merchant called Edward Winslow. Bradford must have smiled.

Lyford was eventually confronted with the irrefutable facts, as collected by Bradford, and banished from the territory of Plymouth Colony. Oldham was banished later. Lyford's wife, Sarah, later testified that her husband was an incorrigible womaniser, in particular with the housemaids, and had fled from Armagh after raping a girl in his parish.

The attempt to bring Plymouth into the Anglican fold, and therefore under the control of the state, had been defeated. It was a historic victory for Bradford. If Lyford had won and New England had become Anglican, then the Great Migration of the 1630s would have gone to Holland, to Arnhem and Rotterdam, the new havens, where some did flee in any case.

There was a final bid to oust Brownism in 1625. This came not from Gorges but from some of the adventurers. They begged the Plymouth congregation to sign up to the French Huguenot church and so renounce 'ye scandalous name of ye Brownists'. This must have been a tempting option and it is a pity that the vote is not known. For the Brownists in New Plymouth did not have a pastor, unlike their sister churches in Leiden, London and Amsterdam, and an English-speaking Huguenot pastor could easily have been found. Moreover, on the *Fortune* and the *Anne* had come the Leiden Huguenots, Hester Cooke and Philip Delano, who would no doubt have been delighted by such a turn of events. Most of all, abandoning the name of 'Brownist' would have unlocked the supplies they sorely needed from the adventurers in London at present scared to invest while Plymouth was in conflict with the court. Nonetheless the proposal was still rejected. The Plymouth congregation decided that, although very close to the Huguenots, they would not renounce their independence. It also has to be remembered that the Pilgrims had an acute sense of English patriotism. They did not want to be ruled by the Dutch or the French.

James Sherley

This principled refusal left the settlers in a disastrous situation. They were virtually a colony of the City of London and the Lyford affair had so alienated the adventurers there now seemed little chance of getting any more supplies. In 1625 Standish travelled to London to beg for supplies but found London in the grip of a deadly plague that was killing thousands. He did get some supplies – but at a punishing 50% interest rate. Not only that but he brought back tragic news. John Robinson was dead, as were Robert Cushman and King James.

His talks with James Sherley, head of the Plymouth Colony adventurers on the finances of the colony were inconclusive and Sherley was seriously ill. Bradford wrote: 'All which things ... it is a marvel it did not wholly discourage them and sink them.'[2]

Bradford identified 1625 as the worst year for the colony but also as the year when the tide turned. It was as if a miracle occurred. The London merchants sympathetic to the settlers came up with a plan for the long-term future of the colony and in 1626 Isaac Allerton, the leading merchant in Plymouth since the death of Carver, was despatched to London for negotiations. It emerged that four merchants – Richard Andrews, John Beauchamp Timothy Hatherley, and James Sherley – were prepared to take over the financing of the colony in return for a six-year monopoly of the fur trade. They would buy up the colony from the remaining investors and then sell it to the settlers. They would also keep the colony supplied, although all supplies would have to be paid for. Before any of this started, however, there had to be intricate negotiations.

The leading light of this rescue plan was James Sherley, the 'Treasurer' (i.e. leader) of the Plymouth Colony adventurers in London. The leading lights after him were John Beauchamp and Timothy Hatherley. All were Brownist members or strong sympathisers and it can be argued, therefore, that by keeping the 'Brownist name' in 1625 the congregation had made the correct decision. Sherley had been the driving-force of Plymouth Colony from the beginning. Bradford says Sherley was 'a chief friend to the plantation' and by 1625 was 'the stay, and life of the whole business'.[3]

Sherley and Beauchamp, before they became business partners in London, were old Brownists from the Exiled Church in Amsterdam, supporters of Ainsworth against Johnson. Beauchamp had started out as a salter but his main business was importing goods from the Netherlands as an 'interloper', wriggling somehow outside the monopolies, just like Weston, while Sherley was a goldsmith trading with the Netherlands at a time when goldsmiths were an integral part of banking and finance. The two became united in London because both had diversified into the fur trade. They lived in Clapham but had townhouses and shops in the City of London. Sherley's goldsmiths' shop was at the 'Golden Horseshoe' on London Bridge while his town house was at the northern end of the bridge in Crooked Lane. Correspondence on Plymouth was addressed to the Golden Horseshoe and therefore the 'headquarters' of the Plymouth Colony Company was on London Bridge (as the headquarters of the Virginia Company was at Thomas Smythe's home). In a letter of 1636 Sherley said he kept all his books in his townhouse in Crooked Lane.

Sherley was ready to emigrate if Charles I proved to be as oppressive as he feared. He wrote to Bradford in 1627: 'Wherefore if the Lord should send persecution or trouble heer (which is much to be feared) and so should put into our minds to flye for refuge, I know no place safer than to come to you...' He was a close friend of Edward Winslow and, when Winslow's daughter, Elizabeth, married in Clapham Sherley was a witness. It should come as no surprise that Clapham was a centre for the manufacture of beaver hats.

The first step towards the settlers gaining control of the colony was buying out the existing investors. Only 42 were left out of the original 70. Some of these were bought out by Sherley himself but 53 'freemen' of the colony (known as the 'Purchasers') bought out the majority, agreeing to pay over several years. Once this was all done, the *Mayflower* joint stock company was wound up in November 1626. It was replaced by twelve 'Undertakers' (eight from New Plymouth and four from London) who agreed to pay off Plymouth's debts in return for trading rights. The four had agreed with Allerton in October to sell the colony to the settlers for £800, to be paid off at £200 per year, but he had promised to take the contract back to Plymouth for ratification before final agreement. Everybody remembered Cushman in 1620. In fact, the settlers were pleased with Sherley's contract (especially as he had bought out some of the investors himself). They signed it and Allerton took it back to London in 1627.

The twelve Undertakers were Sherley, Andrews, Beauchamp and Hatherley, plus Alden, Allerton, Bradford, Brewster, Howland, Prence, Standish, and Winslow. There was expectation that the settlers would pay off the £800 soon, but the debt was not liquidated until the 1640s and even then Bradford, Prence, Standish and Winslow had to contribute their own property.

In 1627 the colony received the benefits of the new financial stability. In the 'Division of Cattle', the cattle were distributed to settlers according to their shareholdings and in January 1628 Plymouth court (the assembly) distributed land, about 20 acres per share, to colonists. There was a general feeling of emancipation and optimism. This was what many of the colonists had come to America for – land and property of their own.

There was one sour aftertaste. When Allerton made his trip to London in 1627 to deliver the signed contract, returning on a fishing fleet, he came back with trading rights to Plymouth Harbour, Cape Cod and the Kennebec River. These could be utilised by the colony or Allerton himself. Shortly afterwards Timothy Hatherley crossed the Atlantic and when he arrived in Plymouth he investigated whether or not Allerton had obtained these rights under false pretences. Allerton had told the investors in London that Plymouth would not be able to pay off its debts unless it was granted extra trading concessions. This damaged Plymouth's reputation but allowed Allerton to make use of the concessions for his own purposes. The result of Hatherley's enquiry was the removal of Allerton as the London agent for Plymouth and the appointment of Winslow in his place.

Plymouth Triumphant

If 1625 had been the worst year for Plymouth (apart from 1621), then 1628 was the best. This year took Plymouth for the first time to a level of economic prosperity, albeit of modest proportions. As Bunker wrote: 'For the *Mayflower* Pilgrims, the trading season of 1628 supplied the reward for eight years of effort.' Not only did they achieve a grain surplus but they sent a huge quantity of beaver skins to England. The policy of friendship with the Indians had paid off: it was the Indians who had taught them how to plant, and how to fertilise the soil with dead fish, and it was the Indians who caught the beaver. They had also benefitted from free trade. They had shaken off the royal monopoly of the Virginia Company with its non-economic objectives and the minor monopoly of the London investors with their short-term aim of quick profits. Now they could set their own targets. They gained other freedoms too. In New England they could hunt in freedom (fowling and fishing), which was forbidden to 'common people' in England, and they were free of landlords. For the first time they did not have to pay rent to anybody. For many of them this was a liberation.

They also achieved freedom of religion. They could practise their Brownism openly here, and increase their numbers, which they could not do in Holland. They were free, above all, from Anglican persecutions, from the whippings, imprisonments and hangings, not to mention freedom from Catholic torture and burnings. The attempted takeover by Lyford had been defeated. This was what they had become Pilgrims for – freedom of religion and freedom of trade.

In 1630 Plymouth received at last a proper patent, to replace the rushed job which was the second Peirce Patent of 1621. The government in England now legalised their existence instead of trying to subvert it. It was called the 'Warwick Patent', being signed by the Earl of Warwick, and was made out in Bradford's name. Naturally he included in it all the First Comers, all who had arrived on the four ships of the *Mayflower* expedition. They were all founders of New England, not just him, and not just *Mayflower* passengers, since on the other three ships had come their wives, children and dearest friends.

The success of the Pilgrims opened a new chapter in British history. In 1628 there had been a huge surge in financial investment in London; an interest in New England had been aroused; in 1629 a Massachusetts Bay Company was founded; and in 1630 a fleet landed around 700 settlers. All seemed well. The *Mayflower* had finally triumphed and this had encouraged others to settle in New England.

Massachusetts Bay

There is no peace for the wicked they say, but there is no peace for the saints either. The mass immigration into Massachusetts Bay ended the isolation of the Pilgrims but also presented them with a new problem, one this time they failed to solve. The majority of the newcomers to Massachusetts Bay were not Brownists but puritans, and puritans were sometimes worse enemies to the Brownists than corrupt, absentee rectors who did not care much either way.

The Plymouth Colony Pilgrims were rapidly outnumbered. By the late 1630s the number of British immigrants in North America had reached about 50,000 and Plymouth was just a small enclave. Maryland became a destination for English Catholics; Virginia was loyal to the Anglican church; Massachusetts Bay was overwhelmingly puritan. The minor Plymouth Colony clung to the values of the *Mayflower* by the skin of its teeth.

The reason for the influx of so many puritans lay in the policies of the British government. The 'Great Migration' was fuelled by two political factors as well as the usual one of economic distress. The first was the oppressiveness of a church led by William Laud, Bishop of London from 1628 and Archbishop of Canterbury from 1633. Laud was not just opposed to Brownists and other separatists but he aimed to drive out of the Church the moderate reformers known as puritans. The second factor was the dissolution of Parliament by Charles I in 1629, with little prospect of a recall in the foreseeable future. This meant there was oppression without any means of constitutional redress, and emigration was therefore an option of natural recourse.

The leader of the Massachusetts Bay Colony was the highly capable John Winthrop to whom the wise and thoughtful Bradford may have seemed rather pedestrian. On the surface Winthrop and Bradford were friendly enough, as in the circumstances they had to be, given their common enemies, and they did share a critique of the Anglican Church and a belief in covenants and the role of congregations, but there was a divide. The Bay settlers were often from a wealthier background than the Brownists and did not have such radical views. It might be said that they tended to be upper middle class while the Brownists tended to be lower middle class. Winthrop was conscious of his superior social status. For example, in 1620 he complained that persons 'of meane respect, quality and condicion' were driving around London in coaches.[4] For Winthrop maximum acquisition of land was a sign of God's blessing and he was often involved in land disputes. It is true that many Brownists were wealthy merchants, such as Allerton, Carver, Hatherley and Sherley, but there is not with them the sense of status that emanates from Winthrop. In his sermon on Christian charity Winthrop said: 'God Almighty in his most holy and wise providence has so disposed of the condition of mankind as in all times some must be rich, some poor, some high and eminent in power and dignity, others mean and in subjection.'

As well as the deficit in social status and in wealth compared to Winthrop in Boston, the Plymouth Pilgrims also lacked, since the deaths of Ainsworth and Robinson, any intellectual firepower. In 1633 John Cotton arrived in Boston, one of the great puritan theologians of the day. Cotton, originally from Derby and educated at Emmanuel College, Cambridge, ably presented the official doctrine of Boston: 'non-separating Congregationalism'. Like other puritans, Cotton would not separate from the Anglican Church, even though they had driven him out, and was strongly opposed to the separatism of the Plymouth Brownists because he believed there needed to be one church that imposed uniformity throughout the state. He soon became Pastor of the Boston church and by 1635 had imposed strict uniformity of baptism and church discipline throughout Massachusetts Bay.

Both Winthrop and Cotton were very scathing about democracy. Robinson had believed in a mixed constitution, as recommended by Aristotle, which might be said to make him one-third democratic. Winthrop, however, said, 'democracy is, amongst most civil nations, accounted the meanest and worst of all forms of government.' Cotton told Lord Say and Sele: 'Democracy, I do not conceyve that ever God did ordeyne as a fit government eyther for church or commonwealth. If the people be governors, who shall be governed?' There is an elitism in the Winthrop-Cotton worldview not found in Brownist ranks, as was illustrated by Winthrop's declaration as he sailed to America on the ship *Arbella*: 'For we must consider that we shall be like a City upon a Hill; the eyes of all people are on us.' This view casts back to mediaeval times, while the Brownist talk of 'freedom from the hierarchy' has a more modern ring.

This difference in emphasis between Boston and Plymouth was reflected in practical policy. Thus Massachusetts Bay did not have Plymouth's aversion to slavery and after their war with the Pequots, they shipped many captured Pequot warriors to the West Indies as slaves. Winthrop kept back one male and two female Pequot slaves for his own use.

Hutchinson and Williams

The differences between the puritan Massachusetts Bay and the Brownist Plymouth Colony can also be seen in the cases of Anne Hutchinson and Roger Williams. Hutchinson and her family, who were keen followers of John Cotton, arrived in Massachusetts Bay from London, probably Stepney, in 1634. Hutchinson started an all-women discussion group, at first for women with babies who were unable to attend all the church service but still wanted to discuss the sermons, as the men did. Hutchinson was taken with Cotton's teaching on the importance of heeding the inner spirit, but the discussions led to the conclusion that the inner spirit should be given priority over religious laws – the Antinomian heresy. Though she was supported by John Wainwright, Sir Henry Vane and the majority of the congregation in Roxbury, Hutchinson was in 1638 put on trial, excommunicated and banished. At first she took refuge on what is now Rhode Island but in 1643, when Winthrop moved to take control of Rhode Island, she fled to Long Island, part of Dutch territory, where she believed she would be safe, only to be brutally murdered, with her children, by an Indian war-party.

Roger Williams, educated at Cambridge and son of a London merchant tailor, had received legal training as an employee of Edward Coke, the most famous lawyer of the day and a campaigner with Edwin Sandys against monopolies. Williams arrived in Boston at the age of 28 and was offered the job of Teacher in 1631, but he declined the position because Boston was 'an unseparated church'. Williams had arrived at a separatist position by the time he and his wife boarded the *Lyon* in December 1630 and three principles were already central to his teachings: separation from the Anglican Church, separation of church and state, and liberty of conscience. This was routine Brownism, but his legal training made his interpretations very precise.

Having rejected Boston, Williams settled in Salem, which, to the disapproval of Boston, had Brownist inclinations. There he questioned the authority of the king when he granted a charter to the Bay Company that bestowed on the colonists the lands of the native Americans. He argued that on strictly legal grounds only a direct purchase from the Indians gave a just title to land and the royal patent was therefore inapplicable. This was John Robinson's line, that land should be purchased directly from the Indians.

Williams then moved on to Plymouth and was accepted there as a Brownist church member. He was an assistant minister there for almost three years but in 1632 he wrote a lengthy tract openly condemning the king's charters and questioning the right of Plymouth to the land of the town without buying it first from the Indians. Legally, it was not enough that Massasoit had agreed they could have it. He went so far as to rule that James had uttered a 'solemn lie' in claiming he was the first Christian monarch to have discovered the land. For Plymouth this was very difficult – their entire strategy since 1616 had been based on assuring the king that, despite their religious views, they were loyal and patriotic subjects. It sounds as if Brewster was Williams's chief critic in Plymouth, detecting in him the same 'rigid separation and anabaptistry' that John Smyth had developed in Amsterdam. By the beginning of 1634, Williams, though many in Plymouth supported him, had moved back to Salem taking some from Plymouth with him. Bradford says he admired Williams, apart from his 'unsettled judgement', and says he left Plymouth voluntarily ('sued for his dismission'). It was all very unfortunate.

Back in Salem, within Massachusetts Bay, Williams caused more controversy by stating that magistrates should not be able to punish persons for religious opinions. As a lawyer, he was a staunch advocate of the separation of church and state. He was convinced there was no scriptural basis for a state church and if magistrates involved themselves in religious matters, then there was, ipso facto, a state church. Since what Winthrop and Cotton were setting up was very close to a theocracy this did not go down well.

Finally, in October 1635, the Boston General Court tried Williams and found him guilty of sedition and heresy. He was condemned for spreading 'diverse, new, and dangerous opinions' and ordered to be banished. Fearing he might be put on a boat back to England to face the tender mercies of William Laud, he journeyed 55 miles through deep snow from Salem to the Wampanoags at their winter camp in Seekonk. Massasoit hosted the refugee, Williams, for three months until spring.

In the spring of 1636, Williams and a number of others from Salem began a new settlement on land which he had bought from Massasoit. However, the Plymouth authorities worried that this was within their land grant and were concerned that his presence there might anger the leaders of Massachusetts Bay. Williams had learnt the language of the Narragansett Indians and he and twelve 'loving friends' therefore established a new settlement Williams called 'Providence' (later Rhode Island) because he felt God's Providence had brought them there. He managed to keep the peace between the Indian inhabitants and his Rhodes Island settlement for nearly 40 years by constant mediation and negotiation.

Williams offered his new settlement, 'Providence Plantation', as a refuge to all those in the world who sought 'liberty of conscience' and he soon attracted an assortment of dissenters. It was grounded in what might be called 'radical Brownism' – Brownism mixed with what Brewster called 'anabaptistry', the egalitarianism that Francis Johnson had rejected in John Smyth and even Robinson had shied away from when he said Leiden was a mixed democracy, not a full democracy. In Providence Plantation from the beginning a majority vote of the heads of households governed the settlement (though that applied only to civil matters, not religious). Newcomers were admitted to citizenship by a majority vote. All religions were tolerated and in 1637 Williams confirmed that his toleration included Jews and Muslims (the 'Turks'). There was formal confirmation of Williams' arrangements in 1640 in a vote by the 39 freemen. Williams had founded the first place in history, it is claimed, where there was religious liberty, separation of church and state, no slavery, and democracy by majority vote. This was a Brownist achievement and would surely have been welcomed by Jacob and Robinson, although it made Plymouth Colony, who were Brownist but not so radical, very nervous. In his history, Bradford tries to grapple with Williams' 'strange ideas' without condemning them.

Plymouth was in an awkward position, given the power and wealth of Virginia to the south and Massachusetts Bay to the north, neighbours on whom they were dependent economically. It was easier for the Brownists in England to defend Williams, and Sabine Staresmore, for example, did not fail to defend Williams against Cotton and Winthrop.

A word of caution is necessary here about the role of Cotton and Winthrop. It might be thought from the above that they were die-hard reactionaries fighting against a democratic future. Far from it. Williams' experiment was in a remote place and on a very small scale and comparing Massachusetts Bay with him, or even with Plymouth, is grossly unfair on Winthrop and Cotton. Relative to Charles I, Winthrop was the enlightened one, just as Charles I was relatively enlightened compared to the rulers of most European countries. In the 1640s it was in fact puritans like Winthrop and the Scottish Presbyterians that led the revolution against Charles. Winthrop's 'New England Way' was regarded by many as a model of progress. Williams, Bradford and Winslow maintained their personal friendships with Winthrop. In 17th-century terms it might have been considered very tolerant of Winthrop that he did not execute rebels like Williams out of hand. It is only in comparison with Holland, the most civilised of the European countries, that Winthrop might be criticised. In ideal worlds there are absolutes, but in the real world everything is relative.

An example of how progressive Massachusetts Bay could be is education. Browne and Barrowe would have been immensely pleased by what they did. Winthrop insisted on universal literacy at a time when in England fewer than 30% of the population could read and write. A 1642 law required all heads of households to teach wives, children and servants how to read and write. In 1647 a law ordered all towns of 50 inhabitants or more to employ a teacher. Plymouth was strong on literacy too – it was a Protestant theme – but in the Bay Winthrop made Barrowe's dream of universal literacy come true.

Lothrop

In the 1630s the virtues of New England were certainly much appreciated by the persecuted back in England, where dissenters were hit by a new wave of persecution unleashed by Archbishop Laud.

The Brownists left behind in Britain who for various reasons had not sailed in the *Mayflower* expedition had struggled to survive. After returning from his experiment in 'Jacobopolis', perhaps ill, Henry Jacob had died in 1624. He was succeeded as Pastor by a former clergyman, John Lothrop, 'a man of tender heart'. (Sometimes his name is spelt 'Lathrop' but 'Lothrop' was his family's preferred spelling.) Lothrop was from Lambeth in South London, near to Southwark.

He followed Jacob's policy of building links with Anglican ministers who were 'true Christians'.

The trouble with Jacob's policy was that while it could work in fairly moderate conditions, such as in the years after James' renunciation of violence against dissenters in 1614, it was not practicable in the period of polarisation initiated by Charles I. An Anglican minister identified as a 'true Christian' by dissenters might become a target for Laud. Moreover, many Brownists thought building links with Anglicans took attention away from the main objective: separation. It was only through separation, creating separate churches, that toleration and religious freedom could be won.

Just before he died, John Robinson made the point that although it was right to be friendly to Anglicans, separatism was still the nub of the issue: In *A Just and Necessary Apology* (1625) he defended 'we hateful Brownists' from the renewed attacks on them for being separatist. He said they did nothing more than Luther and Calvin had done when they separated from a corrupt church. The Church of England, although it had many good members and had played a historic role, was nonetheless only 'Babylon', and Christians must distance themselves from it.

In 1630 a John Duppa (or Dupper) broke away from 'mild' Lothrop in favour of unadulterated separatism. It was felt that the Anglican Church of Laud was beyond all hope of reasoning. Duppa, billed in the 1640s as a 'tub preacher', had notable support: Sabine Staresmore (the negotiator for the Pilgrims), the Chidley family (who became Levellers), Rice Boye (from Wiltshire Brownists), Thomas Pride (he of the famous Purge) Ralph Grafton (a rich upholsterer of Cornhill), David Brown, John Jerrow and Samuel Eaton. Naturally, they were all targets for Laud. They took elaborate precautions. Katherine Chidley said members not only used false names but went about in disguise, even wearing wigs, to escape the attentions of 'Bishops' bloodhounds' (secret agents).[5] In the end, in one raid, Laud's agents arrested most of them.

Laud had Lothrop and his church members arrested too. In reality there may not have been much difference between them, perhaps it was only emphasis. Brownist breakaways were usually amiable – it was in the nature of Brownism that all congregations had autonomy – and the Duppa breakaway seems not to have been acrimonious. Often a breakup was caused simply by a growth in numbers that could not easily be accommodated in the clandestine meeting spaces. The only breakup that was really acrimonious was that of Ainsworth and Johnson in 1610.

Laud had been Bishop of London since 1628 but, whatever his inclinations, he did not indulge in major persecution until after

Parliament had ceased to sit in 1629. Even then, it was not easy, since the Brownists were clever with their wigs and frequent changes of meeting-place. Finally, in 1632 Laud was able to announce a major breakthrough. He had seized a 'conventicle' of 26 in 'Newington Woodes' and a raid on a private house in Blackfriars belonging to Humphrey Barnet, a brewer's clerk, had netted 42 Brownists (though 18 escaped). They were all imprisoned. The 42 included Praise God Barbone, who later gave his name to Cromwell's Barebones Parliament. After he became Archbishop of Canterbury in 1633 Laud was able to promote his persecutions on a national scale. There were imprisonments, brandings, nose-slittings, public whippings, and the cutting off of ears.

On his release from prison in 1634, Lothrop, his family and other church members (amounting to about 30 in all) emigrated to America on the *Griffin*. They reached Boston in September but almost immediately headed south for Plymouth Colony. They settled in Scituate, where they founded a Brownist church with Lothrop as its first Pastor. There was no denying the continuity with the London church: Lothrop had taken with him Jacob's sacramental vessels: pewter tankard, plates and baptismal bowl. In 1639 they left Scituate and moved to Barnstable, on Cape Cod, a final and successful move.

As Lothrop was crossing the Atlantic in one direction, Winslow was crossing it the other way and walked straight into Laud's wave of persecution when he visited London on business in 1634. He was arrested and consigned to the Fleet prison accused of acting as if he were a minister in New England, preaching, and marrying people unlawfully. He sent in a 'petition' for release which was eventually successful, though only after many weeks. He explained in his petition that when Plymouth had no minister appointed, civil marriages had to be performed by the Governor or Assistant Governor. He said King James had granted Plymouth Colony 'liberty of conscience' (an exaggeration) and there was no evidence that Plymouth had ever been disloyal to the king. Indeed, they even required their Indian allies to swear loyalty to the king. He also reassured them that the Brownists in Plymouth never publicly denounced the Church of England. He finished by saying New England was threatened by the French and the Dutch (another exaggeration), and he really must get back there to repel the king's enemies.

Hampden and Burton

Up until 1637 Laud's crackdown on all separatists and puritans and Charles I's dismissal of Parliament had met with little resistance, but suddenly there was a change of mood. The turning point was embodied in the cases of John Hampden (1637), Bastwick, Burton and Prynne (1637), and John Lilburne (1638). These all became popular heroes and martyrs for the cause.

The Hampden case related to 'Ship Money', an ancient tax that Charles I had discovered which entitled him, without consulting Parliament, to raise taxes for the maintenance of the navy. In 1635 John Hampden, a respected MP, refused to pay. In 1637-38 legal proceedings against him resulted in a trial and it was this trial that evoked tremendous popular support for Hampden.

There was a New England connection. In 1629 Hampden, a puritan, had been involved in the discussions about the Massachusetts Bay Company and the Earl of Warwick later granted him land in Connecticut. Like many figures in the opposition to Laud and Charles, he probably contemplated emigration.

In 1637 three oppositionists, John Bastwick, Henry Burton and William Prynne, who had all written against the policies of Laud and Charles, were convicted of sedition, fined £5000 each, sentenced to life imprisonment and ordered to lose their ears. As well as losing his ears, Prynne also had the letters, 'SL', for 'Seditious Libeller', branded on his cheek with a red-hot iron.

John Rushworth described the grisly scene:

Mr Burton spake much while in the pillory to the people. The executioner cut off his ears deep and close, in a cruel manner, with much effusion of blood, an artery being cut, as there was likewise of Dr Bastwick. Then Mr Prynne's cheeks were seared with an iron made exceeding hot which done, the executioner cut off one of his ears and a piece of his cheek with it; then hacking the other ear almost off, he left it hanging and went down; but being called up again he cut it quite off.

The outrage over the savage sentences imposed on Bastwick, Burton and Prynne came from two sources: from the crowds who gathered in sympathy and from the middle-class puritans they represented. The latter reacted not so much against the savagery, since JPs regularly had members of the lower classes flogged, branded and mutilated, but from horror that such things had been done to a middle-class person. Laud had overreached himself: Bastwick and Prynne were not even radicals.

In 1638 John Lilburne, who was a radical oppositionist, was betrayed by an informer and arrested. After he was imprisoned, he was fined £500, tied to the back of a cart and lashed every three or four paces (by a corded and knotted three-thonged whip) from the

Fleet River almost two miles to Westminster, where he was put in the stocks. He was followed by large and sympathetic crowds every step of the way.

In the mid-1630s it had looked as if Laud's policies in England were now so entrenched that emigration was the only alternative for puritans, Brownists and the Anabaptist sects, but there was a change of mood in 1637. Enough, it seems, was enough. The Brownist church in London was suddenly restored. A new Pastor, Henry Jessey, was chosen. Jessey had been going to America to join Lothrop but he, along with others, suddenly changed his mind. The Venetian Ambassador found it disturbing that Bastwick, Burton and Prynne received such widespread sympathy. He found it ominous that women and children in the street collected the blood of the victims as the blood of holy martyrs.[6]

8

The *Mayflower* Returns to London

In 1637 the new Brownist church in London, led by Pastor Henry Jessey, was a continuation of the Lothrop church and in the tradition of Jacob, so scholars often refer to it as the Jacob-Lothrop-Jessey Church. The church was an instant success and despite an early attempt to break it in a raid by the Bishop of London's officers on a meeting in Queenhithe in 1638, it seems to have rapidly spread across the country, as Johnson's church had spread across the country at the turn of the century. Congregations appeared in Llanvaches, Bristol, Stockport, and in Missenden, Buckinghamshire (in the same district of Chiltern as Jordans, which claimed to have the *Mayflower* timbers).

One result was that in 1639 a William Wroth founded the first independent Brownist church in Wales. Wroth had been the Anglican rector of Llanvaches in Monmouthshire since 1617 and when he made his move Henry Jessey was despatched from London to help set up a gathered church in Llanvaches. At the same time a Brownist church was emerging in Bristol and another in Stockport. They are counted as Brownist because they seem to have been covenanted and were in alliance with Jessey. Tolmie wrote that the gathered church in Missenden, Buckinghamshire, was probably also Brownist but it is difficult to be sure because some gathered churches were Anabaptist. There is a problem with his own suggestion that the English church in Arnhem might be counted as Brownist. This is doubtful since the wealthy congregation in Arnhem contained members who denounced Brownism (Philip Nye, Thomas Goodwin). Arnhem may therefore be better categorised as radical-puritan. Nonetheless, even if Anabaptist or radical-puritan, these were all centres of resistance against Laud.

Jessey was born in Yorkshire in 1601 and was educated at St John's College, Cambridge. He lived at first in Suffolk and was ordained an Anglican minister in 1627. Like so many others, he then fell victim to Laud's drive for national uniformity and was deprived of his living in Aughton, Yorkshire, in 1634. After moving to London he was poised to emigrate to New England, probably to join Lothrop in Scituate, but instead was caught up in organising the agitation in London on behalf of Bastwick, Burton and Prynne. This seems to have led him into accepting the dangerous job of becoming Pastor to the 'Remnant' of Lothrop's London church. If Laud had calculated that his barbaric treatment of Bastwick, Burton and Prynne would have a deterrent effect, he would have been disappointed in the case of the Brownists. As Robinson had written, the Brownists had a special type of 'perseverance'.

Was the Brownist church led by Jessey any different from the church led by Robinson, Jacob and Lothrop? Underground churches leave no records and their public writings have to avoid censorship but sometimes it is possible to learn from attacks on them by their enemies. Ephraim Pagitt in his pamphlet, *Heresiography* (1647), described the Brownists as separatists who oppose the payment of tithes; refuse to take communion with any 'profane persons'; believe everybody may preach; believe there should be equality within the church; believe in civil marriage; excuse those who live with women not their wives; and direct venomous language against Anglicans and Presbyterians. This was a hostile caricature which failed to mention covenants and consent of congregations but does contain familiar elements that are recognisably Brownist. Jacob and Robinson would not have liked a reversion to venomous language against Anglicans, which they had banned, but this reversion was no doubt prompted in the 1630s by the harsh policies of Laud.

In 1637 Jessey's Brownist church made rapid strides straight away because it had a ready-made campaign. They won support for Bastwick, Burton and Prynne and used it to expose the tyranny of the 'hierarchy' of bishops. In the course of the campaigning they developed certain tactics used later in the revolution: public fasting, popular petitions and mass lobbying. In 1641 when Spilsbury's congregation (including John Lilburne, the future Leveller, his wife, Elizabeth, and his sister, Elizabeth) were arrested they used those methods to secure their quick release. The same non-violent tactics enabled Bastwick, Burton and Prynne to return to London in triumph. They could carry this off because they were allied with puritans inside the Anglican Church also bitterly opposed to Laud; and this was only possible because Robinson and Jacob had found a way for Brownists to be separatist but non-sectarian. The Jacob-Lothrop-Jessey church was able to work with all Anglican ministers adjudged to be 'true Christians'.

This approach by the Jessey Church was so successful that already by 1640 the congregations were too large for meetings to be easily concealed from Laud's informers. As often happened with underground churches, they then amicably agreed to divide in half: they did not usually 'split'. One half went with Praise-God Barbone to Fleet St, on the western side of the City, while the other half stayed in the east in the Liberty of the Tower with Henry Jessey. There was also a Brownist church on the south side of the river in Deadman's Place, Southwark, from 1640 onwards. At the house of Richard Sturges in Deadman's Place in 1641 65 Brownists were arrested. By the end of 1641 there were separatist congregations (Brownist or Anabaptist) springing up on all sides, often led by maverick individuals such as Vincent the Cobbler who in 1641 was preaching 'Brownistical opinions' at St George the Martyr in Southwark without the authorisation of the rector. Parliament stopped them being arrested.

Thus the Jessey Church played a major role in the resistance to Charles I's attempt to rule without Parliament and it discredited Laud, the Archbishop upon whom Charles so much relied. Murray Tolmie wrote of Laud: 'Reviewing his career while sitting in the Tower awaiting trial ... Archbishop Laud was inclined to blame the "Brownists" as the chief cause of his downfall.' Decisive, he thought, was the Brownist organisation of support for Bastwick, Burton and Prynne, which had rendered him odious throughout England.[1] Laud was executed on Tower Hill in January 1645.

Scottish Covenanters

While Jessey was away in Wales helping Wroth, a crisis was building in London. Given the previous narrative, it might have been expected that a revolution against Charles I might have broken out in the East Midlands, in East Anglia or in London, but instead it broke out in Scotland. The reason for this is to be found in the nature of Archbishop Laud's enterprise. Backed by Charles, he wanted to impose uniformity of worship throughout the kingdom in accordance with the Arminian emphasis on state control and in accordance with Charles' inclination to move in the direction of Catholicism. Laud's policy, however, proved counter-productive. The puritans, who posed no real threat as they were not separatists, Laud drove out of the church and now, similarly, his uniformity stirred up a hornet's nest in Scotland where they had their own Presbyterian church government.

In 1638 the opponents of Charles in Scotland subscribed to a manifesto that denounced Catholicism (which they thought Charles wanted to impose) and vowed to defend 'true' Christianity. Their manifesto was a 'National Covenant' and its supporters were called the 'covenanters'. When Charles despatched an army against them in 1640 it was defeated and to obtain more funds he had to recall Parliament in London. The MPs, hostile after eleven years of not being consulted, refused to grant him the war chest. When Charles tried to dissolve Parliament, the MPs refused to be dissolved. The outcome of this confrontation was a revolution. Charles withdrew from London in 1642 and raised his standard in Nottingham, thus beginning the Civil War. More men died in the English Civil War, as a proportion of the British adult population, than were killed during the World War of 1914-18.

The City

For Parliament the key to success in their contest with the king was backing from the City of London. Later, the City was to cut back on its support, when the revolution became too radical for its tastes, but in the early years it was a leading force because it wanted to break the dominance of the court and the state church in favour of Parliament. Through Parliament would come the free trade and free enterprise many in the City hoped for. As Asa Briggs wrote: 'It was unquestionably of crucial importance to the success of the Parliamentary cause ... that rich London was behind it from the start and remained so.'[2]

Initially, in 1640 there was ambiguity on the part of the City. Robert Ashton has written that at one time historians took the straightforward view that the City represented Big Business and naturally resented the restrictions imposed by Crown and Church. However, Valerie Pearl, pointing to the apparent royalism of the City in 1640, in 1961 advanced the thesis that the City of London tended to be on the royalist side as it was closely bound by the king's grant of monopolies and patents. Ashton, after analysing the whole history of the relations between the Crown and the City, arrived at the conclusion that support for the Crown ebbed and flowed. If the City felt confidence in the king then they could be royalist but when the chips were down, this was not what they felt about Charles I.[3] In the City elections of December 1641 the City's Common Council was captured by radicals. From then on, the City was solidly on the side of Parliament.

The situation in 1642, on the brink of a devastating civil war, was therefore one in which the Brownists and the City merchants were on the same side. This reconstituted the alliance that had led to the *Mayflower* expedition in 1620-23. Both dissidents and traders were exasperated by the restrictions on freedom imposed by the court, the church and the monopolies (unless they had secured a patent themselves). There was a good example of this during the 'December Days' of

1641 when Parliament's Grand Remonstrance was being printed and tumultuous crowds assembled at Westminster in support of the radicals in the House of Commons. Who was organising these massive demonstrations? Two Common Councilmen from the City. They had contrived the demonstrations, canvassing from door to door to call out City apprentices, according to City accounts. Yet Charles had been informed by his advisers that the demonstrators were a 'multitude of Brownists, Anabaptists and other sectaries', he said.[4] Who was telling the truth? It would surely be surprising if Jessey's Brownists had not played a prominent role since they had been organising mass lobbies since 1637. The answer seems to be that many of the City apprentices were Brownists or Brownist sympathisers and the City Councilmen were adept at 'contriving' them onto the streets.

With the MPs and the City both giving discreet encouragement (Brownists arrested being swiftly released) it is little wonder that in the 1640s gathered churches consisting largely of Brownists and other separatists spread rapidly across maritime London, wherever merchants were clustered. Already by 1642 at least seven separatist churches had appeared. The ones that were definitely Brownist comprised Jessey's one in the Liberty of the Tower, the one led by Praise-God Barbone in Fleet St, and one at the house of John Sturges in Deadman's Place, Southwark. The other four are unclear and may well have been Anabaptist: the one led by John Dart in Southwark; one led by Thomas Lambe in Whitechapel; one led by John Spilsbury in Ratcliffe; and another in Goat Alley, off Whitecross Street in the City.

Lambe's Church and the Pamphlet Explosion

The most famous, or notorious, in the early 1640s was the gathered church founded by Thomas Lambe and his wife, Dorcas, in Whitechapel. He was a soap-boiler from Colchester, a stronghold of Brownism. From Colchester the Childleys and Duppa had come, as did Menasseh Kempton, who sailed to New Plymouth on the *Anne*, and John Crackstone, who sailed as a passenger on the *Mayflower*. Mary Sherley, wife of James Sherley, the great benefactor of New Plymouth, was also from Colchester. Thomas and Dorcas arrived in London in 1639. He and Dorcas had been excommunicated in Colchester for refusing to have their baby baptised in the parish church and in 1637 he had been denounced by an informer for 'boyling of sope on a Sunday'. Now, in 1641, he organised a gathered church in the parish of Whitechapel, where Elizabeth and Stephen Hopkins of the *Mayflower* had lived. It was duly raided and about 60 church members were arrested. Nonetheless, later in the same year he organised a church in Bell Alley, off Coleman Street, in the City and this became the largest and greatest of the gathered churches. It boasted the most famous woman preacher in London, Mrs Attwood.

In 1646, in his book, *Gangraena*, Thomas Edwards, self-appointed scourge of all separatism (the 'gangrene'), whether Brownist or Anabaptist, assessed this popular church. He discovered that Lambe's church in the City was attended, by 'young youths and wenches'; it was debating 'theological' questions that should be reserved for ministers; it allowed 'mechanicks', and even women, to speak; and sometimes, he alleged, decisions were taken by a vote. He felt the entire social order was in mortal danger.

The Brownist press also played a significant role in the revolution, passing on *Mayflower* values. In 1642 they had the same publisher as in the *Mayflower* days, John Bellamy. A hostile pamphleteer described his shop in Cornhill as the 'Brownists Nest wither all the Brethren flutter'. He had dropped out of Brownist membership in 1626 because after Jacob died he felt the church was reverting from semi-separatist to strict separatism, but he still published Brownist pamphlets.

In 1642 Bellamy was elected a Common Councilman and served on one committee that was organising the fortification of the City against the advance of the royal army, and on another organising the suppression of 'scandalous' pamphlets and books. For the latter committee Bellamy was clearly the man best qualified for the job, but he was faced by a huge task. The number of pamphlets published in London rose from 22 in 1640 to 1,966 in 1642. All over London people were reading. Christopher Hill wrote about those years: 'Broadsides were read in taverns even to the illiterate ... all sorts of heresies were spread abroad – Socinianism, the Koran, free love, polygamy, divorce, the perfectibility of man.'[5]

Two pamphlets by a Brownist woman, published in 1642 and 1644, seem to be mildly critical of Jessey. Sara Jones, arrested in 1632 and 1634, was the daughter of a liveryman in the Drapers Company, an Alderman and a former Mayor of London. She seems to agree with Bellamy that Jacob's position has been diluted and there is no longer a positive effort by the Brownists to win over Anglicans. She mentions some 'sermon-gadding' but wants Brownists to do more than that and reach out to Anglicans who are true Christians. She says Anglicans should be allowed to take the covenant and yet stay in the Church of England. Stephen Wright suggested Jones was being critical of Jessey's tolerance of Anabaptists and Seekers.[6] He was perhaps edging closer to the ultra-radicals and she was firing some warning-shots.

The Returners

All this turmoil, even before the civil war broke out, attracted much interest in New England, especially when the Scottish army defeated the royal army at Newcastle in 1640 and the king's chief minister, Strafford, was impeached for high treason by the Long Parliament. 1640 was a historic watershed for New England. Investors and prospective emigrants lost their interest in America as events in London absorbed all attention. In 1620-40 thousands had migrated to New England and few came back. In 1637 so many emigrants crossed the Atlantic that Dod even worried that none of the godly would be left in Britain. Now history reversed itself. In 1640-60 more people left New England each year than came back. In the 1640s it has been estimated that a quarter of the population of New England returned home, either to fight against the King for Parliament or to utilise the freedoms which the revolution had opened up.

There were more mundane reasons for the Great Remigration. As the Laud loyalists were removed from their posts in the church those returning home, who perhaps had been driven out of their livings, could hope to be vicars and rectors again; similarly, as the royal monopolies and trade restrictions were dismantled, New England merchants could hope for business opportunities.

The majority who returned in the 1640s probably returned not for military but for commercial, religious and political reasons. The most famous *Mayflower* returner was Edward Winslow, a former Governor of Plymouth. He did not intend to stay when he arrived in London in 1646 but became caught up in the politics and never returned. Others returned because they were being persecuted by the puritans in Massachusetts Bay.

What did it feel like to go and come back? There is not much documentation of the phenomenon, especially as before the period of the revolution writing tended to be impersonal. However, Susan Hardmore Moore in her *Pilgrims: New World Settlers and the Call of Home* (2007) gives a striking example.

It so happens that in 1673 *The Legacy of a Dying Mother to her Mourning Children*, the deathbed reflections of Susanna Bell was printed, written down by someone unknown, probably at Susanna's home in Seething Lane in the City of London. Susanna was born in Bury St Edmund, Suffolk, in 1604. It was her husband, Thomas, who wanted to emigrate, it seems for a mixture of financial and religious reasons. These two motives were not discrete. Religion and commerce were interconnected. Merchants felt they were held back by the ungodly hierarchy running the church and ungodly monopolists running the economy. In a godly place the godly would prosper.

When Thomas suggested they emigrate to New England Susanna objected: 'I and my friends were very averse unto it. I, having one child, and being big with another, thought it to be very difficult to cross the seas with two small children.' Her reasoning seemed sound but then her baby unexpectedly died. Distraught, she prayed to God and 'begged earnestly of him, to know why he took away my child, and it was given to me, that it was because I would not go to New England.'[7] They sailed for New England in 1634.

Susanna and Thomas settled in Roxbury, near Boston, a town with a typical 'gathered church'. The covenant administered by the church restricted its membership to those who could show that God had truly entered their heart. Tom was accepted but she was not. In Roxbury every settler had to attend a Sunday sermon but only those of 'proven' spiritual enlightenment could become church members and receive communion. It was not until 1636 that Susanna was admitted as a church member.

Thomas prospered as a merchant in just the trades that New England had been set up for. He exported fish, moose skins and timber for masts while importing canvas, cotton, hats, shoes, soap and lead shot. It was the typical trade of a developing country, exchanging natural resources for manufactured goods. His sound reasons for emigrating had been validated. He could now trade, and worship, as he wished.

In the summer of 1642, after the revolution but before the Civil War, Thomas joined a stream of settlers sailing home. For him, it seems, his reasons for leaving had been removed. England was being liberated. Susanna seems to have been more cautious (again). She and the children did not accompany Thomas back to London until 1647 – after Laud had been executed and the king defeated. They settled in Seething Lane (in the parish of St Hallows Barking) where one of their neighbours was the diarist, Samuel Pepys.

To fight, one had to return. Officially, New England stayed neutral during the Civil War, out of fear of spreading the Civil War to America. If New England backed Parliament then royalist, Anglican Virginia would back the king and they would have to fight each other. Anyone who wanted to engage in the conflict therefore had to return. New England was united in its support for Parliament. Naturally Plymouth and its offshoots, with their *Mayflower* and Brownist roots, supported Parliament and the City, but Massachusetts Bay was just as strongly in support. Winthrop rejoiced at the news of every victory by the forces of Parliament.

As a rule, it was individual young men who decided to take a boat to England in order to fight but in 1643 a merchant called Stoughton returned from a trip to London intent on mass recruitment. He took back many volunteers from Boston and in the summer of 1644 they all enlisted in a new regiment of foot raised by Thomas Rainsborough.[8] The hundreds of New Englanders who now joined the New Model Army created by Fairfax played a significant role in the victory of

Parliament in the Civil War simply because every man in New England, if only for hunting, knew how to handle a gun. This is how Isaack de Rasieres, who visited Plymouth in 1627, described church on Sunday: 'They assemble by beat of drum, each with his musket or firelock, in front of the captain's door; they have their cloaks on, and place themselves in order, three abreast, and are led by a sergeant without beat of drum. Behind comes the governor, in a long robe; beside him on the right hand, comes the preacher with his cloak on, and on the left hand, the captain with his side-arms and cloak on, and with a small cane in his hand; and so they march in good order, and each sets his arms down near him.'[9] During the early years of Plymouth Colony, failing to bring your gun to church was an offence for which you could be fined 12 pence. A surprise attack by the French or Spanish, or by pirates, was always possible.

In 1649 Parliament, after the execution of King Charles, declared England a 'Commonwealth'. When a Commonwealth navy was established, to replace the one run by royalists, around 30 New England men became naval officers. Unlike the Boston men recruited by Stoughton those in the navy tended to be of more radical views. The man put in charge of Britain's naval finances was a New Englander, Richard Hutchinson (the brother-in-law of Anne) who had returned to England around the time of her murder in 1643. His boss in the navy was Sir Henry Vane, ex-Governor of Massachusetts and a sympathiser of Anne. Richard Hutchinson had links with the Brownist church in Stepney, as did Edward Witheridge, a merchant-mariner from Boston who attended at Stepney and joined the Commonwealth navy. It shows what an important role New Englanders played in Cromwell's navy that when in late 1652 the navy appointed three new Commissioners, all of them were New England men.

Decline of Plymouth

One of the reasons for leaving Plymouth Colony and heading for London was economic decline and, Bradford noted, the decay of the *Mayflower* values brought over by the Pilgrims. In London, by contrast, the Jessey church was riding high and the idea of separatism seemed triumphant, with Brownist, Baptist and other separatist churches sprouting up on every side. It was not just *Mayflower* people but *Mayflower* values that were returning to London.

Already before the 1640s Plymouth's economy was being outstripped by its puritan rivals in Massachusetts Bay. Boston had a far better harbour and was better situated than Plymouth, 1640 was a year of economic slowdown and Plymouth's cattle trade with Massachusetts Bay suddenly collapsed.

William Bradford lamented the spiritual and moral decline in Plymouth Colony in the 1640s. As the Pilgrim 'Old Comers' died out or returned to England the spiritual force of the original covenant (that 'sacred Bond', he called it) began to decay. It became less important to the new generation. In 1642 there was an outbreak of inexplicable 'wickedness' he recalled: unprecedented levels of drunkenness, fornication, adultery and buggery. There was even bestiality: a youth allegedly had sex with a mare, a cow, two goats, five sheep, two calves and a turkey. He was executed, in accordance with the laws of Moses. But the worst blow was the death of William Brewster in 1644, in some ways the founder of Plymouth Colony. A man of rich experience, he lived in London and Holland before Bradford and many others were born and was a driving force behind what became the *Mayflower* expedition. Bradford said his moving sermons and prayers used to rip the hearts of the congregation.

As Plymouth declined, Massachusetts Bay became not just economically but also politically dominant. It was bad news. In 1641 Massachusetts became the first English colony to pass laws legalising slavery and these laws were applied to Plymouth and Connecticut in 1643 with the creation of the alliance known as the 'United Colonies of New England'. As the puritan intolerance spread to Plymouth there was a reaction. In 1645 the majority in Plymouth church drew up a petition for the Massachusetts Bay General Court to grant 'full and free tolerance of religion to all men that will keep the civil peace, with no exception for Turk, Jew, Papist, Arian, Socinian, Nicolaitan, Familist'. The three leaders of Plymouth – Bradford, Prence and Winslow – begged that the motion not be put to the vote. Bradford says this was because they feared political repercussions, but certainly Edward Winslow and Prence, perhaps Bradford too, were against general toleration. Nonetheless, though the vote was not taken, the incident showed that the *Mayflower* values of the Pilgrims were still alive in Plymouth Colony. The vote was not taken because the majority favoured toleration.

Winslow

It was Winslow who led the way in adopting a hardline position that would have been anathema to Jacob and Robinson. He had been drifting closer to the Massachusetts position ever since the Pequot War and had become a personal friend of Winthrop. He had even tweaked the historical record and claimed (pointing to the 'semi-separatism' adopted in 1616) that Robinson had ceased to be a separatist. This was despite the fact that Robinson had in one of his last letters made it abundantly clear he was just as separatist as before, whatever his willingness to engage with Anglicans in a friendly way. Winslow, rather disingenuously, cited as evidence that Robinson was not a separatist the fact that he had allowed into Plymouth Colony members of the Dutch Reformed Church (Godbert Godbertson and Moses Simonson) and that he also permitted Huguenots to take communion in Plymouth (Samuel Terry, Hester Mahieu Cooke and Philip Delanoy). Winslow would have known that Robinson was making the point that Huguenots and the Dutch Reformed Church were acceptable to the Pilgrims (with minor differences) but the Anglican Church was not.

So opposed was Winslow to toleration that he even considered moving to Massachusetts if the Plymouth Court (as their assembly was called) permitted it.[10] Winslow opposed any extension of democracy to non-freemen since, if non-freemen had the vote, they would vote for toleration. There was a logic behind his position. If there were toleration, then Catholics and Anglicans (neither of whom believed in toleration) might flock to Plymouth and radical puritans such as he and Winthrop might find themselves whipped, mutilated, even hanged. They had the memory of Lyford in their minds.

Winslow also indulged the position of Massachusetts Bay on slavery and its hard line against the Indians. This was not the same man who wrote *Good Newes*. His son, Josiah Winslow, followed in his father's footsteps. When Governor in 1676, Josiah approved the sale of 110 defeated Indians to be shipped abroad as slaves. He had the head of 'King Philip', the defeated Indian leader, displayed on a pike at Plymouth Colony for many years. This was not at all comparable to what Myles Standish had done in 1623, which was a raid in support of friendly Indians against hostile ones, and yet John Robinson had even disapproved of that.

Rebecca Fraser has suggested that perhaps Winslow was seduced by the intellectual sophistication in Boston, where Cotton was one of the foremost puritan intellectuals, respected on both sides of the Atlantic. It was perhaps more that the puritans' intellectual horizon was narrow compared to the rich culture the Pilgrims had absorbed in tolerant Holland. Through Ainsworth they had absorbed the Hebrew theology of Maimonides; Robinson had debated not only Anglicanism with Jacob but Mennonite Anabaptism with Twisck; Brewster in the 1580s had mixed in the humanist circle around Sidney; and though William Bradford was self-taught he regularly cited not only the Bible but pagan authors such as Pliny, Plato and Marcus Aurelius. The Pilgrims had a more tolerant breadth of view. Willison warned readers not to confuse the *Mayflower* Pilgrims with Winthrop's puritans: 'The Pilgrims were far less strait-laced and sanctimonious. There was a humanity in them that the puritans lacked. The Plymouth Colony did not follow the Bay Colony in executing "witches", hanging Quakers, or passing laws against "gay apparel".[11]

Response in London

The response in London to New England was mixed. New Englanders were proving invaluable in the New Model Army, many of them giving outstanding service and becoming officers. They had a commitment others lacked. For puritans fighting on the side of Parliament New England was an inspiration. Winthrop had demonstrated the huge benefits to be gained by overthrowing the hierarchy of bishops, running a decentralised church, and keeping their own laws outside the king's reach. In 1645 Hugh Peter from New England, the agent of Massachusetts Bay in London, told Parliament: 'I have lived in a country where in seven years I never saw a beggar, nor heard an oath, nor looked upon a drunkard.'[12] He argued that London's poor could benefit from New England's full employment.

It was only on matters of liberty that New England fell short. So harassed was Roger Williams in 1643 that he travelled to London to obtain a charter that would protect Rhode Island from the encroachments of its more authoritarian neighbours – Massachusetts, Connecticut and New Haven. Though hounded out of Massachusetts and cold-shouldered in Plymouth, he found in London that his patent was granted by Parliament without much trouble.

In his *The Bloudy Tenent of Persecution* (which MPs in London were not so happy with) Williams took aim at both Winthrop and Laud: 'God requireth not an uniformity of religion to be enacted and enforced in any civil state; which enforced uniformity (sooner or later) is the greatest occasion of civil war, ravishing of conscience, persecution of Christ Jesus in his servants...' In his reply in 1647 Cotton expressed a fear that England's puritan revolution over in London was in danger of becoming democratic. He reminded London that monarchy and aristocracy were ordained by Scripture, but as for democracy, 'If the people be governors who shall be governed?'[13] Significantly, it was Sabine Staresmore, the former negotiator for the Pilgrims, who now stepped forward and defended Williams against Cotton. For him it was clear, even if it was now less clear in declining Plymouth, that the *Mayflower* values of 1620 were not represented by Cotton and Winthrop. Some were pleased by the intolerance of New England. Thomas Edwards wrote in 1647: 'In New-England they will not suffer Brownists, Anabaptists, Antinomians. Mr Cotton, the greatest divine in New-England, and a precious man, is against tolerations.'[14]

There were some in New England who resisted Cotton. In 1645 Nehemiah Bourne in Boston petitioned the General Court to repeal the law banishing Anabaptists but this was rejected. He argued that the law was offending the godly in England and some churches in England were refusing communion to New Englanders. He was almost certainly referring to the Jessey church in London. It was in that year that Jessey and other Brownists had accepted baptism (though not in place of the covenant for the admission of members) as events brought the two separatist traditions into closer alliance.

Stephen Winthrop agreed with Bourne. He was worried that New England's intolerance would deter further emigration to Boston. Many Londoners were criticising New England for its severe laws against the Anabaptists: 'It doth discourage any people from coming to us for fear they should be banished if they dissent from us in opinion.' George Downing, Winthrop's nephew, was much more forthright, writing to his revered uncle that New England's 'law of banishment for conscience ... makes us stink everywhere'.

As Tinniswood wrote: 'No one wanted to admit it. Not to themselves, and certainly not to the formidable Governor Winthrop. But for men in search of liberty, old England offered more.'[15]

The Quakers

More damage to the reputation of New England was yet to come. In 1652 a new force appeared on the scene in the north of England: the Quakers, a sect that drew on Brownist separatism, Anabaptism and Antinomianism. In 1656 two Quaker missionaries, Anne Austin and Mary Fisher, arrived in Boston. They were imprisoned on arrival, quarantined and then deported. Undeterred, the Quakers kept going back, despite prison and repeated whippings. Anne Hutchinson's younger sister, Katherine, protested in 1658 against the ill-treatment of the Quakers. She paid the same price. She was stripped to the waist and publicly whipped ('ten red stripes').

In 1659-61 four Quakers were hanged in Boston. They included Mary Dyer, a follower of Anne Hutchinson. Dyer said the puritans of New England were behaving worse than had the bishops of Old England. The puritan name, she said, stank 'all over the world because of cruelty'.[16] For her 'in and about Boston [was] the bitterest and darkest professing place.'[17]

The Quakers had become the natural successors to the Brownists. Their beliefs were the logical extension of Robinson's 'progressive revelation'. They followed the spirit within them and not just the literal text of the Bible, so they searched for, and expected, 'more truth'. As every individual had access within themselves to the words of Christ this led Quakers to support freedom and equality. From the beginning they were internationalist and supportive of women.

They were also, like the Brownists, a closed group of believers, not some 'national church' with a membership open to everyone who attended. This picked membership made the Quakers, as it once had the Brownists, formidable opponents.

In Plymouth Colony, though not Plymouth itself, the *Mayflower* values of civil toleration still held up. The majority disapproved of Quaker theology but did not support persecution. Barnstable, Duxbury, Rhode Island and Scituate all tolerated Quakers. Plymouth did fine and imprison Quakers, though without executing any. Timothy Hatherley, from the Brownist stronghold of Southwark and, with Sherley, the financial saviour of the Pilgrims in the 1620s, refused to accept this and resigned from the Plymouth Colony Court rather than be party to any persecution, even if only fines and imprisonment.

Hatherley was joined in his protest by James Cudworth and several others. Cudworth was a Fellow of Emmanuel College, Cambridge, who in 1611 had married at St Mary Newington (then in Newington Butts on the periphery of Southwark) a Mary Machell, former nurse to Prince Henry, and probably the granddaughter of John Machell, a clothier, and Sheriff of London. Cudworth had emigrated to New England in 1634 and settled in Scituate, founded by Hatherley. In 1634 they had welcomed the arrival in Scituate of John Lothrop, the Pastor of Southwark's Brownist Church, who had been forced to emigrate with some of his flock for fear of further imprisonment. In 1635 a covenant for the church in Scituate had been agreed and Lothrop had become its minister. Since then Scituate had led the way in Brownist toleration.

In 1657 Cudworth, alone of all the New England Commissioners, refused to sign a letter to Rhode Island demanding they suppress Quakers. In 1658 he wrote a letter to London detailing the harsh and, he thought, illegal measures being taken against Quakers and other opponents of the puritan majority. He wrote that 'the Antichristian persecuting spirit is very active ... he that will not whip and slash, banish and persecute men that differ in matters of Religion, must not sit on the Bench...' He had been deprived of his captaincy, he told London, because he had entertained 'some Quakers at my house'.[18]

In 1660 Cudworth was actually disenfranchised from Plymouth Colony. Isaac Robinson, son of Pastor John, was also stripped of his citizenship when he declined to become a persecutor of Quakers. Nonetheless, the letters from Cudworth and Hatherley to London did have a belated effect. In 1661 Charles II stopped the execution of any more Quakers in New England. The historical irony was profound. New England, once the land of liberty, was now not only less liberal than London but less liberal than the king.

Bradford

It would have been interesting to know how William Bradford would have dealt with the Quaker crisis, but he died in 1656. Re-elected Governor of Plymouth Colony 30 times, Bradford was a pragmatist who had gone along with the downward trend. His genius was to keep Plymouth Colony united. Since 1620, even 1616, the Pilgrims had been playing down their radical roots. Bradford's own unpublished history, *On Plimmoth Plantation*, had avoided explicit mention of Brownism (he says 'the cause') or of executions and martyrs. This was understandable. At first, they had needed the king's blessing to emigrate; then the patent of the Virginia Company; and then the goodwill of the City investors. Bradford began writing his history in 1630 and perhaps from the start, given his unifying impulses, his intention had been to write a history acceptable to the puritan settlers as much as to the Brownists. In the 1640s he had still felt unable to take a vote if it might offend the rich merchants of Boston.

Nonetheless, in 1646 he was ecstatic on hearing the news that in London the Anglican hierarchy of bishops had been removed. In 1645 Archbishop Laud had been executed. His beheading on Tower Hill had taken place after a trial 'in which the prosecuting attorney, his old adversary William Prynne, would employ evidence from the prelate's diary, including accounts of erotic dreams involving the Duke of Buckingham, to devastating effect'.[19] That led the way to the removal of all the bishops. Bradford saw it as victory for the movement that had started in the late 16th century by 'ye little handful amongst the rest, the least amongst the thousands of Israel'. As Peter Westbrook wrote: 'The puritan Revolution was a culmination, he correctly thought, of the movements in whose beginnings he had had a role, however humble and obscure.'[20]

Winthrop, Cotton and Winslow had the same ecstatic reaction but then there opened up a difference between their approach and his. This arose because a Scottish Presbyterian, Robert Baillie of Glasgow, tried to demonstrate that Independency, or the 'New England Way', which was now emerging as the victor in the Civil War, was but a branch of Brownism, and Brownism was but a branch of Anabaptism. Baillie explained that this disease, Brownism, had been transferred to New England by John Robinson but it had now returned to infect Old England. Cotton indignantly rushed to defend Massachusetts and in 1648 published his response in *The Way of Congregational Churches Cleared*. Cotton denied outright any link between puritans in Massachusetts and separatists such as Browne, Barrowe, Robinson and Plymouth Colony. The 'New England Way', was inspired not by

Robinson but by godly divines such as William Ames, Paul Baynes and Robert Parker.[21]

Bradford knew that what Cotton wrote, though it might be true for Boston, was not true for Plymouth Colony, which was where New England had begun. The *Mayflower* expedition, without which the Great Migration of 1630 would have been impossible, had come from the Brownists and the London merchants. It was not acceptable that his own mentors, Brewster and Robinson, should be characterised in discussion as a 'disease'.

Bradford's philosophy, it appears from his writings, was not to offend anybody and so 'study unity, not division' (Robinson's advice, though in fact Robinson was not afraid to offend if it was really necessary). Bradford's solution in this case, as he was still Governor, was to pass on to the younger generation in Plymouth the truth about what happened. He organised a dialogue with 'Som Younge men' in 1648 and repeated it in 1652. He told them the true pedigree of the Plymouth Colony, and therefore of New England. He explained that Johnson, Ainsworth and Robinson were indebted to Barrowe, Greenwood and Penry. Nobody, he claimed, was indebted to Browne (an 'apostate' like Judas), because separatist ideas did not actually start with Browne but rather with the earlier 'Separated Church whereof mr fitts was Pastour'; and before him, 'in the time of Queen Mary', Mr Rough and Cuthbert Simson. Bradford could not resist telling his young listeners that behind Fitz, Rough and Simson stood the real founders of separatism: the separatist Moses, the separatist Prophets and the separatist Jesus. All of them had broken away from the established church of their day.[22]

It is not clear what Bradford thought would happen to his esoteric information. Did he just hope it would be handed down through the generations? In his final years he seems depressed, perhaps at the thought that the old ideals of the *Mayflower* had ebbed away and, since *On Plimmoth Plantation* did not tell the whole truth, the truth would die with him. The problem for him was that even in the late 1640s 'Brownist' was still a term of abuse. In the late 1640s Cotton would not even accept the description 'Independents', which smacked of separatism, but used the term, 'congregationalists'. To the end Bradford was always constrained by his official position in the state: he remained as Governor until his death in 1656 and never published anything.

The Levellers

By the late 1640s New England had ceased to be a source of inspiration for radical ideas but in London the struggle for liberty continued to flourish and indeed became more radical. In 1647 the 'Levellers' produced their proposed 'Agreement of the People'. They called for: peace, an end to the Civil War; freedom of religion; tolerance; an extension of the vote, and equality under the law. These topics were discussed at the famous Putney Debates by officers of the New Model Army, including Cromwell.

The Levellers, like the Quakers, were also a successor-group to Brownist and Anabaptist separatism. They rejected the name of 'Leveller', a term invented by their enemies, and just as the Brownists had called themselves 'so-called Brownists', and the Quakers 'so-called' Quakers, so John Lilburne, a leading light of the Levellers, felt obliged to say: 'Levellers so-called'. The Levellers wanted not to make everybody the same, as their enemies implied by the nickname, but to assert the 'natural rights' of all: religious toleration, equality under the law, and extension of the vote from the very few to all adult male property holders.

Although they usually came from separatist backgrounds, whether Brownist or Anabaptist, the Levellers did not present their arguments in religious terms. They took up the Brownist argument that separatism was not just separation from the church but also separation of church from state. If church questions were to be debated in religious terms, it followed that state questions should be debated in secular, rationalistic terms. This use of 'reason' had first been evident in Henry Jacob's *Humble Supplication for Toleration and Liberty* in 1609, but now a limited toleration had been achieved it made practical sense to use secular language for secular matters. Religious language divided an audience with varied religious beliefs, but secular language did not.

Even so, the Levellers had an uphill struggle for their 'natural rights'. In 1648, Lilburne wrote, the debate in London was between Parliament and the Army, but also, within those institutions, between Levellers, Independents and Presbyterians.[23] The Levellers feared the Presbyterians, strong in Scotland and well supported in England, might be just as oppressive as the Anglicans, and they feared the 'Independents' (as the radical puritans in the army were called) might be just as tyrannical as the king. The Levellers believed they were the moderates in this situation and they published a newspaper called *The Moderate*. They said putting the king on trial was illegal and so was any purging of MPs from Parliament, let alone any dissolution of Parliament. In calling for free trade and an end to monopolies, they said they were only following majority opinion in the City of London.

In 1648, as the political situation grew more and more polarised, the Levellers became more and more isolated. Lilburne described in *Legal Fundamental Liberties* (1649) how he and other Levellers had arranged a meeting with some Independents at the Nag's Head

Tavern by Blackwell Hall (the hall of the cloth merchants, right next to the Guildhall): 'They plainly told us the chief things first to be done by the Army was first to cut off the king's head, etc, and force and thoroughly purge, if not dissolve, the Parliament. All of which we were all against...'[24]

The Levellers had their own taverns. The royalist newsletter in 1647 reported that the Leveller junta of Tobias Box (army agitator), John Lilburne (veteran protestor) and 'Southwarkian Rabbi Overton' met their followers in the 'two Houses of the Leveller Parliament' – the Windmill and Whalebone taverns in Lothbury (close to the Guildhall and Coleman Street).

The Levellers occupied this 'moderate' position just as the Brownists had been the moderates between the puritans and the Anabaptists. John Rees, historian of the Levellers, says it is possible to see a direct line of descent from the Brownist gathered churches to the Levellers even in organisation: 'Some church-learnt methods of association were transferred into political life.'[25] The Leveller, William Walwyn, silk merchant and doctor, author of the *Power of Love* (1643) and *The Compassionate Samaritan* (1644) praised the contribution made by the Brownists and Anabaptists to rational discourse. Walwyn said they were the only ones attached to reason and tolerance and it was only through these that England would resolve its problems. He was impressed that Brownists and Anabaptists were 'mild discoursers' and 'rationall examiners of those things they hold for truth' and are 'every one able to give an account of their tenets (not relying upon their Pastors as most men in our congregations doe).' If anyone doubts this, he says, they should simply attend any Anabaptist or Brownist meeting, 'which are open to all-comers'.[26]

Walwyn placed his finger on a characteristic of the Brownists dating back to the manifesto of 1596 by Ainsworth and Johnson; the debate between Jacob and Johnson in 1599; between Robinson and Jacob (with Ames and Parker) in 1610, and the debate between Robinson and the Anabaptist, Peter Twisck, in 1618, after which Robinson seems finally to have fully accepted the idea of general toleration. From the beginning Robinson was broad-minded: during the dispute in 1610 at Leiden University between Episcopius (Arminian) and Polyander (Gomarist) the students of one refused to attend the lectures of the other, but Robinson attended the lectures of both professors.[27] It is true that Barrowe, Greenwood and Penry had an uncompromising and confrontational style but once in Holland, under the influence of Dutch culture, the Brownists adopted the more civilised approach that Walwyn admired.

Richard Baxter, the puritan army chaplain, also testified to the influence of the Brownists on the Levellers and other radical groups.

He recalled how he was astonished to discover that the army was full of Independents, Anabaptists, Antinomians and Arminians, with representatives even in the highest ranks. These radicals 'most honoured the Brownists, Anabaptists and Antinomians. But Cromwell and his Council took on them to join to no party, but to be for the liberty of all.' Baxter said the majority of the soldiers followed Cromwell's line. They were 'for liberty of conscience, as they called it' and the leaders of these radicals 'were men that had been in London, hatched up among the old Brownists'.[28]

Southwark and Coleman Street

As well as drawing upon Brownist and Anabaptist ideas, the Levellers had the same geographical base as the Brownists: amongst the mariners in Stepney; in City areas such as Coleman Street and, most consistently, in Southwark. Nick Bunker refers to their 'semi-secret congregation based in Southwark, south of the Thames, a twilight place where people did unofficial things'.[29] Mary and Richard Overton had a Leveller printing-press in Southwark, for which they were arrested and imprisoned. It was in Southwark that the Leveller leaders, Lilburne and Walwyn, were parliamentary candidates. This was no accident. It so happened that the parliamentary franchise for the borough of Southwark was vested in its householders, giving Southwark one of the most democratic electorates in England. Pointing to this, the Levellers demanded extending the same Southwark franchise to all householders throughout Britain. Thus the model for democracy and freedom, in the 19th century accepted by the whole country, was based on practice in Southwark, which in the early 17th century was the centre in London of the Brownist church.

In the late 1640s the main centre for the Levellers was Coleman Street, just east of the Guildhall and just west of the Dutch Church in Austin Friars; in fact, the radical movement in the City was more and more concentrated in that area. That is the area where the Leveller and Independent taverns were. At one stage the Brownists were meeting in Swan Alley, off Coleman Street and the Anabaptist, Lambe, had his church in Bell Alley, also off the street. There were two reasons why Coleman Street was such a den of radicals. Firstly, the church of St Stephen Coleman had a history of radical ministers since it was one of only a few parishes in London with the right to elect its own minister. Secondly, Coleman Street was where the returners from New England tended to live. Many had emigrated to New England from there in 1633 when the minister of St Stephen Coleman, John

Davenport, had emigrated. In addition, several friends of Winthrop lived there, such as Nathaniel Barnardiston.

In 1646-47, when Edwards published his *Gangraena*, an 800-page attack on the Independents from a Presbyterian point of view, he identified Coleman Street, Southwark, Stepney and Whitechapel as the most subversive districts in the London area, but it was Coleman Street he identified as the worst, infested as it was with the pernicious doctrine of toleration. His text was not strong on the rational arguments that the Brownists and the Levellers promoted, but he was strong on allegations of Anabaptist ministers fondling comely maidens, and he mixed this with social snobbery, revealing that most of the 'sectaries' were just uneducated shoemakers, milliners and soap-boilers. Edwards believed toleration was a laxity that would lead to social breakdown. If ideas of free thought took hold in the country, he warned, men would not be able to control their wives. He traced the history of pernicious toleration to various churches in the City of London but in particular 'back to Coleman St Ward and the former New Englanders who had gathered there'.[30]

Katherine Chidley

Edwards was particularly irate with a Brownist woman in Coleman Street who in 1641 had answered an attack he made on the separatist churches. Katherine Chidley's rejoinder was called *The Justification of the Independent Churches*. She criticised him again in her pamphlet, *New Year's Gift* (1645), a defence of toleration. She had joined Jacob's church in the 1620s over a feminist issue, not baptism but the practice of 'churching', the ceremony wherein a blessing is given to mothers after recovery from childbirth, which she regarded as a financial ploy by the clergy at women's expense. She and Daniel therefore refused to attend church, which was illegal.

In the 1630s the Chidleys had been members of Duppa's church and had lived in Southwark St Saviour briefly before moving to Coleman Street. Thomas Edwards in *Gangraena* described Katherine as a 'brasen-faced audacious old woman resembled unto Jael'. Jael, a feminist icon, hammered a tent peg through the head of an enemy general while he was asleep. It is interesting that Edwards described her as a 'Brownist' in 1646 after she and Jessey had accepted baptism in 1645. This shows it was clear to everyone at the time that Jessey was still a Brownist, though personally accepting baptism.

Chidley's writings were in the Brownist tradition.[31] She included Jews and Anabaptists in the toleration that she demanded. It was also typical of the Brownist movement that she organised demonstrations and petitions. In 1649 Katherine organised a protest by 'some hundreds of women' against the imprisonment of John Lilburne. When sent away from Parliament without a reply to their requests they kept going back day after day, even when the guards drew pistols. In the end the sergeant of the House of Commons was instructed to deliver a message to the women from the House as follows: 'That the matter they petitioned about was of an higher concernment than they understood; that the house gave an answer to their husbands, and therefore desired them to go home, and look after their own business, and meddle with their housewifery.'

This provoked Katherine and the other women (including Elizabeth Lilburne) to draw up a *Humble Petition of divers well-affected women of the Cities of London and Westminster*. It is a historic feminist document that pointed out that women were creations of God as well as men and in any case: 'Have we not an equal interest with the men of this Nation, in those liberties and securities contained in the Petition of Right, and the other good laws of the land?' In 1653 Lilburne was on trial again and so Katherine organised another mass petition, which attracted the signatures this time of over 6000 women, not just hundreds. On reaching Parliament they were told that the MPs could not possibly receive their petition, 'they being women, and many of them wives'.

Robert Baillie paid a huge compliment to the Brownists and the Anabaptists (the two now being called 'Independents' rather than 'separatists') when he wrote his *Dissuasive from the errors of the time* (1645). He reported that 'of late' the Independents in London have allowed women to preach to their congregations and 'none of the Independents neither in New England or Holland, neither the Brownists of Amsterdam, did ever give unto any woman any public Ecclesiastick power. In this our London Independents exceed all their Brethren...'

Toleration Act

In 1649 a 'Commonwealth' was declared and Britain went into a republican period where Parliament, and then Cromwell, ruled without a king. It was in this period that the old 'sectaries' – Anabaptists, Brownists and smaller sects – faded away to be replaced in the 1660s by the 'Nonconformist' churches that were to play such a large part in British history until the 20th century. Of the main Nonconformist churches, the Presbyterians kept the same name, the Quakers were brand new, the 'Anabaptists' became 'Baptists', New England became 'Congregationalist' (from 1648) and the old Brownists were dispersed amongst the other four. The official turning-point was the Toleration Act of 1650. This repealed the recusancy laws of Elizabeth I which had criminalised 'recusants' who did not attend their parish church. The Act thereby ended the obligation to conform to the state church and instead merely obliged citizens to worship God each week in some place. This was what the Brownists had been asking for since Robert Browne. Their pioneering demand had been the right to form churches separate from the state church – this was now a reality and all the other churches were for ever in their debt. The Brownists had won. It was now time for the name of 'Brownist' to disappear from history. They had outlived their historical usefulness. As ever, extinction is the price of success.

Jessey and Judaism

Jessey's Brownist church had begun to converge with the Baptists, as they were so close politically, in the early 1640s, and in 1645 Jessey himself was baptised by the Baptist minister, Hanserd Knollys. This did not mean Jessey became a Baptist. John Smyth had said in 1609 that baptism should replace the covenant but Jessey did not say that: he left baptism, infant or adult, open to personal choice and the covenant stayed. Jessey remained a Brownist into the 1650s because the covenant was a condition of membership but baptism was not. Llanvaches and Thomas Ewins in Bristol followed his lead. Jessey himself continued much as before. He conducted the services at St George the Martyr on Sunday morning and then in the afternoon was Teacher at one City church and preacher at another. As the Brownists did not approve of tithes, three jobs were needed to provide a reasonable income.

From around 1644 Jessey became very interested in gaining readmission to England for the Jews. The Brownists had always been close to the Sephardi Jews in Amsterdam, using the same accommodation and learning from each other in debate. Jessey always carried a Hebrew Bible with him. The events of 1642 had led to the liberation of all the persecuted religious groups except for two: the Catholics and the Jews. It was politically impossible to tolerate Catholics – Catholic Spain was still feared as a military threat – but Jessey and the Brownists felt that now was the time to readmit the Jews, who had been banned from England since 1290.

There had been an appeal to readmit the Jews in a book, *Religious Peace*, published in 1614 by Leonard Busher, a Londoner in Delft who knew John Robinson and perhaps Thomas Helwys. His book was an appeal for general toleration and was dedicated to James I, who had told Parliament that year: 'No state can evidence that any religion or heresy was ever extirpated by the sword or by violence.'

At around the same time John Traske was calling for readmission of the Jews not so much for toleration in general but because he admired and imitated the Jews. He was not only a 'philosemite' but a 'Judaiser'. His aim was to bring about convergence between Christianity and Judaism. When the Court of the Star Chamber found he was following certain practices in the Old Testament, they punished Traske by having him whipped, with a letter 'J' branded on his forehead and his ears nailed to the pillory. Later, he became a Brownist. The problem with the Judaisers, as far as the authorities were concerned, was that they did not want to convert Jews to Christianity but hoped for a merger between the two religions. Hamlet Jackson, another Judaiser, ended up as a converted Jew in Amsterdam.

Jessey loved Hebrew, admired the Old Testament, as all Brownists did, and was 'philo-semitic' like his contacts, John Dury and Nathaniel Holmes. All three lobbied for readmission of the Jews to England. John Dury, from Edinburgh, was one of the great intellectuals of the day. He was brought up in Leiden and attended Leiden University when Robinson was there. Like Jacob and Robinson, he was intent on uniting all Protestants and Jews. He campaigned for a College of Jewish Studies and corresponded with Menasseh ben Israel, whom he met as early as 1644. That was the year when interest in readmitting the Jews began to grow in London, and in 1646 Busher was reprinted. The revolution of 1642 had changed the atmosphere in Britain and tolerance was on the agenda, to the disgust of Thomas Edwards, who wrote an attack on Busher's book.

Adler says Jessey was a millenarian and believed the Second Coming was imminent. The Messiah would soon appear and initiate 1000 years of peace and happiness. He therefore observed the Sabbath on a Saturday, as well as on a Sunday, hoping for the reconciliation of the Jews and Christians rather than one simply converting the other. For this he was nicknamed 'Jessey the Jew'.[32] In correspondence with Menasseh, he found Menasseh also argued for Jewish-Christian rapprochement rather than one converting the other. That is why Jessey says to the Jews in his *The Glory and Salvation*: 'If I found more truth on your side than on that of the Christians, all advantages, all honour, and all riches in the world would not prevent me from embracing your truth.'[33]

The parents of Menasseh ben Israel had fled from the Spanish Inquisition to Madeira and then to Holland. A boy prodigy, he wrote his first book at the age of 17 and later in life had his portrait painted by Rembrandt. Like Jessey, he also believed the coming of the Messiah was imminent and that this would trigger a thousand years of peace. Yet there was a very important difference. Whereas Jessey believed that when the Jews arrived in England there would be a reconciliation of some sort that would trigger the return of the Messiah, Menasseh believed that the Messiah would come when Jews were dispersed all over the world. He believed that, as it was established that the American Indians were the lost tribe of Israel, England was now the only country in the world where Jews needed to go for the fulfilment of the prophecy. Once the Jews were established in England, the Messiah would appear.

The first petition for readmission was submitted in January 1649 to Thomas Fairfax's Council of War by Joanna and Ebenezer Cartwright, two English Baptists living in Amsterdam. It included a plea that Jews also be helped to return to the Holy Land. In 1650 Menasseh wrote *Hope of Israel* (in Dutch and Latin), saying Jews would not be redeemed until they were 'spread out to the ends of the earth' and in 1651 he met English diplomats in Amsterdam who urged him to apply to the British government for readmission. After *Hope of Israel* was published in English in 1652 the Council of State issued a passport to Menasseh allowing him to enter England legally and in 1653, when Samuel, Menasseh's son, visited England, accompanied by merchant, David Dormido, serious discussion of readmission began. This was a historic turning-point. In London there were about 20 Marrano families (Jews who feigned conversion to Christianity) but, apart from such anomalies, no Jewish community had lived in England for 363 years.

Before Menasseh's *Hope of Israel* appeared Jessey had published *Glory and Salvation of Jehudah and Israel* (1650), dedicated to the Sephardi Jews of Amsterdam in general and to Menasseh ben Israel in particular, and aimed at securing reconciliation between Christians and Jews. It considered the conversion of the Jews to Christianity in this sense: he argued the imminent Messiah expected by the Jews would be Jesus Christ and he tried to prove that from the Jewish scriptures. The point was that whoever the Messiah was, it was the same Messiah coming to both communities. It is sometimes asked why, if Traske, Jessey and Dury wanted a merger of Judaism and Christianity, they nonetheless used the word, 'conversion'. The answer is that it was often a token to appease church censorship. The Virginia Company had done the same. They always included 'conversion of the Indians' in their pamphlets, to ensure publication, but made no attempt to convert any Indians.

The Whitehall Conference

In 1655 Menasseh ben Israel came to London for a conference at Whitehall organised by Oliver Cromwell and backed by Henry Jessey, the Brownists, some Baptists, the Quakers and various philo-semitic intellectuals such as John Dury. Jessey seems to have stage-managed events in London after the arrival of Menasseh; he was one of the organisers of the conference itself.[34] It is to Jessey that historians are indebted for the conference report.[35] He met with opposition straight away, first of all in the shape of an anti-semitic pamphlet from William Prynne, hero of the resistance to Charles I, for whom Jessey and the Brownists had campaigned, at the risk of imprisonment or worse, back in 1637. Cromwell could not understand how dissidents such as Prynne who had for decades suffered from intolerance themselves could now be intolerant towards others. He had asked that year: 'Is it ingenuous to ask liberty, and not to give it? What greater hypocrisy than for those who were oppressed by the bishops to become the greatest oppressors themselves as soon as their yoke was removed?'[36] For Jessey a man like Cromwell was easy to access. Cromwell had Brownists around him and, writes Bunker, he 'was more or less a Brownist himself'.[37]

The Whitehall conference met in December and the arguments in favour of readmission, marshalled by Jessey and his supporters, were as follows. It was first of all pointed out that Jews were now in dire straits in Poland, Lithuania and Russia. Jews were starving in Jerusalem, despite attempts to get aid through. It was the duty of Christians to help those in distress. (As Jessey was at this time fund-raising for the impoverished Ashkenazi Jews of Jerusalem, this was no doubt a point on which he was able to supply details.)

In France, Spain and the West Indies, the conference was told, Jews had to wear a badge which exposed them to mockery and violence. In scripture God was always displeased by anybody being unkind to Jews, even when he was displeased with them himself. The persecution and execution of Jews in Catholic countries should remind us of what had happened in England under Queen Mary. England and the Jews also had something in common. God had elevated the Jews to be a Special People and in the last century, as was well known, God had elevated England to the same status.

The above can be taken to have been Jessey's arguments. Some at the conference wanted readmission so Jews could be converted to Christianity. Others argued that Jews would benefit the national economy by reducing prices of imports. Cromwell avoided the vested interests and argued for the readmission of Jews on scriptural grounds, and he had lawyers there who backed readmission on legal grounds.

Nonetheless, despite all these arguments for readmission, both the clergy present and the merchants were opposed, and they formed the majority. The merchants strongly opposed readmission because they feared Jewish trading would have an adverse impact on them. Many of the churchmen said they favoured readmission in principle but set stiff conditions impractical to meet. Cromwell's view that Jews should be readmitted without restriction was a small minority. Near the end, Cromwell decided to stop the conference to prevent a negative vote. Menasseh was disappointed, for it seemed that of those in power in London 'only Cromwell himself appears to have favoured immigration for the Jews.'[38]

As there had been no vote against, but matters had been left in limbo, the supporters of the Jews now lobbied for their cause. A letter was circulated from John Dury in Cassell, Germany, to Samuel Hartlib in London, entitled 'Whether it be lawful to admit Jews into a Christian Commonwealth?' and dated 8 January 1656. It said all the Calvinist states admit Jews but not all the Lutheran. In Germany most Protestant states admitted Jews, 'but they mark them out so as to make them contemptible.' Dury said the main argument for readmission should be Christian compassion: the Jews are 'banished from the country of their inheritance, and made pilgrims and wanderers through the world; a people in misery and distress, and so an object of hospitality...' We Gentiles also owe them a debt: the oracles of God were conveyed through them to us. These are the true reasons for admission, Dury says, not reasons of trade or to convert them to Christianity. It should be made clear to the Jews 'that it is not for any profit, which they can bring to the state, that they are admitted; but for a desire in us, for doing them good...'

Margaret Fell of the Quakers had a different angle. Quakers wanted to win over the Jews but not to Christianity, rather to a common mysticism found in Judaism (for example, in Maimonides) as much as in Christianity. This would probably have been the position of Ainsworth. She published her *A Loving Salutation to the Seed of Abraham among the Jews* in Aldersgate, London, in February 1656 and it was translated first into Dutch and then into Hebrew, probably by Spinoza, a Quaker sympathiser.

Sally Bruyneel wrote that at the time it was widely believed that, as England was the first truly Christian nation on earth, the Messiah would return within England's shores. Fell believed the Messiah, in the shape of the Inner Light, had already returned. She felt: 'Christ had already returned in the Spirit to the hearts and minds of his true followers...' The Amsterdam Jews said they had nothing against anything in her pamphlet, except that Margaret Fell believed the Messiah had recently arrived, whereas they believed he was yet to come. The Quaker, Richard Hubberthorne, thought there was a mystical connection between Jews and Quakers and Quakers should become 'true Jews', or at least 'inward Jews'. In the late 1650s the Quaker, Samuel Fisher, lived in Holland as a Jewish Quaker, attending synagogue.

After all this, Cromwell was left with the problem of what to do next. Tolmie has written that Cromwell was a man of 'unusually broad sympathies'.[39] For example, he backed the performance in 1656 of the first English opera, *The Siege of Rhodes* by William Davenant, a Royalist and a Catholic whom Milton had helped get released from the Tower. It was performed in Rutland House, Aldersgate St, London. Theatres and plays had been banned by the puritans mainly because they were bawdy and connected with the court, but they did love music – especially Cromwell, who arranged musical concerts in the Cockpit at Whitehall and had a small orchestra at his daughter's wedding to accompany the dancing.

The Whitehall Conference did achieve one thing: it noted that 'there is no law that forbids the Jews return into England.'[40] This enabled Cromwell to achieve readmission though the judiciary, to whom he made his views clear. Later in 1656 war broke out with Spain and Antonio Robles from Spain declared himself a Jew, not a Spanish Catholic, in order to avoid being classified as an enemy alien. He was not penalised and a precedent was established. In 1657 Solomon Domido, nephew of Menasseh ben Israel, was admitted to the Royal Exchange without having to take the Christian oath. Cromwell had achieved the de facto readmission of the Jews.

By December 1656 Jews had acquired a house in Creechurch Lane, which became their synagogue until the great Bevis Marks synagogue was built. In January 1657 the first services began, which was a very historic moment given that Jews had been banned from the country for 366 years. So as to help Menasseh with expenses in London Cromwell had granted him a state pension of £100 per year, but in November 1657 Menasseh died in Holland. It was in Middelburg, appropriately enough, the early haven of the Brownists.

The readmission of the Jews was not quite Jessey's last achievement. In 1657-58 he raised further funds (£300) for the Ashkenazi Jews in Jerusalem. After that, with Cromwell's death, he had little scope for action and in 1661-62, once the monarchy was restored, he was ejected from his ministry at St George the Martyr church in Southwark and imprisoned for pamphlets judged to be anti-government in tone. When he died in 1663 his body lay 'in state' at Woodmongers Hall in Duke's Place, in the heart of the Jewish community, just a few paces from the Cree Church Lane synagogue and a few hundred yards from what is now the Bevis Marks synagogue. Such was the veneration for his name that the funeral was attended by nearly 5000 people. David Katz wrote that Henry Jessey was among Israel's greatest 17th-century benefactors, 'a powerful advocate of Jewish readmission.'[41] He was also the last, but not the least, of the Brownist leaders and a fit representative of the Pilgrim tradition, since the Jews, as Dury had pointed out, were 'pilgrims and wanderers' too.

The Brownists, whose first church in London was in 1592, had now reached the end of the road. They had helped initiate the revolution on the streets of London with their fasts, lobbies and petitions; they had brought down Laud and with him the whole hierarchy of bishops; they had served with returners from New England in Cromwell's New Model Army; they had been pioneers and fore-runners of the separated churches known as the Congregationalists, the Baptists and now the Quakers. They had helped bring about, with others, the Toleration Act of 1650; and now they had with Menasseh and Cromwell secured the historic return of the Jews to England. Their Brownist ancestors in London, Amsterdam and Leiden, especially the Hebrew scholar, Ainsworth, would have been well satisfied with the fruits of their labours.

The Restoration

In September 1658 Cromwell died and the Commonwealth crumbled into dust. It turned out that he had been the only thing holding it together. After negotiations with Charles Stuart, son of Charles I, it was decided that the monarchy, on certain conditions, would be restored. Charles set out from Scheveningen in Holland and entered London on 29 May 1660. It now looked as if all the achievements of the 1642 Revolution might be dismantled.

As part of the agreement in Holland Charles granted an amnesty to nearly all the Commonwealth's supporters, but there were 49 designated 'regicides' who were specifically excluded. A Fifth Monarchist leader, Thomas Harrison, considered very dangerous, was the first regicide to die and he received a 'traditional' execution. He was 'half-hung', then he was 'drawn and quartered' while still conscious (he 'saw his bowels thrown into the fire').[42] Others were simply beheaded, and the majority were either given life imprisonment or banned from holding office ever again. The corpses of Oliver Cromwell and Henry Ireton were granted the distinction of 'posthumous executions': they were disinterred, hung up and decapitated, with their heads stuck on spikes.

Of those with New England connections, Hugh Peter, a prominent returner, had his head cut off and held up aloft on a spear to the cheers of the crowd. Henry Vane, a former Governor of Massachusetts and a giant in the history of parliamentary sovereignty, was not condemned as a regicide, but was instead executed for treason. Three of the regicides fled in time to New England and were warmly welcomed in Boston by Governor John

Endecott, who protected them from arrest when royal warrants arrived. The London government tried, but was never able to find them in the vast spaces of New England.

The former Brownist ministers were by now mostly dispersed amongst the Baptists, Congregationalists and Quakers. They were punished by ejection from their livings. Henry Jessey was ejected as minister of St George the Martyr but continued as a preacher at St Hallows the Great. After being three times arrested (he wrote pamphlets, it was alleged, with an anti-government tenor) he died in 1663. In 1661, while Jessey was in prison, an anti-semitic pamphlet appeared asking for the Jews to be expelled once more.

Not all the opponents of the Restoration walked quietly into oblivion. In 1661 armed men appeared on the streets and swiftly took possession of St Paul's churchyard. It was the Fifth Monarchists from Coleman Street, the 'headquarters of the revolution', where the New England returners had held sway during the heady days of the 1640s. Their millenarian leader, Thomas Venner, was a returner from Massachusetts Bay, opposed to the slave trade and to the undemocratic rule of Cromwell, who had testified in court to the inspiration he had received in New England.

Venner now conducted a bloody rearguard action starting in St Paul's and retreating yard by yard back to Coleman Street. His band numbered only about 50 men and they were heavily outnumbered by the soldiers pouring into the City, but his rebels comprised New Englanders and veterans of Cromwell's New Model Army, professional soldiers determined to make their heroic last stand in Coleman Street, the 'impregnable fortress of the revolution'. Venner was wounded 17 times before anyone could capture him. He and twelve others were executed, and their heads displayed on London Bridge.[43] In their manifesto, *A Door of Hope*, which they had scattered around the streets of the City, the Fifth Monarchists explained that they were bringing 'true reformation out of the American Wilderness in order to emancipate the world'.[44]

1637 The Brownist (Jessey) Church

There is no certainty about actual membership of the church (by covenant) for those listed below and some who were definitely members may have been members only for a short time. There are no records. In the case of those who accepted adult baptism in the course of the 1640s, some (like Jessey himself) did so as a personal choice and did not regard baptism as a replacement for the covenant. Others took the view that their baptism made them Baptists and ended their Brownist membership. It is usually impossible to distinguish between these two groups. Murray Tolmie has used circumstantial evidence to recognise Brownist members and that is all that can be done in many cases. The dates refer to mention of the entry's name in lists of Brownists.

Allen, William	Brownist then Anabaptist.
Barbone, Praise-God	1632-49. Had gathered church in Fleet St.
Barrett, George	Teacher, 1653.
Batty, William	1634 to Gatehouse. 1638 joined Spilsbury.
Blaiklock, Samuel	1641-42 Teacher. Council of New Model Army.
Chidley, Daniel	1626 recusant. 1632 bd son, Daniel, at St Botolph Aldgate. 1632 Freeman of Haberdasher Co. 1639 bd son, Daniel, Southwark St Saviour. 1646 still described as a Brownist. 1649 A Master of the Haberdasher Company.
Chidley, Katherine	Wife of Daniel. *c.*1620 refused 'churching'. 1641 published *Justification of the Independent Churches.* 1645 *A New Year's Gift.* In 1645 she accepted baptism, like Jessey, but in 1646 still described as a Brownist. 1649 and 1653 organised protests in defence of John Lilburne, the Leveller who became a Quaker.
Chidley, Samuel	Son. Treasurer for the Levellers.
Chillenden, Edward	Brownist, then Anabaptist.
Chitwood, Mrs	1639
Cradock, Walter	1638. In 1639 with Jessey and Wroth founded the Llanvaches church in Wales.
Dart, John	Had gathered church in Southwark either Brownist or Anabaptist.
Denne, Henry	Brownist, Anabaptist, Leveller.
Dry, Sister	1637
Eames, Samuel	1641-42.
Fenner, John	1636. 1638 to Gatehouse for separatism. 1639 to Amsterdam.
Glover, Mr	1637, 1641.
Gun, Thomas	1640-41 of Southwark. 1643-44, 1646.

Highland, Samuel	1640s said to be Pastor of Brownist church in Southwark. 1654 Fifth Monarchist in Southwark.
How, Samuel	1632-41 of Southwark.
Jessey, Henry	1601 b West Rowton, Yorkshire. 1618-24 St John's, Cambridge. 1624-33 in Suffolk. 1626 MA at Cambridge. 1627 Ordained. 1633 To Aughton, Yorkshire. 1634 deprived of living in Aughton. 1635 moved to London with Boynton. 1636 moved to Hedgley House, Uxbridge. 1637 wanted to emigrate to New England but became Pastor of Lothrop's church instead. 1638 arrested in raid by the Bishop's 'pursuants'. 1639 helped found Llanvaches Independent church, Wales. *c.*1640 in Tower Liberty. 1640 imprisoned in Tower of London. 1645 bp by Knollys. 1650 His *The Glory of Iehudah and Israel*. 1650s minister at St George the Martyr, Southwark; Teacher in Coleman Street; preacher at All Hallows the Great. 1658 raised funds for Jews in Jerusalem. 1660 arrested. 1663 funeral attended by nearly 5000, bd Bethlem, Bishopsgate.
Jones, Sarah	1632 arrested. 1640 arrested at Tower Hill. 1642 *The Relation of a Gentlewoman.* 1644 *To Sions Virgins.* In the 1650s seems to have become a Quaker.
Kiffen, William	1633. 1641 arrested in Southwark and imprisoned in White Lion. 1644 'Anabaptist'. Freeman of Leathersellers Co. Rich merchant and leading Baptist.
Knollys, Hanserd	1641 member of Jacob-Jessey church. 1643, 1644: Anabaptist.
Lambe, Dorcas	Wife of Thomas.
Lambe, Thomas	From Colchester, a Brownist centre. *c.*1640 led gathered church in Whitechapel, London. As a Baptist led famous gathered church in Bell Alley, off Coleman Street. A Leveller.
Larner, William	Printer, Brownist and Leveller.
Lovell, Mrs	1638

Manning, Edward	1637
Manning, Judith	1641-42.
Norwood, Mrs	1638 joined Spilsbury.
Overton, Henry	Bookseller in Pope's Head Alley. In Jessey's church. Leveller.
Overton, Mary	Wife of Richard. A Leveller.
Overton, Richard	Not known definitely whether he started a Brownist like Henry, but close. Member of Lambe's church. A Leveller.
Patience, Thomas	1643-44.
Pawle, Anne	1640
Penn, Henry	1638
Pickering, William	1632. George Fox's 'Uncle Pickering'?
Price, Mary	1635
Russell, William	1638 of Candlewick St.
Sheppard, Thomas	1633, 1635, *c*.1639. Leather-dresser of Southwark St Olave. 1642 was bp.
Smith, R	1637
Snow, William	1636 Gatehouse prison. Of Southwark.
Spencer, John	1639 of Crutched Friars.
Staresmore, Sabine	Seems to have joined, or been close to, the Jessey Church after emigration of the Duppa Church.
Sturges, Richard	Had house in Deadman's Place in Bankside, Southwark, which was raided in 1641.
Teballs, Thomas	1640 weaver in Bernondsey.
Tolderoy, Jone	*c*.1641, 1655.
Vincent the Cobbler	1641 preached 'Brownistical opinions' at St George the Martyr.
Webb, John	1641 arrested in Southwark. 1646 atheist.
'Widow White'	1633
Wilson, Susan	1632, 1640. All Hallows Barking.
Wilson, Thomas	1632, *c*.1633. 1638 joined Spilsbury.
Wroth, William	1639 with Jessey and Cradock founded the Llanvaches church in Wales, opening up Wales to Brownist separatism.

9

The *Mayflower* Vindicated

At first sight it must have looked as if the restoration of the monarchy in 1660 would mean the defeat of Parliament, whatever promises were made by King Charles. Defeat for Parliament would surely mean an end to the aspirations that lay behind the *Mayflower* expedition: toleration in religion, free trade and Parliamentary supremacy in politics. These were the aims of the Edwin Sandys group in the 1620s. In fact, appearances, often deceptive, were especially deceptive in this case. The king and the Church were both indeed restored to their previous status, but without their previous power. It turned out that the power in the land after 1660 belonged to the more rational religionists, the merchants in the City of London, and their representatives in the Westminster Parliament.

In April 1660 Charles had actually set out the profile of this new order in the Declaration of Breda, an agreement he had made in the Netherlands before returning to London. He would rule with leniency and tolerance; there would be liberty of conscience; and Anglican church policy would not be harsh. He would not exile past enemies or confiscate their wealth. For all his opponents there would be pardons, except for those designated 'regicides'. Above all, Charles promised to rule in co-operation with Parliament. As Hill wrote:

> In 1660 the old order had not been restored: neither prerogative courts nor the Court of Wards nor feudal tenures. Royal interference in economic affairs did not return ... by the end of the century industrial freedom had been won, monopolies had been overthrown, government interference with the market, including the labour market, had ended.[1]

This promising start to the new reign was promptly derailed, though not by Charles. The problem was the new Parliament, which contained so many Royalists – some bent on revenge – it was known as the 'Cavalier Parliament'. More royalist than royalty and more vindictive than the king, this Parliament insisted on a system of discrimination and persecution against the dissenters. In 1661 a Corporation Act excluded dissenters from participation in local government. In 1662 an Act of Uniformity ejected from their livings some 2000 clergy who dissented from a revised Anglican prayer book. Those who would not conform were now called 'Nonconformists' (a term that replaced 'dissenters'). In 1664 a Conventicle Act forbade all unofficial religious meetings ('conventicles') of more than five people. In 1665 a Five Mile Act forbade dissenting ministers from travelling within five miles of their former places of ministry and it also forbade them to teach in schools. These four Acts became known as the 'Clarendon Code' since they were introduced, very reluctantly, by the king's first minister, the Earl of Clarendon. The king and Clarendon were both nervous. Charles II wanted peaceful moderation and an enjoyable life with his mistresses. This was not how Breda had intended things to be.

Parliament's policy seemed at first like a repeat of Whitgift and Laud – but this was deceptive too. No wave of executions and banishments emerged from new laws. Nonconformists could not hold office or assemble for open worship, but that had not been allowed by the Dutch to Brownists in Leiden. Locally, Parliament found there was no effective way of enforcing church attendance. The poorest had probably never attended and after 1660 general defiance by the middle-class sects meant attendance became unenforceable. Nobody in authority locally wanted a return to the persecutions of Laud or the violence of the Civil War. In practice, though organised furtively, gathered churches did exist: 'In place of a single state church based on compulsory geographical communities of families – parishes – we get religious toleration – membership of congregations by individuals who chose them.'[2] There was nothing much the Cavalier Parliament could do. It was not possible in practice to reverse toleration. Even under Charles II the Brownist separatists had substantially won, and the *Mayflower* passengers would have felt justified by history. It was the same with freedom of the press. That too in its essentials proved irreversible, even though initially under Charles II it was severely restricted.

As the Marquis of Halifax wrote: 'The liberty of the late times gave men so much light, and diffused it so universally among the people, that they are not now to be dealt with as they might have been in an age of less inquiry.'[3] Adam and Eve had once again eaten the fruit from the tree of knowledge and there was no way the Cavalier Parliament could put the fruit back on the tree.

Society had changed in a fundamental way and there was nothing the MPs or the king could do about it. The balance of power had shifted since 1642. The City of London merchants, ever increasing their economic power because of the long-term boom in London since the 1550s, now exercised preponderant financial influence, and they had no interest in persecutions. As there was no Church High Commission any longer to impose the censures of the church, and none of the other prerogative courts had been restored, the legislation of Parliament was now dependent on the judgement of the common-law courts. In all urban areas, not just the City, the magistrates and constables were from the trading or merchant class and they were reluctant to persecute. Burning people in the High Street was bad for business.

It was the same with trade itself. The medley of adventurers who despatched the *Mayflower* in 1620 were now calling the tune. After 1660 the old monopoly trading companies declined. In 1671 the Eastland Company lost its monopoly when Parliament established free trade in the Baltic. In 1689 the old Merchant Adventurers lost their monopoly and the cloth trade at last became free. This was due not just to the decline of the royal court but also to the emergence of a strong navy under Cromwell. He had made Britain a naval power on a level with the Dutch, and ships could now be protected from pirates by the British navy. The Merchant Adventurer convoys (not always effective anyway) were no longer even needed.

It slowly dawned upon the country, within Parliament and without, that what had happened in 1642-1660 may well in fundamentals be irreversible. In one way the regicides had been proved right. Once an Archbishop of Canterbury has been decapitated, followed by a king, the spell was broken for ever – no ruler would ever again feel they were appointed, or protected, by God. The old mystique was shattered. The doctrine known as the 'Divine Right of Kings' fell into the executioner's tray along with the head of Charles I.

Jews and Quakers

A good example of how difficult it was to reverse the results of the revolution is the case of the Jews. Their readmission had been supported not only by Cromwell but by Jessey's Brownists, Margaret Fell's Quakers, and by certain enlightened Anglicans and Royalists. Charles II had himself been helped in exile by Jews attached to his wife, Catherine of Braganza. Therefore, when in 1660 there immediately popped up a petition from some London merchants asking for the exclusion of the Jews all over again, Charles ignored it, and nothing happened. Again in 1673, when opponents of the Jews managed to get Jews holding a meeting in Duke's Place (haven of the Pilgrims) indicted for alleged rioting, the Privy Council intervened, stopped the proceedings and nothing further happened. There was no appetite to reopen old controversies.

The restoration was also unable to reverse the rise of the Quakers. Like the Jews, whom they strongly supported, Quakers not only survived the restoration but flourished. By 1670 there were about 50,000 Quakers, over 1% of the British population. They refused to accept any compromises but on the other hand remained pacific and industrious. The Quakers replaced the Brownists as the standard-bearers of separatism.

Recruits came to the Quakers from the old 'sectaries' (small fringe groups in the Anabaptist tradition like the Seekers) but also from former Brownists and Levellers. In 1656, not long before he died, the Leveller leader, John Lilburne, declared his adherence to Quakerism. The 'Digger', Gerard Winstanley, who believed in direct action, did likewise. On the Brownist side, the brothers of *Mayflower* passenger John Howland, Henry and Arthur, became Quakers.

Quakerism was not an easy option. Throughout the 1660s and 1670s the Quakers, as well as some other Nonconformists, were beaten up, stoned and imprisoned, as well as being discriminated against by the Clarendon Code. In some cases, in England and New England, only the intervention of Charles II saved their lives. Nonetheless, they were not driven totally underground as the Brownists were by Elizabeth, James and Charles I.

They were, however, forced to emigrate. Like their Pilgrim predecessors, the Quakers took ships to America. By the 1670s emigration to America was as huge as it was in the Great Migration of the 1630s. The worst moment for the Quakers came during the time of the 'Popish Plot', an anti-Catholic scare in 1678-81. As they believed in toleration for Catholics as well as for other faiths, the Quakers fell foul of an anti-Catholic hysteria that swept the country. That meant they were targeted not just by Anglicans but by other Nonconformists as well. The number of Quakers seeking emigration soared.

In 1681 Charles granted to the Quaker William Penn a royal charter to found 'Pennsylvania' (not, it should be said, Penn's choice of name but the king's). Like Roger Williams, Penn wanted the territory to be a refuge for persecuted people. He offered liberty of conscience to all religions and genuine trial by jury. He also offered love and friendship to the American Indians since God 'hath made us not to devalue and destroy one another, but live soberly and kindly together in the world'.[4] He promised as well that in Pennsylvania 'no law can be made, nor money raised, but by the people's consent'.

These are all *Mayflower* values and the last one, affirming government by consent, is to be found in the *Mayflower* Compact. As *Mayflower* values, they can be traced back to Henry Jacob and John Robinson (as well as to certain Anabaptists) and, specifically, Penn's 'open-door' policy recalls that of the Brownist Roger Williams in founding Providence Plantations in the 1630s.

In 1681 Penn agreed the Treaty of Shackamaxon with Tamanend, leader of the Delaware Indians. The Quaker settlers agreed to purchase Indian land. Penn told the Delaware: 'I desire to enjoy it with your consent that we may always live together as neighbours and friends.' It was the first treaty signed between Indians and a state in North America. Later, the French philosopher Voltaire, noting that the Quakers always refused to swear oaths, commented piquantly that this was the only treaty never sworn to – and never broken. For 75 years peace with the Indians was maintained in Pennsylvania, as it was in Plymouth Colony from 1620 until 1675. The Quakers became the successors of the *Mayflower* Pilgrims, carrying out the same policies of tolerance and rule by consent. Through the medium of the Quakers, Pilgrim values, which had faltered in New England, were transmitted into the 18th century and beyond.

The 1688 Revolution

In 1688 James II issued a 'Declaration of Indulgence' removing restrictions on both Catholics and Nonconformists. This offer of toleration appeared even-handed, but it was distrusted as a ruse to bring back Catholic supremacy. In June seven bishops were imprisoned in the Tower of London when they refused to have the Declaration of Indulgence read out in churches. Remembering what had happened under Mary and Charles I the bishops were not taken to prison through the crowded streets but by boat along the Thames. This did not work out. Crowds of sympathisers lined the banks of the river and cheered on the bishops from there. What a turn of events was this – Anglican bishops were now popular. They were standing up against tyranny instead of participating in it. When, at the end of June, the defiant bishops were acquitted by the Court of the King's Bench, Londoners went wild with celebration: bonfires were lit; guns were fired; and bells were rung as the crowds thronged the streets.

James had camped his army on Hounslow Heath just outside London so as to strike fear into the hearts of any Londoners who might think of opposing him but, instead. the enthusiasm of Londoners for their Anglican bishops was communicated to the troops. James had now aligned Protestant merchants, London crowds and disaffected troops. A letter was sent to William of Orange asking him to invade

England and rescue the English from their government. One of the seven signatories was Henry Compton, Bishop of London.

The Dutch Prince, William of Orange, was married to Mary Stuart, daughter of James, and was therefore legally capable of claiming the throne (just about) if it became vacant. The Dutch government favoured invasion since they could not afford to have a Catholic ally of Louis XIV of France, who was a constant threat to the Netherlands, on the English throne. They also worried, as did the seven bishops (and all the governments of Europe), that the huge crowds in London might augur another radical revolution such as the one in 1642. In this sense the 'Glorious Revolution' of 1688, which now began, was a soft, pre-emptive revolution to forestall a hard one.

On 5 November 1688, William's army landed in Torbay, Devonshire, and he began his march on London. When James II found that the City of London, as was to be expected, refused to support him but backed the revolution, he fled. This too was bungled and in Kent he was swiftly captured. William, however, 'connived' at the escape of his father-in-law to Catholic France. On 21 April 1689 William III and Mary II were crowned as king and queen.

A Victory for Toleration

From the perspective of the *Mayflower* Pilgrims the most important piece of legislation passed after the 1688 Revolution was the Toleration Act (1689). The Act gave wide-reaching toleration to Nonconformist religion. Catholics were still not tolerated but all Protestant churches were granted freedom to worship as they liked. This was the greatest achievement for the movement of which the *Mayflower* Pilgrims were the pioneers. It might be argued that founding the first permanent settlement in New England was greater but, if the Brownists had been granted toleration in 1592, then they would not have had to emigrate to Amsterdam, Leiden or New England. If the Pilgrims had been granted such toleration in Leiden, then there may never have been a *Mayflower* voyage. Toleration was what they had always wanted.

The Toleration Act was a key moment. In 1600 all English people had been deemed members of the state church, dissent was heavily punished, heretics were still burnt at the stake, and suspected traitors were tortured. After the Act of 1689, 'Protestant dissent was legally tolerated: the Church could no longer burn, the state no longer tortured.'[5] It brought to a victorious conclusion the struggle started by Fitz, Browne, Greenwood, Barrowe and Penry. As Doran and Durston say: 'With the passing of the Toleration Act of 1689, Separatism finally achieved its objective and Nonconformists were given the right to go their own way outside the established church.'[6]

John Robinson was also vindicated. Ashton wrote that the principles Robinson contended for 'had spread throughout England, and a considerable portion of America'.[7] Nor would he have been surprised by how long their victory had taken. Robinson had once reflected: 'Religion is not always sown and reaped in one age. One soweth and another reapeth.'[8] William Bradford also referred to the *Mayflower* Pilgrims as but 'stepping-stones' in history. It had taken almost a hundred years since the 1592 church had been founded and since, in Amsterdam, they had encountered Dutch toleration.

The 1688 Revolution had its own philosopher of toleration, John Locke. In 1683 he too had fled to the Netherlands and encountered Dutch toleration. He had engaged with the circle of the Spinozists (though Spinoza had died in 1677), advocates of toleration, a democratic assembly and the separation of church and state. It will be remembered that Spinoza, a rationalist who was almost an atheist (in the end expelled from the Amsterdam synagogue), had been an admirer of Margaret Fell and the Quakers and a supporter, with Jessey and Dury, of a rational convergence between Judaism and Christianity. In his *The Reasonableness of Christianity* (1695), Locke reflected this view of the world. He contended for religious toleration, for the use of reason, for a balanced constitution and for the natural rights of all.

What connected Locke, Quakers, Brownists and dissident Sephardi Jews like Spinoza? The answer was given by the Leveller and silk merchant, William Walwyn, back in the 1640s. He said, it will be remembered, that of all the religious groups the Brownists and the Anabaptists, were 'rationall examiners of those things they hold for truth'. Brownists like Jessey and Quakers like Fell opened up a route to rationalism offered by none of the other Nonconformist groups.

There was a price the Nonconformists had to pay for toleration. They were allowed their own places of worship in the towns but not allowed to attend university, hold office in government or enter the professions. And yet, in the circumstances, this was no great imposition. The freedom to worship as they pleased was all the Brownists had asked for. Discrimination in the professions had to be preferable to whipping, branding and decapitation.

One irony: it was not just Nonconformist churches that benefited from the Act. The victory of the separatist movement created the modern Anglican Church – relatively tolerant, no longer the persecuting organisation it had been under Elizabeth, James and Charles. The cheering of the bishops by the London crowds was a sight that had opened up a new era for Anglicanism.

Victory for Free Trade

As has been noted more than once, the progress toward toleration was always interwoven with progress towards free trade. At every stage the Brownists and Pilgrims received backing from merchants or trading interests in high places. It is no surprise therefore that the 1688 Revolution freed up trade.

An Act of Parliament of 1689 'permitted anyone to export cloth anywhere'.[9] Though the Act gave certain exemptions, which allowed monopoly companies to continue, it made a breach in principle, sweeping away the old privileges of the Merchant Adventurers (now operating under the name of the 'Hamburg Company'). The big exception was the East India Company, which survived the 1688 Revolution and kept its monopolistic features.

It was not just the export of cloth. As Davis says, from the 1690s on 'nearly all trade was carried on by individual merchants free of regulations, or by great joint-stock companies whose capital was gathered to meet special needs.'[10] The interloper, Thomas Weston, and his *Mayflower* clients, would have felt at home in this freer environment. By 1695 the number of joint-stock companies in England had grown from just 11 in 1689 to around 100. In 1694 the Bank of England itself was founded as a joint-stock company. At first the embryonic institution only issued bank notes and handled government loans but soon it was creating money itself above the level of its deposits. No other country had such a bank, not even Holland.

By 1700 it had become accepted that 'trade must be the principal interest of England'. By then 'industrial freedom had been won, monopolies had been overthrown, government interference with the market, including the labour market, had ended.'[11] All this flowed from the victory in the 1688 revolution of Parliament, and the commercial interests it represented, over the Crown. It was just as historic as the Act of Toleration. All the apparatus of state control had to be dismantled. As Hill says, if Stuart state control had worked, then the Industrial Revolution could never have happened.[12]

The way mercantile and commercial values always worked side by side with toleration and free speech is illustrated by the demise of censorship. Before 1688 censorship had been exercised through the Stationers' Company, acting through the Licensing Act of 1662. This Act lapsed in 1695, not in response to some liberal campaign, such as Milton's in his *Areopagitica*, but merely in a quiet response to pressure from profit-seeking printers and booksellers.[13] From 1695, instead of fearing the Stationers on the one hand and relying on aristocratic patrons on the other, writers and artists could now earn money simply by selling their own work. Authors still had to negotiate severe laws of libel but the principle of freedom was established.

Victory in New England

In 1689 John Locke's *Letter Concerning Toleration* had urged that the same freedoms be extended to American colonists. No man, he wrote, should be deprived of liberty on account of religion, 'not even Americans'. During the years since 1620 New England had forgotten the *Mayflower* values of Henry Jacob and John Robinson and become a persecuting state, and now this was put right. In 1776 it would be the other way around. The Americans would have to remind the British of the freedoms which they had forgotten.

In 1689 Massachusetts rose against the royal Governor imposed by James II and arrested him, and the other colonies followed suit. Massachusetts was expecting its old charter to be restored, but William III resisted this, since it would mean a continuation of the harsh puritan regime. After much debate in London, Massachusetts and Plymouth were combined together into one unit, the 'Province of Massachusetts Bay' (1691). Eligibility for voting was now to be decided by land ownership, not by religious criteria. This expanded the vote to three-quarters of adult males. The colony kept its elected assembly, the General Court, and it chose the Governor's Council, but the Governor appointed by London had veto powers in the last resort. The worst aspect of this from the puritans' point of view was that they had to accept freedom of worship and follow the same policy of toleration already adopted in London. The resulting settlement was very close, says MacCulloch, to 'the obstinate individualism and separatism of the Plymouth Pilgrim Fathers (an ethos which Winthrop and his covenanting congregations deplored)'.[14]

The puritans seem to have had great psychological difficulties in dealing with the 1691 settlement. They could not resist, since the majority excluded from power had probably always favoured more toleration. Now, as Quaker and other missionaries entered Boston with impunity, their power crumbled away. Scapegoats were sought. The minister in Salem Village (now called Danvers) declared that witches had appeared in the village and were spreading evil. The execution of witches began. To save themselves from execution some of the accused women denounced others as accomplices and soon there was a mass hysteria of serial denunciation, leading to the execution of 19 'witches' and the accusation of 150 more. To protest against the witch-hunt was to expose oneself to the accusation of complicity. It was 1693 before Governor Phipps took a firm line and stopped the trials. With calm restored, an investigation was launched; the trials were found retrospectively to have been unlawful, all those accused were exonerated, and in 1711 compensation was paid to their surviving heirs.

The notorious 'Salem witch trials' of 1692 were the last spasms of a puritan culture introduced by Winthrop in 1630. During the 1630s it had driven into the wilderness Anne Hutchinson and Roger Williams, and in the 1650s it had hanged Quakers, but in 1691 it had been defeated by reforms from London that had stripped away its power. Although the puritans had always been united with the Pilgrims against the common enemy of royal despotism and church 'hierarchy', and although they used a covenant like the Pilgrims and at least on paper deferred to their congregations, they had always identified with state authority and denounced separatists. They well understood that separatism by definition means toleration. Their views came from God, were correct, and it was morally wrong, they thought, to tolerate falsehood.

From the beginning their outlook seems to have been connected with disdain for women and the poor. The Salem trials seem to have been a frenzied backlash following their loss of power. From the beginning the women had borne the brunt of puritan authoritarianism, from Anne Hutchinson's all-women discussion circle to the persistent Quaker, Mary Dyer, and now had been the turn of the poor women in Salem. Of 19 hanged as witches, 14 were women and 5 were men.

There was an (almost) endearing postscript to this terrible story. In 1700 Samuel Sewall attacked slavery in *The Selling of Joseph*. It is the earliest recorded anti-slavery tract published in what is now the USA. Sewall also expressed his concern for women's rights. It transpired that his liberalism stemmed from a tormented conscience – he was a judge in the Salem witch trials.

The 1691 settlement and the infamy of the Salem witch trials vindicated the *Mayflower* Pilgrims and the Brownist church. Jeremy Bangs says there was no witchcraft hysteria or sectarian killings in New Plymouth; nor was there in Scituate, an offshoot of New Plymouth, where James Cudworth opposed the persecution of Quakers.[15] When Isaac Robinson, John's son, arrived in New England after his father's death, he also opposed the persecution of Quakers. Significantly, he moved to the more liberal towns of Scituate and Barnstable, as Plymouth lost its way. These were the towns of John Lothrop, Brownist Pastor from the Southwark Church in London, the church of Henry Jacob, Henry Jessey and Sabine Staresmore. Jacob had won over Robinson to toleration of Anglicans who were 'true Christians', Jessey had secured with Menasseh the readmission of the Jews, and Staresmore had via Naunton secured the 'connivance' of James I to the Brownist emigration. These were the real victors in the historic settlement of 1691.

The 'Glorious Revolution' (a term already used by John Hampden in 1689) brought vindication and posthumous victory to the *Mayflower* Pilgrims. A few, however, were still alive. In fact, Richard More, last surviving male passenger, did not die until *c*.1695 and Mary Allerton, the last surviving passenger of all, lived until 1699. Appropriately enough, the news of the 'Glorious Revolution' was brought to New Plymouth by John Winslow, son of John Winslow Sr and Mary (Chilton) Winslow, both passengers on the *Mayflower*.

Although Richard was the only one of the tragic More children to survive the first winter in New Plymouth, not enough is known to ascertain whether he ever found his mother, Katherine More, or his father, Jacob Blakeway. He did return to London as a sailor and in 1645 he married, bigamously it seems, at St Dunstan, Stepney ('church of the sailors'). Later he was criticised in New England for 'licentiousness' and in 1688 censured by Salem magistrates, at the age of 74, for his 'gross unchastity'.

Mary Allerton, who had sailed on the Mayflower at the age of three or four, died as Mary Cushman after marrying Thomas Cushman, son of Robert. She lived uneventfully, it appears, blessed by at least 50 grandchildren. Richard and Mary are healthy reminders that many *Mayflower* passengers lived what George Eliot called 'unhistoric lives'.

London Vindication

In 1688-92 the *Mayflower*, the City adventurers and the Brownist separatist movement received their first vindication. Later, they were also to be hailed in America for their Mayflower Compact and for their infusion into American life of democratic ideals. They have a legacy in New England of monuments and memorials. What did they leave behind in London?

Most of central London has connections with the *Mayflower*. The voyage was a London expedition, with a London ship and a London crew, financed and organised in the City of London, with about 65 of the final 102 passengers recruited in London and embarked from London, that is to say, within the borders of London as it is now. It was London that was listed by the Port of London in 1620 as the home port of the *Mayflower* and the ship sailed to America from London. Southampton, Dartmouth and Plymouth were only brief stops on the way. The only place of equal importance to London in the *Mayflower* story is Leiden, and the nearby port of Delfshaven, where the *Speedwell* embarked with, according to the estimate by Banks, the remaining 37 passengers.

This does not mean that other places were unimportant. Southampton was very involved because supplies were loaded there and it was the appointed meeting-place with the Leiden Pilgrims on board the *Speedwell*. Plymouth in Devon was the last stopping-point (apart perhaps from picking up fresh water in Cornwall) before crossing the Atlantic, and the Pilgrims retained the name of Plymouth for their place of disembarkation in New England. As for the East Midlands, East Anglia and Kent, they are of great genealogical and historical interest to the *Mayflower* descendants, but they have only a slight connection with the voyage of the *Mayflower* in 1620.

The problem with London is that, due to the Great Fire of 1666 and then the bombing of London in the wars of the 20th century, few 17th-century buildings remain. Nonetheless, there are still very many sites that bear witness to the presence of the *Mayflower*, the crew, the adventurers, the passengers, and the Pilgrim Church. (There are over 60 listed in the Appendix.)

The most important area for *Mayflower* history was the City of London itself. The founding of New England by the Pilgrims was perhaps the City's greatest achievement. The adventurers who subscribed to the Virginia Company and those who financed the *Mayflower* usually belonged to one of the great City companies and their magnificent livery halls, often architectural treasures, are still open to visitors, although because of the Great Fire or bombing, they may not be in the same streets now as they were in 1620. The Drapers Hall, Fishmongers Hall, Haberdashers Hall, Ironmongers Hall (that of Thomas Weston), Mercers Hall (home to Merchant Adventurers) and Merchant Taylors Hall date back to the 17th century and are all related in some way to the story of the *Mayflower*. The companies with a particular commercial interest in the voyage of the *Mayflower* were the Fishmongers (the *Speedwell* was bought for fishing), the Skinners (specialists in furs), the Haberdashers (they sold the beaver hats) and the Feltmakers (hats). They looked to import from America large quantities of fish and fur. They must have been delighted to hear that the *Mayflower* had anchored in the area marked 'Plymouth' on John Smith's map. The rivers there were said to host beaver and Cape Cod was not called Cape Cod for nothing.

Apart from the livery halls there are several London churches with *Mayflower* links. For example, the church of St Mary le Bow has an impressive statue of John Smith outside and nearby a plaque to Milton, a champion of toleration. At St Bride's there is a bust of Virginia Dare, first British child born in America, and a reredos in honour of Edward Winslow, a Governor of Plymouth Colony, whose parents married in that church and who was an apprentice in Fleet St.

The most important church is the Dutch Church in Austin Friars. This is a beautiful modern church, but with a pillar of the original

17th-century church preserved in a planter. It has an old altar stone dating from the 13th century, and a 17th-century paten and chalice probably used by those Pilgrims who could visit London with impunity. It has an image of William the Silent, a hero to the Pilgrims, and a stained-glass window depicting William and Mary, the saviours of the Pilgrim cause. The church also owns a three-volume work signed by Thomas Weston, proving he attended in company with Dutch merchants.

A site of great historical importance is the Bevis Marks synagogue. It is on the same site as the old complex of tenements known as Heneage House. Banks said that Heneage House 'may well be designated as the only Pilgrim shrine in London', used as it was by the Southworth family, Robert Cushman, John Carver, and probably by William Bradford, William Brewster, Thomas Weston, John Greenwood, and John Penry.

Since Heneage House was amidst the Jewish area after 1656 it is also highly likely that Henry Jessey visited it when fund-raising for the Jewish community in Jerusalem. He might perhaps have been pleased to learn that the first draft of the Balfour Declaration was made in the home of Moses Gaster, Rabbi of Bevis Marks. He never saw the synagogue himself. After 1688, the Quakers, probably urged on by Margaret Fell, helped the Sephardi Jews raise money to build Bevis Marks and the synagogue was actually built by a Quaker, Joseph Aris. It is impressive, and the oldest synagogue still in use in Britain. The interior, which is very different from the Sephardi synagogue in Amsterdam on which it was alleged to have been modelled, has with its dark, high wooden seats the look of an English Nonconformist, especially Quaker, meeting-house. Jeremy Bangs suggests that perhaps the Pilgrims, as the first to have Nonconformist churches, introduced high-backed benches grouped around pulpits and the Quakers followed their lead. In that case, the Bevis Marks synagogue follows the style of the Pilgrims and is a glorious example of a Brownist meeting-house.

Across the river In South London there is the reconstructed Globe theatre of William Shakespeare, who wrote two plays that have a Mayflower connection. *Twelfth Night* has a line that refers to 'Brownist' and *The Tempest* is linked to the Bermuda shipwreck of Stephen Hopkins. Southwark Cathedral nearby unites the parishes of St Saviour and St Olave, within whose boundaries the Brownist church was very active: Roger Rippon, Henry Jacob, Robert Browne and Francis Johnson were all there.

Between the two lies the Clink Prison, in Clink Street, where so many Brownists suffered and sometimes died. It was in that prison the famous *Confession* of 1596 was co-authored by Francis Johnson and it was there that Barrowe paid a visit to Greenwood and was arrested himself. In August 1961 Donald Smith, US Consul General, unveiled a plaque of remembrance in Clink Street, whose (slightly inaccurate) inscription read:

> Fifty yards eastwards of this spot there stood the Clink Prison where in the years 1586 to 1593 JOHN GREENWOOD and HENRY BARROWE founded a church (today the Pilgrim Fathers' Memorial Church) from those imprisoned for refusal to obey the Act of Uniformity of Worship. They, with John Penry, a member of the Church, were Martyred for Religious Liberty. Francis Johnson was the first Minister. This Church helped to secure the sailing of the *Mayflower* (1620) and a number of its members were among the ship's company.

It was also in Southwark St Saviour that a permanent place of worship was found for the Pilgrim Church, in Deadman's Place, west of the Clink, and this church seems to have continued until the 1970s and even, loosely, down to the present day. A strict line of descent is not really provable as the church in Deadman's Place left no records. However, it seems indisputable that in and around the parish of Southwark St Saviour (now Southwark Cathedral) there was a strong congregationalist-baptist tradition dating back to the 17th century. The chain of descent for this church, based on the researches of John Waddington in the mid-19th century, looks like this: Roger Rippon 1592 > Henry Jacob 1616 > John Lothrop 1624 > Henry Jessey 1637 > Deadman's Place from 1640 > Union St 1788 > Buckenham Square, New Kent Rd 1864 > Great Dover St 1956 > Hampton St 1971. The last is now part of the United Reformed Church and does not claim to be a direct descendant. The Reverend Peter Stevenson, who has written the history of this church,[16] says the only link left, apart from the property held, is a congregational polity.

Waddington's findings were greeted with much enthusiasm by Samuel Morley and Thomas Binney, two of the leading anti-slavery campaigners of the day. The anti-slavery movement and those who campaigned for native Americans were champions of the *Mayflower* because the record of the Pilgrims in their treatment of both oppressed groups was superior to that of other colonists.

The anti-slavery supporters of the Pilgrims, led by Benjamin Scott, a City financier and ardent supporter of the *Mayflower* cause, fund-raised to build the successor-church to Union St, in Buckenham Square on the New Kent Road. This church continued until it was destroyed by bombing in 1940. It was replaced in 1956 by the

'Pilgrim Fathers Church' in Great Dover Street, opened by the US Ambassador, Winthrop Aldrich. The inscription on its memorial stone said:

To the memory of: Robert Browne, Francis Johnson, Henry Barrowe, John Greenwood, John Penry. The Inspirer, the First Minister and the Martyrs of the Gathered Church in Southwark 1592.' The church received greetings from both the Queen and President Eisenhower addressed to 'The Pilgrim Fathers memorial Church in London.

Eisenhower wrote on 10 October 1956: 'As co-heirs of a great tradition, this congregation has a secure place in the hearts of all who cherish the spirit of religious liberty. Long ago, when the *Mayflower* carried early pilgrims from your church to our shore, they helped to establish one of the strongest bonds which unite the people of our two Nations.' (There is a surviving silent film of this 1956 opening.)

In Rotherhithe there is St Mary's Church, where Christopher Jones is buried and where children of his were baptised. There is a monument to Jones in the churchyard and nearby an amusing statue of a *Mayflower* Pilgrim reviewing with a young boy what has happened in America since 1620. The *Mayflower* pub is not authentic but is full of *Mayflower* memorabilia and has a restaurant with a list of the Mayflower passengers on the wall.

Conclusion

Between 1620 and 1642 nearly 80,000 people left Britain, and about 58,000 of them went to North America or the Caribbean. Why were 102 passengers on the *Mayflower* remembered more than all the others?

David Hume, in his classic *History of England* (1754-62), analysed the 17th century as a struggle for freedom against royal despotism and this analysis still has the ring of truth. He also identified who won the struggle. Using the looser definition of 'puritan' (very strict Protestants), he wrote: 'So absolute indeed was the authority of the crown, that the precious spark of liberty had been kindled, and was preserved, by the puritans alone; and it was to this sect, whose principles appear so frivolous, and habits so ridiculous, that the English owe the whole freedom of their constitution.'[17]

Hume was not concerned with who exactly the 'puritans' were, but a hundred years later Benjamin Scott, a Chamberlain for the City of London (1858-92), became interested in the *Mayflower* after the publication of William Bradford's history in 1856. At that time Bradford was regarded as an English author as much as an American, and the *Mayflower* as an episode in English history as much as American. If a British soldier had brought Bradford's manuscript to London, then that was thought to be a reasonable decision.

Benjamin Scott was a highly regarded City financier who ran the new Bank of London and was able to get the City through Black Friday, the financial panic of 1866. He was also a social reformer who campaigned for state education and green open spaces. His campaign against brothels and prostitution ran aground after he found both institutions had strong support in high places. In 1866 he published *The Pilgrim Fathers neither puritans nor Persecutors* and declared in a lecture that the Pilgrims were of a 'freer, more catholic spirit' than the puritans and the freedoms they promoted led to free trade and free speech. He helped raise funds for the remains of the Pilgrim Fathers Church in Southwark and promoted 'Pilgrim' values in the City.

Scott's interpretation of the Pilgrims was taken one step further in the 1890s. Charles Firth and the very eminent historian, Samuel Gardiner, reappraised the Levellers after the discovery of the 'Putney Debates' manuscript in the library of Worcester College, Oxford. This research on the Levellers showed the links between the Levellers and the Brownist gathered churches. By the late 1930s a picture had emerged of the role played by the Brownists and the New Englanders in the English Civil War. The Brownists in London and the families of the Pilgrims in New England had united to support Parliament. Interwoven with this analysis was the work of the American, Charles Banks, who had researched the key role of London and the City in the *Mayflower* expedition. All these trends in scholarship pointed to a story of the *Mayflower* that was embedded in British history and embedded in London history. It was a story about those who had campaigned against the Stuart kings for freedoms: for freedom of trade, freedom of enterprise, freedom of worship, freedom of speech, freedom of Parliament, freedom of the press.

In America the *Mayflower* had also been given a liberal interpretation in the course of the 19th century. In 1820 American statesman Daniel Webster, well before the full publication of Bradford's history, had contrasted the attitude of the 'Forefathers' to slavery with the developments further south in Virginia. The Pilgrims were driven by 'principles of civil and religious liberty' and lived 'under a condition of comparative equality'.[18] Webster was a campaigner for the anti-slavery movement and wanted to stress that the Forefathers were exponents of liberty and did not condone slavery. French historian Alexis de Tocqueville took up the theme in his *Democracy in America* (1835). For the same reason, Abraham Lincoln in 1863 praised the Pilgrims, celebrated the voyage of the *Mayflower* and even made 'Thanksgiving' a national holiday. The *Mayflower* became an icon of freedom because, unlike later settlers, the Pilgrims had not indulged in slavery and had avoided war with the Indians. In Britain they had asked for freedom, and in America they had not encroached on the freedom of others.

The trouble was that all this lavish praise of the Pilgrims was more than their simple story could bear. Extravagant claims were made for the *Mayflower* that were hard to sustain and when in 1936 the distinguished American historian, Samuel Morison, addressed the subject he had easy targets. He felt able to pour scorn on the obvious myths that the Pilgrims were somehow precursors of independence, or the founders of democracy, or inventors of constitutional government, or the prophets of free enterprise. From there Morison moved on to destroy the 'myths' created by Benjamin Scott. He claimed the *Mayflower* was not regarded as important in its time and that historians were agreed on the insignificance of the voyage. New England was largely populated from the Colony of Massachusetts Bay and it was the Bay that forged its distinctive character; while it was in Rhode Island and Maine, not in Plymouth, that the seeds of democracy and religious liberty were planted. Scott had distorted history when he said the Pilgrims were not puritans and created the liberal 'myth' of the broad-minded Robinson and his freedom-loving followers. If the *Mayflower* had sunk in the Atlantic the history of New England would have, in its essentials, remained the same.

Morison admitted that this left him with a problem: if the *Mayflower* was so insignificant, then why had it captured the imagination of the world? He had an answer. First of all, it was William Bradford's history that had inspired so much interest, not the *Mayflower* itself. Though he was unfair and partisan, Bradford did show the perseverance and courage of the Pilgrims, fortified as they were by their Christian faith. This faith was displayed already in Leiden, said Morison, when they 'resisted the typical refugee vice of whining, railing, and complaining'. Secondly, it was because Winthrop's colonists created a God-fearing culture in New England. God approved New England, and it was God who made the *Mayflower* famous – for their impressive feats of faith and endurance during the voyage and then for the 'miracle' of their survival after landing in Plymouth. Their legacy was to inspire the whole of America with their faith in God.[19]

Although not everyone followed Morison in invoking God, his thesis that the *Mayflower* was historically insignificant became widely accepted after 1945. It became routine to debunk the 'myths' of the 'Pilgrim Fathers'. As Bangs says, by the end of the 20th century historians had judged the Pilgrims as 'small, unheroic, and pathetically insignificant'.[20] To some extent this was a class question. Willison, who had stressed that Jamestown was the first sustained settlement in America, not New Plymouth, and Massachusetts Bay the most economically successful, dismissed the Pilgrims as a group of 'simple and humble folk of plebeian origin'. Another reason was the Cold War. Neither in Britain nor in the US was it any longer attractive to have persecuted radicals ('refugees') in one's ancestry. It was worrying that the Pilgrims denounced 'the hierarchy' and in New Plymouth briefly practised (Plato's) 'communism'. The name 'Leveller' sounded rather socialist (though in fact the Levellers were fairly moderate liberals). In London no one wished to be reminded that London's greatness was built by risk-taking financiers, dubious interlopers and puritan merchants, and not by common-sense British chaps of pragmatic and sound judgement.

The distinguished Dutch historian, Schulte Nordholt, took a similar approach to Morison in a lecture delivered in 1992. Like Morison, he compared the Pilgrims in New Plymouth unfavourably with Winthrop's colony in Boston. There were settlers in North America before the Pilgrims came (Jamestown, Newfoundland fishermen, the Dutch settlers in Niuew Nederland in 1614) and Boston afterwards was far more successful than they were. That made them 'an undistinguished group'.[21] The Pilgrims were also very mediocre in their aspirations compared to Winthrop's puritans. He said: 'The puritans laid the foundation for the idealistic America, which had the pretension of a special mission for the world. The Pilgrims on the contrary wanted no more than to lead a quiet and peaceful life.' All the Pilgrims ever wanted was to go back to England and practise their religion without persecution, whereas Winthrop's puritans had a determination to be the 'city on the hill'. The puritans looked forward, in effect, but the Pilgrims 'did not want to improve the world'. Schulte Nordholt, like Morison, took care to leave the Pilgrims with a saving grace. He liked the flexibility of Robinson's belief in progressive revelation: Robinson is quoted as saying how regrettable it was that, just as Lutherans would not go beyond what Luther said, the Calvinists would not go beyond what Calvin said: 'they stick fast where he left them.'

The reason Morison, Schulte Nordholt and others took such a dismal view of the Pilgrims was partly because they failed to see them from a British and a London perspective and therefore discounted the long history of struggle from 1553 to 1688. The Brownist church first raised the separatist flag in the reign of Mary I and did not achieve final victory until the reign of Mary II.

The 'undistinguished group' were regarded as dangerous revolutionaries by Whitgift, and in London three were executed and dozens died in prison, even though they were not heretics but merely wanted a semi-democratic polity. This 'insignificant' body then produced, via Ainsworth, Jacob and Robinson, a more tolerant and open-minded version of 'puritanism' and in 1620 founded New England, thus making Winthrop's Great Migration possible. In 1650 and then in 1688 it was the more moderate Plymouth Colony line that prevailed over the 'successful' Winthrop line, which was by then thoroughly disgraced. Their Brownist movement disappeared after 1650 simply because toleration was winning, and they had outlived their historical usefulness.

It is strange to say that Brownists 'did not want to improve the world'. Rule by congregation implied democracy; separatism necessitated toleration; Browne was an educationalist and Barrowe wanted education everywhere ('in every citie'); Johnson denounced tithes, lavish retinues, absentee ministers and the churching of women; Jacob called for toleration; Robinson told the Pilgrims in Southampton to have only governors 'which your selves shall make choice of for that worke'; Bradford complained of the 'hard' exploitation in Leiden; and Jessey campaigned for the emancipation of the Jews.

The charge of insignificance, let alone that of 'undistinguished' insignificance, is an odd one. Despite Schulte Nordholt, popular admiration for the *Mayflower* continues unabated, and it is not for sufferings on the voyage or the 'miracle' of their disembarkation, as Morison believed. People know that they founded New England and opened up the coast from Boston to New York; it is known from the annual celebration of Thanksgiving that they, like John Smith before them, enjoyed friendly relations with the Indians; it is known that they left England as refugees and were harried almost into extinction in Holland; it is known they did not practise slavery; it is known that the Mayflower Compact, although not democracy, represents government by consent; and known that Bradford left an account written in gorgeous prose. For most people, that is plenty. How then can 21st-century beneficiaries of the freedoms the Pilgrims fought for justify the belittling of the Pilgrim cause? It is not as if the critics of the Pilgrims have themselves suffered imprisonment for their beliefs, built a town with their bare hands in the snow, or written on goatskin, by candlelight, a masterpiece of world literature. Perhaps the patronising talk of 'myths' and 'insignificance' is all of a piece with a superior disdain for the Pilgrims as, in Winslow's words, a 'poor persecuted people'.

Whatever the underlying reason, from the 1980s onwards the Pilgrims were increasingly subjected to criticism. They could be accused of almost anything, however unlikely. As undifferentiated 'puritans', they were held responsible for the puritan persecutions in

New England from Williams to Salem, and they were held responsible, as the first successful colonists in New England, for colonialism, slavery and the genocide of the native Americans.[22]

Behind all these disputes lies a fundamental mismatch in the perceptions of the disputing parties. The clue to the yawning divide between Scott, who had romanticised the Pilgrims into significance, and Morison, who had sanctified them out of significance, lies in Morison's claim that if the ship had sunk in the Atlantic then nothing much in history would have changed. This may or may not be true, but it is not the issue. The ship is not honoured for what it did but for what it represented. To claim that the voyage of the *Mayflower* led directly to American independence, modern democracy, respect for human rights or free-market capitalism is to claim too much. It did none of those things. In the same way as the fall of the Bastille in Paris represents victory over injustice, and Magna Carta represents the rule of law, the *Mayflower* represents the struggle for freedom. The voyage was not a determining factor in history, as some have foolishly claimed, nor merely a symbol, as some have foolishly assumed, but a representation – an inspiring image, emblem, or icon – for all the forces of freedom that drove the Pilgrims forward. Because they stood for so many types of freedom – free trade for the adventurers, free speech and free assembly for the religious, freedom for refugees, freedom for slaves and rights for Indians – they stood for freedom as a whole.

What was lost when Morison shot down Scott was historical context. He dug up the Pilgrims from their roots in London and transplanted them to Heaven, just as he removed, when editing Bradford's history, the page where Bradford expressed his delight at the overthrow of the bishops and deposited it in an appendix. It was a shame he tampered with Bradford because Bradford had a wise understanding. He understood that what mattered in human affairs was not necessarily what people directly caused, though that also mattered, but what they stood for and the direction in which they pointed. In the 1650s he was deeply despondent but never, it seemed, in total despair because he regarded the Pilgrims only as 'a stepping-stone'. It was enough that they offered a practical route for others to follow. He also believed in the value of inspiration. He wrote in 1630, as boats packed with migrants were sailing into New England, the colony that the Pilgrims had founded: 'Thus out of small beginnings greater things have been produced ... and as one small candle may light a thousand, so the light here kindled hath shone into many, yea in some sort to our whole nation...'[23]

Bradford's nation was England. The forces struggling for freedom were the City investors in London, the London dissidents of the

Jacob church, and the doughty Pilgrims across the sea in Leiden. All three worked hand in hand, although by no means in agreement, united by the struggle against the royal court, the state church and the state-controlled economy. They recognised in each other's causes the mirror image of their own, and all they asked for was freedom to pursue their trade deals or practise their religion.

It was for liberty that the *Mayflower*, 'a fine ship' as Weston said, laden heavy with the twin causes of trade and toleration, sailed out of the Thames in 1620. Anchored in London, it was intimately engaged with the City's adventurers, its financiers, its livery companies, its apprentices, its underground churches, its homeless orphans, and its dense, plague-riddled alleyways. All had legitimate aspirations. Once the *Mayflower* is seen as the icon of a broad movement for liberty, and not just as another voyage which had this or that effect, then 1620 may be reaffirmed, on both sides of the Atlantic, as a justly celebrated date in the history of the world.

The London Legacy

This lists the sites in London definitely, or very probably, connected with the Brownists or *Mayflower* in some way. The persons named with the sites also have a definite, or very probable, connection.

Camden

The British Museum, Bloomsbury, has a letter by Francis Johnson.

The City

All Hallows Barking. Where John Greenwood was buried, William Penn was baptised and Governor Thomas Prence was a young parishioner.

Bevis Marks Synagogue, Aldgate. In Heneage Lane, on part of the site of Heneage House. Built at end of 17th century, it is said to have been modelled on the Sephardi synagogue in Amsterdam, but the builder was a Quaker and its style is one the Pilgrims and the Quakers would have approved. Alice and Edward Southworth certainly lived in Heneage House and it is likely that visitors included William Bradford, John Carver, Robert Cushman, John Greenwood, Henry Jessey, John Penry and Thomas Weston.

Drapers Hall, Throgmorton St. Has fine paintings and 17th century building. Daniel Studley, Randall Thickens, William Harris.

Duke's Place, Aldgate. Centre for dissidents, the Dutch and the Jews. It originally included Heneage House.

Dutch Church. Beautiful modern church, it has a pillar of the original church preserved in a planter. Underneath the communion table is the old altar stone dating from the 13th century. It also has a paten and chalice dating back to the 17th century. Has an image of William the Silent, hero of the Pilgrims. The name of every minister since its foundation in 1550 is engraved on the wall near the main entrance and a stained glass depicts the history of the Dutch Church, starting with Edward VI. Another such window depicts William and Mary.

Fishmongers Hall. At London Bridge, on original site. Impressive paintings and silverware.

Fleet Prison. Off Farringdon St (east side) but not commemorated.

Guildhall. At the centre of the City. Its library has the records of the livery companies.

Haberdashers Hall. In West Smithfield. They sold the beaver hats. Richard Andrews. Edward Boyes. Daniel Chidley.

Ironmongers Hall. In Shaftesbury Place off Aldersgate St. Thomas Weston's Hall, not on the original site but still impressive.

King William St. The 1592 Pilgrim Church met in a house on the spot now occupied by No. 80 King William St, at the intersection with Nicholas Lane.

Mercers Hall. In Ironmonger Lane, home of the Merchant Adventurers.

Merchant Taylors Hall. In Threadneedle St. John Pocock. John Slaney.

Minories Holy Trinity. Humility Cooper.

New Bridge St. A plaque commemorates Bridewell Palace Hospital, on which site was also the infamous Bridewell women's prison and the orphanage. The former gatehouse still survives.

Skinners Hall. At Dowgate Hill. Has a 17th century building.

St Andrew Undershaft. John Allerton, John Tilley.

St Bartholomew the Great, Smithfield. Christopher Martin, Thomas Rogers, John Hooke.

St Bartholomew's Hospital, West Smithfield: memorial to the Marian Martyrs, including John Rough and Cuthbert Simpson, looked upon by Bradford and Robinson as the pioneers of their church.

St Botolph Billingsgate. John Howland.

St Bride: Winslow's parents were married here. He may well have attended when an apprentice. Has a reredos in honour of Edward Winslow and statue of Virginia Dare, the first British child born in America.

St Giles Cripplegate. John Hooke

St Giles in the Fields. Dr Giles Heale.

St Katherine Coleman. Stephen Hopkins.

St Martin in the Fields. Richard Warren.

St Mary le Bow. Has a fine statue of John Smith and a plaque to Milton is nearby. Smith delivered a sermon there promoting migration to America and John Pocock, the Adventurer, lived nearby.

St Michael Wood St, Cripplegate. Edward Leister.

St Paul's churchyard. Where many books and pamphlets were sold *c*.1620, including emigration literature. The Pilgrims called it Paul's churchyard.

St Swithin Cannon St. Robert Coppin.

Stationers Hall. In Ave Maria Lane, near St Paul's, 17th century.

Wood Street Prison, Cripplegate. Sabine Staresmore, Henry Jacob.

Islington

St Mary. Degory Priest.

Lambeth

Clapham. Home of Beauchamp and Sherley.

Lambeth Palace. Has documents relating to the *Mayflower*. In 1967 it held an exhibition of 'Pilgrim Fathers' documents including John Greenwood's *Answer to George Giffard* (1590); Barrowe's *Plain Refutation of Giffard* (1591); the *Examinations* of Barrowe, Greenwood and Penry (1587-89); Barrowe's *True Description*; Henry Jacob's appeal to James I (1609) with margin notes by the king; and other works by Penry and Browne, including Penry's last letter. Most fascinating is the 3-volume *Works of St Basil the Great* donated to the Dutch Church by Thomas Weston and inscribed 'Ex dono Thoma Weston'.

Lewisham

St Nicholas Deptford. Richard Clarke, Richard Gardiner, John Parker – Ely?

Richmond

National Archive at Kew has the petition to Elizabeth by the Brownists asking to emigrate.

Southwark

Clink Prison. Where John Greenwood, Henry Barrowe, Francis Johnson were inmates. Henry Jacob, who lived nearby, visited. The remains of Winchester Palace, of which the Clink Prison was a part, are still visible.

Coverdale plaque, Borough High St. This commemorates the first complete English Bible printed in Britain (1535), the Coverdale Bible, which has on its title page, 'Imprinted in Southwark in St Thomas' Hospital'.

Crossway Church. In Hampton St, Elephant and Castle. Crossway took over the Pilgrim church and still owns the Great Dover St building. It has loaned the communion plate (the oldest Nonconformist communion plate extant) to the Victoria and Albert Museum and the Pilgrim Church's font to a church in Wandsworth. Of wood, it has a lid said to be made of Plymouth Rock. The communion plate is dated to 1691. But in fact, only one item of the set is 1691 (though all the communion cups bear the date of 1691) so it was probably this that Jonathan Owen presented to the church and the other 3 are later copies. Crossway Church is now a United Reformed Church.

Deadman's Place. Site of the Pilgrim Church (1640s – 1788), now buried under a car park in Thrale St behind the Novotel.

Globe Theatre. Shakespeare's *Tempest* drew inspiration from the voyage to America of the *Sea Venture* (1609). *Twelfth Night* mentioned the Brownists. In Park St there is a memorial site which was once, with the Pilgrim church in Deadman's Place, part of the Barclay Brewery.

Greenland Dock, Rotherhithe. Formerly the only creek or inlet on the peninsula so probably where the *Mayflower* was berthed.

Harvard Library. Has plaque to John Harvard. Has documents with Browne's signature binding him to good behaviour while Headmaster of St Saviour.

King's Bench Prison. On north side of Angel Place, Borough High St, where the Harvard Library is now. John Penry and others held there.

Marshalsea Prison. On north side of Mermaid Court, Borough High St. There died John Udall, ally of the Brownists. He was buried in the churchyard of St George the Martyr.

Mayflower pub. Changed its name to Mayflower only in 1957. There is no evidence of any connection with the *Mayflower*, but it is a pleasant pub full of *Mayflower* memorabilia, including a list of passengers in the restaurant.

Mayflower tree. Tree planted in 2018 outside the church of St George the Martyr in honour of Henry Jessey, who campaigned for tolerance of Jews and Muslims. Rabbi Morris of Bevis Marks synagogue attended, as did an Imam, and representatives of Christian groups, including Quakers, a Zoroastrian and Peter Stevenson of Crossway Church.

Pilgrim Fathers Church. The building remains, on the corner of Great Dover St and Sturgeon St, of the 4th 'Pilgrim Fathers Church' building opened in 1956 by US Ambassador, Winthrop Aldrich. The Ambassador was given a golden key to open the church door, as a gift, but he later returned it to the church. It cannot now be found and neither can the illuminated model of the *Mayflower* ship or the church's archives or the letter from Queen Elizabeth II. This church had a 'Mayflower Museum' but it was only one room. There is a silent film on You-Tube of the 1956 event. The upper floor of the building is now flats while the downstairs is currently leased out to a travel company. In New England the West Parish Congregational church in Barnstable was the sister church of the Southwark church. Barnstable traces its history back to the founding of the Jacob church in 1616 and can prove its direct descent. In 2016 it celebrated its 400th anniversary.

Pilgrim's Pocket statue. Striking statue showing a boy and a Pilgrim surveying American history since the Mayflower.

Queen's Head Inn. Plaque at 103 Borough High St says (rather inaccurately) that the inn was 'owned by the family of John Harvard founder of Harvard University'.

St George the Martyr. John Udall, Henry Jessey, John Penry.

St Mary Magdalen, Bermondsey. James Janeway, John Penry.

St Mary Rotherhithe. Christopher Jones and family, Thomas Gataker and John Clarke. Has Christopher Jones statue by Jamie Sergeant (1995). Has blue plaque (2004) commemorating the *Mayflower*.

St Olave. Demolished 1926. John Harvard (bp), Timothy Hatherley, John Billington and family (= 5), Earl of Sussex at Bermondsey House.

St Saviour, now Southwark Cathedral. Roger Rippon, Henry Jacob, Francis Johnson, Edward Philips (minister, 1588-1602), George Yeardley, Robert Browne, Edward Doty, perhaps Mary Brewster connected. John Harvard was pupil in the church school. Harvard Chapel in the North Transept. Edmund Shakespeare bd there, 1607. Stained glass window to William Shakespeare and statue to him. North entrance door has theme of pilgrimage.

St Saviour and St Olave School for Girls on the New Kent Rd has a plaque to the *Mayflower* in its grounds. There used to be a sundial mounted on a large stone with the Mayflower ship on one side and on the other an inscription by the Trustees of the Pilgrim Fathers Memorial Church but the whereabouts of this are currently unknown.

St Saviour and St Olave School: present building at Tower Bridge was built in 1893-96, though the school was founded in 1571. Robert Browne taught at this school and was headmaster. John Harvard was a pupil. It is now the Lalit Hotel, but they have kept a room named the Headmaster's Study.

Surrey Lock. If the Mayflower was broken up locally, as seems likely, then it would probably have happened here or at Fortune Dock to the west. At this site was Beatson's Yard where the Temeraire was broken up 200 years later.

Thomas a Watering. At the junction of Albany Rd and Old Kent Rd. Where Penry was executed and where Chaucer's Pilgrims proceeded to Canterbury.

Union St Chapel. This was the site of the Pilgrim Church (1788-1864) that succeeded Deadman's Place. The original gates and drive are still in place.

Tower Hamlets

Blackwall. Departure point for passenger and cargo ships leaving on long-haul journeys to America or Asia. Headquarters of the East India Company. Had a good road leading into London. Probably the *Mayflower* embarked its passengers there, or in Wapping.

St Dunstan, Stepney. John Allerton, Alice and John Rigsdale.

St Mary Matfelon Whitechapel. Now part of Altab Ali Park. Nothing left of the original church. Stephen Hopkins, Elizabeth, (plus Damaris, Constance, Giles, Oceanus), John Howland, John Turner.

Notes

Preface

1. Bangs, Jeremy: Pilgrim Edward Winslow (2004), p.xxviii.

1. The Origins of the Mayflower

1. Alford, Stephen: London's Triumph (2017):
2. Hill, Christopher: The Century of Revolution (1980 ed. of 1961), pp. 20-23.
3. Marshall, Peter: Heretics and Believers: A History of the English Reformation (2017), p.105.
4. Hanbury, Benjamin: Historical Memorial (1839), pp.1-2.
5. Adair, John: Puritans (1998 ed. of 1982), p 86.
6. Gurney, David: Education and the Early Modern English Separatists (1998) p. 282
7. Gurney, David: Education and the Early Modern English Separatists (1998), p. 53.
8. Burrage, Champlin: Early English Dissenters in the Light of Recent Research (2001 ed. of 1912), pp.69-70.
9. George, Timothy: John Robinson and the English Separatist Tradition (1982), pp. 14-16.
10. Hill, Christopher: Some Intellectual Consequences of the English Revolution (1980), p. 13.
11. Bredwell, Stephen: The Rasing of the foundations of Brownisme (1588).
12. Linebaugh, Peter & Rediker, Marcus: The Many-Headed Hydra (2012 ed. of 2000), p. 65.
13. Sprunger, Keith: Dutch Puritanism (1982), p.29.
14. Punchard, George: History of Congregationalism (1865) p. vi.
15 Tomkins, Stephen: The Journey to the Mayflower (2020), pp. 108-109.
16. Adair, John: Puritans (1998 ed. of 1982), p. 110.
17. Adair, John: Puritans (1998 ed. of 1982), p.106.
18. Evans, James: Emigrants: Why the English Sailed to the New World (2017), p.98.

19. Gurney, David: Education and the Early Modern English Separatists (1998), p.203.
20. Gurney, David: Education and the Early Modern English Separatists (1998), p.214.
21. Bradford, William: Conferences (1648-51).
22 Culpepper, Kenneth Scott: One Christian's Plea (2006), p. 83
23. Gurney, David: Education and the Early Modern English Separatists (1998), p. 159.
24. George, Timothy: John Robinson and the English Separatist Tradition (1982), p.81.

2. *The London Church*

1. Haefili, Evan: New Netherland and the Dutch Origins of American Liberty (2012), pp. 75-76.
2 See Culpepper, Kenneth Scott: One Christian's Plea (2006), p. 128ff.
3. Bradford, William: Conferences (1648-51).
4 Culpepper, Kenneth Scott: One Christian's Plea (2006), p. 120ff.
5. Bradford, William: Conferences (1648-51).
6 Culpepper, Kenneth Scott: One Christian's Plea (2006), pp. 89-90.
7 Fairlambe, Peter: The Recantation of a Brownist (1606).
8. Culpepper, Scott: Francis Johnson and English Separatist Influence (2006), p.215.
9. Bunker, Nick: Making Haste from Babylon (2011 ed. of 2010), p.149.
10. Culpepper, Scott: Francis Johnson and English Separatist Influence (2006), p.206.
11. Bradford, William: Conferences (1648-51).
12. Bradford, William: On Plymouth Plantation (2006 ed. of 1856), p.404.
13. See Gray, Adrian: From Here We Changed The World (2016), p.11 & p.113.
14. Bradford, William: On Plymouth Plantation (2006 ed. of 1856), pp.35-36.
15. Robinson, John: Justification of Separation (1610).
16. George, Timothy: John Robinson and the English Separatist Tradition (1982), p. 78.
17. Bradford, William: On Plymouth Plantation (2006 ed. of 1856), p.40.
18. Bangs Jeremy: Strangers and Pilgrims (2009). p.62.
19. See Culpepper, Scott: Francis Johnson and English Separatist Influence (2006).
20. Lee, Jason: The Theology of John Smith (2003), pp.46-47.
21. Wright, Stephen: The British Baptists and Politics (2002), pp.34-35.
22. Bradford, William: On Plymouth Plantation (2006 ed. of 1856), p.48.
23. George, Timothy: John Robinson and the English Separatist Tradition (1982), p. 178.
24. Boddie, John: Seventeenth Century Isle of Wight County (1938), pp.20-21.
25. Lee, Jason: The Theology of John Smith (2003), pp. 57-58.
26. Hanbury, Benjamin: Historical Memorials (1839), pp.230-31.
27. Hanbury, Benjamin: Historical Memorial (1839).

3. The London Company

1. Johnson, Caleb: Here Shall I Die Ashore (2007), p.41.
2. Linebaugh, Peter & Rediker, Marcus: The Many-Headed Hydra (2012 ed. of 2000), p. 13.
3. Evans, James: Emigrants: Why the English Sailed to the New World (2017), pp. 89-90.
4. Evans, James: Emigrants: Why the English Sailed to the New World (2017), p. 90.
5. Davis, Ralph: The Rise of the Atlantic Economies (1973), pp. 85-86.
6. Bradford, William: On Plymouth Plantation (2006 ed. of 1856) p.87.
7. Coleman, Donald: The Economy of England 1450-1750 (1977), p.59.
8. Levett, Christopher, A Voyage into New England (1624), quoted in Bridenbaugh, p. 407.
9. Haley, Kenneth: The Dutch in the Seventeenth Century (1972), p. 45.
10. Boddie, John: Seventeenth Century Isle of Wight County (1938), p.30.
11. Boddie, John: Seventeenth Century Isle of Wight County (1938), p.21.
12. Bangs, Jeremy: Strangers and Pilgrims (2009) p.681.
13. Ashton, Robert (ed.): Introduction to The Works of John Robinson (2015 ed. of 1851).
14. Bradford, William: On Plymouth Plantation (2006 ed. of 1856), p.48.
15. Bradford, William: On Plymouth Plantation (2006 ed. of 1856), pp.55-56.
16. Bradford, William: On Plymouth Plantation (2006 ed. of 1856), pp.53-58.
17. Winslow, Edward: Hypocrisie Unmasked (1646).
18. Punchard, George: History of Congregationalism (1865), p.363.
19. Tolmie, Murray: The Triumph of the Saints (1977), p.15.
20. Tolmie, Murray: The Triumph of the Saints (1977), p.16.
21. Burgess, Walter: John Robinson, Pastor of the Pilgrim Fathers (1920), pp.140-141.
22. Tolmie, Murray: The Triumph of the Saints (1977), p.13.
23. Bangs, Jeremy: Strangers and Pilgrims (2009) p.416.
24. Boast, Mary: The Mayflower and Pilgrim Story (1995 ed. of 1970), p.22.
25. Bradford, William: On Plymouth Plantation (2006 ed. of 1856), p.77.
26. Bridenbaugh, Carl: Vexed and Troubled Englishmen 1590-1642 (1968), p.10.
27. Bangs, Jeremy: Strangers and Pilgrims (2009), p.587.
28. Bradford, William: On Plymouth Plantation (2006 ed. of 1856), p.72.
29. Hill, Christopher: Century of Revolution (1980 ed. of 1961), p.35.
30. Hill, Christopher: Century of Revolution (1980 ed. of 1961), p.31.
31. Bridenbaugh, Carl: Vexed and Troubled Englishmen 1590-1642 (1968), p.193.
32. Hill, Christopher: Hill: Century of Revolution (1980 ed. of 1961), p.76

4. The Mayflower in London

1. Bradford, William: On Plymouth Plantation (2006 ed. of 1856), p.76.
2. Bunker, Nick: Making Haste from Babylon (2011 ed. of 2010), p.292.
3. Bradford, William: On Plymouth Plantation (2006 ed. of 1856), p.75.
4. Minchinton, Walter: in The Fontana Economic History of Europe: The Sixteenth and Seventeenth Centuries ed. by Carlo Cipolla (1974), pp. 109-10.

5. Morison, Samuel (ed.): Of Plymouth Plantation by William Bradford (1953), p.54 fn.
6. Hills, Leon & Hills, Leon Clark The History and Genealogy of the Mayflower Planters and the First Comers (1936-41), p.40-41.
7. Banks, Charles: The English Ancestry and Homes of the Pilgrim Fathers (2006 ed. of 1929), p.16.
8. Gataker, Thomas: A Discours Apologeticall (1654)

5 *The Mayflower Sails from London*

1. Parker, Geoffrey: in The Fontana Economic History of Europe: The Sixteenth and Seventeenth Centuries ed. by Carlo Cipolla (1974), p. 554.
2. Tinniswood, Adrian: The Rainborowes (2014 ed. of 2013), p.69.
3. Harris, G G: Trinity House of Deptford Transactions 1609-35 (1983), p.138.
4. Turack, Daniel: Freedom of Movement: The Right of a UK Citizen to Leave his Country (1970).
5. Bradford, William: On Plymouth Plantation (2006 ed. of 1856), pp.91–92.
6. Woodhouse and Roots: Puritanism and Liberty (1992 ed. of 1938), p. 45.
7. Bradford, William: On Plymouth Plantation (2006 ed. of 1856), pp.103-106.
8. Banks, Charles: The English Ancestry and Homes of the Pilgrim Fathers (2006 ed. of 1929), p.11.
9. Bridenbaugh, Carl: Vexed and Troubled Englishmen 1590-1642 (1968) pp.179-80.
10. For greater detail, see Donald Harris: The More Children and the Mayflower (1999).
11. Bridenbaugh, Carl: Vexed and Troubled Englishmen 1590-1642 (1968), pp. 5-8.
12. Bradford, William: On Plymouth Plantation (2006 ed. of 1856), pp.125-127.
13. Bangs, Jeremy: Strangers and Pilgrims (2009), p.261.
14. Acton, John: Lectures on Modern History (1956 ed. of 1906), p.200.
15. Morison, S: The Pilgrim Fathers: Their Significance in History (1937), pp.9-10.
16. Mourt, G: Mourt's Relation (1865 ed. of 1622), p.6.
17. Bangs, Jeremy: Strangers and Pilgrims (2009), p.624.
18. Bangs, Jeremy: Strangers and Pilgrims (2009), p.620.
19. Bemiss, Samuel: The Three Charters (2007 ed. of 1957).
20. Butman and Targett: New World, Inc. (2018), p.289.
21. Bradford, William: On Plymouth Plantation (2006 ed. of 1856), p.22.
22. Bridenbaugh, Carl: Vexed and Troubled Englishmen 1590-1642 (1968), pp. 10-11.
23. Morton, Nathaniel: New England's Memoriall (1854 ed. of 1669), p.22.
24. Ford, Worthington (ed.): Of Plimmoth Plantation by William Bradford (1912 ed. of 1856), vol 1, p.192, fn. 3.
25. Mourt, G: A Relation or Journall (1865 ed. of 1622), p.143.
26. Mourt, G: A Relation or Journall (1865 ed. of 1622), p.145.
27. Mourt, G: A Relation or Journall (1865 ed. of 1622), pp.146-147.

28. Mourt, G: A Relation or Journall (1865 ed. of 1622), pp.148-149.
29. Bangs, Jeremy: Strangers and Pilgrims (2009), p.15.
30. Bradford, William: On Plymouth Plantation (2006 ed. of 1856), p.114.
31. Bradford, William: On Plymouth Plantation (2006 ed. of 1856), p.87.
32. Winslow, Edward: in Mourt's Relation (1865 ed. of 1622), p.129.
33. Winslow, Edward: in Mourt's Relation (1865 ed. of 1622), pp.133-135.
34. Winslow, Edward: in Mourt's Relation (1865 ed. of 1622), p.133.
35. Bunker, Nick: Making Haste from Babylon (2011 ed. of 2010) p.67.
36. De Baar: Pilgrim Fathers in Holland (2002), p.29.

6 Family and Friends

1. Banks, Charles: The English Ancestry and Homes of the Pilgrim Fathers (2006 ed. of 1929), p.viii.
2. Winslow, Edward: Good Newes from New-England (1624).
3. Westbrook, Perry: William Bradford (1978), p.91.
4. Mourt, G: A Relation or Journall (1865 ed. of 1622), p.141.
5. Harris, G G: Trinity House of Deptford Transactions 1609-35 (1983), pp.70-71.
6. Smith, John: Travels and Works II, pp.722-23.
7. Cushman, Robert: in Mourt's Relation or Journall (1865 ed. of 1622), pp.151-154.
8. Prory, John: in Three Visitors to Early Plymouth (1997).
9. Smith, John: True Travels, Adventures, and Observations (1630).

7 The Mayflower Hanging by a Thread

1. Bradford, William: On Plymouth Plantation (2006 ed. of 1856), pp.195-196.
2. Bradford, William: On Plymouth Plantation (2006 ed. of 1856), p.231.
3. Bradford, William: On Plymouth Plantation (2006 ed. of 1856), p.231.
4. Bridenbaugh, Carl: Vexed and Troubled Englishmen 1590-1642 (1968), p.180.
5. Rees, John: The Leveller Revolution (2017 ed. of 2016), p.38.
6. Rees, John: The Leveller Revolution (2017 ed. of 2016), p.29.

8 The Mayflower Returns to London

1. Tolmie, Murray: The Triumph of the Saints (1977), p.46.
2. Briggs, Asa: A Social History of England, p 159.
3. See Ashton, Robert: The City and the Court (1979).
4. Linebaugh, Peter & Rediker Marcus: The Many-Headed Hydra (2012 ed. of 2000), pp.69-70.
5. Hill, Christopher: Some Intellectual Consequences of the English Revolution (1980), p.49.
6. Wright, Stephen: Sarah Jones and the Jacob-Jessey Church: The Relation of a Gentlewoman (2004).
7. Moore, Susan Hardmore: Pilgrims: New World Settlers and the Call of Home (2007), p.2.

8. Adair, John: Puritans (1998 ed. of 1982), p.178.

9 James, Sydney (ed): Three Visitors to Early Plymouth (1997).

10. Bangs, J: Pilgrim Edward Winslow (2004), p.411.

11. Willison, George: Saints and Strangers (1966 ed. of 1945): p.xi.

12. Adair, John: Puritans (1998 ed. of 1982), p.229.

13. Tinniswood, Adrian: The Rainborowes (2014 ed. of 2013) p.157.

14. Tinniswood, Adrian: The Rainborowes (2014 ed. of 2013), p.156.

15. Tinniswood, Adrian: The Rainborowes (2014 ed. of 2013), p.308.

16. Evans, James: Emigrants: Why the English Sailed to the New World (2017),: p.224.

17. Bremer, Francis: Puritanism: A Very Short Introduction (2009), p.89.

18. Bangs, Jeremy: The Town Records of Sandwich 1620-92 (2014).

19. Vallance, Edward: A Radical History of Britain (2010 ed. of 2009), p 141.

20. Westbook, Perry: William Bradford (1978), p.86.

21. George, Timothy: John Robinson and the English Separatist Tradition (1982), p. 4.

22. Bradford, William: Conferences (1648-51).

23. Woodhouse, Arthur & Roots, Ivan: Puritanism and Liberty (1992 ed. of 1938), p.347.

24. Woodhouse, Arthur & Roots, Ivan: Puritanism and Liberty (1992 ed. of 1938), p.342.

25. Rees, John: The Leveller Revolution (2017 ed. of 2016), pp.59-60.

26. Walwyn, William: The Compassionate Samaritane (1644).

27. George, Timothy: John Robinson and the English Separatist Tradition (1982), p.175.

28. Baxter, Rchard: Reliquiae Baxterianae (1696).

29. Bunker, Nick: Making Haste from Babylon (2011 ed. of 2010), p.25.

30. Donoghue, John: Fire under the Ashes (2013), p.170.

31. See Gillespie, Katharine: Katherine Chidley (2009).

32. Adler, Jonathan: Jessey the Educator and Jessey the Jew in Jewish Historical Studies, vol. 47 (2015).

33. Jessey, Henry: The Glory and the Salvation of Jehudah and Israel (1650).

34. Katz, David: Sceptics, Millenarians and Jews (1990), p.165.

35. Jessey, Henry: Narrative of the late Proceeds at White-Hall concerning the Jews (1656).

36. Roots, Ivan: Speeches of Oliver Cromwell (1989), speech 22 January 1655.

37 Bunker, Nick: Making Haste from Babylon (2011 ed. of 2010), p.77.

38. Bruyneel, Sally: Margaret Fell and the End of Time (2010), p.126.

39. Tolmie, Murray: The Triumph of the Saints (1977), p.5.

40 Katz, David: Philo-Semitism and the Readmission of the Jews (1982), p.9.

41. See Katz, David: Philo-Semitism and the Readmission of the Jews (1982).

42. Tinniswood, Adrian: The Rainborowes (2014 ed. of 2013), p.333.

43 Donoghue, John: Fire under the Ashes (2013), p.283.

44. See Medley, William: A Door of Hope (1661).

9 *The Mayflower Vindicated*

1. Hill, Christopher: God's Englishman (1972 ed. of 1970), pp. 246-248.
2. Hill, Christopher: Some Intellectual Consequences of the English Revolution (1980), p.79.
3. Hill, Christopher: Some Intellectual Consequences of the English Revolution (1980), p.50.
4. Evans, James: Emigrants: Why the English Sailed to the New World (2017), p.227.
5. Hill, Christopher: Century of Revolution (1980 ed. of 1961), pp.2-3.
6. Doran, Susan and Durston, Christopher: Princes, Pastors and People (1991), pp.196-197.
7. Ashton, Robert (ed.): Introduction to The Works of John Robinson (2015 ed. of 1851)
8. Robinson, John: Justification of Separation (1610).
9. Coleman, D.C.: The Economy of England 1450-1750, p. 149.
10. Davis, Ralph: The Rise of the Atlantic Economies (1973), p.209.
11. Hill, Christopher: God's Englishman (1972 ed. of 1970), pp.246-248.
12. Hill, Christopher: The Century of Revolution (1980 ed. of 1961), p.35.
13. Hill, Christopher: Some Intellectual Consequences of the English Revolution (1980), p.51.
14. MacCulloch, Diarmaid: Reformation (2004 ed. of 2003), p.544.
15. Bangs, Jeremy: Strangers and Pilgrims (2009), p.677.
16. See Stevenson, Peter: This is the Church that God built (2018).
17. Hume, David: History, volume 5, chapter 40.
18. Webster, Daniel: The Plymouth Oration, 22 December 1820.
19. Morison, Samuel (ed.): Of Plymouth Plantation by William Bradford (1953), pp.1-21.
20. Bangs, Jeremy: Strangers and Pilgrims (2009), p.viii.
21. Schulte Nordholt: The Pilgrim Fathers in Holland (2002), p.10.
22. See Reilly, Danny & Cushion, Steve: Telling the Mayflower Story (2018).
23. Bradford, William: On Plymouth Plantation (2006 ed. of 1856), p.289.

Select Bibliography

This is but a fraction of the voluminous *Mayflower* literature. CUP = Cambridge University Press; GSoMD = General Society of Mayflower Descendants; MHS = Massachusetts Historical Society; NEHGS = New England Historic Genealogical Society; OUP = Oxford University Press; SLSL = Southwark Local Studies Library; and ed. = edited, or edition.

Primary Sources

AINSWORTH, Henry & JOHNSON, Francis: *True Confession* (1596, 1598).

AINSWORTH, Henry & JOHNSON, Francis: *An apologia or defence of such true Christians as are commonly (but unjustly) called Brownists...* (1604)

AINSWORTH, Henry: *The Communion of Saincts* (1607)

AINSWORTH, Henry: *Counterpoyson* (1608)

ASHE, Simeon: *The Narrative of the Life and Death of Mr Gataker* (sermon 1654, in *Grey Hayres Crowned with Grace*,1655).

BARROWE, Henry: *A True Description* (1589)

BARROWE, Henry: *Plain Refutation of Giffard* (1591).

BELL, Susanna: *The legacy of a dying mother to her mourning children* (1673)

BRADFORD, William: *Of Plimmoth Plantation* (Boston: MHS, 1912 ed. of 1856)

BRADFORD, William: Of Plymouth Plantation (New York: Knopf, 1953 ed of 1856)

BRADFORD, William: *Of Plymouth Plantation* ((Xlibris, 2006 ed. of 1856)

BRADFORD, William: Conferences *Between Some Young Men Born in New England and some Ancient Men who Came out of Holland* (1648-1651).

BRADFORD, William: in *Mourt's Relation or Journall* (Boston: John Kimball Wiggin, 1865 ed. of 1622).

BREDWELL, Stephen: *The Rasing of the floundations of Brownisme* (1588).

BRIDGE, William: *The Wounded Conscience Cured* (1642).

BROWNE, Robert: *A Treatise of Reformation without Tarying for Anie* (1582).

BUSHER, Leonard: *Religion's Peace, or a Plea for Liberty of Conscience* (1614)

CAMDEN, William: *Annales Rerum Gestarum Angliae et Hiberniae* (1615-19).

CHILDE, John: *New Englands Jonas Cast up at London* (1647).

COTTON, John: *The Keys of the Kingdom of Heaven* (1644).

CROMWELL, Oliver: *Speeches of Oliver Cromwell* (1989) by Ivan Roots.

CUSHMAN, Robert: *The Sin and Danger of Self Love: A Sermon* (1622).

CUSHMAN, Robert: *Reasons and Considerations*, in *Mourt's Relation or Journall of the Plantation at Plymouth* (Boston: John Kimball Wiggin, 1865 ed. of 1622).

DUNTON, John: *A True Journal of the Sally Fleet* (1637).

DURY, John: *A Case of Conscience* (letter, 1656).

DURY, John: *Whether it be lawful to admit Jews into a Christian Commonwealth* (1656)

EDWARDS, Thomas: *Gangraena* (1646)

FAIRLAMBE, Peter: *Recantation of a Brownist* (1606).

FELL, Margaret: *A Loving Salutation to the Seed of Abraham* (1656).

FELL, Margaret: *For Menasseh Ben Israel* (1656)

FOXE, John: *Actes and Monuments* (aka the *Book of Martyrs*) (1563).

GATAKER, Thomas: *Marriage Duties* (1620).

GATAKER, Thomas: *A Serious and Faithful Representation* (1648).

GATAKER, Thomas & CLARKE, Samuel: *A Martyrologie* (1652).

GATAKER, Thomas: *A Discours Apologeticall* (1654).

GREENWOOD, John: *Answer to George Giffard* (1590)

HAKLUYT, Richard: *Divers Voyages Touching the Discovery of America* (1582).

HARCOURT, Robert: *Relation of a Voyage to Guiana* (1613).

HARLEIAN MISCELLANY: Pamphlets and Tracts, Vols VII & VIII (London: 1811).

HELWYS, Thomas: *The Mystery of Iniquity* (1612).

HILTON, William: *Letter to his family* (1621).

HOLMES, Nathaniel: *Ecclesiastica Methermeneutica* (1652).

HUBBERTHORNE, Richard: *An Answer to a Declaration* (1659).

JACOB, Henry: *Against Master Francis Johnson and others of the Separation commonly called Brownists* (1599)

JACOB, Henry: *An Humble Supplication for Toleration and Liberty* (1609)

JESSEY, Henry: *The Glory and the Salvation of Jehudah and Israel* (1650).

JESSEY, Henry: *Narrative of the late Proceeds at White-Hall concerning the Jews* (1656).

JOHNSON, Francis: *A Treatise of the Ministry of the Church of England* (1595).

JOHNSON, Francis & AINSWORTH, Henry: *True Confession* (1596).

JOHNSON, Francis: *Answer to Master Jacob* (1600).

JOHNSON, Francis and AINSWORTH, Henry: *An apologia or defence of such true Christians as are commonly (but unjustly) called Brownists...* (1604)

LEVETT, Christopher, *A Voyage into New England* (1624).

LILBURNE, John: *The Freeman's Freedom Vindicated* (1646)

LILBURNE, John: *The Foundations of Freedom* (1648)

LOCKE, John: *Letter concerning Toleration* (1689).

LOCKE, John: *Two Treatises of Government* (1690).

MARPRELATE, Martin: *The Marprelate Tracts* (ed. by Joseph Black, OUP, 2008)

MATHER, Cotton: *Magnalia Christi Americana* (1702).

MEDLEY, William: *A Door of Hope* (1661)

MENASSEH ben ISRAEL: *Spes Israelis* (1650)

MENASSEH ben ISRAEL: *Vindiciae Judaeorum* (1656)

MILTON, John: *Areopagitica* (1644).

MORTON, Nathaniel: *New England's Memoriall* (1854 ed. of 1669).

MORTON, Thomas: *New English Canaan* (1637).

MOURT, G: *A Relation or Journall* (Boston: John Kimball Wiggin, 1865 ed. of 1622).

MUN, Thomas: *A Discourse of Trade from England Unto the East Indies* (1621).

MUN, Thomas: England's Treasure by Foreign Trade (1628).

OVERTON, John: *An Appeal* (1647).

PAGITT, Ephraim: *Heresiograph: or, A Description of the Hereticks and Sectaries* (1645).

PARKER, Henry: *Of a Free Trade* (1648).

PENN, William: *A Further Account of the Province of Pennsylvania and Its Improvement* (1685).

PENRY, John: *Last letter* (1593).

PORY, John: Letter (1623)

PRATT, Phineas: *Declaration of the Affairs of the English People that First Inhabited New England* (1662).

RALEIGH, Walter: *Discoverie of the Large, Rich and Bewtifull Empyre of Guiana* (1596).

ROBINSON, John: *The Works of John Robinson* (3 vols, 2015 ed. of 1851).

ROBINSON, John: *A Defence of the Doctrine Propounded by the Synod of Dort* (1624).

ROBINSON, John: *A Justification of Separation* (1610).

ROBINSON, John: *A Just and Necessary Apology* (1625).

SALTMARSH, John: *Smoke in the Temple* (1646)

SMITH, John: *Travels and Works of Captain John Smith*, ed. by Arber & Bradley (John Grant, 1910).

SMITH, John: *Generall Historie of Virginia, New England etc.* (1624).

SMITH, John: *A Description of New England* (1616).

SMITH, John: *True Travels, Adventures and Observations* (1630).

SPARKE, A: *Greevous Grones for the Poore* (1621).

TAYLOR, John: *Booke of Martyrs* (1639).

TRAPNEL, Anne: *The Cry of a Stone* (1654).

WALWYN, William: *The Compassionate Samaritane: Liberty of Conscience Asserted and the Separatist Vindicated* (1644).

WHISTON, Edward: *The Life and Death of Mr. Henry Jessey* (1671).

WILLIAMS, Roger: *The Bloody Tenent of Persecution* (1644)

WINSLOW, Edward: in *Mourt's Relation or Journall* (Boston: John Kimball Wiggin, 1865 ed. of 1622).

WINSLOW, Edward: *Good Newes from New England* (London, 1624).

WINSLOW, Edward: *Hypocrisie Unmasked* (London, 1646).

WINSLOW, Edward: *New England's Salamander Discovered,* (London, 1647).

WINSLOW, Edward: *Glorious Progress of the Gospel Amongst the Indians* (1649).

WOOD, William: *New England's Prospect* (1634).

Secondary Literature

ADAIR, John: *Puritans: Religion and Politics in Seventeenth Century England and America* (1998 ed. of 1982).

ACTON, John: *Lectures on Modern History* (London: Macmillan, 1956 ed. of 1906).

ADCOCK, Rachel: *Baptist Women's Writings in Revolutionary Culture 1640-1680* (London: Ashgate, 2015)

ADLER, Jonathan: *Jessey the Educator and Jessey the Jew* (*Jewish Historical Studies*, vol 47, 2015).

ALFORD, Stephen: *London's Triumph: Merchant Adventurers and the Tudor City* (Penguin, 2018 ed. of 2017).

ANDERSON, Virginia: *New England's Generation: The Great Migration and the Formation of Society and Culture in the Seventeenth Century* (Cambridge: CUP, 1991).

ANDREWS, Charles (ed.): *The Fathers of New England: A Chronicle Of The Puritan Commonwealths* (1918).

APPELBAUM, Robert & SWEET, John W: *Envisioning an English Empire: Jamestown and the Making of the North Atlantic World* (University of Pennsylvania, 2005)

ARBER, Edward: *The Story of the Pilgrim Fathers* 1606-23 (Boston and New York: Houghton Mifflin, 1897).

ARBER, E & BRADLEY, A G (eds): *Travels and Works of Captain John Smith* (1910).

ASHTON, Robert: *The City and the Court 1603-1643* (Cambridge: CUP, 1979).

ASHTON, Robert (ed.): *The Works of John Robinson, Pastor of the Pilgrim Fathers* (London: 1851).

BAAR, P J M de: *The Pilgrim Fathers in Amsterdam, Leyden and Delfshaven* (in Stichting Oudse Hollandse Kerken: *The Pilgrim Fathers in Holland*, 2002 ed. of 1993).

BAKER, William: *The Mayflower and Other Colonial Vessels* (London: Conway Maritime Press, 1983).

BANBURY, Philip: *Shipbuilders of the Thames and Medway* (Newton Abbot: David & Charles, 1971)

BANGS, Jeremy: *The Seventeenth Century Records of Scituate, Mass.* (Boston: NEHGS, 1997-2001).

BANGS, Jeremy: *Indian Deeds: land transactions in Plymouth Colony 1620-1691* (Boston: NEHGS, 2002).

BANGS, Jeremy: *The Pilgrim Edward Winslow: New England's First International Diplomat* (Boston: NEHGS, 2004).

BANGS, Jeremy: *Strangers and Pilgrims, Travellers and Sojourners: Leiden and the Foundation of Plymouth Plantation* (Plymouth, Ma: GSoMD, 2009).

BANGS, Jeremy: *The Town Records of Sandwich 1620-92* (Leiden: Leiden American Pilgrim Museum, 2014).

BANKS, Charles Edward: *The English Ancestry and Homes of the Pilgrim Fathers* (Baltimore: Genealogical Publishing, 2006 ed. of 1929).

BANKS, Charles: *The Planters of the Commonwealth 1620-40* (Baltimore: Genealogical Publishing, 1972 ed. of 1930).

BANKS, Charles E: *Topographical Dictionary of 2885 English Emigrants to New England 1620-1650* (Baltimore: Genealogical Publishing, 1976 ed. of 1937).

BARBOUR, Philip (ed.): *The Complete Works of Captain John Smith* (London: University of North Carolina, 1986).

BECK, Edward: *Memorials to Serve for a History of the Parish of St Mary Rotherhithe* (Cambridge: CUP, 1907).

BELDEN, Albert: *Prison Church and Pilgrim Ship* (London, in SLSL, booklet, 1958).

BELDEN, Albert & FIELD W: *A Southwark Ship A Southwark Church* (London, in SLSL, booklet, 1950).

BIRCH, Thomas: *The Court and Times of James I Illustrated by Authentic and Confidential Letters* (London: Henry Colburn, 1848).

BOAST, Mary: *The Mayflower and Pilgrim Story: Chapters from Rotherhithe and Southwark* (London: London Borough of Southwark, 1995 ed. of 1970).

BODDIE, John: *Seventeenth Century Isle of Wight County, Virginia* (Baltimore, Genealogical Publishing 1973 ed. of 1938).

BOULTON, Jeremy: *Neighbourhood and society: A London suburb in the seventieth century* (Cambridge: CUP, 1987).

BOYER, Carl: *Ship Passenger Lists: national and New England, 1600-1825* (Newhall: Carl Boyer, 1977)

BRADDICK, Michael: *The Common Freedom of the People: John LIlburne and the English Revolution* (Oxford, OUP, 2018)

BREMER, Francis J: *John Winthrop: America's Forgotten Founding Father* (New York: OUP, 2003).

BREMER, Francis J: *Puritanism: A Very Short Introduction* (New York: OUP, 2009).

BREMER, Francis J: *Puritan Crisis: New England and the English Civil Wars* (New York: Garland, 1989).

BRENNER, Robert: *Merchants and Revolution* (London: Verso, 2003 ed. of 1993).

BRIDENBAUGH, Carl: *Vexed and Troubled Englishmen 1590-1642* (Oxford: Clarendon Press, 1968).

BRIGGS, Asa: *A Social History of England* (London: Penguin, 1991 ed. of 1983).

BRUYNEEL, Sally: *Margaret Fell and the End of Time* (Waco: Baylor University, 2010)

BUNKER, Nick: *Making Haste from Babylon: The Mayflower Pilgrims and Their World* (London: Pimlico, 2011 ed. of 2010)

BURGESS, Walter: John Robinson, *Pastor of the Pilgrim Fathers* (London: Williams and Norgate, 1920).

BURRAGE, Champlin: *Early English Dissenters in the Light of Recent Research* (2001 ed. of 1912).

BUTMAN, John & TARGETT, Simon: *New World Inc* (London: Atlantic Books, 2018)

CAFFREY, Kate: *The Mayflower* (New York: Stein and Day, 1974)

CANNADINE, David (ed.): *Oxford Dictionary of National Biography* (Oxford: Oxford University Press, 2004).

CARRINGTON, Roger: *Two Schools: a Short History of the St Olave's and St Saviour's* Grammar School Foundation (St Olave's Grammar School, 1962).

CLEAL, Edward: *Story of Congregationalism in Surrey* (London: John Clarke, 1908).

COCKSHOTT, Winifred: *Pilgrim Fathers: their Church and Colony* (1909).

COFFEY, John: *John Goodwin and the Puritan Revolution* (Woodbridge: Boydell Press, 2006).

COLDHAM, Peter W: *The Complete Book of Emigrants: 1607-1660* (Baltimore, Md.: Genealogical Publishing, 1987).

COLEMAN, Donald: *The Economy of England 1450-1750* (London: OUP, 1977).

COLLINSON, Patrick: '*From Cranmer to Sancroft*' (London: Hambledon Continuum, 2006).

COMO, David: *Blown by the Spirit: Puritanism and the emergence of an antinomian underground in pre-Civil-War England* (Stanford: Stanford UP, 2004).

CRESSY, David: *Coming Over: Migration and Communication between England and New England in the Seventeenth Century* (Cambridge: CUP, 1987).

CULPEPPER, Scott: *Francis Johnson and English Separatist Influence: the Bishop of Brownism's Life, Writings and Controversies* (Macon, Mercer University Press, 2006).

CULPEPPER, Kenneth Scott: *One Christian's Plea: The Life, Ministry, and Controversies of Francis Johnson* (dissertation, Baylor University, 2006).

DAVIS, Kenneth: *America's True History of Religious Tolerance* (Smithsonian magazine, October, 2010).

DAVIS, Ralph: *The Rise of the Atlantic Economies* (London: Weidenfeld & Nicolson, 1973).

DEETZ, Patricia Scott & DEETZ, James: *Passengers on the Mayflower* (Plymouth Colony Archive Project, online, 2000).

DEXTER, Henry Martyn and DEXTER, Morton: *The England and Holland of the Pilgrims* (New York: Houghton, Mifflin & Co.,1905).

DEXTER, Henry M (ed.): *Mourt's Relation, or Journal of the Plantation of Plymouth* (Boston: John Kimball Wiggin, 1865 ed. of 1622).

DILLON, Francis: *A Place for Habitation: The Pilgrim Fathers and their Quest.* (London: Hutchinson, 1973).

DOLBY, Malcolm: *William Bradford of Austerfield: His Life and Work* (Doncaster Library Services, 1991).

DONOGHUE, John: *Fire under the Ashes* (London: University of Chicago, 2013).

DUESING: *Counted Worthy: The Life and Work of Henry Jessey* (2012).

DUNTHORNE, Hugh: *Britain and the Dutch Revolt 1560-1700* (Cambridge, CUP, 2013)

DURSO, Keith: *No Armor for the Back: Baptist Prison Writings* (2007).

EVANS, James: *Emigrants: Why the English Sailed to the New World* (London: Weidenfeld & Nicolson, 2018 ed. of 2017).

EVANS, James: *Merchant Adventurers: The Voyage of Discovery that Transformed Tudor England* (London: Weidenfeld & Nicolson, 2013).

FORD, Worthington (ed.): *Of Plimmoth Plantation* by William Bradford (Boston: MHS,1912 ed. of 1856).

FRASER, Rebecca: *The Mayflower Generation: the Winslow Family and the Fight for the New World* (London: Vintage, 2018 ed. of 2017).

GAY, Peter: *A Loss of Mastery: Puritan Historians in Colonial America* (Berkeley: University of California Press, 1966).

GEORGE, Charles & Katherine: *The Protestant Mind of the English Reformation 1570-1640* (Princeton: Princeton University Press, 1961).

GEORGE, Timothy: *John Robinson and the English Separatist Tradition* (Macon: Mercer University Press, 1982).

GILL, Crispin: *Mayflower Remembered: A History of the Plymouth Pilgrims* (Newton Abbot, David & Charles, 1970).

GILLESPIE, Katharine: *Katherine Chidley* (Routledge, 2016).

GODFREY, Dennis: *Clink; the Story of a Forgotten Church* (London, 1965).

GOMEZ-GALISTEO, Carmen: *Early Visions and Representations of America* (London, Bloomsbury, 2013).

GRAY, Adrian: *From Here We Changed the World* (Retford: Bookworm, 2016).

GREIL, Ole Peter: *Dutch Calvinists in Early Stuart London: the Dutch Church in Austin Friars* (Leiden: E. J. Brill, 1989).

GREEN, H & WIGRAM, R: *Chronicles of Blackwall Yard* (London: Whitehead, Morris & Lowe, 1881).

GURNEY, David: *Education and the Early Modern English Separatists* (London: University of London, 1998).

HA, Polly: *English Presbyterianism, 1590-1640* (Stanford: Stanford University Press, 2011)

HAEFELI, Evan: *New Netherland and the Dutch Origins of American Religious Liberty* (Philadelphia: University of Pennsylvania, 2012).

HALEY, Kenneth: *The Dutch in the Seventeenth Century* (London: Thames & Hudson, 1972).

HANBURY, Benjamin: *An Historical Research Concerning the Most Ancient Congregational church in England, shewing the claim of the Church worshipping in Union St, Southwark, to that distinction* (London: 1820).

HANBURY, Benjamin: *Historical Memorial Relating to the Independents, or Congregationalists* (London: 1839-44).

HARRIS, Donald: *The Mayflower Descendants* (1993-94).

HARRIS, Donald: *The More Children* (1999).

HARRIS, G G: *Trinity House of Deptford Transactions* (London: London Record Society, 1983).

HARRIS, John: *Saga of the Pilgrims* (1983).

HARRIS, J Rendell: *The Finding of the Mayflower* (1920).

HARRIS, J Rendell: *Souvenirs of the Mayflower Tercentenary* (1920).

HARRIS, J Rendell: *The Last of the Mayflower* (1920).

HESSAYON, Ariel: *The Resurrection of John Lilburne, Quaker* (London: *Journal of the Friends Historical Society*, vol 68, 2017).

HIGHAM, Florence: *Southwark Story* (Hodder and Stoughton, 1955).

HILL, Christopher: *God's Englishman: Oliver Cromwell and the English Revolution* (London: Pelican: 1972 ed. of 1970).

HILL, Christopher: *The Century of Revolution: 1603-1714* (London: Routledge Classics, 2002 ed. of 1961).

HILL, Christopher: *Some Intellectual Consequences of the English Revolution* (London: George Weidenfeld & Nicolson, 1980).

HILL, Christopher: *Milton and the English Revolution* (London: Faber and Faber, 1979 ed. of 1977).

HILLS, Leon & HILLS, Leon Clark *The History and Genealogy of the Mayflower Planters and the First Comers* (1936-41).

HILTON, Christopher: *Mayflower: The Voyage that Changed the World* (2005).

HODGES, Margaret: *Hopkins of the Mayflower: Portrait of a Dissenter* (1972).

HODGSON, Godfrey: *A Great and Godly Adventure* (2006).

HOWARD, Alan: *Art and History in Bradford's Of Plymouth Plantation* (1971).

HUBBARD, William: *General History of New England* (1815, but 17th century MS).

HUME, David: *History of England* (1754-62).

ISRAEL, Jonathan: *The Dutch Republic: Its Rise, Greatness and Fall, 1477-1806* (Oxford: OUP, 1998 ed. of 1995).

ISRAEL, Jonathan: *A Revolution of the Mind: Radical Enlightenment and the Intellectual Origins of Modern Democracy* (Princeton: Princeton University Press, 2010).

JAMES, Sydney (ed.): *Three Visitors to Early Plymouth* (Applewood, 1997 ed. of 1963).

JENNINGS, Francis: *The Invasion of America: Indians, Colonialism and the Cant of Conquest* (1975).

JOHNSON, Caleb: *The Mayflower and her Passengers* (Xlibris, 2006).

JOHNSON, Caleb: *The Complete Works of the Mayflower Pilgrims* (internet, CD ROM).

JOHNSON, Caleb (ed.): *Of Plymouth Plantation* by William Bradford (Xlibris, 2006).

JOHNSON, Caleb: *Here Shall I Die Ashore* (Xlibris, 2007).

JOHNSON, R C: *The Transportation of Vagrant Children from London to Virginia* (1970).

JONES, A T: *Notes on the Early Days of Stepney Meeting* (1887).

JONES, Lincoln: *Colonel Thomas Rainsborough* (Wapping: History of Wapping Trust,1991).

KATZ, David: *Philo-Semitism and the Readmission of the Jews* (1982).

KATZ, David: *Sceptics, Millenarians and Jews* (1990).

KENT HISTORY CENTRE, Maidstone: Cranfield Papers and Port of London records.

KESTEVEN, G R: *The Mayflower Pilgrims* (1966).

KING, Jonathan: *The Mayflower Miracle* (1987).

KIRK-SMITH, Harold: *William Brewster: The Father of New England* (Richard Kay, 1992).

KREY, Gary Stuart de: *Following the Levellers* (Palgrave Macmillan, 2017-18).

LEE, Jason: *The Theology of John Smyth* (Macon, Mercer University Press, 2003).

LENG, Tom: *Disorderly Brethren: The Merchant Adventurers of England* (2015).

LENG, Thomas: *Fellowship and Freedom: The Merchant Adventurers and the Restructuring of English Commerce, 1582-1700* (2020).

LEYNSE, James: *Preceding the Mayflower* (1972).

LINEBAUGH, Peter & Rediker, Marcus: *The Many-Headed Hydra* (London: Verso, 2012 ed. of 2000).

LINGELBACH, W E: *The Merchant Adventurers of England: Their Laws and Ordinances (Transactions of Royal Historical Society*, vol xvi, 1970 ed. of 1902).

LIU, Tai & LIU, Dai: *Puritan London* (Newark, University of Delaware Press, 1986).

LONDON COUNTY COUNCIL: *Survey of London volumes 22 & 25: Bankside (1950) and St George's Fields (1955)*.

LONDON METROPOLITAN ARCHIVES, Farringdon: Church of England parish registers for St Mary Rotherhithe, St George the Martyr, St Olave, St Saviour and the City churches.

LONDON PUBLIC RECORD OFFICE, Kew: High Court of Admiralty Records.

MACCULLOCH, Diarmaid: *Reformation* (London: Penguin, 2004 ed. of 2003).

MACKENNAI, Andrew: *The Story of the English Separatists* (1893).

MAITLAND: *History of London* (1739).

MANNING, Brian: *The English People and the English Revolution* (London: Heinemann Educational, 1976).

MARBLE, Annie: *The Women who Came in the Mayflower* (1920).

MARSHALL, Peter: *Heretics and Believers: A History of the English Reformation* (2017).

MATTHEWS, A G: *The Congregational Churches of Staffordshire* (1924).

MAYBURY, Richard: *The Great Thanksgiving Hoax* (1999).

MINCHINTON, Walter: in *The Fontana Economic History of Europe: The Sixteenth and Seventeenth Centuries,* ed. by Carlo Cipolla (1974 ed.).

McNALLY, D: *Political Economy and the Rise of Capitalism: A Reinterpretation* (1988).

MOORE, Susan Hardman: *Pilgrims: New World Settlers and the Call of Home* (London: Yale University Press, 2007).

MOORE, Susan Hardman: *Abandoning America: Life-stories from Early New England* (Rochester: Boydell Press, 2013).

MORISON, Samuel: *The Founding of Harvard College* (Massachusetts, 1935).

MORISON, Samuel: *The Puritan Pioneers: Studies in the Intellectual Life of New England in the 17th Century* (New York: New York University Press, 1936).

MORISON, Samuel: *The Pilgrim Fathers: their Significance in History* (Concord, Society of Mayflower Descendants, 1937).

MORISON, Samuel (ed.): *Of Plymouth Plantation* by William Bradford (New York: Knopf, 1952)

MURDOCK, Kenneth: *Literature and Theology in Colonial New England* (Cambridge, Mass.: Harvard University Press, 1949)

NUTTALL, Geoffrey: *Visible Saints: The Congregational Way: 1640-1660* (1957).

NUTTER, Bernard: *Story of the Cambridge Baptists* (2011 ed. of 1912).

PARKER, Geoffrey: in *The Fontana Economic History of Europe: The Sixteenth and Seventeenth Centuries* ed. by Carlo Cipolla (Collins, 1974).

PEARL, Valerie: *London and the Outbreak of the Puritan Revolution* (London: OUP, 1961).

PESTANA, Carla Gardina: *The English Atlantic in an Age of Revolution 1640-1661* (London: Harvard University Press, 2004)

PHILBRICK, Nathaniel: *The Mayflower: A Story of Courage, Community and War* (London: Penguin, 2007 ed. of 2006).

PICARD, Liza: *Restoration London* (London: Phoenix Press, 1997).

PICARD, Liza: Elizabeth's London (London: Phoenix, 2004 ed. of 2003).

PORTER, Roy: *London: A Social History* (London: Penguin Books, 2000).

PRINCE, Thomas: *Chronological History of New England 1602-1730* (1736).

PRÖGLER, Daniela: *English Students at Leiden University 1575-1650* (Burlington, Ashgate Publishing, 2012).

PUNCHARD, George: *History of Congregationalism* (New York, 1865).

REES, John: *The Leveller Revolution: Radical Political Organisation in England, 1640-1650* (London, Verso, 2017 ed. of 2016).

REILLY, Danny & CUSHION, Steve: *Telling the Mayflower Story* (London, Socialist History Society, 2018).

RENDLE William: *Old Southwark and its People* (London, 1878).

RENTON, Peter: *The Lost Synagogues of London* (London, Tymsder Publishing, 2000).

ROSENMEIER, Jasper: *With My Own Eyes: William Bradford's Of Plymouth Plantation in Typology and Early American Literature* (1972).

ROWSE, Alfred: *The Elizabethans and America* (Macmillan, 1959).

RYNE, Alec: *Protestants* (2017).

SCHULTE NORDHOLT, J W: *On the Move as Pilgrims* (in Stichting Oudse Hollandse Kerken: *The Pilgrim Fathers in Holland*, 2002 ed. of 1993).

SHORTO, R: *Amsterdam: A History of the World's Most Liberal City* (London: Little, Brown, 2013).

SMITH, Bradford: *Bradford of Plymouth* (1951).

SMITH, J Rider: Foreword to *A Southwark Ship A Southwark Church* (1950) by Belden, A.

SPRUNGER, Keith: *Other Pilgrims in Leiden: Hugh Goodyear and the English Reformed Church* (*Church History*, Vol 41, March 1972).

SPRUNGER, Keith: *The Learned Doctor, William Ames* (University of Illinois, 1972).

SPRUNGER, Keith: *Dutch Puritanism* (Leiden: Brill, 1982).

SPRUNGER, Keith: *Trumpets from the Tower: English Puritan Printing in the Netherlands 1600-1640* (Leiden: Brill, 1994).

SRINIVASAN, Bhu: *Who paid for the Mayflower?* (Foundation for Economic Education, 2018).

STEPHENSON, Walter: *Norwich and the Pilgrim Fathers* (Norwich, Jarrold & Sons, 1920).

STERN, P J and WENNERLIND, C: *Mercantilism Reimagined: Political Economy in Early Modern Britain and its Empire* (OUP USA, 2013).

STEVENSON, Peter: *This is the Church that God Built* (Exeter, 2018).

STONE, Peter: *History of the Port of London* (Barnsley: Pen and Sword, 2017).

STOPES, Charlotte C: *The Life of Henry, third Earl of Southampton* (Cambridge: CUP, 2013 ed. of 1922).

STRATTON, Eugene: *Plymouth Colony: Its History and People, 1620-1691* (Salt Lake City: Ancestry, 1986).

TAMMEL, Johanna W & BANGS, Jeremy: *The Pilgrims and other People from the British Isles in Leiden 1576-1640* (Peel: Mansk-Svenska Publishing, 1989).

TINNISWOOD, Adrian: *The Rainborowes: Pirates, Puritans, and a Family's Quest for the Promised Land* (London, Vintage, 2014 ed. of 2013).

TOLMIE, Murray: *The Triumph of the Saints: The Separate Churches of London 1616-1649* (Cambridge: CUP, 1977).

TOMKINS, Stephen: *The Journey to the Mayflower* (Hodder & Stoughton, 2020).

TURACK, Daniel: *Freedom of Movement: The Right of a UK Citizen to leave his Country* (in *Ohio State Law Journal*, vol 31, 1970).

TYACKE, Nicholas: *The Fortunes of English Puritanism* (London: Dr Williams' Trust, 1989).

USHER, Roland: *The Pilgrims and their History* (Williamstown: Corner House, 1984).

VALLANCE, Edward: *A Radical History of Britain* (Abacus, 2010 ed. of 2009).

VRIES, de & WOUDE, van der: *The First Modern Economy* (Cambridge: CUP, 1997).

WADDINGTON, John: *Surrey Congregational History* (London: Jackson, Walford & Hodder, 1866).

WADDINGTON, John: *The Church of the Pilgrim Fathers* (SLSL, booklet, 1851).

WADDINGTON, John: *John Penry the Pilgrim Martyr* (London: W. & F. G. Cash, 1854).

WAITE, Gary: *Jews and Muslims in Seventeenth Century Discourse* (Routledge, 2018).

WALKER, Thomas: *Clapham and the Mayflower* (London: Clapham Society, 2015).

WALKER, Williston: *The Creeds and Platforms of Congregationalism* (New York: C. Scribner's Sons, 1893).

WEBSTER, Daniel: *The Plymouth Oration*, 22 December 1820.

WESTBROOK, Perry: *William Bradford* (Boston, Mass.: Twayne, 1978).

WHITTOCK, Martin: *When God was King* (Oxford: Lion Hudson, 2018).

WILLEN, Diane: *The Godly Friendship of Thomas Gataker and William Bradshaw,* The Seventeenth Century, Volume 34: number 3 (2019), pp.305-327 (London: Routledge, Taylor & Francis, 2019).

WILLIAMS, David: *Milton's Leveller God* (McGill-Queen's University Press, 2017).

WILLISON, George F: *Saints and Strangers: The Story of the Mayflower and the Plymouth Colony* (London: Heinemann, 1966).

WOODHOUSE, Arthur & ROOTS, Ivan: *Puritanism and Liberty* (London: J. M. Dent & Sons, 1992 ed. of 1938).

WRIGHT, Stephen: *The British Baptists and Politics 1603-49* (Semantic Scholar, internet, 2002).

WRIGHT, Stephen: *Sarah Jones and the Jacob-Jessey Church: The Relation of a Gentlewoman* (British Library Journal article, 2004).

YOUNG, Alexander: *Chronicles of the Pilgrim Fathers of the Colony of Plymouth* (Boston, Mass.: Little & Brown, 1844).

ZAHEDIEH, N: *The Capital and the Colonies: London and the Atlantic Economy 1660-1700* (Cambridge: Cambridge University, 2010).

Index